The Trail Ahead

Dr. Dave Smith

The Trail Ahead

ISBN: 978-1-63073-404-6

Faithful Life Publishers & Printers
North Fort Myers, FL 33903

FaithfulLifePublishers.com
info@FaithfulLifePublishers.com
888.720.0950

Cover design: Dannah Bottrell
Editing: Jodi Raasch

For additional copies contact:
Saddle Up Ministries
P. O. Box 527
Lancaster, KY 40444
saddleupmin@gmail.com

Scripture quotations are from the King James Version

Published in the United States of America.

25 24 23 22 1 2 3 4 5

Dedication

It is with an overflowing heart that I would like to dedicate ***The Trail Ahead***, to our two children, Davina Jo Bottrell and Jeremy Lynn Smith. For over thirty years our children faithfully stood by our sides and served diligently with my wife and me. No two children could have been any more faithful servants of the Lord in times of testing, times of exhaustion, times when we did not know what we were going to do. My faith was often strengthened by the faith of our children, and their determination to press on. Many times, in my mind I hear each of them say, Dad, the Lord will help us, Dad, we can do it, Dad, I am praying for you, my dad is not a quitter; and the phrases of encouragement kept going. To this very day as Mrs. Smith and I watch our children's lives, along with their mates and children, we see their faithfulness to the Lord and their dedication to live for Him and serve Him, and that is such a strengthening to us.

Ephesians 6:1-3, *"Children, obey your parents in the Lord: for this is right. Honour thy father and mother; (which is the first commandment with promise;) That it may be well with thee, and thou mayest live long on the earth."* These words express my heart, and with great pleasure and thankfulness I dedicate this book to Davina and Jeremy. Thank you for being who you are and what you are for the Lord and for mom and dad.

I love you!

Dad

Testimonials

What People Are Saying About the Writing of Dr. Dave Smith

"This book was given to me by a dear church friend. Once I started reading and "listening," I knew others needed the same joy I had with reading this book. It's a daily reminder of how much God loves us. It would remind me of days past, and how God protected me then, as He does today. This devotional book was written with honesty, and it was like I was with Bro. Smith as he experienced what he was writing about. I'd smile as I was reading because of the "realness" of how the subject was presented. The last statement for each day always had me ponder with joy! I love it and look forward to reading it daily.

— Angie Tedder

Happy to see another book by Dr. Dave Smith. What a blessing to daily walk through the Scriptures with his first devotional, ***In The Saddle***. Bro. Dave's personal downhome, thought-provoking style of writing offers valuable lessons in wisdom on how to live more faithfully.

— Bill and Elaine Kunert

Bro. Dave Smith has a knack for tying his rich life of diverse experiences with Scriptural examples, applying the Word of God in an uplifting and challenging manner. Through his devotionals, he encourages his readers to follow God's path and fulfill our purpose by focusing on the pattern of the life of our Lord and Saviour, Jesus Christ. We have certainly benefitted from these daily exhortations.

— Kevin and Chrissy Udd

Our family has been blessed by Bro. Smith's devotional book ***In The Saddle***. The beginning of this year we were at a crossroads in our life. God used this devotional to help us discern God's will for our lives. We love his personal stories and the simple applications he makes that can be applied to our lives personally. We believe Bro. Smith really walks with the Lord.

— Hudak Family

Dr Dave Smith has a special walk with the Lord. He is a true servant of the Lord. His devotional helps me start my day in the right direction. I've developed a closer walk with the Lord since using his devotional. I highly recommend his writings.

I always enjoy reading Dr. Dave Smith's books. I can hear the tone of his voice as he expresses himself in his writing. In one of his books, ***In the Saddle***, he talked about feeding the horses and other animals. When reading this, you can almost smell the hay, corn, and oats in the barn. Dr. Smith tries to see everything through God's eyes. As our society is picking up speed, rolling down the hill toward pre-modern tribalism that thrives on stories which border on myth and fiction, it is more important than ever to tell the story of the Bible. Dr. Smith's books are soul winning books and he is a true servant of the Lord. In reading this book, his words will encourage you to have a close walk with God.

— Kenneth E. Watts

Acknowledgements

All of us in life owe so much to so many people that have helped us and encouraged us, and most of all have believed in us. I know that nothing gets done without the strength from the Lord and the many blessings that He bestows on us. I would like to thank several people that were an encouragement to me, in believing that the Lord could use me to write the devotionals included in ***The Trail Ahead***.

Mrs. Smith, my wife that has loved me and believed in me for over fifty years. Thank you, honey, for daily listening to what I was writing as we read the Bible together, prayed together and you patiently listened to what I had written for the day. You have encouraged me and lovingly walked with me every day.

Miss Jodi Raasch, has been so kind and so patient to read every word I wrote and to patiently correct, edit and proof every devotional. Her humble spirit was such an encouragement to me as I would check how the proofing and editing was coming. Thank you, Miss Jodi.

No one anywhere has a granddaughter like I do. She did all the computer work, designed the cover, made suggestions, encouraged me, and above all was very patient. Thank you Dannah for all the coordination between all involved in making ***The Trail Ahead***, a reality. Thank you, Snooks.

Thank you, Pastor Fugate, for your words of encouragement to keep writing. I love and appreciate my Pastor and his love and sacrifice, and for always being there.

Mrs. Robert Steffen took time early every morning to post every devotional I have written for our Sunday School class. You have faithfully been there and were always so positive about what I had written.

There are so many others that have encouraged me to keep writing. You purchased ***In The Saddle***, and so often sent me a text or gave me a call. Thank you for the kind words, encouraging words and appreciation. Lord Bless you all in a special way.

Thank you, Bro. Jim Wendorf and Faithful Life Publishers, for bringing into completion ***The Trail Ahead***. May the Lord continue His blessing on you and your ministry.

January 1

Genesis 1-3 | Psalm 1 | Proverbs 1 | Matthew 1-2

Jesus First

Good morning and a Happy New Year! Another year of life begins. This could be the year, the day, the hour, and the very moment of the return of our Lord and Saviour, Jesus. Let us decide to stay ready. Let us start this new year by considering that every day is made by God for a specific purpose.

We begin to read about God's creation in Genesis 1:10, "And God called the dry land Earth; and the gathering together of the waters called he Seas: and God saw that it was good." God does not make bad days. Focus on the words, "and God saw that it was good." Genesis 1:11, "And God said, Let the earth bring forth grass, the herb yielding seed, and the fruit tree yielding fruit after his kind, whose seed is in itself, upon the earth: and it was so." Genesis 1:12, "and God saw that it was good." Genesis 1:31, "And God saw every thing that he had made, and, behold, it was very good." All that God created was not just good, "it was very good." Nothing of God's is ever messed up until we listen to the flesh, be led away by the flesh and try to satisfy the flesh. Man and God had a wonderful relationship and we still can today. Please get it in your mind that God wants a relationship with us today and every day. Perfect creation, perfect relationship, perfect satisfaction, perfect contentment, until Genesis 3:5, "For God doth know that in the day ye eat thereof, then your eyes (flesh) shall be opened (revealed), and ye shall be as gods, knowing good and evil." I thought about the word "gods" with a lower case "g." No authority, no power, no control, just empty and yet full of self. Man then hid himself from God, and sin fell on all of mankind, but God has never failed. Matthew 1:21, "And she shall bring forth a son, and thou shalt call his name Jesus: for he shall save his people from their sins." It is only Jesus that gives us true strength to fight the flesh. Look again why He came, "for he shall save his people from their sins." Let us be alert to the flesh. Proverbs 1:10, "My son, if sinners entice thee, consent thou not." Proverbs 1:23, "Turn you at my reproof: behold, I will pour out my spirit unto you, I will make known my words unto you."

Make this year a year to put all things aside and put Jesus first. Stay faithful in reading and studying God's Word. This world will soon pass, but our relationship with Christ should be growing stronger. Psalm 1:2, "But his delight is in the law of the LORD; and in his law doth he meditate day and night." God loves us and just as He walked with Adam in the garden, He hungers to walk with us. Just like He spoke with Joseph and Mary, He hungers to speak with us. His Word is a guide for us to make it through this sinful world. Time in prayer is to tell Him how we love Him and need Him. Let Him guide you this year and may this be the most blessed year of your life.

Make this year a year to put all things aside and put Jesus first.

January 2

Genesis 4-6 Psalm 2 Proverbs 2 Matthew 3-4

Walking With the Saviour

Good morning! Early in my Christian life, I wish there had been someone who would have taken the time to teach me how to have a walk with God. I believe deep down in the heart of every person who has trusted Christ as their personal Saviour, is a desire to know Christ in a very personal way. To know Him is to walk with Him, learn from Him, obey Him and strive to please Him in every area of our life.

The first two sons of Adam and Eve set a foundation to learn from in having a walk with God. Genesis 4:3, "And in process of time it came to pass, that Cain brought of the fruit of the ground an offering unto the LORD. Cain brought "fruit of the ground," fruit that the ground had produced, but there was no giving of life. Genesis 4:4, "And Abel, he also brought of the firstlings of his flock and of the fat thereof. And the LORD had respect unto Abel and to his offering." The key here is easy to understand if we take the time to look. "Firstlings of his flock and the fat thereof." This pictures the best of the flock. Blood was sacrificed. This was the second sacrifice in the Bible because God killed an animal to make clothes for Adam and Eve after they sinned in the garden, and now their son Abel brought a blood sacrifice of the best. This is a perfect picture of Jesus being given as a sinless sacrifice for the sins of the world. The best that you and I have is ourselves. Not that we sacrifice ourselves but we put Christ first place in our life. We see also in Genesis 5:24, "And Enoch walked with God: and he was not; for God took him." Enoch's priority of life was a walk with God. Man on the earth kept getting more wicked and God was ready to destroy what He created because as Genesis 6:6 records for us, "And it repented the LORD that he had made man on the earth, and it grieved him at his heart." We see God's heart "grieved," which means saddened, suffering sorrow, feeling pain. Then God saw the lives of those who walked with Him. Genesis 6:8, "But Noah found grace in the eyes of the LORD." Genesis 6:9, "and Noah walked with God." Genesis 7:22, "Thus did Noah; according to all that God commanded him, so did he."

You are sitting reading this little devotional because in your heart you have a desire to walk with God. Don't lose that desire, don't quit giving your best, don't quit striving to please the Lord. As Jesus told the disciples in Matthew 4:19, "Follow me, and I will make you fishers of men." Make it a priority of daily life to read God's Word. Learn to meditate on verses the Lord gives you. Spend time learning to pray and carrying your burdens to Him. Praise Him and praise Him every time you can. Proverbs 2:7, "He layeth up sound wisdom for the righteous: he is a buckler to them that walk uprightly." There is always something special from God when we put Him first place. Psalm 2:11, "Serve the LORD with fear, and rejoice with trembling." I love the three words we read in Genesis 7:22 about Noah, "so did he." May it be said of us, "so did they." Enjoy your walk with the Saviour today.

There is always something special from God when we put Him first place.

January 3

Genesis 7-9 Psalm 3 Proverbs 3 Matthew 5

Make Today Count

Good morning! God has a plan for each of us and I have purposed not to mess up God's plan. By saying what I just said, I realize I am a sinner but there is a great desire in my heart to always stay in the perfect will of God, or plan of God, for my life. I do not want to drift away from the Lord or ever get out of His will. As I was turning on the lights to begin my private time with the Lord this morning, I was in the kitchen getting something to drink and I noticed a cup that my wife had setting out. I had not seen this cup before and it is not like my wife to leave something setting out. I picked up the cup and read a statement printed in very small letters on the side of this cup. The words that were printed read like this, "Make Today Count." I set the cup back down and went to my time of prayer and I could not forget that statement, "Make Today Count." I wrote it down on a piece of paper, "Make Today Count."

In our reading today, Noah had only one chance to do the will of God. The rain was going to come. All the inhabitants on the earth were going to die. The earth was going to be covered with water as never before. God was asking Noah to build something that he had never seen. Noah had to make each day count. He had to do what he was told to do and how he was told to do it. Noah had to "Make Today Count." Genesis 7:16, "And they that went in, went in male and female of all flesh, as God had commanded him: and the LORD shut him in." Noah had to "Make Today Count." The flood came, the water subsided, and all inhabitants of the ark left and we read what Noah immediately did. Genesis 8:20, "And Noah builded an altar unto the LORD; and took of every clean beast, and of every clean fowl, and offered burnt offerings on the altar." He immediately did "Make Today Count." God then made a covenant with Noah and put a bow in the sky, which we call the rainbow.

Matthew 5:13, "Ye are the salt of the earth." Matthew 5:14, "Ye are the light of the world." Matthew 5:44, " But I say unto you, Love your enemies, bless them that curse you, do good to them that hate you, and pray for them which despitefully use you, and persecute you." God is telling us to "Make Today Count." We might not have a tomorrow, a next week, a next month, a next year. We might not even have a next moment. We must "Make Today Count." You might be saying this morning, what can I do? Proverbs 3:9, "Honour the LORD with thy substance, and with the first fruits of all thine increase." Be where you need to be, doing what you need to be doing and "Make Today Count." Oh, that we would have an urgency of being in God's will, doing God's will. Psalm 3:4, "I cried unto the LORD with my voice, and he heard me out of his holy hill. Selah." "Make Today Count!!"

Be where you need to be, doing what you need to be doing and "Make Today Count."

January 4

Genesis 10-12 Psalm 4 Proverbs 4 Matthew 6-7

Pot Holes

Good morning! Pot holes, pot holes, pot holes, and more pot holes. Now that is a funny way, or a different way, to start out with a morning devotional. Most all of my life I have lived in a place where I have to drive daily on a gravel road. The lane to the camp is gravel and the drive up to our house is gravel. It would be very nice, less muddy, less dusty if it was paved with black top or concrete, but that is very expensive so we continue to drive on gravel. Along with a gravel road come "pot holes." These are holes that develop because of a soft spot in the surface, a moving of the ground from freezing and thawing. You can fill the pot holes and they will come back. You can use a box blade, which we have at the camp, and pull it behind the tractor and tear up the "pot hole" and the area around the hole and come back and smooth the loosened gravel out, and still after a short while the pot holes will come back. Even a hard surface road can get "pot holes" in it. If you live on a gravel road or a gravel lane, you are always going to be filling and repairing "pot holes."

Man has always tried to figure out how to do everything and accomplish everything without God. Genesis 11:4, "And they said, Go to, let us build us a city and tower, whose top may reach unto heaven; and let us make us a name, lest we be scattered abroad upon the face of the whole earth." Man has always tried to replace God, reject what God says to do, try to live the Christian life the way they want instead of living like God wants them to live. Man continually tries to justify his actions. Let us face the fact of human life. Life is full of "pot holes." We are weak and HE is strong. We constantly fail and we need God's strength. Man cannot and will not ever replace the need for God. Man is full of "pot holes" that only God can repair. Can I just very simply say it? "Pot holes" are areas of sin in our life. Today I will try to repair some pot holes in the camp's lane and when I do, they will eventually come back. God watched as man tried to build this tower. Man thought they had life figured out without a relationship with God. Genesis 11:6, "And the LORD said, Behold, the people is one, and they have all one language; and this they begin to do: and now nothing will be restrained from them, which they have imagined to do." Man had no controls on their actions. We are weak and we need God in every area of our life.

God has given us a way to repair our "pot holes" of life. This repairing is of Him and for Him. Matthew 7:7, "Ask, and it shall be given you, seek, and ye shall fine; knock, and it shall be opened unto you." Matthew 7:8, "For every one that asketh receiveth; and he that seeketh findeth; and to him that knocketh it shall be opened." The "pot holes" of life are to be and can be repaired by God. Proverbs 4:18, "But the path of the just is as the shining light, that shineth more and more unto the perfect day." It is God that lighteth the path and when He shines the light, we see the "pot holes" of life. Look today, my brother and sister, and ask God to show you the "pot holes" that you have. Proverbs 4:26, "Ponder the path of thy feet, and let all thy ways be established." When the "pot holes" begin to develop in the road, we try to avoid them. The "pot holes" will get bigger and more will develop if they are not filled and repaired. The same is true in our lives. I am thankful the Lord always makes a way for us to see and allow Him to repair the "pot holes" of our lives. Psalm 4:3, "But know that the LORD hath set apart him that is godly for himself:

the LORD will hear when I call unto him." Got any "pot holes?" Then let the Lord fill them and repair them.

We are weak and we need God in every area of our life.

January 5

Genesis 13-15 Psalm 5 Proverbs 5 Matthew 8-9

Build Your Nest

Good morning! Well, I am a little late but the bird feeders for winter are up and the birds of many colors are starting to come in. I was in the back of the camp property, and flying out of the woods where I was, was a beautiful bright red male cardinal. As I headed back toward the barn, a flock of geese came flying over. We did not read about birds in our reading this morning, but the word "migration" did come to my mind. Walking with the Lord daily is to keep going where you are being fed. As it caught my interest, I began to read about why birds migrate. I found some interesting thoughts and comparisons. Birds migrate for two main purposes, food and nesting. Many migrate because of temperature, but most because of food and nesting. Genesis 13:1, "And Abram went up out of Egypt." Genesis 13:4, "Unto the place of the altar, which he had made there at the first: and there Abram called on the name of the LORD." Abram went to the place where he had built an altar, where God had met with Him.

My brother and sister, we have too much drifting around and starvation because God's people are not staying in the place where they receive the preaching, teaching, spiritual feeding, and fellowship that each of us need. A bird will migrate to sustain their life, but we as God's people will drift and die. As we read on in Matthew this morning, we read where blind men and others came to Jesus to be healed. They knew where to go to receive the healing of God. Matthew 9:28, "And when he was come into the house, the blind men came to him: and Jesus saith unto them, Believe ye that I am able to do this? They said unto him, Yea,

Lord." Matthew 9:29, "Then touched he their eyes, saying, According to your faith be it unto you." I found it interesting that birds that migrate do not go back to a nest. They go to where they know food is and they know there will be material to make a nest. Birds that do not migrate are being fed and they have a nest. God calls some people to go to the mission field and other places of service, but too many move before they know that they will have a place of spiritual feeding and a place to call a spiritual home. Birds that migrate know where they are going and why they must go. Proverbs 5:21, "For the ways of man are before the eyes of the LORD, and he pondereth all his goings." Let God be the only guide that you have.

Fathers and mothers, get your children in the place where they are spiritually growing in the Lord. Build a nest for your family to be a place of spiritual strength for each family member, and be involved. I love to listen to the birds in the morning. They seem to be content and in the place they know they are to be. Psalm 5:3, "My voice shalt thou hear in the morning, O LORD, in the morning will I direct my prayer unto thee, and will look up." Psalm 5:8, "Lead me, O LORD, in thy righteousness because of mine enemies; make thy way straight before my face." Oh, what the birds of the sky can teach us. Build your nest in the right spot and there will be the food supply that you need. See you in church.

Build a nest for your family to be a place of spiritual strength for each family member.

January 6

Genesis 16-17 Psalm 6 Proverbs 6 Matthew 10

Determination

Good morning! Thank the Lord for mommas that were tough; those who stood firm and unwavering but had a tender heart. This morning as I was reading, a word came to my mind and I wrote the word down, and then heard a voice in my mind that said, "you need to look it up." If mom said to do it, you better do it. She is in Heaven and my life is daily revealing the input of my father and mother. The first word this morning that I looked up was the word, "determination." The meaning of determination is: firmness of purpose; the act of deciding definitely and firmly, fixed intention to achieve a desired end.

Why did Abram listen to his wife Sarai, when it came to going to her maid? Genesis 16:2, "And Abram hearkened to the voice of Sarai." Why did Adam listen and partake of the fruit that Eve gave him? Genesis 3:6, "she took of the fruit thereof, and did eat, and gave also unto her husband with her; and he did eat." Our flesh is weak. There must be a firm and determined walk with God to live the victorious life in Christ. We must have a daily "firmness of purpose." Every day and every moment of every day, we must be determined to do right in the eyes of God. Abram was a man, just like you and me. Genesis 17:1, "And when Abram was ninety years old and nine, the LORD appeared to Abram, and said unto him, I am the Almighty God; walk before me, and be thou perfect." When Abram and Sarai lost their faith, or their faith was weakened, they sinned. We need to look at two things in Genesis 17:1 to build a determination in our walk with God. The words "Almighty God" means "El Shaddai," which means, "Strong One," "Nourisher," "Strength-giver," "Satisfier." God wanted to be and wants to be our "El Shaddai," but we must be determined to allow Him and to follow Him. The word "perfect" in Genesis 17:1 means sincere or upright. Are we fully given to Christ? Is our life's desire to please the Lord in everything? Jesus told His disciples in Matthew 10:16, "Behold, I send you forth as sheep in the midst of wolves: be therefore wise as serpents, and harmless as doves." He told them to be determined to be what they needed to be to spread the gospel. Proverbs 6:23, "For the commandment is a lamp; and the law is light; and reproofs of instruction are the way of life." The writer in Proverbs 6 just repeated to us that we must be determined to allow the light to shine when the sin of the world darkens, and the light of the law will guide us. When we do wrong, accept the "reproofs" or correction.

Our country is covered with telephone poles. Those poles bring power and phone lines to us. Those power poles were not grown in their spots, but a hole was dug deep to withstand many things. Just think, those poles withstand all the elements of the weather. Those poles withstand time and often a vehicle bumping into them, as well as the weight of the lines. The utility poles stand because they were buried deep in the ground, and for many of them a guide wire was attached to give them stability. When the utility poles were put in the ground, there was a determination to do everything possible to give them a long life of service. We need to bury ourselves deep in the Word of God, stabilize ourselves in a prayer life that keeps us on our faces with God and have a determination to serve Christ with all of our life. "El Shaddai" is there for us. Psalm 6:2, "Have mercy upon me, O LORD; for I am weak: O LORD, heal me." That is where we need to start, on our knees before God. Let us be determined to stand firm for Christ and for His glory.

Every day and every moment we must be determined
to do right in the eyes of God.

January 7

Genesis 18-19 Psalm 7 Proverbs 7 Matthew 11

Listen to the Cry

Good morning! Have you ever been on a trail deep in the woods and heard the cry of some animal or bird? Have you ever listened late in the evening or early in the morning, deep in the woods, and the silence of the time is broken with the cry of an animal? I have heard a little fawn deer cry for its mother. I have heard the cry of a coyote for the pack. I have heard the cry of a rabbit caught. I have watched as a hawk has swooped down from being perched high in a tree and caught a field mouse, and heard the screech of both the hawk and the mouse. I asked myself this morning, what cry does the Lord hear in our day?

We read this morning in Genesis 18:20, "Because the cry of Sodom and Gomorrah is great, and because their sin is very grievous." Does God hear the cry of us, the born again, for the salvation of the lost? Does God hear us cry for His mercy to save our nation and this world we live in? Is the cry of sin louder than the cry of the saved to plead mercy for the lost and dying? Abraham pleaded with God for mercy. The count began in Genesis 18:23, "Wilt thou also destroy the righteous with the wicked?" Fifty, forty-five, forty, thirty, twenty; verse 33, "I will not destroy it for ten's sake." Ten could not be found. I wrote in my notes this morning in red letters to myself, "listen to the cry." Matthew 11:15, "He that hath ears to hear, let him hear." Matthew 11:24, "But I say unto you, That it shall be more tolerable for the land of Sodom in the day of judgment, than for thee." A call often used when hunting for coyotes is a call called, "rabbit in distress." That call of the "rabbit in distress" draws in the coyotes. We must listen to the cry of a lost world and reach them in every way that we can. Those who are saved have the promise of Heaven, but the world has no hope. We must hear the "call of distress" of this lost world. Proverbs 7:24, "hearken unto me now therefore, O ye children, and attend to the words of my mouth." Listen to the distress call of broken marriages, children who have no one to love them. Hear the cry of those addicted, hear the cry of a community that has no church, hear the cry of a people in a tribe with no one to share the love and salvation of Jesus.

Listen to the cry that God is letting you hear this morning and respond to that cry by giving your all to it. Psalm 7:11, "God judgeth the righteous, and God is angry with the wicked every day." God is calling today for us to hear "the distress call" of this world that needs Christ. We must do what we can, be where we need to be, doing what we need to be doing. Oh, the call of a fawn, the call of an animal in distress! Much greater is the call of a lost and dying world. Hand out a tract today. Take time and share the gospel. Call and invite someone to church. Make a hospital visit. Send a card or text to someone today. What cry are you hearing this morning? If you are not hearing a cry, it is because you have been caught in a trap by the devil. You see, he has the best bait in his traps. Seek the face of God so you can get out of Satan's trap and listen for the voice of God. Here should be your cry; Psalm 7:1, "O LORD my God, in thee do I put my trust." Stop, take time, and ask the Lord to let you hear the cry.

God is calling today for us to hear "the distress call"
of this world that needs Christ.

January 8

Genesis 20-22 Psalm 8 Proverbs 8 Matthew 12

Right is Always Right

Good morning! I am not sure where it was that I first heard this quote, but it has been said by many different people many times and I feel it is good for us to read it and hear it this morning. "Wrong is never right and right is always right, and wrong is always wrong." Another quote is, "It is never right to not do your best and it is always wrong to not try and do your best." I am very thankful that I have often heard these quotes and they hold a very deep place in my mind and heart. I dislike very much the statement, "it is close enough," or "it is alright for what we are doing." Why do we not want to do our best and be our best when we do anything? Truth is truth and a lie is a lie.

As we read this morning, this is the second time Abraham has feared for his life and told a lie about his wife Sarah being his sister. The first time was in Genesis 12 and now in Genesis 20:2, "And Abraham said of Sarah his wife, she is my sister: and Abimelech king of Gerar sent, and took Sarah." Tell the truth no matter the consequences. The world knows when we are not real, honest or truthful in our testimony for Christ. Abraham was found out in Genesis 20:9, "Then Abimelech called Abraham, and said unto him, what hast thou done unto us? And what have I offended thee, that thou hast brought on me and on my kingdom a great sin? Thou hast done deeds unto me that ought not to be done." Genesis 20:10, "And Abimelech said unto Abraham, What sawest thou, that thou hast done this thing?" I stopped my reading after this verse and thought, is America in her condition and the world in its sinful state because of the lack of Christians being what we should have been and should be? Great mission works around the world were started years ago and now almost nothing is even close to the gospel reach it should be. In America, churches are closing their doors instead of reaching people for Christ. Great revivals in the past we read about, and now today we hear excuse after excuse as to why folks are not in church, let alone serving

God. What happened to your faith, Abraham? What happened to your courage to do God's will, Abraham? Genesis 20:11, "And Abraham said, Because I thought, Surely the fear of God is not in this place; and they will kill me for my wife's sake."

Thank the Lord for conviction of the Holy Spirit in our hearts, and for obedience when we see that we are not what God wants us to be and He has to give us a kick in the seat of our pants to get us back on the right track. Sarah became with child and Isaac became the next great step of faith for Abraham. We read in Genesis 22:16, "for because thou hast done this thing, and hast not withheld thy son, thine only son." Genesis 22:17-18, "That in blessing I will bless thee, And in thy seed shall all nations of the earth be blessed; because thou hast obeyed my voice." Let us fully do right in every area of our life. Matthew 12:30, "He that is not with me is against me; and he that gathereth not with me scattereth abroad." God loves us and wants to use us and bless us. Proverbs 8:17, "I love them that love me; and those that seek me early shall find me." Proverbs 8:32, "blessed are they that keep my ways." I can remember the fear of falling off of a horse. What often happens to people is they never get on and enjoy the ride. I have fallen off a few times and been bucked off a couple of times, but I sure enjoy the ride when I am on a horse, and my fear was always less when I got back on. Praise the Lord that He has given us time to live right and do right. Let us get up and get back on that pony and enjoy the ride. Psalm 8:1, 9 says, "O LORD our Lord, how excellent is thy name in all the earth!"

Praise the Lord that He has given us time to live right and do right.

January 9

Genesis 23-24 Psalm 9 Proverbs 9 Matthew 13

God of the Impossible

Good morning! Seeing the impossible is believing the possible. Just when we think it can't be is when it can be. When we think there is no way, that is when there is a way. When we think it is the end, that is when it is really the beginning. Quit believing it will not work and get busy working. You will never get me to believe God can't when I know He can. The servant was given the orders and he thought it was an impossible task. How would you like to go get somebody you have never seen, have no idea their name or where they live, you know nothing about them, their family, their location, and you are told to go get them? I love the words of Abraham in Genesis 24:7, "The LORD God of heaven, which took me from my father's house, and from the land of my kindred, and which spake unto me, and that aware unto me, saying." Wow, what a testimony of knowing God can!

Do you find yourself doubting? Do you find yourself at the end of your rope? Do you find yourself having no hope? Hang on and see God. Just about the time you and I do not think things are possible is when God does the impossible right before our eyes. The servant was to seek a bride for Abraham's son Isaac. Abraham gave the servant some boundaries. We must be in the will of God to have the faith we need in God. Sin will never give us clear spiritual sight. Genesis 24:27, "And he said, Blessed be the LORD God of my master Abraham, who hath not left destitute my master of his mercy and truth: I being in the way, the LORD led me to the house of my master's brethren." The key part of this verse is, "I being in the way, the LORD led me." We know how the Lord led the servant and prepared Rebekah to be where she was, and prepared the heart of her family, and everybody's willingness and blessing. God is ready to do the impossible when we are where we are supposed to be, doing what we are supposed to be doing, the way He told us to do it. Matthew 13 is full of parables for people to see and understand the truth Jesus is teaching, and Matthew 13:23 sums up His teaching. "But he that received seed into the good ground is he that heareth the word, and understandeth it, which also beareth fruit, and bringeth forth, some an hundredfold, some sixty, some thirty." When our faith is in God to do the impossible, He will do the possible. Proverbs 9:9, "Give instruction to a wise man, and he will be yet wiser: teach a just man, and he will increase in learning."

God knows exactly where we are and what we are going through. Let God be God and watch Him do the impossible. Quit fretting and get in the place you are to be, doing what you are to be doing. If you are being and doing what God has for you, then keep on. Psalm 9:12, "he forgetteth not the cry of the humble." Keep on. The impossible will soon become the possible. Don't forget what the servant of Abraham said, "I being in the way, the LORD led me."

When our faith is in God to do the impossible, He will do the possible.

January 10

Genesis 25-26 Psalm 10 Proverbs 10 Matthew 14

Spiritual Strengthening

Good morning! Mrs. Smith and I were grocery shopping and she asked if we could stop by a couple of other stores. As we were looking at things in this discount store, or should I say, as I was following Mrs. Smith through the store like a little pup . . . . Just kidding, I love the time we get to spend together and it does not matter what we are doing, I just love the time we are together. I just like looking at trucks more than junk. Please do not tell her I used the word "junk." You have heard it said, "one man's junk is another man's treasure." As we were shopping, I noticed a lady picking up all kinds of things and taking a picture with her phone of the codes on the back of each item. Mrs. Smith told me that she was price checking. She was looking for the best value to be able to save money.

As I read this morning, I am afraid we have too many Christians who are spiritually "price checking." We read this morning of two brothers, Esau and Jacob. Both of these young men are like our children, both were different. Esau came in from the field and was very hungry and asked Jacob to prepare him some stew. Genesis 25:31-32, "And Jacob said, sell me this day thy birthright. And Esau said, Behold I am at the point to die: and what profit shall this birthright do to me." Esau was the oldest and as we read, his dad Isaac was closer to Esau, and Rebekah loved Jacob. Esau, being the first born, was in line to receive the birthright, or control of the future of the family's inheritance. The sad part of the story is found in Genesis 25:34, "thus Esau despised his birthright." He put his fleshly desires over spiritual desires. We all will find ourselves in this position as human beings. Let us look at what the birthright was going to give in comparison to our inheritance as being a Christian. When we put our inheritance through Christ first place, we have spiritual, physical, emotional leadership and receive blessings from our walk and relationship for Christ. Esau surrendered it all for a bowl of stew by pleasing the flesh. Matthew 14:15, "send the multitude away, that they may go into the villages, and buy them victuals."

The disciples were focused on the physical needs of the people and not the spiritual strengthening that they were getting from being with and listening to the teachings of Christ. Look what happened when Christ said in Matthew 14:16, "But Jesus said unto them, They need not depart; give them to eat." Jesus blessed five loaves and two fishes to feed five thousand hungry people. They could have left and went to town to get food, but they were more interested in being with Jesus. God will take care of us when we put our relationship with Him first and foremost. Proverbs 10:3, "The LORD will not suffer the soul of the righteous to famish." We need spiritual and physical strength, but it is more important to put the spiritual over the physical and the blessings of God will come. Proverbs 10:22, "The blessing of the LORD, it maketh rich, and he addeth no sorrow with it." Our flesh is weak and that is the greatest battle fought over every addiction that human flesh can have. Psalm 10:17, "LORD, thou hast heard the desire of the humble: thou wilt prepare their heart, thou wilt cause thine ear to hear." May the Lord hear our spiritual plea so much more than our physical plea. Seek Him and He promises to take care of your every need. Put Christ first and He will give you the strength for the needs that you have. He blesses the physical work of those who put Him first.

When we put the spiritual over the physical, the blessings of God will come.

January 11

Genesis 27-28 Psalm 11 Proverbs 11 Matthew 15

A Hunger for God

Good morning! I often ask myself this question that I am going to ask you. What do you hunger for in life? Each of us have priorities. What are your priorities centered around? Yes, young newly married couples often hunger for the day that they are able to purchase their first home. Teens hunger for that day they get their driver's license, or they are able to get their first car. Mothers and fathers hunger for the day to simply enjoy life with their children and grandchildren and not push to just exist in life. As I use the word "hunger" this morning, let us take time and define this word. The first thought that comes to our mind is the lack of food or the feeling of starving. I want us to think of this part of the definition: desiring eagerly, longing for, craving. To some, the gift of salvation is nothing more than an assurance they are going to Heaven when they die. To some, salvation is a growing relationship with Christ, wanting to know more about Him, desiring to please Him in areas of their life. To others it is a heart-yearning desire to know Him, yield to Him, walk with Him, allow Him full control and leadership.

I do not know where you are, but I do know that I want to give Him full control of my life today, tomorrow and the rest of my life. In our reading today we see a father who appears to be close to his last days. His eyesight is dim, he is tired, weary, and wants to pass on his blessing to his son. The passing of the birthright was the heritage of the family. We have the promise of God to Abraham, passed on to his son Isaac and now ready to be passed on to either Esau or Jacob. Isaac wants it passed on to Esau and his wife Rebekah wants it passed on to Jacob. We must look and think about God's will and put things in perspective and bring us into these thoughts: venison being prepared over goats from the flocks that God had blessed, a birthright that had already been despised or was not wanted by Esau. Genesis 25:34, "thus Esau despised his birthright." Another son who was a "supplanter" or deceiver was Jacob. What can we learn? We see a comparison of desire of earthly matters over spiritual matters. Let me say it this way, things I want over what God might want. How can we put both in their proper place? Notice the statement mentioned by Isaac the father, "Who art thou" (Genesis 27:18, 32). Jacob is blessed and his dad tells him in Genesis 28:1, "Thou shalt not take a wife of the daughters of Canaan." Jacob is obedient and does not. On the other hand, we see Esau rebel and take a wife of Canaan. The passing of the birthright should have been a public event of the entire family and not just between a son and his father. The home is split, and mom wants the birthright to go to the son that she favors. We truly cannot see life through our own eyes. We must hunger to see through the eyes of our Lord and hunger to be in His perfect will.

Many lives have missed the will of God because of wanting to please man instead of God. We sought success of this world instead of God's blessing. We put self in front of God. Jesus told the Pharisees in Matthew 15:6, "Thus have ye made the commandment of God of none effect by your tradition." Be careful of this world and its ways twisting the will of God for your life. Proverbs 11:18, "The wicked worketh a deceitful work: but to him that soweth righteousness shall be a sure reward." Proverbs 11:23, "The desire of the righteous is only good: but the expectation of the wicked is wrath." There is so much to learn from today's Scripture reading, so let us bring it down to hungering to know God and His will. Mom and dad, do not live your will in your children's life, but daily pray for them to walk with God and to know His will. Young person, do not live to please mom and dad, live to know God's will for your life. One thing I know for sure, a prayer life that supersedes all we can do or think is where we will find the will of God. To please God is to be in God's will. To live in God's Word is to be in God's will. To spend time in prayer with God is to be in God's will. Psalm 11:7, "For the righteous LORD loveth righteousness, his countenance doth behold the upright." Let God show you, "who art thou." Hunger for God and His will.

We must hunger to see through the eyes of our Lord and to be in His perfect will.

January 12

Genesis 29-30 Psalm 12 Proverbs 12 Matthew 16-17

Living God's Plan

Good morning! In the life of a Christian, we must always keep in the front of our mind that God sees way beyond what we see. Too many become discouraged and want to give up because they only see what is in front of them. The older we get, the better we are able to see that the way we think things should work out is not always the way the Lord works things out. God knows His plan. We just need to live His plan His way. Jacob is now heading out into life. We need to remember the words in Genesis 28:20, "If God will be with me, and will keep me in this way that I go, and will give me bread to eat and raiment to put on." Genesis 28:22, "of all that thou shalt give me I will surely give the tenth unto thee." God has His plan, His method, His way, and we just need to yield to all that He has for us and before us. Genesis 29:25, "What is this thou hast done unto me? Did not I serve with thee for Rachel? Wherefore then hast thou beguiled me?"

Sometimes we feel like God is not hearing our prayers, but He is. We are just not getting the results we want. Jacob did get Rachel. Look at Genesis 29:27, "Fulfil her week, and we will give thee this also for the service which thou shalt serve with me yet seven other years." Genesis 29:28, "And Jacob did so, and fulfilled her week: and he gave him Rachel his daughter to wife also." The custom in the land was to give the older daughter in marriage first. Leah was the rightful first to be given. Jacob's eyes were on what he wanted and what he wanted was not the right order of events. I am afraid that most of us think we know what we want, when we want it, and how we want it and the truth is, we do not. Let us live for God to have His way in our life. Matthew 16:26, "For what is a man profited, if he shall gain the whole world, and lose his own soul? or what shall a man give in exchange for his soul?" Man does whatever he has to do to get his own way, and that way is not God's way. Man is snared in selfishness. Proverbs 12:13, "The wicked is snared by the transgression of his lips: but the just shall come out of trouble." Proverbs 12:20, "Deceit is in the heart of them that imagine evil: but to the counselors of peace is joy."

This world is wicked and selfish, and its goal is to get all it can gain. Look at the condition around the world. Millions are starving and the few of leadership are basking in wealth. Common sense has turned into no sense at all. Psalm 12:1, "Help, LORD; for the godly man ceaseth; for the faithful fail from among the children of men." We need another generation to wait on God. Go through every step God wants to take you through to stay in the perfect will of God, to obtain the perfect will of God. God knows His plan. Just stay in His plan for your life. Be patient and learn to wait on Him. Know God is never late. God's way is the only way. God knows what we are going through so go through it and be blessed in God's time.

God has His plan, His method, His way,
and we need to yield to all that He has for us.

January 13

Genesis 31-32 Psalm 13 Proverbs 13 Matthew 18

Come Back Home

Good morning! There is nothing like going home after a day at work, after a long trip, after a day at school. In our reading today, we see Jacob now heading back home. Genesis 31:11, "And the angel of God spake unto me in a dream, saying, Jacob: And I said, Here am I." Genesis 31:13, "I am the God of Bethel, where thou anointedst the pillar, and where thou vowedst a vow unto me: now arise, get thee out from this land, and return unto the land of thy kindred." For the saint of God, this world is just temporary and Heaven is our eternal home where we will one day go.

What about your relationship with Christ today? Have you drifted away from where you know God wants you? Do you struggle with returning to a fellowship with Christ because you seem to be so far away? All of us have bumps in our lives when it seems we read the Bible and struggle to get anything from our reading. We have excuse after excuse why we are not in church. We used to go to every service, now we are only making one time a week or maybe two. It seems as though the devil has just parked on you, and you cannot get back up. Can I encourage you this morning to come back home? Come back to where you know you should be. Matthew 18:11, "For the Son of man is come to save that which was lost." Look at the wording of this verse. "Save that which was lost." God knows where we are and where we should be. He is reaching out to each of us today and saying, "come home." Matthew 18:12, "How think ye? If a man have an hundred sheep, and one of them be gone astray, doth he not leave the ninety and nine, and goeth into the mountains, and seeketh that which is gone astray?" You might not be far away from God now, but always be careful of drifting away and always know you can "come home." Proverbs 13:1, "A wise son heareth his father's instruction: but a scorner heareth not rebuke."

I wish it had not happened, but I remember that awful day when dad and I got in an argument. My mom came into the room as I told my dad I was leaving, and to this day I remember my mom standing there with tears flowing down her face and saying, "David, please do not leave." I walked out and headed down the road, not knowing where I was going. Oh, the awful feeling in my heart that day. Oh, the emptiness I felt. Dad came trying to find me in the car. I remember those words he said that day. "David, please come on back home." I did return, I asked forgiveness, and I am thankful for a dad and mom that said, "come home." Psalm 13:1, "How long wilt thou forget me, O LORD? forever? how long wilt thou hide thy face from me?" God has not hidden from us. It is us hiding from God or thinking we can hide from Him. Come home! Please don't ever leave. Stay true and faithful to Him. He loves us.

I went to our piano this morning and picked up the hymnal and turned to "Lord, I'm Coming Home." "I've wandered far away from God, Now I'm coming home; The paths of sin too long I've trod, Lord, I'm coming home. I've wasted many precious years, Now I'm coming home; I now repent with bitter tears, Lord, I'm coming home. I've tired of sin and straying, Lord, Now I'm coming home; I'll trust Thy love, believe Thy word, Lord, I'm coming home. My soul is sick, my heart is sore, Now I'm coming home; My strength renew, my hope restore, Lord, I'm coming home. The chorus: "Coming home, coming home, Never more to roam; Open now Thine arms of love, Lord, I'm coming home."

If you have not left, then stay there, but if you have drifted, come on home. There is no place like being in the perfect will of God. I call it home until I leave this world and head to my Heavenly Home. Have a blessed day.

God is reaching out to each of us today and saying, "come home."

January 14

Genesis 33-35 Psalm 14 Proverbs 14 Matthew 19

Emotions Under Control

Good morning! So much is in our reading each day. I trust as you read the Word of God that you are taking time to stop and think about what you are reading. Reading the Bible and reading through the Bible is tremendous, but it is God's will and way to speak to us personally. Picture with me this morning two children fighting over something. It could be a toy, it could be that one got something first, it could be that one got in trouble with their parents and the other did not. They are siblings and they are in a bad argument. There are words said that can never be taken back. Have you ever been there? I pray not.

Esau and Jacob have not seen each other in a long time and Jacob is heading to the homeland. Coming toward the caravan of Jacob's family and herds is four hundred men with Esau in the lead. Can you feel the fear? Their parting years ago was not a good parting. Now they face each other, and listen to the conversation. Genesis 33:8, "And he (Esau) said, What meanest thou by all this drove which I met? And he said, These are to find grace in the sight of my lord." Genesis 33:9, "And Esau said, I have enough, my brother; keep that thou hast unto thyself." Genesis

33:10, "And Jacob said, Nay, I pray thee, if now I have found grace in thy sight, then receive my present at my hand: for therefore I have seen thy face, as though I had seen the face of God, and thou wast pleased with me." Who is it that you love and have not seen or spoken to in years because of some falling out or disagreement long ago? We live in an attacking, ungodly, high tempered time in our world. No one is perfect and without error. We who are God's people need to live in wisdom from the Lord and not let our emotions get out of control. What is it that you are holding onto that is causing you to miss the full joy of a life in Christ? A young man came to Jesus in Matthew 19:16, "what good thing shall I do, that I may have eternal life?" Jesus spoke with him about keeping the commandments and the young man said, "All these things have I kept from my youth up: what lack I yet?" (Matthew 19:20). Matthew 19:21, "If thou wilt be perfect, go sell that thou hast, and give to the poor, and thou shalt have treasure in heaven: and come and follow me." The word "perfect" is what we need to look at. "Perfect" means full development, growth in maturity of godliness.

You know, when we lose our tempers or have a major battle with another person, we really have shown our immaturity. We need to heed to the words, "anger and sin not." Proverbs 14:10, "The heart knoweth his own bitterness." Proverbs 14:14, "The backslider in heart shall be filled with his own ways." Proverbs 14:21, "He that despiseth his neighbour sinneth: but he that hath mercy on the poor, happy is he." How about mercy on the one you have had a disagreement with? It has been said it takes more of a man to disagree and hold your tongue and walk away, than to stand there and argue. I am not talking about compromise. I am talking about being Christ-like and using wisdom. I am thankful for the final meeting of Esau and Jacob. They parted in peace that day and if you remember before they met, God talked with Jacob and said in Genesis 35:10, "And God said unto him, Thy name is Jacob: thy name shall not be called any more Jacob, but Israel shall be thy name: and he called his name Israel." We need our heart cleansed of all bitterness and anger. Psalm 14:5, "God is in the generation of the righteous." You might have been wronged in a very hurtful way. Give it to the Lord and go on for God. God's mercy and grace is sufficient. Let us be the generation of righteousness. Walk in the spirit and do not have a chip on your shoulder of the flesh. Learn to say, I am so sorry, please forgive me.

God's people need to live in wisdom from the Lord
and not let emotions get out of control.

January 15

Genesis 36-38 Psalm 15 Proverbs 15 Matthew 20

Are You Jealous?

Good morning! Attacked by dogs. Now before you begin to wonder what kind of attacks, I am talking about my dogs, not a wild pack of dogs. I walk out the door and if they are not waiting, in a very short period of time they will be there. Their tails will be wagging and as I reach down to pet one, the other will crowd in to be petted. When I feed them, they will each start eating and then they will go and check each other's bowl to see what the other dog was fed. Jealousy, jealousy, jealousy.

We see a process of where jealousy takes us in today's reading. All of us fight jealousy and if it is not controlled it will lead us down a dangerous path. Joseph was the youngest brother and was loved in a very special way by his father Jacob, or Israel. This special love created a jealous spirit in his other brothers. Genesis 37:4, "And when his brethren saw that their father loved him more than all his brethren, they hated him, and could not speak peaceably unto him." A jealous spirit creates envy within us. Genesis 37:11, "And his brethren envied him." God had a very special plan for Joseph's life and unbeknown to Joseph, his training for greater days was about to begin. Before we have victory there will always be battles. It was not that God was not going to use Joseph's brothers, it was that they were jealous and then envious of what God was doing in his life. The same can happen to us. Where does envy take us? Genesis 37:18, "they conspired against him to slay him." Genesis 37:20, "Come now therefore, and let us slay him, and cast him into some pit." They did not kill Joseph, but they did sell him and tried to cover up their sin. We see five dangerous steps that each of us can take if our spirit is not controlled and directed toward what Christ is doing in our lives. Jealousy leads to envy, envy leads to hatred, hatred leads to destruction or the desire to destroy, and then comes conspiracy or lies, gossip or anything to destroy a person, which in time will really destroy us. We need to wake up and enjoy the blessings of others even if these blessings do not come our way. We must know that God will bless us according to His will in our lives. Our Scripture today in Genesis is also a picture for us to see the life of Christ on this earth. Matthew 20:18, "Behold, we go up to Jerusalem; and the Son of man shall be betrayed unto the chief priests and unto the scribes, and they shall condemn him to death." We must protect our heart, attitude, and spirit. Proverbs 15:14, "The heart of him that hath understanding seeketh knowledge: but the mouth of fools feedeth on foolishness." Proverbs 15:26, "The thoughts of the wicked are an abomination to the LORD: but the words of the pure are pleasant words."

I love both of my dogs. One is a lot older than the other and will probably die before the younger dog and when that happens, I will watch the younger dog go into morning for the loss of its companion. Why allow a wrong spirit to lose a friendship? Why allow jealousy to destroy a good team? Why try to get revenge because you were not promoted like another coworker? Be careful and learn to give your situation and circumstance to the Lord. Psalm 15:3, "He that backbiteth not with his tongue, nor doeth evil to his neighbor, nor taketh up a reproach against his neighbor." Psalm 15:4, "he honoureth them that fear the LORD." I love both dogs. You are needed on the team. Your family will always be your family. Be careful and love beyond the hurt.

We need to enjoy the blessings of others
even if these blessings do not come our way.

January 16

Genesis 39-40 Psalm 16 Proverbs 16 Matthew 21

Teach Responsibility

Good morning! There is no greater joy as a parent, teacher, leader, trainer, or anyone trying to instruct another, than to see them learning and completing a task or responsibility just the way they were told. I can remember teaching our children different tasks to teach them responsibilities. Learning to do a task creates within a person a sense of accomplishment. Doing things for our children and not making them responsible is holding their maturity back. Many a child has not been taught to be responsible and now they are dependent on someone else or the government and possibly both.

We see in the Scriptures this morning the trust that came to Joseph because of how he accepted responsibility. Genesis 39:3, "And his master saw that the LORD was with him, and that the Lord made all that he did to prosper in his hand." Even when Joseph was cast into prison, he was given great responsibility. Genesis 39:22, "And the keeper of the prison committed to Joseph's hand all the prisoners." The key to learn here is why this happened. Genesis 39:23, "because the LORD was with him, and that which he did, the LORD made it to prosper." We as parents and leaders must teach responsibility or we will destroy and cripple those for whom we are responsible. In Matthew we read about Jesus sending two disciple to find and get an ass for Jesus to ride upon to enter Jerusalem. Can you imagine if the disciples said, we can't, where do we look, how should we bring the ass back, how do we lead him, and so on? Matthew 21:6, "And the disciples went, and did as Jesus commanded them." We must teach responsibility in helping others to learn to walk with God, have victory over the flesh, and how to walk with God in His will. Proverbs 16:9, "A man's heart deviseth his way: but the LORD directeth his steps." Psalm 16:11, " Thou wilt shew me the path of life: in thy presence is fullness of joy; at thy right hand there are pleasures for ever more."

Who has God put in your path to help them grow in the Lord? Growing is learning to take responsibility and watching God bless a life. It is not being hard but loving them beyond where they are and encouraging them to grow.

Growing is learning to take responsibility and watching God bless a life.

January 17

Genesis 41-42 Psalm 17 Proverbs 17 Matthew 22

Perfect Will of God

Good morning! I so enjoy feeding the birds this time of year. We have several feeders that I keep sunflower seeds in for the birds. Yesterday as I went out to fill one of the feeders, I noticed some very loud singing of a couple of birds. I just stopped in my tracks and listened. I could not spot the birds, but I moved very slowly so as not to be a distraction and just to keep enjoying their singing.

This morning in our reading is a very important phrase for all of us. Genesis 41:16, "And Joseph answered Pharaoh, saying, It is not in me: God shall give Pharaoh an answer of peace." Look at the phrase, "It is not in me." Pharaoh had a dream and we read in Genesis 41:38, "And Pharaoh said unto his servants, Can we find such a one as this is, a man in whom the Spirit of God is?" Pharaoh was looking for someone to explain his dream and the question is asked, is there anyone that can? Joseph is now brought before the king and, as we know, the butler remembered his dream that Joseph explained. Genesis 41:39, "And Pharaoh said unto Joseph, Forasmuch as God hath shewed thee all this, there is none so discreet and wise as thou art:." I can just see the humility in Joseph as the king expresses himself to Joseph. As I listened and looked for the birds singing, I thought, they are just doing what they were created to do. Oh, that we would walk with God and seek to do what He has created us to do. Doing what God's will is for us should be the greatest desire of all of us. They asked Jesus, "which is the great commandment in the law?" (Matthew 22:36).

Matthew 22:37, "Jesus said unto him, Thou shalt love the Lord thy God with all thy heart, and with all thy soul, and with all thy mind." Stop and think of every bird or animal that God created. They all do what they were created to do. How about us? The happiest Christians are those who are in the perfect will of God for their life. Proverbs 17:22, "A merry heart doeth good like a medicine: but a broken spirit drieth the bones." The most miserable Christians are those waiting for somebody to do something for them, or they are in depression because nobody notices them.

Those birds were singing as loud as they could because they were doing what God created them to do. Get busy doing what God has put in front of you and watch the Lord bless it and you. Psalm 17:7, "Shew thy marvelous lovingkindness, O thou that savest by thy right hand them which put their trust in thee." I thought as I stood there, not wanting to disturb those singing birds. They were not singing to impress anyone, they were not singing for pay, they were not singing to be acknowledged, they were not singing to be liked. They were just singing because that is what the Lord created them to do. Joseph did what God gave him the wisdom to do. How about you and me deciding that we need to be always doing what God created us to do, the way He wants us to do it, where He wants us to do it? Look very close to things around you and you might just find God's will for your life.

The happiest Christians are those who are
in the perfect will of God for their life.

January 18

Genesis 43-45 Psalm 18:1-15 Proverbs 18 Matthew 23

Be a Blessing

Good morning! Who have you shown a personal interest in lately? Has the Lord laid a certain person on your heart, and you checked on them, or sent them a note to see how they were doing? When was the last time you sat down and wrote a handwritten note to someone?

As I was reading this morning in Genesis 43:7, "The man asked us straitly of our state, and of our kindred, saying, Is your father yet alive? Have ye another brother?" Jacob has heard that Joseph wants to see Jacob's youngest son Benjamin, and Jacob is telling his sons, I have lost Joseph and now I cannot lose Benjamin. He makes this statement in Genesis 43:6, "Wherefore dealt ye so ill with me, as to tell the man whether ye had yet a brother?" When we talk to others, do we show a personal interest in them? Are there people who have visited church and we do not take the time to go out of our way to greet them and show an interest in them? Could it possibly be the reason some folks have no interest in church, because no one shows an interest in them? Could the reason you do not have many friends be because you never ask about others? Because you only see yourself and your situations? Jacob caught his breath and listened to his sons tell the full story. Isn't that just like us? We react before we hear the whole story. Then we see interest respond to interest and love respond to love. Genesis 43:11, "take of the best fruits in the land in your vessels, and carry down the man a present, a little balm, and a little honey, spices, and myrrh, nuts, and almonds:." Genesis 43:12, "And take double money in your hand." They did, and listen to Joseph's response when the brothers get back to Egypt. Genesis 43:27, "And he asked them of their welfare, and said, Is your father well, the old man of whom ye spake? Is he yet alive?"

There is a multitude of blessings in being a blessing to others. We need to quit thinking about ourselves and our problems and be an encourager to others. Find others' needs and see your own needs met. Reach out to others and watch others reach out to you. Matthew 23:12, "And whosoever shall exalt himself shall be abased; and he that shall humble himself shall be exalted." Quit asking others to feel sorry for you, pity you, baby you. Seven times we see this phrase in Matthew 23, "Woe unto you scribes, and Pharisees, hypocrites!" A statement we read in Proverbs 18:24 is so very true, "A man that hath friends must shew himself friendly." Seek out people you do not know in church and Sunday School and introduce yourself to them and show an interest in them. Always make visitors feel welcome. Do not feel like I have been hard on you this morning. Read with me Psalm 18:15, "Then the channels of waters were seen, and the foundations of the world were discovered at thy rebuke, O LORD, at the blast of the breath of thy nostrils." Jesus' life was spent for others. Let your life come alive by seeing and ministering to others and their needs.

There is a multitude of blessings in being a blessing to others.

January 19

Genesis 46-48 Psalm 18:16-36 Proverbs 19 Matthew 24

An Expression of Love

Good morning! When you wake up during your night of sleep, what do you do? Please do not think me inappropriate. I am talking about the Lord waking you to speak with you. Throughout the Bible we read of men being awakened during their sleep and the Lord speaking to them, as well as during a dream. We read this morning in Genesis 46:2, "And God spake unto Israel in the visions of the night, and said, Jacob, Jacob. And he said, Here am I." I have made a habit for many years that when I am awakened during the night, I ask the Lord if He needs to tell me something, or does He just want me to tell Him I love Him? Last night was one of those nights I seemed to awaken every hour, and I simply told the Lord how much I love Him. Should we express our love to Him more than we are? I love to end every call to my wife, children, and grandchildren with the words, "I love you."

When that love relationship grows with our Heavenly Father, there is a greater desire for obedience. Genesis 46:3, "And he said, I am God, the God of thy father: fear not to go down into Egypt; for I will there make of thee a great nation:." For a young child to obey their parents is a sign of love for the parents. Yes, I know the child does not want to get in trouble, but as a child grows in a relationship with their parents there is a desire to please and that desire to please is an expression of love. Jacob was going to have to move from Canaan to Egypt at the age of 130 years. To move at any age is difficult, but at 130 years old is very difficult! Jacob's love for God and God's love for Jacob is the key. Genesis

46:4, "I will go down with thee into Egypt; and I will also surely bring thee up again." God was telling Jacob that things were going to be okay. Is our love for God the missing ingredient in our lack of faithfulness and service? To begin the day in the Bible is an expression of love for God. To spend time in prayer is an expression of love to God, saying we want to spend time communicating with Him. Always spend the first time of your prayer time in praise and thanksgiving to the Lord for who He is and what He is. Jesus is coming soon and our watching for Him is also an expression of our love for Him. Matthew 24:42, "Watch therefore: for ye know not what hour your Lord doth come." Matthew 24:44, "Therefore be ye also ready: for in such an hour as ye think not the son of man cometh." A young man that loves a young lady will be on time to see her when he told her he would be. To be ready and busy waiting for the Lord is a tremendous way for us to show our love for the Lord. Excuses will not keep the love in a relationship growing. We need to keep reminding ourselves that excuses are often a coverup for sin. Proverbs 19:3, "The foolishness of man perverteth his way: and his heart fretteth against the LORD." Yes, my love for God is shown in my actions to God. Psalm 18:30, "As for God, his way is perfect: the word of the LORD is tried: he is a buckler to all those that trust in him."

Last night, I did not go to a private place and get on my knees, but just in the dark of the night I said, Father I love you. Yesterday while driving the truck, I spent time speaking to the Lord and just telling Him I love Him. When I got home and had to split some wood, I just stopped and told Him how I love Him. I was not 130 years old when Mrs. Smith and I had to make a major move in our lives, but I was 54, and we moved because we loved Him and wanted to be in His perfect will. It was hard, but we did it because we love Him. Let us love the Lord and express our love in every way we can.

To be ready and busy waiting for the Lord
is a tremendous way for us to show our love for Him.

January 20

Genesis 49-50 Psalm 18:37-50 Proverbs 20 Matthew 25

What Energizes You?

Good morning! I love talking to children. I love seeing them get excited. Sunday night I saw a little boy with some other children and as I walked by, I saw him look at me and I called him by name and stopped and sat down to talk with him. We talked about different things, but then I asked him how his puppy is, and I called his puppy by name. His eyes got big, and the chatter began. It was like energy came to him in our conversation. What energizes you when it comes to the things of the Lord, or is your Christian life just struggling along?

Jacob made a statement in Genesis 49:1, "And Jacob called unto his sons, and said, Gather yourselves together, that I may tell you that which shall befall you in the last days." Again, in Genesis 49:2, "Gather yourselves together, and hear, ye sons of Jacob; and hearken unto Israel your father." "Gather yourselves together," and then he challenges them with two words, "hear" and "hearken." Listen to me and do what I am telling you. Have you forgotten that God wants to use you? Do you need to refocus and get your focus back on God, and get a new excitement about what God wants to do in and through you? When I sat there and talked with that little fellow about his puppy, an excitement and enthusiasm and a little light came on and he wanted to tell me all that his puppy is doing. Jacob was telling his sons that he was leaving but God had a purpose for each one of them, and they needed to live out God's purpose. Quit getting caught up in the things you cannot change or fix and live God's purpose for your life. We have heard many messages on how God is an investor so let us review a couple of verses. In Matthew 25:21, 23, the master is complimenting his faithful servant; "Well done, thou good and faithful servant: thou hast been faithful over a few things, I will make thee ruler over many things." Do not waste your life doing nothing or very little for God. Praise the Lord for your faithfulness, but what are you doing as God has given you time to grow and time to serve? Proverbs 20:4, "The sluggard will not plow by reason of the cold; therefore shall he beg in harvest, and have nothing." Quit giving excuse and get busy. Take another breath, go forward. Get up in the morning and get in the Word of God and spend that time in prayer. Get that joy of the Lord fired up in your life.

Proverbs 20:13, "Love not sleep, lest thou come to poverty; open thine eyes, and thou shalt be satisfied with bread." Live like God is alive and in control. Psalm 18:46, "The LORD liveth; and blessed be my rock; and let the God of my salvation be exalted." I told my wife how much I enjoyed and was blessed talking with this little fellow. She said, "Honey, that is why older people always get a smile on their face when they hold a baby. It is life, and life brings life." Get some life in your walk with God today. I think Mrs. Smith could have used another word other than "older." Maybe I just need to accept the fact and keep being around young people. May our lives produce for the Lord in serving the Lord. Have a blessed day.

Live like God is alive and in control.

January 21

Exodus 1-3 Psalm 19 Proverbs 21 Matthew 26

Seeking His Blessing

Good morning! Years ago, my wife and I were on a vacation out west in several states. I am always captivated in watching the herds of buffalo and elk. Just last night driving to church, I said to my wife, look up at that hillside. Standing there in the reflection of the setting sun were five deer. I slowed down and they watched what we were going to do as we drove on. Herds of cattle, herds of buffalo, herds of elk and even groups of deer; they all have something in common. They multiply and multiply and multiply. Yes, each one was created for a food supply, and it is their nature to keep multiplying. That is the way the Lord created it to be.

We read this morning in Exodus 1:7, "And the children of Israel were fruitful, and increased abundantly, and multiplied, and waxed exceeding mighty; and the land was filled with them." Because of this increase in number, the Egyptian Pharaoh became fearful. Did you ever ask yourself why the Egyptians were not multiplying as fast as the children of Israel? One reason is God's blessing. We have the promise of God's blessing as a child of God. Even in trials and persecutions we have God's promise. The problem is, we are like the Egyptians. We are not seeking the blessings of God and we are doing all that we do in the flesh. The more the children of Israel grew, the more they were afflicted by the Egyptians, but the more God blessed. Exodus 1:12, "But the more they afflicted them, the more they multiplied and grew." There are great blessings awaiting us in spreading the gospel of Jesus Christ. May we seek the face of God and may He hear our pleas to help us spread His Word of salvation to this lost and dying world. No, the world will not like it, but God will bless it. Each fall there are large roundups and hunts to keep the herds of buffalo, elk and deer thinned down to control the population and to preserve the feeding areas for these herds. You know, every year the herds build back, and many years they are greater than they were the year before. In that hour of trial for the Lord Jesus in Matthew 26:53, He said before those that wanted to destroy him, "Thinkest thou that I cannot now pray to my Father, and he shall presently give me more than twelve legions of angels?" We are not buffalo or any animal that roams the prairies and forests, but we are the children of God and God's blessings are waiting for us to receive as we are obedient to the will of God. Proverbs 21:21, "He that followeth after righteousness and mercy findeth life, righteousness, and honour."

I love to hear a bull elk give his call to a herd of cows, letting them know that he has claimed and fought other bulls for his own. I love to hear the grunting sound of a cow buffalo as she is grazing and calling her new calf to come along. My brother and sister, God will bless our efforts to share the story of God's gift of salvation. May we do as the words of Psalm 19:14, "Let the words of my mouth, and the meditation of my heart, be acceptable in thy sight, O LORD, my strength, and my redeemer." May we seek the blessings of God by being obedient to the will and purpose of God for our life. Have a blessed day spreading the gospel.

There are blessings awaiting us in spreading the gospel of Jesus Christ.

January 22

Exodus 4-6 Psalm 20 Proverbs 22 Matthew 27

God Almighty

Good morning! Oh, how I was blessed from our reading today. Today is one of those days that I just want to keep reading and studying. Do not just read to check off a box on your daily schedule, but read to learn, grow, and come closer to the Lord. Dive into the Word of God to learn, grow and live the Christian life in a closer walk with the Lord. We all get discouraged. We all sometimes ask ourselves why we are going through what we are going through. I believe there are also times we question what the Lord is trying to do in our lives when it seems that we are up against a wall, and we cannot see anything positive in front of us.

Moses had gone to the leaders of the children of Israel, and they had been instructed that God was going to lead them to the Promised Land and out of Egypt. Moses and Aaron went to Pharaoh and that made Pharaoh mad, and more pressure was put on the children of Israel. The children of Israel were now mad that Moses showed up and caused this greater burden to be placed upon them. In Exodus 5:22, Moses asks the question, "why is it that thou hast sent me?" Exodus 6:1, "Then the LORD said unto Moses, Now shalt thou see what I will do." Please read slower now and get the impact of what God is about to say. Exodus 6:2, "And God spake unto Moses, and said unto him, I am the LORD." Exodus 6:3, "And I appeared unto Abraham, unto Isaac, and unto Jacob, by the name of God Almighty." Now let us take a moment and remember back in Genesis 17:1 where God identified himself as El-Shaddai. He told Abraham that He is the Almighty God. Now let us finish the verse in Exodus 6:3, "but by my name JEHOVAH." God is the God of all sufficiency and now He said He was becoming their LORD to show His power and goodness. He would keep His promises of being their deliverer and take them out of bondage and to the Promised Land that He had provided for them. GLORY!! Thank the Lord for your salvation, but God wants and desires to be our LORD and take us to His promises. When Jesus hung on the cross, the centurion looked at Him and "saw the earthquake, and those things that were done. Then they feared greatly, saying, "Truly this was the Son of God." (Matthew 27:54).

My brother and sister, He gave each of us who know Him the perfect gift of salvation, but He is waiting for us to fully give ourselves to Him so that He can be God Almighty in our lives. Proverbs 22:20, "Have not I written to thee excellent things in counsels and knowledge." Proverbs 22:21, "That I might make thee know the certainty of the words of truth." God wants to do great things in our lives, but more than doing great things, He is looking to be "God Almighty." Psalm 20:6, "Now know I that the LORD saveth his anointed; he will hear him from his holy heaven with the saving strength of his right hand." I encourage you to take this moment and say, Father, I surrender my will and my ways to have YOU be the "God Almighty." Let Him have full control. Have a blessed day.

More than doing great things in our lives,
God is looking to be "God Almighty."

January 23

Exodus 7-8 Psalm 21 Proverbs 23 Matthew 28

What Are Your Goals?

Good morning! At the end of each year, or very early in the beginning of a new year, we set goals. These goals could be personal, family, ministry, or business. I believe we should set goals and keep looking at the goals we set throughout the year to make sure we are moving toward accomplishing them. As I was reading this morning, I asked myself, have

I been setting goals in the wrong way, or do I need to take more time in setting the goals I set?

We see in our reading this morning that Moses and Aaron are now going before Pharaoh to ask permission to let the children of Israel go from the bondage of the Egyptians. Exodus 7:4, "But Pharaoh shall not hearken unto you, that I may lay my hand upon Egypt, and bring forth mine armies, out of the land of Egypt by great judgments." Before Moses and Aaron went before Pharaoh, God let these men know that Pharaoh was not going to let the people go. I thought, why go through the process, Lord? Just get to what you want and be done with Pharaoh and the Egyptians. That is when it hit me. God's way and will is not always our way and will. God has His purpose, and that purpose is not always for us to see or to understand. Listen to the following statements. Exodus 7:5, "And the Egyptians shall know that I am the LORD." Exodus 7:17, "Thus saith the LORD, In this thou shalt know that I am the LORD." Even Pharaoh's own magicians went to him and told him that these were acts of God. Exodus 8:19, "Then the magicians said unto Pharaoh, This is the finger of God."

The world wants to control us. The world will allow us to be Christians, but they want the total control of our Christianity. The world says it is okay to be a Christian, but do not tell us we are wrong, and do not tell us how to live. The world wants us to compromise and that is why many do compromise, just to get along with the world. Exodus 8:25, "And Pharaoh called for Moses and for Aaron, and said, Go ye, sacrifice to your God in the land." Do you see the words, "in the land?" Pharaoh would let them have their religious services, but he would have control over where they had them. Exodus 8:32, "And Pharaoh hardened his heart at this time also." We must realize we will never have the total approval of the world, and this is where we must always stay alert to the sly workings of the devil. Even when the soldiers felt the earthquake, saw the stone rolled away and saw that the tomb of Jesus was emptied, they knew it was God but they were paid money and told to tell a lie. Matthew 28:13, "Saying, Say ye, His disciples came by night, and stole him away while we slept." Matthew 28:15, "So they took the money, and did as they were taught: and this saying is commonly reported among the Jews until this day."

Keep your focus. What is God's purpose for you? What is God's will for all of us? What is the foremost goal of every Christian that hungers to do God's will? Matthew 28:19, "Go ye therefore, and teach all nations." What really spoke to me this morning is that my goal setting should be knowing God's will and setting the goals to accomplish God's will. We are not alone in serving God in God's will. Matthew 28:20, "lo, I am with you alway." That is how missionaries can go around the world to win the lost to Christ. My brother and sister, the world is a liar. It wants what it wants and God will have His way. Proverbs 23:23, "Buy the truth, and sell it not; also wisdom, and instruction, and understanding." May our goals each day be the will of God. Psalm 21:3, "Be thou exalted, LORD, in thine own strength: so will we sing and praise thy power." Do not be caught in the trap of compromise with the world. Live for Christ and His will to be done.

Our goal setting should be knowing God's will
and setting goals to accomplish His will.

January 24

Exodus 9-11 Psalm 22:1-21 Proverbs 24 Mark 1

A Tender Heart

Good morning! Each time I read in Exodus about Moses and Aaron going before Pharaoh, I think to myself how slow of a learner Pharaoh was. He knew God was going to have the victory, and yet he fought it the whole way. Even his magicians came to him and told him to let the people go and yet his heart, time and again, got hard and he would not let them go. I often check my own heart to see if it is getting hard. We must keep a tender heart toward the Lord to keep growing in Him and to stay in His will for our life. God wants to use each of us. Do not focus on how, when, or where God will use you. Just maintain and grow in Him to be used.

Listen to Exodus 9:16, "And in very deed for this cause have I raised thee up, for to shew in thee my power." We do not always know what "very deed" is, but we do know that we have life to be used. Exodus 10:2, "And that thou mayest tell in the ears of thy son, and of thy son's son, what things I have wrought." God has a purpose, and it is not always for us to know, but live by and for God's purpose. We read in Mark chapter one of God the Father speaking to Jesus, and the Bible records those words for us to read and to know. Mark 1:11, "Thou art my beloved Son, in whom I am well pleased." Now we see what God does to Jesus and how He wants the separation from the world for each of us. Mark 1:12, "And immediately the Spirit driveth him into the wilderness." We need to always be in church and learning and growing plus daily be in the Word of God, learning and growing. Jesus set an example for us to follow. Mark 1:35, "And in the morning, rising up a great while before day, he went out, and departed into a solitary place, and there prayed." If Jesus felt this time of separation and preparation was important, how about us? Proverbs 24:5, "A wise man is strong; yea, a man of knowledge increaseth strength." This verse teaches us the importance of learning and that learning makes us stronger in the Lord. Generations before us had a belief and trust in God. Psalm 22:4-5, "Our fathers trusted in thee: they trusted, and thou didst deliver them. They cried unto thee, and were delivered: they trusted in thee, and were not confounded."

This world we live in is so mixed up and far from God. There is a fear today of the unknown and the unseen and yet there is not the turning to God. What an opportunity there is before us! It is God that does the saving, but never forget He wants to use each of us. Moses and Aaron were the tools that God used. God is looking and willing to use any of us as we go to that "solitary place" and learn from Him, as we spend time in His Word and in prayer to Him. He is waiting for you. Get to the "solitary place" and grow in the LORD. You ask, where is the "solitary place?" It is any private place that you and the Lord can be alone, and you have a complete focus in heart, mind, and spirit, on the Lord. Please know He is there and wants to be with you. Seek Him today.

We must keep a tender heart toward the Lord
to keep growing in Him and to stay in His will.

January 25

Exodus 12-13 Psalm 22:22-31 Proverbs 25 Mark 2

An Orderly Life

Good morning! You know everything in life has order. That is the way God made it to be. A tree will have buds before the leaves grow on the limbs. The seasons will always come in order. The sun will always rise before it sets. Yes, everything of God is in order. What about our lives? Is there order in our walk and service for the Lord? As we read in Exodus 12 and 13 this morning, we see order in God telling the children of Israel how to prepare to leave Egypt. Let us take a brief look at the order of preparation that God gave them. Exodus 12:5, "Lamb without blemish." Exodus 12:5, "Male of the first year." Exodus 12:6, "Keep it up until the fourteenth day." Exodus 12:9, "Eat not of it raw." Exodus 12:10, "let nothing remain." Exodus 12:11, "And thus shall ye eat it; with your loins girded, your shoes on your feet, and your staff in your hand; and ye shall eat it in haste: it is the LORD's Passover." Exodus 12:15, "Seven days shall ye eat unleavened bread." Exodus 12:22, "none of you shall go out at the door of his house until the morning." Look back to Exodus 12:7, "And they shall take of the blood, and strike it on the two side posts and on the upper door post of the houses, wherein they shall eat." The death angel would pass that night and where there was blood on the door post, the angel would pass by but not at the homes where the blood was not applied. Order must be done God's way.

I remember in the 7th grade when I started taking wood shop and then welding and metal shop. All our tools had to be put back in the exact place they came from. Each tool was to be used for the purpose it was made and to be used in the way it was to be used. There is order all around us. Streets have a name in every community. Laws are given for us to obey. God has an order that He wants us to follow so that He can use us and bless our lives. A man had palsy that we read about in Mark chapter 2, and when four men took him to see Jesus to be healed, there was no way they could get him to Jesus. They took him up on the roof, removed a portion of the roof and let Him down. The Bible tells us in Mark 2:5, "When Jesus saw their faith." The man was healed, and Jesus told him, "thy sins be forgiven thee." These men knew what needed to be done, and it had to be done God's way through their faith in God. God needs to see order in our lives. All of us are a work in progress, but God is daily looking to see us desiring to walk with Him and making some changes along with order in our lives. Proverbs 25:4, "Take away the dross from the silver, and there shall come forth a vessel for the finer." The "dross" is the impurity of the metal.

We have to get the disorder out and put order in our lives. If all of creation has order, how about us? May I suggest order in every day's beginning? Make it a point to take the time to read the Bible on a schedule, during an appointed time every day. We are a generation that has lost the principle of earlier generations of going to bed when it is time to go to bed and being able to get up and read the Word of God before the day begins. Please do not say you can't. To have order in our life is a work in progress. Where do we start? Psalm 22:26, "The meek shall eat and be satisfied: they shall praise the LORD that seek him: your heart shall live for ever." Did you see the word "meek?" That is for you and me to humble ourselves. I challenge us to make time to work on order in our lives, and watch the blessings come. The first blessing will be learning from the Bible. The next is we will be accomplishing more things in our lives. Let us take time this morning and check to see what is out of order and make a list of areas that we need to get back in order, and then start working on the list. Remember, God has an order for everything.

God has an order that He wants us to follow
so that He can use us and bless our lives.

January 26

Exodus 14-15 Psalm 23 Proverbs 26 Mark 3

Why Look Back?

Good morning! Well, I pray that you will read the entire devotional this morning, because I am going to start out with something that might be a little too strong for some stomachs, but it is Bible and I have learned a new truth. Proverbs 26:11, "As a dog returneth to his vomit, so a fool returneth to his folly." Most all of us have seen a dog or a cat eat their own vomit. I have seen it many times and every time I think, how awful and how can they do it? Well, there is a very good reason and picture for us to see in all of our Scripture this morning. Dogs have a very keen ability to smell and when they vomit, it is the food that they just ate, and it was not digested. Their smell lets them know that it is good food, so they eat it again.

How did the children of Israel want to stay in Egypt after all they had been through? Exodus 14:12, "Is not this the word that we did tell thee in Egypt, saying, Let us alone, that we may serve the Egyptians? For it had been better for us to serve the Egyptians, than that we should die in the wilderness." An addicted person is thankful and rejoicing when they trust Christ, but then the battle comes when the old friends and the flesh put the pressure on. The flesh says, it was better than what you are going through now. When the children of Israel faced their first trial after leaving Egypt, they looked back instead of looking forward and letting their faith in God grow. Did God deliver them when they were obedient to proceed? Yes, He did. They then came to the waters of Marah and they were bitter. Exodus 15:23, "waters of Marah, for they were bitter." Moses cried unto the Lord, Exodus 15:25, "And he cried unto the LORD; and the LORD shewed him a tree, which when he had cast into the waters, the waters were made sweet." Every trial and testing we go through is to make us stronger and have greater faith in the Lord. Exodus 15:26, "If thou wilt diligently hearken to the voice of the LORD thy God, and wilt do that which is right in his sight, and wilt give ear to his commandments, and keep all his statutes, I will put none of these diseases upon thee, which I have brought upon the Egyptians: for I am the LORD that healeth thee."

Why look back? Why eat the vomit of past sin? Why quit on what God is doing in your life? Why turn to the world and its wicked deceitful ways? You are a child of God, so live like it. Mark 3:35, "For whosoever shall do the will of God, the same is my brother, and my sister, and mother." So you and I come to something we cannot cross; look to the

Lord. So you come to bitter water of temptation and trial; look to the Lord. Psalm 23:4, "Yea, though I walk through the valley of the shadow of death, I will fear no evil: for thou art with me; thy rod and thy staff they comfort me." The next time you get sick from a pet returning to his vomit, just look at yourself returning to a sin you once did or coming to a body of water that you thought you could not cross. Let us decide to keep going through each battle and grow in the Lord.

Every trial and testing we go through is to make us stronger and have greater faith in the Lord.

January 27

Exodus 16-18 Psalm 24 Proverbs 27 Mark 4

Our Motive for Obedience

Good morning! If we know what is right, then why do we struggle to do right? I asked myself this question this morning. It is not that I do not always want to do right, it is that I sometimes struggle in my flesh. I thought about one of the dogs I have. Does it obey only for reward, or does it look for reward because of obedience? I asked myself the same question. Do I do what is right because I know God will bless, or do I love God and obey Him because that is a show of my love for Him? Exodus 16:28, "And the LORD said unto Moses, How long refuse ye to keep my commandments and my laws?" The children of Israel were continually complaining about how their needs were going to be met, instead of just being obedient to God and then He would provide their needs. Exodus 18:19, we read how Moses' father-in-law challenged Him to teach and train others to be obedient to God and then the work of God could grow. "Be thou for the people to Godward, that thou mayest bring the causes unto God." Exodus 18:20, "And thou shalt teach them ordinances and laws, and shalt shew them the way wherein they must walk, and the work that they must do."

You know, when a dog obeys his or her master, they both enjoy each other's companionship better. When your dog is disobedient, you get frustrated, impatient, and maybe even regretful you have the pet. That is why many people do not have animals, because of the added responsibility. Let us think about ourselves personally. Do we do what God wants because we love God, or do we do what we do because we are looking for God to bless our lives? What if we did not see the blessings of God for a while, or what if we did not see God answer our prayers in the way we wanted? How is our attitude then? Mark 4:2, "And He taught them many things by parables, and said unto them in his doctrine." The word "doctrine" means teachings. Mark 4:3, starts out with one word, "Hearken," meaning to be in complete submission and understanding. Mark 4:12, "That seeing they may see, and not perceive; and hearing they may hear, and not understand; lest at any time they should be converted, and their sins should be forgiven them." Jesus is saying that through the doctrine or teachings they will learn, be convicted of sin, and be saved. Oh, that we would learn and obey!

Proverbs 27:23, "Be thou diligent to know the state of thy flocks, and look well to thy herds." A shepherd will know the needs of his flock and tend to those needs. Our Shepherd has provided us His Word, the Bible, and our love for Him should bring about our daily reading, studying, and applying the teachings to our life. Do we obey for reward, or do we receive the rewards of a faithfulness to God because of our obedience? Psalm 24:4-5, "He that hath clean hands, and a pure heart; who hath not lifted up his soul unto vanity, nor sworn deceitfully. He shall receive the blessing from the LORD, and righteousness from the God of his salvation." Would you not like God to do something very special for you just because He has seen your love and obedience to Him? Think about how you are living. Ask yourself the question this morning, am I obedient to God because of the rewards I desire or is my love for God and desire to please Him causing me to be obedient? Something to think about.

Do we obey for reward, or do we receive the rewards because of our obedience?

January 28

Exodus 19-20 Psalm 25 Proverbs 28 Mark 5

Making Memories

Good morning! The large flakes of snow have fallen, and I have memories of sledding down a hill, making a snow fort, making the pile of snowballs, getting ready for the big snowball fight of the year. As I looked out in the dark earlier this morning, I saw the birds by the bird feeder picking at the snow to get down to the seeds in the feeders. My mind is full of memories today of winters and large snowfalls of the past.

I imagine in my mind the memories of the children of Israel as they remember the day that they approached Mount Sinai and they were all going to hear the voice of God. We read earlier all that God spoke to Moses, and then he told it to the people, and this is how they responded. Exodus 19:8, "And all the people answered together, and said, All that the LORD hath spoken we will do." The boundary was set around Mount Sinai. Exodus19:12, "And thou shalt set bounds unto the people round about." Moses now goes alone to be with God and in Exodus 20, the law is given. We read in Exodus 20:20, "Fear not: for God is come to prove you." All of us have memories of things that the Lord has done in our lives. The day we received Christ as our Saviour, the day we were obedient and followed the Lord in baptism, the day we got our first Bible, but what about today? Are the memories only memories or are they benchmarks of growth in our life? The law was to help all of us grow in Christ, for it reveals sin to us and gives us guidelines to grow in Christ. I read on in Mark 5 and as I read, I pictured the woman with an issue of blood who pushed her way through the crowd just to get to Jesus, and just to touch Him. Mark 5:28, "If I may touch but his clothes, I shall be whole." She did and, as you know, she was healed, just from the touch of the Saviour's clothes. As years passed in her life, I wonder if the memory of that day kept her faith growing in the Lord. Proverbs 28:9, "He that turneth away his ear from hearing the law, even his prayer shall be abomination." I trust you are not turning away from the Lord. Please keep growing and being faithful to the Lord. Proverbs 28:20, "A faithful man shall abound with blessings." Proverbs 28:26, "He that trusteth in his own heart is a fool: but whoso walketh wisely, he shall be delivered."

Keep daily walking in the Lord and building memories of all that the Lord is doing. When those days of testing come, keep moving because of what you have seen the Lord do before. Remember He will do it again and, most of the time, in a greater way. Psalm 25:15, "Mine eyes are ever toward the LORD; for he shall pluck my feet out of the net." The snow will melt away, but the memories of the sun glistening on it, like it is a field of diamonds, will last. May your daily walk with God be a walk of making memories that are to be stepping stones of all that the Lord is doing in your life. Have a blessed day in the Lord.

Keep daily walking in the Lord and building memories of all that the Lord is doing.

January 29

Exodus 21-22 Psalm 26 Proverbs 29 Mark 6

Committed to the Master

Good morning! Wow, the Scriptures are full and overflowing! We must pay attention to each word and allow the Holy Spirit to speak to us. What a joy to hold the Words of God in our hands! My thoughts this morning start at the words of a servant that could be set free and be on his own, but we read how if he desires, he can stay committed to the master. Did you catch what I just said? If the servant desires, he can stay committed to the master. There are many who are thankful they are saved, but to make that commitment takes character. I have often heard said, I want to come to Sunday School, but we have trouble getting up. I am just not a morning person. It is a fight getting the children up and ready. Sunday is the only day I have to sleep in. Two hours is just too long for the children to sit still for Sunday School and church.

Exodus 21:5, "And if the servant shall plainly say, I love my master, my wife, and my children; I will not go out free." Look at those words, "I love my master, my wife, and my children." This servant wanted to stay under the master's authority, control, responsibilities, etc. Oh, that our love for the Master would cause a love even greater than this servant had! In Mark 6:45, we read how Jesus said, "And straightway he constrained his disciples to get into the ship, and to go to the other side." The words "straightway" and "constrained" shows a powerful urging. Is our lack of obedience to God really a personal character problem? We all will do what we want to do. I have said it before, "good intentions never accomplish anything." All of us get sick, have family situations, but what is it when we do not? Proverbs 29:1, "He, that being often reproved hardeneth his neck, shall suddenly be destroyed, and that without remedy." What happened to young people who are now destroying property of others and burning cities? It is like they were never taught discipline, self-control, appreciation, respect, and the list goes on. Proverbs 29:15, "The rod and reproof give wisdom: but a child left to himself bringeth his mother to shame." Proverbs 29:17, "Correct thy son, and he shall give thee rest, yea, he shall give delight unto thy soul." Who is training children today? What is training children today? Are we as parents and grandparents teaching and building character in the next generation?

I cannot encourage enough for each of us to work on our own character and the character of those whom we are responsible for. Psalm 26:11, "But as for me, I will walk in mine integrity: redeem me, and be merciful unto me." It starts with each of us personally. As I read Psalm 26:12, "My foot standeth in an even place." Let us start with a self-evaluation and begin with our personal relationship with Christ. No excuse but a fresh commitment to be honest with ourselves. Allow God to hear us say "forgive me" and start moving in the right direction. If you are going in the right direction, stay in the race to the end when we all stand face to face with our Saviour.

There are many who are thankful they are saved,
but to make that commitment takes character.

January 30

Exodus 23-24 Psalm 27 Proverbs 30 Mark 7

Personal Revival

Good morning! I saw a picture of a family with their hands all on top of each other with the father's hands first laying on an open Bible, then the mother's hands and then each child. My heart was so moved as I thought about all the Word of God teaches us and how the Lord ordained the family and the guidelines that are laid out for us.

Exodus 24:7, "And he took the book of the covenant, and read in the audience of the people: and they said, All that the LORD hath said will we do, and be obedient." Oh, that we would read, study, and apply all that is within the pages of Scripture! What is the problem with us? Do we continually give excuse why we can't, or should I say why we will not, be faithful to God and the teachings of His Word? Mark 7:20-23 spells things out very clearly for each of us. "And he said, That which cometh out of the man, that defileth the man. For from within, out of the heart of men, proceed evil thoughts, adulteries, fornications, murders, Thefts, covetousness, wickedness, deceit, lasciviousness, an evil eye, blasphemy, pride, foolishness: All these evil things come from within, and defile the man." Sin is ruining us, and it constantly must be purged through the reading, teaching, and preaching of the Word of God. Oh, my friend, we need to heed the Word of God and put our priorities of life in second place and put God first in everything. Proverbs 30:12, "There is a generation that are pure in their own eyes, and yet is not washed from their filthiness." Let Jesus save you today if you have not asked Him to forgive you of your sins. Let Him come into your heart and save your soul. For those of us saved, there must be a continual revealing and cleansing of this old flesh and our sinful hearts. May our hearts be as we read in Psalm 27:8, "When thou saidst, seek ye my face; my heart said unto thee, Thy face, LORD, will I seek."

As I looked at the picture of the hands of each family member all laying on the Word of God, I said to myself, let a revival start in my heart and sweep to each member of our family. May that be the prayer of each of us. May there be a reviving to the things of God in each of us. A freshness about our church attendance, a freshness toward the reading of the Word of God, and a fresh surrendering of our heart to do and live the Word of God in every way we can. Psalm 27:14, "Wait on the LORD: be of good courage, and he shall strengthen thine heart: wait, I say, on the LORD." Be patient as you read the Word of God, be patient in your prayer life, be patient in your daily walk with God and see Him come forth like never before in your life. Lord, start a revival in me, and let it flow through me. Lord bless you.

May there be a reviving to the things of God in each of us.

January 31

Exodus 25-26 Psalm 28 Proverbs 31 Mark 8

Set in Order

Good morning! I hear the wind blowing outside, the rain, sleet, and a little snow in the air, and then I read about the children of Israel in the wilderness. I read about the construction of the tabernacle, the furniture, the ark and all the adornments, along with the making of the materials that will be the borders and that beautiful curtain that will separate the holy place from the most holy place. I ask myself, how was all this done in the wilderness? Their dedication to be what God desired for them to be and their obedience to do what God told them to do, how God told them to do, brings a great conviction on me.

Exodus 25:16, "And thou shalt put into the ark the testimony which I shall give thee." I asked myself this morning, Dave Smith, what kind of testimony is being recorded about you? You and I have entertained the thought of quitting, giving up. Making statements like "things are too tough." I read three words that we need to take a long look at this morning. Exodus 26:17, "set in order." To accomplish what the Lord had asked them to do, they had to set a lot of things in order. Is your life "set in order?" God cannot and will not be what we need Him to be if things in our lives are not "set in order." Exodus 26:30, "And thou shalt rear up the tabernacle according to the fashion thereof which was shewed thee in the mount." This is why it can never be stressed enough regarding the importance of a daily walk with the Lord, and faithfulness in God's house every time the church doors are open to learn and grow in the way that God has instructed us to be. We must daily "set in order" our lives in accordance to God and His Word. We read in Mark 8:33 the words Jesus said to Peter when he was rebuked by Jesus. Jesus was talking about how "the Son of man must suffer many things, and be rejected of the elders, and of the chief priests, and scribes, and be killed, and after three days rise again" (Mark 8:31). Then Jesus says, "thou savourest not the things that be of God, but the things that be of men." We must "set in order" our lives. Mark 8:34, "Whosoever will come after me, let him deny himself and take up his cross, and follow me." Mark 8:35, "For whosoever will save his life shall lose it; but whosoever shall lose his life for my sake and the gospel's, the same shall save it."

Oh, the wonderful words of Proverbs 31:8,9 "Open thy mouth." Let us learn to grow in the Lord and be obedient to what we are being taught and what we are daily learning in a walk with the Lord. God will speak if we listen. Psalm 28:2, "Hear the voice of my supplications, when I cry unto thee, when I lift up my hands toward thy holy oracle." Right now, let us reach out to the Lord so that we can "set in order" our lives for God. His order is always the right order. Picture with me the presence of God in that beautiful tabernacle in the wilderness and then think with me that same presence of God lives within the heart and life of everyone who has trusted Christ as their Saviour. May we daily "set in order" our lives for the cause of Christ.

We must daily "set in order" our lives in accordance to God and His Word.

February 1

Exodus 27-28 Psalm 29 Proverbs 1 Mark 9

Thick as Soup

Good morning! Are you ready to begin another day with a walk with the Lord? I am so very thankful we have the living Word of God to read, study and apply to our lives. For all of us who know the Lord and are trusting in Him, it seems there are those days that He seems far from us, but He is not. As I was driving the other day it was around noon and you could hardly see five car lengths in front of you. It was in the middle of the day and the sun would have been at its brightest, but the warm air had brought a ground cover fog that was thick as soup. Now that is an expression that has passed down through time. I hope you will add it to your statements that you will pass on in life. Yes, "thick as soup." I could not see very far ahead, so I had to slow down the speed I was traveling. That is not what I wanted to do, but to be safe that is what I had to do.

The Christian life is a battle because we fight a daily battle of sin. Life sometimes with its trials seems to be "as thick as soup." You cannot see very far ahead, so you have to slow down and trust in the Lord and wait on Him. As our reading took us to Exodus chapters 27 and 28, I noticed these words mentioned twenty-five times, "And thou shalt." Just three words, but a powerful lesson. I did not know what was ahead in the fog, so I had to slow down and keep my eyes on the road and be very cautious for oncoming traffic, as well as traffic coming from a side road. As a Christian, we must keep our eyes on Christ because we do not know what the devil is going to throw at us and we do not always know what temptation is going to appear right before us. What we must do is the "thou shalts." By this I mean we must daily do what we know is always right to do. Life is a path that is not always clear but staying with Jesus on the path of life will cause us to have His strength, His protection, His guidance for every situation. We must keep Christ first and foremost in every area of our lives. As we read about Aaron's priestly garments this morning, we read in Exodus 28:26, "And thou shalt make a plate of pure gold, and grave upon it, like the engravings of a signet, HOLINESS TO THE LORD." This was to be a gold plate right on the very front of his mitre that he was to always wear as he presented himself before the Lord. When life becomes "thick as soup," we can have clear eyesight when we walk with the Lord and put Him in first place and in the forefront of our lives. Mark 9:23, "If thou canst believe, all things are possible to him that believeth." We need to keep growing in our faith in God. The father who brought his son to Jesus cried out in Mark 9:24, "I believe; help thou mine unbelief."

Oh yes, life will get as "thick as soup," but keep putting your trust in the Lord. Proverbs 1:7, "The fear of the LORD is the beginning of knowledge: but fools despise wisdom and instruction." The worst thing I can do in driving on a road in the fog is to stop. A car might be coming and then my stopped car appears in front of it and that oncoming car cannot stop and hits me. When the Christian walk and growth seems to get "as thick as soup," just keep looking to the Lord. He will give guidance and strength. Psalm 29:11, "The LORD will give strength unto his people; the LORD will bless his people with peace." Remember when life gets "as thick as soup," keep on going. You might have to slow down more than you want but keep walking with the Lord and He will safely guide you through those trials and temptations. We need to be thankful that He is always there and even in the "thick of soup," learn to call upon Him. When you and I cannot see because things are as "thick as soup," know HE always sees and has perfect sight.

When the Christian walk gets "as thick as soup,"
just keep looking to the Lord.

February 2

Exodus 29-30 Psalm 30 Proverbs 2 Mark 10

Time To Get Up

Good morning! Do you ever find yourself being stubborn? I do not want to do what I know I need to do. I read in a book yesterday that a person does not have trouble getting up because they are tired. A person has trouble getting up because they enjoy the comfort of the bed more than getting up and getting done what needs to be done. I have thought a lot about that statement. We enjoy what we are doing more than what we should be doing.

As I began the reading this morning in Exodus 29, I saw this phrase, "And this is the thing that thou shalt do." These were instructions for worship and to understand the coming Messiah who would fulfill the will of God for salvation to all mankind. They were also instructions on obedience to follow God in holiness and a set apart life. Let us look at the entire verse; "And this is the thing that thou shalt do unto them to hallow them, to minister unto me in the priest's office." Look at the word "hallow," which means to make holy or set apart for holy use. That is God's purpose and plan for us, to be set apart and holy in His eyes. The children of Israel were learning proper worship in the wilderness, and it started with preparation of the priests which would perform the functions of sacrifices and worship for the people. Exodus 29:20, "Then shalt thou kill the ram, and take of his blood, and put it upon the tip of the right ear of Aaron, and upon the tip of the right ear of his sons, and upon the thumb of their right hand, and upon the great toe of their right foot." Okay, let us look at the blood being applied and the picture for us to see. The "ear" is to stress the importance of proper listening to God. The "thumb" teaches us proper worship and service for God, and the blood being applied to the big toe of the right foot pictures a need to have a sure walk with God. All we learn in our walk with God is not just for us, but to live and teach to our families and to others. Exodus 29:29, "And the holy garments of Aaron shall be his sons' after him, to be anointed therein, and to be consecrated in them." Salvation is for all mankind. Man refuses to humbly come to God so man makes the gift of salvation and a growth in Christ so difficult, which it is not, because that is where lies the victory in the Christian's life. Mark 10:26-27, "And they were astonished out of measure, saying among themselves, who then can be saved? And Jesus looking upon them saith, With men it is impossible, but not with God: for with God all things are possible."

Is extra time in a warm soft bed and the comfort of those covers more important in our day than learning how to walk and have victory in a life with Christ? Proverbs 2:1-2, "My son, if thou wilt receive my words, and hide my commandments with thee; so that thou incline thine ear unto wisdom and apply thine heart to understanding." Read on down to Proverbs 2:5, "Then shalt thou understand the fear of the LORD and find the knowledge of God." This morning the temperature is very cold, the wind is blowing, and the bed felt so good. Yet before the day starts, each of us must get our strength, guidance, and preparation to face the day from the Lord. We need to get up, wake up, and have that daily walk with the Lord. Sing a chorus, praise the Lord for a while, and prepare to meet thy God. Psalm 30:4, "Sing unto the LORD, O ye saints of his, and give thanks at the remembrance of his holiness." Have a very blessed day in the Lord.

We need to get up, wake up, and have that daily walk with the Lord.

February 3

Exodus 31-33 Psalm 31 Proverbs 3 Mark 11

The Lord's Day

Good morning! Picture with me a Saturday evening before it gets too late, the family getting their clothes pressed and ready for church on Sunday morning. The call of dad is heard saying, "Get everything ready for Sunday and when you get done, come to the living room for us to have family devotions and prayer. We have to get to bed early to be ready to get up and be at church on time." Sunday morning arrives, the smell of fresh coffee and the noise of each calling out when they are finished in the bathroom. Dad lets everybody know what time it is and when the car will be pulling out for church. The focus early Saturday night was for church Sunday. Now we all know that is not the true picture in every home, but I ask the question, should it be?

Exodus 31:13, "Verily my sabbaths ye shall keep." Exodus 31:15, "Six days may work be done; but in the seventh is the sabbath of rest, holy to the LORD." Exodus 31:17, "for in six days the LORD made heaven and earth, and on the seventh day he rested, and was refreshed." We now live in a world that runs seven days a week and twenty-four hours a day. Many people have to work on Sunday just to provide services for the rest of us, such as hospitals, police and fire protection, utilities, etc., but society has turned Sunday into a holiday instead of a holy day. When Sunday started turning into a holiday, we also began to see the attitude toward worship change just like what happened to the children of Israel in our reading this morning. They were in Egypt and their worship turned into the actions they learned while in Egypt. Exodus 32:17, "And when Joshua heard the noise of the people as they shouted, he said unto Moses, There is a noise of war in the camp." Wrong attitude toward the sabbath brought wrong worship, wrong music, idol worship and nakedness. We read on in Mark as Jesus came to the temple and He saw all that was going on. Mark 11:15, "And they come to Jerusalem: and Jesus went into the temple, and began to cast out them that sold and bought in the temple, and overthrew the tables of the money changers, and the seats of them that sold doves." Mark 11:17, "Is it not written, My house shall be called of all nations the house of prayer? But ye have made it a den of thieves."

May I suggest that we evaluate our faithful attendance and attitude toward the Lord's Day? Do we look forward to worshipping the Lord, or are our minds on entertainment and on what we want to do the rest of the day? Should our focal point each week and each day be on worshipping the Lord? Proverbs 6:7, "In all thy ways acknowledge him, and he shall direct thy paths. Be not wise in thine own eyes: fear the LORD, and depart from evil." Oh, that our attitudes and actions would be looking forward to the day and time we can join together as a family, as brothers and sisters in Christ, and worship the Lord together in His house! Psalm 31:19, "Oh how great is thy goodness, which thou hast laid up for them that fear thee; which thou hast wrought for them that trust in thee before the sons of men!" May we set the example of being early each time the doors are open at our church. May we be prepared and ready to join together in singing hymns and have Bibles open when the message is being preached. May we put worship in a spot of priority in our lives. Read those words again with me from Exodus 31:13, "Verily my sabbaths ye shall keep." Oh, that we may all join together as believers in Christ and worship and bring praise to our Lord God. See you in church.

Our focal point each week and each day should be on worshipping the Lord.

February 4

Exodus 34-35 Psalm 32 Proverbs 4 Mark 12

Mixing and Baking

Good morning! Do you like cake? After beginning my Bible reading this morning, a verse stirred a thought in my mind. Exodus 35:21, "And they came, every one whose heart stirred him up, and every one whom his spirit made willing." I have watched many times as my wife, and years ago my mother, would begin the process of making a cake or preparing to bake cookies. You do know that the greatest cookies ever baked are oatmeal raisin cookies. I can smell them baking. I pictured in my mind this morning a bowl on the counter with all the ingredients being added to prepare to bake a beautiful, delicious oatmeal spice cake. As the ingredients go into the bowl, it is not yet a cake.

The children of God were being instructed of what was needed to construct the tabernacle, and their hearts were being stirred to bring items and to learn what to do. They became involved in God's plan and will. Exodus 35:29, "The children of Israel brought a willing offering unto the

LORD, every man and woman, whose heart made them willing." I asked this morning, is it a cake or is it not a cake? Many have come to know Christ as their Saviour but have failed in allowing their heart to be stirred for God, and yet many have had their heart stirred for God, but failed or just quit when they had to go through the oven of trials and testings. There will be no cake if the ingredients stay in the mixing bowl, or even if the ingredients do get poured into the pan to be baked, but never get put in the oven. Think about a cake being prepared, put into the oven, but the oven never gets turned on. The process of making and baking a cake must be complete to enjoy that delicious oatmeal spice cake. Mark 12:30, "And thou shalt love the LORD thy God with all thy heart, and with all thy soul, and with all thy mind, and with all thy strength: this is the first commandment." That is the full process of being what God has made us to be. Proverbs 4:11, "I have taught thee in the way of wisdom; I have led thee in right paths." Proverbs 4:13, "Take fast hold of instruction; let her not go: keep her; for she is thy life."

Why not be all that God desires for us to be? We are not a cake mix. We have been washed by the blood of the Lamb and given life to live and be used for the glory of God. Psalm 32:8, "I will instruct thee and teach thee in the way which thou shalt go: I will guide thee with mine eye." I remember watching and sticking my finger in the dough and having Mrs. Smith say, "Get your finger out of the dough. You can have a cookie when they are baked." Let God do the mixing and baking in your life. Let Him put the ingredients in that you need and go through the baking process to be the blessing that God wants you to be. Enjoy the oatmeal spice cake today or whatever kind of cake you think is best. There is a beautiful aroma from that cake and those cookies being baked. If you are in the oven today, remember God is watching and with you in the baking process. Have a blessed day.

We have been washed by the blood of the Lamb
and given life to be used for the glory of God.

February 5

Exodus 36-38 Psalm 33 Proverbs 5 Mark 13

A Specific Purpose

Good morning! If you have some type of writing instrument close to you, please look at it for a moment. No matter the type of pen, there is a point that you write with. It could be a gel roller, a fountain tip, a felt tip, or a very familiar ink pen. All of them are different, but the use is the same, and all those writing instruments have many parts that must fit together. The tabernacle that we have been reading about had many parts and pieces, and they all had to fit together. My son and son-in-law are cabinet makers. I have watched them take multiple pieces of raw mill cut wood and work so diligently to cut, shape, sand, check and recheck for an exact fit. It is amazing to me how a simple writing instrument can have multiple pieces and be put together to write perfectly, and that rough sawn wood can be worked with to make a beautiful cabinet or piece of furniture.

The work of preparing each curtain, badgers skin, piece of furniture, perfect color of something, perfect shape and placement of something, a perfect loop, a perfect ring, were all for a specific purpose. Exodus 38:21, "This is the sum of the tabernacle, even of the tabernacle of testimony, as it was counted, according to the commandment of Moses, for the service of the Levites, by the hand of Ithamar, son to Aaron the priest." I thought about the phrase, "this is the sum." This is the purpose, this is the reason, this is what is completed, this is why it was done, this is for this use. We might say it often and yet I do not know if we do say it often enough, but God has a perfect plan and purpose for each of us. God is going to have His way, so why do we not just surrender and allow Him to sand us, shape us, develop us so that the pieces can fit perfectly together for God's plan? Jesus is coming soon, and God's plan is coming together for you and me and this world that we live in. Mark 13:31-33, "Heaven and earth shall pass away: but my words shall not pass away. But of that day and that hour knoweth no man, no, not the angels which are in heaven, neither the Son, but the Father. Take ye heed, watch and pray: for ye know not when the time is." Mark 13:37, "And what I say unto you I say unto all, Watch." The pieces are all coming together for God's purpose. We should be listening, observing, and allowing God to do His work in His way, so that all things work God's way. Proverbs 5:1-2, "My son, attend unto my wisdom, and bow thine ear to my understanding: That thou mayest regard discretion, and that thy lips may keep knowledge."

Every writing instrument was made for the purpose of writing. Every cabinet and every piece of furniture was made for the use that it was manufactured for. How about you and me? Have we allowed the Lord to shape the details in us? To form us the way He wants for His will and His purpose? Psalm 33:4, "For the word of the LORD is right; and all his works are done in truth." Psalm 33:9, "For he spake, and it was done; he commanded, and it stood fast." A beautiful cabinet started from pieces of rough wood. An ink pen that fits your hand and writes the letters or notes for you is used for the purpose that it was made. May I ask each of us this morning, are we allowing the Lord to shape us, mold us, put us together in the way that His purpose can be fulfilled in our life? The chair you are sitting in right now started out as rough materials, but it was shaped, molded, and put together to be used as it is right now. A writing pen and a cabinet are far different from each other, like you and me, but each has its purpose. May we purpose to be His purpose. Have a very blessed day.

We should be allowing God to work in His way,
so that all things work God's way.

February 6

Exodus 39-40 Psalm 34 Proverbs 6 Mark 14

Proper Maintenance

Good morning! I always spend time in prayer before I begin the reading of my Bible. I desire to begin each day with the Lord and I spending time together, asking Him to reveal sin that I have not gotten right or that I do not know about and need to confess. Most of my time in the beginning is praising Him. You know, I have learned the more I praise Him, the less time I spend on things I feel I need to pray about. It is like it does maintenance on my heart that needed to be done. As I finished praying, my mind went back to the late fifties when I began to get an interest in doing maintenance and learning as much as I could about cars and trucks, learning how to maintain them to keep them going. I was not able to drive yet, but I had an interest in how they worked and as I learned how they worked, I learned the importance of maintenance.

Our walk with God must be maintained. We are not a machine, but if we are not careful, we can get out of tune spiritually. Did you ever notice when your car begins to break down, you begin to start thinking about getting another car? Or at least you ask yourself if the cost of maintaining the car is going to cost more than getting another car. Exodus 39:43, "And Moses did look upon all the work, and, behold, they had done it as the LORD had commanded, even so had they done it: and Moses blessed them." I noticed all down through chapters 39 and 40 phrases such as, "according to," "as the LORD commanded Moses," even with the lamps to be set in order," "set," "put," referring to the fact that everything with the tabernacle had to be right and had to be maintained. Sometimes we as God's people do not realize the importance of maintaining our walk and service for the Lord. Exodus 40:16, "Thus did Moses: according to all that the LORD commanded him, so did he." As we read on in Mark chapter 14, we see Jesus is sending disciples to prepare the upper room for the Passover. Mark 14:15, "And he will shew you a large upper room furnished and prepared: there make ready for us." Did you notice the words, "make ready?" Mark 14:16, "And the disciples went forth, and came into the city, and found as he had said unto them: and they made ready the Passover." We now picture Jesus with the disciples praying in the garden, about to be betrayed, and we read in Mark 14:38, "Watch ye and pray, lest ye enter into temptation. The spirit truly is ready, but the flesh is weak." Think about those words, "watch ye and pray." We need to maintain a walk of preparation with the Lord. We are challenged in Proverbs 6:20-21, "My son, keep thy father's commandment, and forsake not the law of thy mother: Bind them continually upon thine heart, and tie them about thy neck." Did you see the words, "bind them continually?" More daily maintenance.

Oh, to keep our walk with God where it needs to be, growing in the Lord and keeping a tender heart to the voice of the sweet Holy Spirit. We maintain our vehicles and our physical health, along with doing the upkeep on our homes, so may we be challenged today to do whatever needs to be done to maintain our walk and relationship with the Lord to keep going strong for Him until He returns. Let us have a spiritual tune up today. As a vehicle needs maintenance, and as we need repairs to our home, we need to see more of the importance of keeping ourselves in spiritual repair. That is why we not only need to be in our Bible and prayer daily, but we also need to be under good Bible preaching and teaching to keep us running in top condition for the Lord. Everything runs smoother and longer when it is maintained properly.

We need to maintain a walk of preparation with the Lord.

February 7

Leviticus 1-3 Psalm 35:1-16 Proverbs 7 Mark 15

In Order

Good morning! When I was eleven years old, I joined the Boy Scouts. I have many good memories of things I learned. Like so many things in life, the Boy Scouts are nothing, and I mean absolutely nothing, today like they were when I was part of them. I am so thankful for the many life lessons that I learned and many of those lessons are still part of my life today. I have said this because of two words that spoke to me this morning in our reading. As we began our Old Testament reading in the book of Leviticus, we see the teachings of the proper way to have the sacrifices for the sins of the people. We know today that the Lord Jesus Christ came and is the Messiah and the perfect sacrifice for our sins and the sins of the entire world. Let us learn today some principles of how Moses was instructing the people.

Leviticus 1:7, "And the sons of Aaron the priest shall put fire upon the altar, and lay the wood in order upon the fire." Isn't that interesting? The wood had to be laid "in order" upon the fire. When I first began to learn to build a campfire for cooking, I was taught how to prepare the fire pit for safety and not just to get any wood, but to learn how to find kindling, dry wood and wood that would make coals for cooking. I also learned different types of fire pits and fire structures to make for different reasons. I wonder, what is not laid in proper order in our daily lives? Now let us look at Leviticus 1:8, "And the priests, Aaron's sons, shall lay the parts, the head, and the fat, in order upon the wood that is on the fire which is upon the altar." Did you see those two words again, "in order?" First the wood must be laid in order, then the bullock sacrifice must be laid in order. We read on about sheep and goats and in verse twelve we see those same two words again, "in order." This fire and these sacrifices had to do with the people's worship. I thought as I read on this morning about the Lord Jesus giving Himself in order for us. He came, He grew, He matured, He served, He bore the shame and He was crucified all "in order" for you and me. The most important is that He arose "in order" for all. Mark 15:37-38, "And Jesus cried with a loud voice, and gave up the ghost. And the veil of the temple was rent in twain from the top to the bottom." Only the high priests could go behind that curtain into the Holy of Holy's, but now our Lord and Saviour set things "in order." We are challenged day after day to keep our lives in spiritual order as we read the Scriptures. Proverbs 7:2-3, "Keep my commandments, and live, and my law as the apple of thine eye. Bind them upon thy fingers, write them upon the table of thine heart."

You know, as I learned more and more about building campfires, I learned more about keeping the wood "in order." I pray that we are getting some principles this morning to help us keep "in order" our lives and service for the Lord. Psalm 35:2-3, "Take hold of shield and buckler, and stand up for mine help. Draw out also the spear, and stop the way against them that persecute me: say unto my soul, I am thy salvation." Oh, that we would evaluate our personal walk with God and get things "in order" the way they should be. It is time for us to look at every area of our life spiritually and make sure things are "in order." To this day when I teach young men on our staff and during the week of camp we call

"Take the Challenge," I stress the importance of making sure the fire pit and safety area around where they are going to build the fire is "in order." Also, before they begin trying to build their fire, I tell these young men to make sure they have kindling, dry wood and a little wood for coals that will make a good cooking fire. I tell them over and over to keep things "in order." May we in our spiritual lives, our service, our walk with God, keep things "in order." May our praise and worship to our Lord always be "in order" to bring glory to our Lord and KING.

It is time for us to look at every area of our life spiritually and make sure things are "in order."

February 8

Leviticus 4-5 Psalm 35:17-28 Proverbs 8 Mark 16

Ignorance Is No Excuse

Good morning! I am not an artist, but I truly enjoy an artist that can make a picture look and feel so real. I have a calendar on the wall by my desk and this month is a picture of horses pulling a sleigh down a snow-covered road and two boys playing with their dog in the snow as the sleigh crosses a bridge. The sun is glistening off the snow. Can you see it in your mind? I also enjoy chalk artists that will tell a story as they are drawing the picture. When they get all done and turn the black lights on and the picture is revealed, or as the chalk drawing is turned over, you see the picture.

As I read the Scriptures this morning, it was like picture after picture was being revealed to me. In Leviticus I kept reading the word, "ignorance." So I took the time and looked in my dictionary and found the definition to be "the negative state of mind which has not been instructed." Let us now look how the word "ignorance" is used in some verses. Leviticus 4:13, "And if the whole congregation of Israel sin through ignorance:." Leviticus 4:22, "When a ruler hath sinned, and done somewhat through ignorance." Leviticus 4:27, "And if any one of the common people sin through ignorance." The question is often asked, what if I do not know that something is a sin? Let me first say that does not mean we have not sinned. To be ignorant is to not know, or not have learned yet. That is why we must read, study, learn and apply the Word of God. That is also why we must have preaching and teaching that names sin and we must learn to listen to the Holy Spirit of God. Leviticus 4:30 and 34, "shall pour out all the blood thereof at the bottom of the altar." I remember seeing a chalk drawing of Jesus on the cross, or an artist's rendering of Jesus on the cross, and when the light was turned on, you could see the blood from Jesus dripping into the ground. My brother and sister, we must not be ignorant of our sins. We must confess and forsake them. Mark 16:14, "Afterward he appeared unto the eleven as they sat at meat, and upbraided them with their unbelief and hardness of heart, because they believed not them which had seen him after he was risen." The disciples had allowed their hearts to be hardened. Proverbs 8:32-34, "Now therefore hearken unto me, O ye children: for blessed are they that keep my ways. Hear instruction, and be wise, and refuse it not. Blessed is the man that heareth me, watching daily at my gates, waiting at the posts of my doors." We must ask the Holy Spirit to reveal sin to us and face the fact it is sin and confess and forsake it. Psalm 35:17, "Lord, how long wilt thou look on?"

Are we going through what we are in our lives, our country, our world because we have not faced up to sin, confessed and forsaken it? Psalm 35:22, "Keep not silence: O Lord, be not far from me." Ignorance is no excuse and in God's eyes ignorance will not be tolerated. Let us all get on our knees and seek the face of our God. Look closely at the artist's drawing; the light is about to be turned on. What would we really see of our lives if the Lord would show us the sin that is hidden? That sin is there. We must seek the face of our Lord and plead with Him for mercy. Some things to think about this morning.

Ignorance is no excuse and in God's eyes ignorance will not be tolerated.

February 9

Leviticus 6-7 Psalm 36 Proverbs 9 Luke 1

A Daily Cleansing

Good morning! Do you have the peace and joy of the Lord? May we ask ourselves this question, are we walking in peace with God? Leviticus 7:11-12, "And this is the law of the sacrifice of peace-offerings, which he shall offer unto the LORD. If he offer it for a thanksgiving, then he shall offer with the sacrifice of thanksgiving unleavened cakes mingled with oil, and unleavened wafers anointed with oil, and cakes mingled with oil, of fine flour, fried." There is a lot to think about in these two verses. Do we have peace with a thankful heart because we do not have sin in our life?

There have been times throughout the years that I have had to call a vet to check an animal, and there have been times I have had to take an animal to the veterinarian because something just did not seem right. As I read the word "unleavened," I thought about no sin. I asked myself and I ask you, are we walking in secret sins or do we see the importance of a daily cleansing from sin? I then thought about the cakes and wafers being mingled with oil, and the thoughts came to me about us being filled and walking in the Spirit of God. Is the Spirit of God having freedom in our lives? I asked the doctor to come and see the animals because I knew there was something not right. Is everything right between you and the Lord this morning? What a miracle of God for Elisabeth and Mary to be told that they both were with child by the Holy Ghost! Listen to Mary's words in Luke 1:46-47, "And Mary said, My soul doth magnify the Lord, and my spirit hath rejoiced in God my Saviour." Did you take time this morning and thank the Lord for the indwelling of the Holy Spirit of God? Oh, that there would be a greater reality of the Holy Spirit within us and more of an urgency to have the sin purged from us. Proverbs 9:8-9, "Reprove not a scorner, lest he hate thee: rebuke a wise man, and he will love thee. Give instruction to a wise man, and he will be yet wiser: teach a just man, and he will increase in learning." God is saying that a wise man will respond when sin is pointed out and a man of pride, or the Bible says a scorner, will hate you for revealing sin in his life.

May we walk in the Spirit, rejoice in the Spirit, learn by the Holy Spirit, serve in the strength of the Holy Spirit and be drawn closer to our Heavenly Father by the power of the Holy Spirit. Psalm 36:9, "For with thee is the fountain of life: in thy light shall we see light." As the priests were to cover the wafers and cakes in oil, may we be covered in the outpouring of the Spirit of God in and through us. Walk with the Lord today. The doctor found what was wrong with the animals. May we look closely at our spiritual condition this morning. May we walk in praise and thanksgiving to the Lord. Think on the words of Mary, "My soul doth magnify the Lord, and my spirit hath rejoiced in God my Saviour."

Did you take time this morning and thank the Lord for the indwelling of the Holy Spirit of God?

February 10

Leviticus 8-10 Psalm 37:1-22 Proverbs 10 Luke 2

The Value of His Word

Good morning! I am so thankful for a warm dry home. As I looked outside, the freezing rain has already begun here at our home. I just sat for a moment by the wood stove and watched as the coals began to catch the wood on fire and the stove began to heat up. I was thinking about a statement I just read in a book that I am reading, "The value of a statement is measured, to a great extent, by the one who makes the statement." I thought about how important it is for us to put the highest value on every word that we read in the Word of God because God Himself is the author.

Leviticus 9:6, "And Moses said, This is the thing which the LORD commanded that ye should do: and the glory of the LORD shall appear unto you." It is a promise, a guarantee from God Himself. Leviticus 10:10, "And that ye may put difference between holy and unholy, and between unclean and clean." These statements by God, recorded by Moses, are to be given the highest value because of Who said them. In our reading we read statements of authority by those that were eyewitnesses to Jesus. Luke 2:17, "And when they had seen it, they made known abroad the saying which was told them concerning this child." The shepherds did this at the very viewing of the baby Lord Jesus. Luke 2:30, "For mine eyes have seen thy salvation," a statement by Simeon as he himself saw Messiah, the Lord Jesus. Luke 2:38, "And she coming in that instant gave thanks likewise unto the Lord, and spake of him to all them that looked for redemption in Jerusalem." Anna, who had waited all those years to see Jesus herself, gives testimony. "The value of a statement is measured, to a great extent, by the one who makes the statement." Listen to the wisdom God gave Solomon. Proverbs 10:14, "Wise men lay up knowledge:." Proverbs 10:16, "The labour of the righteous tendeth to life: the fruit of the wicked to sin." Proverbs 10:21, "The lips of the righteous feed many: but fools die for want of wisdom."

What words are you listening to? What authority are you giving things you listen to in the news? What does a young person really know in comparison to a saint who has lived for the Lord almost eighty years and stayed faithful to the Lord and His Word? Psalm 37:18, "The LORD knoweth the days of the upright: and their inheritance shall be for ever." God is keeping score. God is in complete control. "The value of a statement is measured, to a great extent, by the one who makes the statement." Stop and think about what and who you are listening to. As for me, I am sticking with the preserved, inherent Word of God.

We must put the highest value on the Word of God
because God Himself is the author.

February 11

Leviticus 11-12 Psalm 37:23-40 Proverbs 11 Luke 3

The Storm Will Pass

Good morning! As I woke this morning, I could hear the ice hitting the window. I got up and went to the wood stove and stirred the coals, added some wood, and opened the front door to the sound of the big trees in the front yard bending and cracking under the weight of the ice that was now clinging to the limbs and branches. I stood out on the front porch briefly and listened as branch after branch cracked and popped and yes, some broke off and hit the icy ground with a thud. I thought as I looked in the darkness with my flashlight and watched the limbs move with the breeze, which limbs will break under the load of the ice? I took my flashlight and put the beam on the smaller willow trees and their limbs were now bent over and touching the ground. The dead or weaker limbs will fall or break off the big maple tree.

All of us are going through a time in our world that is hard to understand unless we hunger to look through the eyes of the Lord and realize that He is in complete control. Young and old Christians alike are going through some puzzling times. Leviticus 11:44-45, "For I am the LORD your God: ye shall therefore sanctify yourselves and ye shall be holy; for I am holy: For I am the LORD that bringeth you up out of the land of Egypt, to be your God: ye shall therefore be holy, for I am holy." These two verses stress to the children of Israel and for us to make application to ourselves to be holy because He is holy, and to separate from the world. As the trees are now under a great stress from the ice storm, they are still standing and I believe they will endure the storm, but you can hear the stress they are under. My brother and sister, we need to focus on being a holy testimony for the Lord and let Him clear sin out of our lives when we go through the storms. John the Baptist said in Luke 3:6, "And all flesh shall see the salvation of God." May we stick with the stuff so that the world can always see Jesus in us. We all know our world is filled with wickedness, but the focus of our lives should be on holiness. Proverbs 11:18, "The wicked worketh a deceitful work: but to him that soweth righteousness shall be a sure reward." Proverbs 11:27, "He that diligently seeketh good procureth favour." The word "procureth" means to get or to gain. In times of trial, let your stand for Christ be strong and stable.

I loved the words of Psalm 37:25 in our reading, "I have been young, and now am old; yet have I not seen the righteous forsaken, nor his seed begging bread." Picture with me an old man sitting at the old country store, with younger men around him, and he speaks slowly these words of wisdom, "Men, I have seen storms like this before and we all made it just fine." I called a young pastor yesterday who the Lord had laid on my heart to pray for, and I decided to give him a call. These were the words he said to me, "Brother Smith, this has been a very tough week and your call means so much to me." As a young pastor, he was going through some battles, and I simply told him I was praying for him and that I was thanking the Lord for him and his wife. The storms of life will all pass, and those who stand with and for Christ will last. Psalm 37:34, "Wait on the LORD, and keep his way." The ice will soon melt and the storms of winter will pass. The storm you are going through now, or will someday, will also pass. Stand faithful to and for the Lord.

May we stick with the stuff so that the world can always see Jesus in us.

February 12

Leviticus 13 Psalm 38 Proverbs 12 Luke 4

Never Rejected by God

Good morning! After reading Leviticus 13 this morning, my heart is so burdened to understand how to greater help people who have the feeling of rejection. I had parents, a brother and sister, grandparents and many family members that loved me. I have children and grandchildren that love me and many friends as well. To think that for over fifty years my wife has loved me and has put up with all that I am not or should have been, and she still loves me. How lonely to have leprosy and to be rejected or sent outside of the people you love and are part of. Leviticus 13:9, "When the plague of leprosy is in a man, then he shall be brought unto the priest." Leviticus 13:14, "But when raw flesh appeareth in him, he shall be unclean." Leprosy is a picture of sin. Sin always brings separation.

I have raised several animals that were rejected by their mother for different reasons. Sometimes they were not strong enough to fight for a place to be fed, or had a birth defect and no one would want them. Whatever the reason, I have enjoyed raising some animals who needed extra care to make it. Look around and take your time to see all that love you. Look at those who spend time with you. Now look at those who seem to have nobody and let your heart and life reach out to them. Can you imagine with me a person that the priest looks at and says those words, "it is leprosy?" I do not know what you are going through today, but there are times all of us have that feeling of loneliness, and the devil makes us think nobody cares. Jesus does, and He has left His Word for us, and the Holy Spirit is there to be a comfort to us. Luke 4:4, "And Jesus answered him, saying, It is written, That man shall not live by bread alone, but by every word of God." We need to first deal with the loneliness through the promises of the Bible. Quit focusing on your feelings and start focusing on all that the Lord has done. Proverbs 12:15, "The way of a fool is right in his own eyes: but he that hearkeneth unto counsel is wise." Proverbs 12:19, "The lip of truth shall be established for ever." The truth is God loves us and will never reject any. Proverbs 12:28, "In the way of righteousness is life." Sin, like leprosy, brought the need for separation.

I remember the day I held a little scrawny calf. The owner said the mother had a rough time in birthing it and that it would not nurse. I remember getting down and lifting that calf, putting it in a warm dry place and bottle feeding it, talking to it, spending time with it, and watching it grow. You might feel down today, but you are not rejected by our Lord. You might be discouraged; look to God through His Word. You might feel puzzled by what God is doing in your life; be patient. Psalm 38:9, "Lord, all my desire is before thee; and my groaning is not hid from thee." Psalm 38:15, "For in thee, O LORD, do I hope: thou wilt hear, O Lord my God." You know, I named that calf and when it would hear its name, that little calf knew I was coming to feed it. It took time, but I sure did enjoy the time with that little calf that was rejected. God is waiting to spend time with you and me. He is ready and waiting to pick us up and to see that we are fed and loved. Christ never said that we were unclean, He just said, "come unto me."

The truth is God loves us and will never reject any.

February 13

Leviticus 14 Psalm 39 Proverbs 13 Luke 5

Clean and in Order

Good morning! I sure am thankful to walk into my closet and find all my shirts and pants washed, ironed, and hanging so neatly. I can go to my dresser and find my clothes washed and folded so neatly. Mrs. Smith will not be very happy that I am bragging on her this way, and she will say that is what a wife is supposed to do. I am so very thankful beyond words that I could be married to a wife that takes things so seriously in taking care of her husband. She often says her greatest calling, next to her walk and service for the Lord, is taking care of her husband and family.

You might be asking yourselves this morning, Bro. Smith, where in the world did you get this out of the Bible reading? Leviticus 14:54-57, "This is the law for all manner of plague of leprosy, and scall, And for the leprosy of a garment, and of a house, And for a rising for a scab, and for a bright spot: To teach when it is unclean, and when it is clean: this is the law of leprosy." Yesterday in our thoughts we talked about leprosy being a sign of sin. Today we see not only sin in a person's life, but sin in our home, our dress (garment), and checking every area of our lives where sin might be. My wife works daily to keep our house clean and in order. She works so hard keeping every room in order, and again I want to say that she will say "it is a privilege to take care of our home and you." Listen to the words that she said, "this is what a wife is supposed to do." I am thankful for my wife in so many ways, but this morning I thought how the children of Israel were to check their homes, their garments, and their skin. We need to take heed and make sure every area of our lives is free of sin and work to keep the sin out and things in order.

I remember in the early days of our marriage when Mrs. Smith taught daily and even worked a part time job just to help meet the needs of our family. Now after all these years she is still pressing to do everything she can to help me keep our house and lives in order serving the Lord. Let us not compare this morning but look at the words, "garment" and "house" and "scab." Looks like we need to look for sin in every area of our lives and responsibilities. Sin is our biggest enemy. We want to use other things in our lives as an excuse for not living and serving our Lord, but we must face sin first. Jesus said in Luke 5:32, "I came not to call the righteous, but sinners to repentance." He came seeking sinners full of sin. Proverbs 13:6, "Righteousness keepeth him that is upright in the way: but wickedness overthroweth the sinner." Proverbs 13:21, "Evil pursueth sinners: but to the righteous good shall be repayed." Sin is destroying marriages, homes, our children, ministries and so on. Mrs. Smith will be the first to say that she fails daily. None of us are perfect. The point to make is we need to check our lives personally, our homes, the places we go, the friends we keep, the music we listen to, the books we read, the time we spend on our phones, what we keep before us; and keep the sin out. Psalm 39:1, "I said, I will take heed to my ways." Psalm 39:12, "Hear my prayer, O LORD, and give ear unto my cry." Psalm 39:13, "O spare me, that I may recover strength, before I go hence, and be no more." My brother and sister, sin is destroying us. Let us make it a point to find the sin, confess, and forsake the sin that is keeping us from victory in our lives.

We need to make sure every area of our lives is free of sin and in order.

February 14

Leviticus 15-16 Psalm 40 Proverbs 14 Luke 6

A Goal for Growth

Good morning! All sports games have a way for each team to earn points, and it is the goal of each team to get more points on the board than the other team. Every sport has a method for the winner to have a goal to reach. No team or team member would have in their mind to go out and lose. A boxer or wrestler has a goal to get more points if there is not a knockout for the boxer or a pin for the wrestler. When a student takes a test, the goal is to get a 100% or at least as many points as possible. Do we have goals that we are trying to reach in the Christian life? The Christian life is not a game, but we do need to have goals. These goals must stay in the front of our lives and our service. To have no goals is to have no growth. The Christian cannot just exist, or we will backslide.

Let me express some thoughts from our Scripture reading today. Leviticus 16:29, "And this shall be a statute for ever unto you: that in the seventh month, on the tenth day of the month, ye shall afflict your souls, and do no work at all." Leviticus 16:31, "It shall be a sabbath of rest unto you, and ye shall afflict your souls, by a statute for ever." The phrase we need to consider this morning is "ye shall afflict your souls." This is saying we need to have time to fast, separate, evaluate, consider, so that our focus can be on a right relationship with the Lord and right goals that we should be reaching to attain. The world and all its frustrations can and will confuse our walk with the Lord if we are not careful. The cares of this world will take first place over a growing relationship with the Lord. The Lord Jesus Himself took time to go away to seek the face of His Father in Luke 6:12, "And it came to pass in those days, that he went out into a mountain to pray, and continued all night in prayer to God." May I suggest for each of us to have a regular set time we separate ourselves to be alone with the Lord and spend time in His Word and with Him in prayer. How about starting with one meal a week? Spend that time alone, reading God's Word and spending time in prayer. Luke 6:46, "And why call ye me, Lord, Lord, and do not the things which I say?" We must have times of mind, heart, and spiritual cleansing. Proverbs 14:26, "In the fear of the LORD is strong confidence: and his children shall have a place of refuge."

A new car, a new home, new clothes, a special trip are not going to bring the peace and freshness that a time alone spent with the Lord will. I am not saying any of those things are wrong, but when was the last time that you on purpose "afflicted your soul?" Fasting is not a punishment. It is a time of spiritual strengthening and refreshing. Fasting allows us to get a fresh look at ourselves in light of what the Lord is seeing and allowing us to see. Fasting is a time of cleansing us from this world and sin. Proverbs 14:34, "Righteousness exalteth a nation: but sin is a reproach to any people." The Psalmist says it best in Psalm 40:3-4, "And he hath put a new song in my mouth, even praise unto our God: many shall see it, and fear, and shall trust in the LORD. Blessed is that man that maketh the LORD his trust." The Christian life is not a game to be played, but it is important for us to have goals to reach in growing and serving the Lord. To keep our focus on things that please the Lord, we need times like Moses wrote about, showing the importance for people of God to "afflict your souls."

To have no goals is to have no growth.

February 15

Leviticus 17-18 Psalm 41 Proverbs 15 Luke 7

Castor and Cod Liver Oil

Good morning! It seems the older I get, the more memories I have of when I was younger and living at home. Mom would say, this will help you, and I thought often, I just want to stay sick instead of taking what you are giving me. I am speaking of taking castor oil and cod liver oil. Now Mrs. Smith and I often use these two oils but when I was younger, I would often do anything not to take them. I think that is like us when we first learn a new truth from the Bible, or we are under conviction of the Holy Spirit because we have been convicted by God's Word and our flesh does not like it.

Leviticus 18 is one of those passages that I am speaking of. It is truth because it is the Word of God, and it is straightforward truth. If we just look at one word, the word "nakedness" is mentioned twenty-seven times in just this one chapter. Leviticus 18:6, "None of you shall approach to any that is near of kin to him, to uncover their nakedness: I am the LORD." That is just where things start and continue all the way down through verse 19. Then in verses 20-23, we see the sins of adultery, abortion, sodomy, and bestiality mentioned. Let me read to you one of the definitions from the Websters 1828 dictionary concerning the word "nakedness": exposed to shame and disgrace, want of covering or clothing. As I read all the definitions, I thought about how our bodies are to be covered and very modest. Boy, that will rub the fur on a cat's back the wrong way, but God does not stop there. Leviticus 18:26, "Ye shall therefore keep my statutes and my judgments, and shall not commit any of these abominations." Well, I went to Webster again for the definition of "abominations": extreme hatred toward a holy righteous God; detestation. Sounds like God is plain and without question in how He feels about nakedness, adultery, abortion, sodomy, and bestiality. I thought how far God's people have gone away from the holy life God expects of us. Luke 7:31, "And the Lord said, whereunto then shall I liken the men of this generation? and to what are they like?" It seems as though this is the generation where every man does that which is right in their own eyes. We cannot hide from God. Proverbs 15:3, "The eyes of the LORD are in every place, beholding the evil and the good." Proverbs 15:9, "The way of the wicked is an abomination unto the LORD: but he loveth him that followeth after righteousness."

I did not like the castor oil or the cod liver oil, but I now have learned the need for them and the help they are to me. Turn, my brother and sister, and know we must stand for holiness unto our God. We need to receive the Word of God and walk and serve in holiness unto a righteous God. Proverbs 15:29, "The LORD is far from the wicked: but he heareth the prayer of the righteous." Mom knew what would help my sickness. God knows what will help a sin sick world. Please do not turn a blind eye to God's Word. Proverbs 15:32, "He that refuseth instruction despiseth his own soul: but he that heareth reproof getteth understanding." There was a time I thought using castor oil and cod liver oil was going to kill me, but it was just what I needed. Psalm 41:4, "I said LORD, be merciful unto me: heal my soul; for I have sinned against thee." We need to just open our hearts and minds to receive the Words of God. Oh, there is no covering up the taste of castor oil and cod liver oil, but it sure did work. God loves you and me and He always knows what is best.

We must stand for holiness unto our God.

February 16

Leviticus 19-20 Psalm 42 Proverbs 16 Luke 8

Leave Some Grain

Good morning on this very cold, icy wintry day in February! Picture this morning us sitting by a fireplace drinking a cup of hot tea, coffee or even a hot cup of chocolate with marshmallows floating and melting on top. Smells good and sure tastes good. Doing things together or doing things for others is the heart of our Lord. Our lives as Christians should be lived for others. I have heard many times, "take time for others and others will take time for you." You might be hurting today, so take time to find someone else hurting and do what you can through a note, phone call or some action to be a blessing to someone else. A farmer needs to glean every bit of grain he can from a field during harvest so that he can pay his bills, have money to live on and be able to buy grain for the next year.

Something very interesting for us to learn is found in Leviticus 19:9-10, "And when ye reap the harvest of your land, thou shalt not wholly reap the corners of thy field, neither shalt thou gather the gleanings of thy harvest. And thou shall not glean thine vineyard, neither shall thou gather every grape of thy vineyard; thou shalt leave them for the poor and stranger: I am the LORD your God." What a needed principle for us to learn today, leaving a certain portion for others or having some of every dollar we earn be used for somebody other than ourselves. Make plans in your financial budget to have a section where you set aside money to be used for others. Jesus sought out those in need. I believe this teaching this morning for us is to reach out to those who are not a family member, but who the Lord brings across our path or lays a burden on our heart to help in some way. How about a person that you see needs a pair of shoes, a new shirt, a new dress, a meal? What about making a big container of chicken soup or a stew and some biscuits or a cake pan full of cornbread? When you deliver the meal, have a card, and include some cash to help them out and be an encouragement. Just think with me and picture it in your mind. The corners of the field were left for others and all the grapes were not picked so others could have some. The grain that was dropped on the ground was left for others. The next time you go to church, do not just go find your seat and sit down. Look around and ask the Lord to show you someone that you can be a blessing to. When you go to the store, smile, be friendly. When going through the drive through to get something, pay for the people behind you.

Leviticus 19:34, "But the stranger that dwelleth with you shall be unto you as one born among you, and thou shalt love him as thyself; for ye were strangers in the land of Egypt: I am the LORD your God." In Luke 8:46, the woman that had the issue of blood for twelve years and just touched the garment of Jesus, caused Jesus to stop and say, "And Jesus said, somebody hath touched me: for I perceive that virtue is gone out of me." There is a "somebody" whom the Holy Spirit is ready to have touch you. The word "virtue" is that Christ-like spirit that should be pouring out of each of us for others. Our spirit should be that of "Lord, please use me in any way you can." Everybody does not need to know. Let God get the glory and let Him bring the blessing to both those in need and you. Proverbs 16:19, "Better it is to be of an humble spirit with the lowly, than to divide the spoil with the proud." May our earnest desire today and every day be for the Lord to use us to be a blessing to others. I thought about the snow and ice on the ground this morning and a deer in the woods coming to that spring and drinking of the fresh water that has not been frozen by the cold. Psalm 42:1, "As the hart panteth after the water brooks, so panteth my soul after thee, O God." Let God use you today and be blessed beyond. Let God use you to be a touch for somebody else. Be that spring of fresh water for a thirsty soul today. Leave some grain for somebody to go and harvest.

Take time for others and others will take time for you.

February 17

Leviticus 21-22 Psalm 43 Proverbs 17 Luke 9

Listening for God

Good morning! It is 13 degrees here at the Ranch this morning. I sat in front of the wood stove as I stoked the fire and stirred the coals. Before I had my prayer time, I sat there and looked into the fire and said, Lord please speak to me in a special way this morning. For us to understand that God wants to speak to each of us is a very important aspect of walking with the Lord. Little did I realize at that time that the Lord was preparing me for His Word this morning.

Leviticus 21:1, "And the LORD said unto Moses, Speak unto the priests the sons of Aaron, and say unto them." Did you see the capital "S" on the word Speak? This shows the personal importance of listening and telling. Leviticus 21:16, "And the LORD spake unto Moses, saying." We see this same phrase in Leviticus 22:1, 17, 26. At this time, God was teaching man to hear from Him personally, and to tell what God was saying to others. Now we turn to our New Testament reading in Luke 9:18, "And it came to pass, as he was alone praying, his disciples were with him: and he asked them, saying, Whom say the people that I am?" The answer is in the very next verse. Luke 9:19, "They answering said, John the Baptist; but some say, Elias; and others say, that one of the old prophets is risen again." God wants so much to be personal with each one of us. We must each day see the importance of getting alone with Him personally and privately. He spoke through men of old. Then Jesus came and walked with man, and after Jesus went to Heaven, the Holy Spirit now indwells every believer in Christ. Let us look how the disciples responded to the question that Jesus asked. Luke 9:20, "He said unto them, But whom say ye that I am? Peter answering said, The Christ of God." As they then followed Jesus, eight days later Jesus took Peter, James, and John to a mount to pray, and listen to what they heard when they awoke from sleeping and saw a cloud where Jesus was. Luke 9:35, "And there came a voice out of the cloud, saying, This is my beloved Son:

hear him." There again God is stressing each of us learning to hear God's voice. Those two words, "hear him" must be stressed today. Luke 9:44, "Let these sayings sink down into your ears."

As I have said many times, God never compromises His principles in His Word. Too many listen to flesh, friends, family, and circumstances instead of learning to hear, understand and discern the voice of God, which is a must for each of us. The more we walk with Him the plainer His voice is to hear. Proverbs 17:28, "Even a fool, when he holdeth his peace, is counted wise: and he that shutteth his lips is esteemed a man of understanding." God and His will is never confusing. We must learn to listen and be quiet, walk patiently to know and be obedient to His voice. I am so thankful how our reading in Psalms this morning gives us a sweet peace. Psalms 43:3, "O send out thy light and thy truth: let them lead me; let them bring me unto thy holy hill, and to thy tabernacles." I can hear those words said by my parents, and now sometimes by Mrs. Smith, "I am speaking to you, are you hearing me?" When we cannot learn to listen to man whom we can see, how will we ever be able to listen to the voice of God whom we cannot see? God is speaking. Are you listening?

The more we walk with Him the plainer His voice is to hear.

February 18

Leviticus 23-24 Psalm 44:1-8 Proverbs 18 Luke 10

A Little at a Time

Good morning! Picture with me this morning a food buffet. We have gone into a buffet that has several lines of food, from salad, vegetables, meat and then over to the dessert area. Our eyes glance over everything. We then have a word of prayer and begin the journey from salad all the way to a dessert. Now, I need you to stop and regroup with me at a table where we sit down and before our eyes is a table where a wife or mother has been in a kitchen and prepared a delicious meal that has been set before us with a meat platter, a couple of different vegetables, and we can smell the aroma of a fresh apple pie cooling in the kitchen. Also on the table is a fresh loaf of baked bread and jersey cow butter setting there waiting to be spread on the warm bread. At the buffet we almost always overeat, and at a home cooked meal we are satisfied and can have room for that delicious pie with a scoop of vanilla ice cream on top.

This morning in our Old Testament reading there is so much for us to digest, and I thought today it is very important for us to not try to understand, or digest, all that is said. At a buffet there is usually so much food it is hard to decide what to eat, or we try some of everything and leave too full and miserable. Eating a home cooked balanced meal, we take our time, enjoy the fellowship, and slowly eat the simple but delicious meal set before us. This morning I have notes dealing with trumpets, sabbath, fasting, oil, lamps, blasphemy, and capital punishment. That is too much to digest at one time. That is why it is important for each of us to take our time in reading and studying the Word of God. The Bible is a well that never runs dry and we must drink one cup at a time, then go back for more. Leviticus 23:24, "a memorial of blowing of trumpets." This one statement is a picture of calling together of the people, and calling them to the Promised Land, a calling together for repentance of sin. That is where we must always start. We must not get frustrated in so much that is before us, but only take what we can receive and then go back for seconds so that we do not get overwhelmed with too much. Jesus said to His disciples in Luke 10:23-24, "Blessed are the eyes which see the things that ye see: For I tell you, that many prophets and kings have desired to see those things which ye see, and have not seen them; and to hear those things which ye hear, and have not heard them."

A child will make themself sick when a lot of candy is before them, but a wise parent will control how much candy the child eats. The child does not get sick, they enjoy a little at a time and the candy lasts longer. More Christians have gotten discouraged and quit because they tried to consume everything that was before them, instead of just eating one meal at a time. May our hearts stay tender and hungry for the things of God. Proverbs 18:15, "The heart of the prudent getteth knowledge; and the ear of the wise seeketh knowledge." Learn to enjoy a little at a time and let what you partake of strengthen you one step, or one spoonful, at a time. Listen, learn, live is the process for all of us. Psalm 44:1, "We have heard with our ears, O God, our fathers have told us, what work thou didst in their days, in the times of old." Generations have gone before us and were faithful to the end. May we grow in our walk with God step by step. See you at God's table.

It is important for each of us to take our time in reading and studying the Word of God.

February 19

Leviticus 25 Psalm 44:9-26 Proverbs 19 Luke 11

Excuses, Excuses

Good morning! How often have we heard the phrase, "It is time to grow up and accept responsibility?" Excuses have never accomplished anything in life. Sometimes I want to pull out my hair (which is getting less by the day and disappearing so fast that I now use a comb to scratch with instead of comb my hair) because of excuses. The Lord made some things very plain in Leviticus 25 this morning and I want to just touch on a couple of thoughts. First, let us ask ourselves why we make excuses for what we make excuse for. Excuse for not getting up out of bed to have personal devotions before the day begins. Excuse why we cannot be someplace on time. Excuse why we have quit something that at one time we obligated ourselves to. Excuse why we fear something that we cannot even control. Excuses never bring comfort. They just cause us to hide from the responsibility or obligation.

Leviticus 25:23, "The land shall not be sold forever: for the land is mine; for ye are strangers and sojourners with me." Look at the word "strangers"; one who belongs to another country. Also take a look at the word "sojourners," meaning temporary resident. We are so controlled by what we think we want or what we think will make us happy and we never truly get the fact of the song, "this world is not my home,

I am just a passing through." Let us read on to Leviticus 25:24, "But the field of the suburbs of their cities may not be sold; for it is their perpetual possession." Okay, let us look at the word "perpetual"; never ceasing, destined to be eternal. Now let us look at the word "possession," meaning having or holding. Our thought from the Scriptures is this world is not our home. We are just passing through to eternity and we must focus on our salvation and relationship with our Lord and eternity in Heaven because that is our permanent dwelling place where we will spend eternity. It is not wrong to have a nice home, nice vehicle, nice clothing, and possessions; but they are all only temporary. Our families, our friendships, our worldly possessions are only temporary, but Heaven is permanent. and we should be building a walk and relationship with Christ and focus on pleasing the Lord first in every area of our lives. Listen to Luke 11:23, "He that is not with me is against me: and he that gathereth not with me scattereth." It sure does not sound like there is any room for excuses. Luke 11:28, "blessed are they that hear the word of God, and keep it." What God gave the children of Israel was to never be sold because it was the Lord's.

The gift of salvation given to all of us who have trusted Christ is to never be put in second place, and we are never to give excuse why we cannot put Him first. Yes, we all get sick and have different situations, but I am talking to you and me about when our flesh controls and not our spirit. When we do what we want instead of doing what we know the Lord wants. Proverbs 19:3, "The foolishness of man perverteth his way: and his heart fretteth against the LORD." Look at the word "perverteth." It means to turn from right to wrong. We must not sell or compromise what we have been given in salvation. Proverbs 19:20, "Hear counsel, and receive instruction, that thou mayest be wise in thy latter end." Proverbs 19:21, "There are many devices in a man's heart; nevertheless the counsel of the LORD, that shall stand." The words of the Psalmist gave me comfort as it was like a breath of fresh air in Psalm 44:18, "Our heart is not turned back, neither have our steps declined from thy way." Let your heart lead and guide you. Psalm 44:21, "Shall not God search this out? For he knoweth the secrets of the heart." We give an excuse because we know we have fallen short, but we must not allow the excuses to control us. Focus on your "perpetual possession," which is Heaven for all eternity. Some things to think about today.

Excuses never bring comfort. They just cause us to hide from the responsibility or obligation.

February 20

Leviticus 26-27 Psalm 45 Proverbs 20 Luke 12

Hold Nothing Back

Good morning! Yesterday before I headed to town a neighbor called and asked if I could bring the tractor and pull them out. I said sure and got ready to head out, but as I walked out the door my eye caught the long icicles above the door. The kid came out in me very fast. Those days of breaking an icicle off the barn's roof and carrying it around and eating it like a piece of candy. I knocked the icicles down and walked on to the barn, and then I began to think about the forming of the icicle. I looked the word icicle up and will give you the official definition: Outdoor temperature is subfreezing but sunshine warms and melts some snow or ice. As it drips off your roof, a water droplet freezes when it loses its heat to the cold air. An icicle starts with a few frozen droplets.

As I read Leviticus 27:28, "Notwithstanding no devoted thing, that a man shall devote unto the LORD of all that he hath, both of man and beast, and of the field of his possession shall be sold or redeemed: every devoted thing is most holy unto the LORD." I stopped and thought a drop of water forms to a beautiful snowflake from a miracle of God, and they say no two snowflakes are the same. These snowflakes stick to a roof and when the sun shines, the snowflakes begin to melt but form a beautiful icicle, and we get to enjoy one drop over and again, plus the beauty of it all. Now we read about "devoted things" being given to the Lord and I thought of those times I have knelt at an altar in church, at a youth conference, mission conference, revival and a multitude of times and just said, "Lord, take me, use me, and you can have all of me." A life given to Christ for the cause of Christ is "most holy unto the LORD." When is the last time you gave yourself freshly to the Lord for His use? Luke 12:37, "Blessed are those servants, whom the lord when he cometh shall find watching." Luke 12:40, "Be ye therefore ready also: for the Son of man cometh at an hour when ye think not." I went outside and walked for a while and saw the sun coming up and thought, it could be today, it could be this very moment. The sun was glistening on the snow and. showing itself through the trees, the hillsides covered with snow sparkled life diamonds. I looked up to Heaven and said, "Lord please use me. I give all again to you." Proverbs 20:27, "The spirit of man is the candle of the LORD."

Turn loose and let God have it all. Let God use you in a way that pleases Him. Psalm 45:1, "My heart is inditing a good matter: I speak of the things which I have made touching the king: my tongue is the pen of a ready writer." Look at the word "inditing," which means to make known formally, to proclaim. As I came back into the house, I looked at more icicles before I came in. From my heart to yours, use this time to give yourself freshly to the Lord. Hold nothing back. He is coming soon, and we must be about His business. There will be more icicles forming today. How about us letting the Lord use us to form something for HIM?

When is the last time you gave yourself freshly to the Lord for His use?

February 21

Numbers 1-2 Psalm 46 Proverbs 21 Luke 13

Enjoy the Journey

Good morning! Mrs. Smith and I have talked often about how our fathers used to plan our family vacations. Even though we did not know each other, our fathers' method of planning a family vacation was so similar. From the roads we were to travel, to the places we were going to stay, the places we were going to see and the destination where we were going to end up. The money was saved and we stayed on the budget. I can remember dad going to the bank and getting the travelers checks. Credit cards were never talked about, and if we did not have the money, we did not buy it.

Starting today, we enter the book of Numbers in the Old Testament. Ending the book of Leviticus, we find the children of Israel at the base of Sinai. Numbers 1:1, "And the LORD spake unto Moses in the wilderness of Sinai, in the tabernacle of the congregation, on the first day of the second month, in the second year after they were come out of the land of Egypt, saying." Now the people are numbered, set in order, told how they are to travel, where they are to camp around the tabernacle when they stop, and all seems to be well. Numbers 2:2, "Every man of the children of Israel shall pitch by his own standard, with the ensign of their father's house: far off about the tabernacle of the congregations shall they pitch." Here is where we need to stop and begin to consider some things. The children of Israel are now about to be in the Promised Land. Do you know if they had gone in a straight line the journey would have only taken two weeks? Just two short weeks to arrive at their destination of the Lord's promise. Our family vacations were two weeks. We are about to see what happens when we do not do God's will, God's way. The truth of life for a Christian is that we must learn how to face sin in our lives and deal with this sin. Luke 13:3 and 5, "I tell you, Nay: but except ye repent, ye shall all likewise perish." Why would we not want God's full blessing? Do we love sin and our lack of obedience more than God's blessings that we could have? Proverbs 21:2, "Every way of man is right in his own eyes: but the LORD pondereth the hearts." Proverbs 21:3, "To do justice and judgment is more acceptable to the LORD than sacrifice."

Our family vacations were always a wonderful time as long as we did what was planned for us. There were times we wanted to stay longer in a place or see something else, but dad would say, we did not plan for that, or not this time, we need to keep moving. God's blessing is always there for those who do what God says, when God says and how God says. Proverbs 21:21, "He that followeth after righteousness and mercy findeth life, righteousness, and honour." Life is a trip for each of us. God has a destination for us. Oh, that you and I would go the path that the Lord has planned for us. There will be a multitude of blessings along the way, and when there seems to be trouble it is time for us to learn and grow. Psalm 46:1, "God is our refuge and strength, a very present help in trouble." There were times on vacation that we might have vehicle trouble, but there was always somebody there to help us. Psalm 46:7, "The LORD of hosts is with us; the God of Jacob is our refuge. Selah." Yes, each of us has a wonderful journey that Christ planned for us. Why don't we decide today that Christ is and knows the way? Enjoy the journey.

God's blessing is there for those who do what God says,
when God says and how God says.

February 22

Numbers 3-4 Psalm 47 Proverbs 22 Luke 14

First Thought of the Day

Good morning! When you awoke this morning, what were your first thoughts? When I say awoke, I mean when you are conscious of what is going on around you. Waking up in the morning is not the same with everybody, as you know. There are some of us who, when our feet touch the floor, our mouth begins to fly open and the words are ready to come out. I have tried and I am learning to keep my big mouth shut and to give my precious wife time to get her thoughts together and to gradually welcome the new day before us. I am so sorry for those like my son-in-law who says, give me time to get my thoughts together. When I awake in the morning, there are thoughts that hit my mind right away. This morning, before I began my prayer time and not knowing what I would be reading in the Scriptures, or not knowing how the Lord was going to speak to me through His Word, I just stopped and thought about what the first thoughts of my mind were this morning. You know, my thoughts were on what I carry a burden about. What is most on my mind? I do not just want to discuss what is on my mind, but ask you what most possesses your thoughts. We all have thoughts about our marriages, our children, our grandchildren, those we love, our places of employment, things we are doing around our homes, etc. But what about our thoughts about spiritual things? What motivates you spiritually? What drives you spiritually? What causes you to carry a spiritual burden? What causes you to be driven to the Scriptures for spiritual guidance?

What I am speaking about is what our reading is about today. Numbers 4:19, "But thus do unto them, that they may live, and not die, when they approach unto the most holy things: Aaron and his sons shall go in, and appoint them every one to his service and to his burden." Okay, some observations. "Appoint them every one to his service and to his burden." Why was this so important? Look at the first part of the verse, "that they may live, and not die." My heart breaks often over Christians who once had a fire to serve the Lord, desired to do something for the Lord, had dedicated or rededicated their life to Christ and now miss church, are late, or just really do not care and constantly are giving excuses. I am not attacking anyone. I beg you to please consider some thoughts. If we as God's people are not carrying a burden and serving, we will lose interest, we will become cold, we will become so empty we see no reason to keep on going. I have seen this pattern too many times. Numbers 4:49, "According to the commandment of the LORD they were numbered by the hand of Moses, every one according to his service, and according to his burden: thus were they numbered of him, as the LORD commanded Moses."

Pastor made a tremendous statement that has stuck with me, "we were not just saved to be saved, we were saved to serve." Webster defines the word "burden" as that which is borne or carried; a load. We are not all preachers, teachers, choir members, deacons, ushers, etc., but we stay alive by carrying a burden or responsibility. Luke 14:27, "And whosoever doth not bear his cross, and come after me, cannot be my disciple." The joy of the Christian life is to be serving. All of us can pass out a tract. All of us can give our testimony of salvation. It is time for us to see if we are carrying a spiritual burden or a spiritual responsibility. Proverbs 22:9, "He that hath a bountiful eye shall be blessed; for he giveth of his bread to the poor." A "bountiful eye," giving of self to others. Carrying a burden will bring life to a life. Psalm 47:6, "Sing praise to God, sing praises: sing praises unto our king, sing praises." A burden or spiritual responsibility will bring joy and joy will produce a song of praise to our Lord. What spiritual burden of responsibility are you carrying today? If none, let us search our hearts and ask the Lord to lay a burden on our hearts, or maybe we need to repent and get busy doing what we know we are supposed to be doing for the Lord. I am thankful what my first thoughts were this morning. They drove me to my knees to seek the Lord.

The joy of the Christian life is to be serving.

February 23

Numbers 5-6 Psalm 48 Proverbs 23 Luke 15

Sin Forsaken

Good morning! Mrs. Smith and I were just talking yesterday about a horse that we had years ago. We called him Big Red. He was a very large horse, but very gentle. He loved all the affection you could give him, but he had a very ornery streak in him. He would get out of the pasture that we had him in, and we would just open the gate and scold him and he would walk back in. I was working on the fence, making some repairs and Mrs. Smith was helping me. Big Red came over, started nudging me with his head and I reached up to pet him. After I rubbed his nose a little bit, I turned to get a tool and he reached behind me and took my pliers. He just stood there and held those pliers in his mouth and when I reached for them, he backed away until I scolded him and he dropped them in my hand. That horse had the most loving but ornery personality. Big Red would get out and he knew he was not supposed to be where he was. Big Red is a horse, but how about us when we do wrong? God calls it sin. Big Red was so tall that he could jump over the fence with no trouble. We had to get rid of him because every time we turned around he was out of his pasture. His bad behavior sometimes was funny but his behavior led us to have to get rid of him.

Numbers 5:6 does not talk about bad behavior; it names it as sin. Numbers 5:6, "When a man or woman shall commit any sin that men commit, to do a trespass against the LORD, and that person be guilty." Let us look at the word "trespass." Trespass means to pass beyond, to go beyond a boundary. We might ask the question, go beyond what? Go beyond guidelines the Lord had set. I know this passage has to do with priests that took a vow, but we must begin to see sin because sin is painted so brightly in our day. Did you also see the words, "any sin that men commit?" It is not my place this morning to begin to list sins of our flesh, but we must live with a walk with God in His Word and accept the revealing of all sins in our lives. Number 5:7, "Then they shall confess their sin which they have done." My brother and sister, sin is destroying lives. Sin must be confessed and forsaken. When a child does wrong, parents should not just laugh or pass over what they did, but teach the child what they did is sin in the eyes of God. We as adults live in such a sin cursed world, and we as God's people must look at life through the eyes of what God sees. God gave a way for us, as our sins were washed away when we got saved. Yet now as we walk in newness of life, when we sin, we must confess and forsake those sins. Luke 15:7, "I say unto you, that likewise joy shall be in heaven over one sinner that repenteth, more than over ninety and nine just persons, which need no repentance." Luke 15:10, "Likewise, I say unto you, there is joy in the presence of the angels of God over one sinner that repenteth."

I will not answer for you, but I want to live in a way that the Holy Spirit of God will point directly to me and the sin that is causing a broken relationship with a Holy God, so that I can confess the sin and walk like I am pleasing the Lord instead of living in sin and trying to run from God. Proverbs 23:17, "Let not thine heart envy sinners: but be thou in the fear of the LORD all the day long." I thank the Lord I can be forgiven. Let us live to praise Him and not forsake Him. Psalm 48:1, "Great is the LORD, and greatly to be praised in the city of our God, in the mountain of his holiness." We need to have a walk with God to face our sin, confess our sin and walk with Him to bring praise to Him. Sin forgiven should be sin forsaken.

Sin must be confessed and forsaken.

February 24

Numbers 7-8 Psalm 49 Proverbs 24 Luke 16

Faithful Servants

Good morning! I want you to think with me about the most frustrating, or least desired, task around your house. A task that gets put off because no one wants to do it. A task that is dirty, hard, and frustrating to do. A task that no one volunteers for and says, I will do it. In every business, every organization, every ministry, there are tasks or work that needs to be done that is often very unrewarding, not personally satisfying, but has to be done and no one wants to do it. Who enjoys cleaning a bathroom? Yet we all are thankful for a clean bathroom. Around every ministry and every place of labor, as well as around every home, there are things that have to be done that no one likes or wants to do.

Can you imagine in our Old Testament reading the beautiful garments the priests wore, the beauty of the temple, the beautiful colors, the ornate beauty in all the craftsmanship? Now think with me when it was time for all the people to move and go forward. Everything was packed up and the sons of Kohath were called to carry everything and to do any maintenance on anything that needed to be repaired. Numbers 7:9, "But unto the sons of Kohath he gave none: because the service of the sanctuary belonging unto them was that they should bear upon their shoulders." They were the men to carry everything. What a privilege to be called by God to serve! God is not looking for those who seek glamor and position. God is looking for those who just want to serve, just want to work. My mind goes to many young people who have come summer after summer to just serve. Ladies got on their hands and knees and scrubbed, young men crawled on their knees and pulled weeds. Every inch of a kitchen was taken apart and areas that will never be seen were scrubbed and sanitized. Wooded areas that were full of briars and weeds and thorns, were cleared by hands and arms that soon showed skin that was opened from the prick of nettles. Stones were hauled to make a trail.

Physical labor has to be done every day and I am afraid the volunteers are often few. Luke 16:11-12, "If therefore ye have not been faithful in the unrighteous mammon, who will commit to your trust the true riches? And if ye have not been faithful in that which is another man's who shall give you that which is your own?"

There is always a place for faithful, humble servants who just want to work. Think with me about church. What if no one set up the chairs, vacuumed the floor, cleaned the bathrooms, emptied the trash, put salt on the ice during the winter and cleared the snow? What about all the repairs that are done that no one knows about? Our country and this world have turned into a place where only the glory is seen, but our forefathers were men and women of sacrifice and labor. There was a drive in them that is far beyond what we see in our society today. Proverbs 24:30-31, "I went by the field of the slothful, and by the vineyard of the man void of understanding; And, lo, it was all grown over with thorns, and nettles had covered the face thereof, and the stone wall thereof was broken down." Oh, that a generation of servers and volunteers would rise again. Walk across a church parking lot and you see a piece of paper, what do you do? See a hymnal laying out on a seat, what do you do? May we raise another generation that hungers to serve and not just be served. Proverbs 24:32, "Then I saw, and considered it well: I looked upon it, and received instruction." We want success. We work for pay to buy more and yet God says in Psalm 49:16-17, "Be not thou afraid when one is made rich, when the glory of his house is increased; For when he dieth he shall carry nothing away. His glory shall not descend after him." We read in the Old Testament reading today 115 verses and just one verse said, "But unto the sons of Kohath he gave none: because the service of the sanctuary belonging unto them was that they should bear upon their shoulders." It takes everybody to make a team, to accomplish a goal, but somebody has to do the physical work and "bear upon their shoulders" the load. Some things to think about this morning. God is looking for laborers. How about us?

What a privilege to be called by God to serve!

February 25

Numbers 9-11 Psalm 50 Proverbs 25 Luke 17

Help Carry the Burden

Good morning! I love watching a team work together. I love any athletic activity when you can see a team working together. A group of firemen arriving at the scene of a fire and each firefighter knowing exactly what to do and following leadership of the commanding officer in charge at the fire. More is always accomplished when all of the team is working together, going the same direction and sharing the same burden to accomplish the same goal. Moses, as the chosen leader by God, arrives at a point of needing others to carry the burden with Him. Numbers 11:15, "I am not able to bear all this people alone, because it is too heavy for me." God shares His plan with Moses in Numbers 11:16, "And the LORD said unto Moses, Gather unto me seventy men of the elders of Israel, whom thou knowest to be elders of the people, and officers over them." Certain men of certain qualities were to come together to carry the same burden.

How about carrying part of the burden of your pastor, church staff, Sunday School teacher, choir director, helping usher or work in the nursery, help on a van or bus route? Help visit absentees of your Sunday School class. Offer to help in cleaning the church. Offer to help in some area of a ministry in your church. Listen what God did with these "seventy men of the elders." Numbers 11:17, "I will take of the spirit which is upon thee, and will put it upon them; and they shall bear the burden of the people with thee, that thou bear it not thyself alone." I know every Sunday School teacher needs help in visiting absentees, and every ministry can always use help in areas that are mostly unknown unless you ask the leader what they need help with. I remember hearing many messages on it is our "duty." That word "duty" carries with it responsibility of helping carry the load. Luke 17:10, "So likewise ye, when ye shall have done all those things which are commanded you, say, We are unprofitable servants: we have done that which was our duty to do." Doing our duty is helping to share the burden. In Luke 17:33, Jesus made it very plain, "Whosoever shall seek to save his life shall lose it; and whosoever shall lose his life shall preserve it." Moses was told by God to seek mature men ready to accept positions of leadership and to fulfill responsibility and be accountable. God was telling Moses to look for faithful men.

There are a couple of farmers around the camp that have told me they are quitting farming because they cannot get anybody to help them with the work. They said there are plenty that want the money, but they cannot show up on time and you cannot count on them to be there when you need them. Proverbs 25:13, "As the cold of snow in the time of harvest, so is a faithful messenger to them that send him: for he refresheth the soul of his masters." You know, I believe one of the keys to revival in our lives and in our churches is to have more of God's people be faithful and help carry the burden of the pastor and other leaders. Share the burdens of the ministry. May all of us join hands in spirit, labor, sacrifice, and commitment to be more involved in carrying the burden of reaching, teaching, training, and sending another generation to reach a lost world for Christ. Psalm 50:14, "Offer unto God thanksgiving; and pay the vows unto the most High." Let us put into action what we have said in our heart and keep the commitment to the Lord that we have made to Him, or maybe it is time, as the old soldier said, to reenlist.

More is always accomplished when all of the team is working together.

February 26

Numbers 12-14 Psalm 51:1-9 Proverbs 26 Luke 18

March On

Good morning! Have you ever climbed a hill just to see what was on the other side? Or looked at a creek and said, I need to cross it and I do not care if I get muddy? Have you ever run a race and you were so thankful you finished? Did you ever take a test that you were concerned you could pass, and when you started taking the test, all the things that you had studied began to come to your mind and you received a very good grade on the test that you so feared? Keep on, my brother and sister in Christ. March on for the cause of Christ. Pick yourself up, wipe the dust off, take a deep breath and get back in the fight for souls for Christ.

God is ready, Moses is ready, and the twelve spies are given the orders. Numbers 13:17, "And Moses sent them to spy out the land of Canaan, and said unto them, Get you up this way southward, and go up into the mountain." Verse 18, "see the land, what it is." Verse 19, "what the land is that they dwell in, whether it be good or bad." Verse 20, "And be ye of good courage, and bring of the fruit of the land." He did not ask them one time, in any form if they thought the land could be conquered, and yet they said after they gave the report, Numbers 13:31, "We be not able to go up against the people; for they are stronger than we." Never turn back, never say you can't, never let the past draw you back from a life in Christ. Quit making excuse why you can't, quit giving in to the flesh. March on for the cause of Christ and the victorious life that is yours. Quit listening to the flesh, quit looking at your circumstances, and march on. Jesus taught the parable of the unjust judge in Luke 18:1, "And he spake a parable unto them to this end, that men ought always to pray, and not to faint." Luke 18:7, "And shall not God avenge his own elect, which cry day and night unto him, though he bear long with them?" We look at things as impossible, but with God there is always a way. Luke 18:27, "The things which are impossible with men are possible with God."

The problem with all of us is that we see what we see instead of asking for the eyes of the Lord to see what He sees. Proverbs 26:12, "Seest thou a man wise in his own conceit? There is more hope of a fool than of him." Let us fall before our Saviour and our King and seek His face as the Psalmist did in Psalm 51:7-8, "Purge me with hyssop, and I shall be clean: wash me, and I shall be whiter than snow. Make me to hear joy and gladness." God is still on His throne, He still hears our prayers, our salvation is eternal. March on in the will of God and take the land of life for souls, and for the cause and will of Christ for your life. See you on the other side of the hill.

March on for the cause of Christ and the victorious life that is yours.

February 27

Numbers 13 Psalm 51:10-19 Proverbs 27 Luke 19

Do What You Can

Good morning! There has never been a greater plea for men and women of God. The cry that has been from creation to this day is the plea for men and women to live, stand and teach another generation to stand for God, the Word of God and in the power of the Holy Spirit of God. I asked myself this morning as I read the Words of God, am I doing what God has given me to do? We talk of the "will of God," but do we live to be and serve in the true "will of God?" As I looked at our Scriptures for reading today, even before I began to read, I thought of the fears in our world and how the devil is doing everything that he and his demons can do to quiet the "will of God" in the lives of all of us. Numbers 13:2, "Send thou men, that they may search the land of Canaan, which I give unto the children of Israel: of every tribe of their fathers shall ye send a man, every one a ruler among them." These were not children that were being sent. These were not unproven men that were being sent. These were men who this verse tells us were "every one a ruler among them." I stopped and asked myself and I ask you this morning, are we doing what God has given us to do in His will for our lives?

Numbers 13:3, "all those men were heads of the children of Israel." These were hand-picked men of leadership and courage. They had positions of respect by the people, men that could be trusted and who had proven themselves worthy of this mission. What happened? Are the same things happening to us today that causes us to have the fear of the unknown, the fear of failing, the fear of pushing on, the fear of standing? What was it that caused them to come back after seeing all that God was ready to give them and yet they said, "Nevertheless" in verse 28? Numbers 13:33, "we were in our own sight as grasshoppers, and so we were in their sight." They were defeated in themselves and lost faith in God. The first thing I thought was, God protected you to go into the land and be a spy and bring back the fruit of the land. God let you see the promise of the land, but you looked at yourselves and lost faith in what God could do.

Let us now look at little Zacchaeus in Luke 19:3, "And he sought to see Jesus who he was; and could not for the press, because he was little of stature." Verse 4 tells us that he "climbed up into a sycamore tree to see him." I have always liked Zacchaeus. I think it is because he was short and I am short and I have always loved his determination. Because of what Zacchaeus did, look what Jesus did in Luke 19:5, "And when Jesus came to the place, he looked up, and saw him, and said unto him, Zacchaeus, make haste, and come down; for today I must abide at thy house." He had determination to do whatever to just see Jesus! Wow! How about you and I be determined to do what God wants? Zacchaeus not only got to see Jesus, but Jesus went to his house and had a meal. My brother and sister, we need to quit looking at why we can't and start doing what we can. Quit giving excuses and become doers. Proverbs 27:18, "Whoso keepeth the fig tree shall eat the fruit thereof: so he that waiteth on his master shall be honoured." God is saying, you do what you can and leave the rest to me. We need to cry out to our Lord this morning in a plea to get a fresh vision of what we can do through the power of God and quit seeing what we do not think we can do. Psalm 51:12, "Restore unto me the joy of thy salvation; and uphold me with thy free spirit." It is time for us to take souls for Christ, climb the mountain and see all that God has for us.

Are we doing what God has given us to do in His will for our lives?

February 28

Numbers 14 Psalm 52 Proverbs 28 Luke 20

Keep Pressing On

Good morning! Did you ever just stop and enjoy the beginning of another day? Today has never been here before and it will never, never return. Too often in life we try to go back. Oh yes, memories are always wonderful for remembering those special times. Yesterday we had the privilege to be with our entire family. Our son and his wife and our daughter and her husband, as well as all the grandchildren. We just got to spend a few hours together and we hung on to every moment. As I read this morning, I thought about the birth of each of our children and the birth of each of our grandchildren. I also thought about the answer of prayer and watching the hand of God in providing the perfect mate for our children. We laughed, told stories, and memories of the past just kept rolling out. You know, not one time did anybody say, I wish we could return to those days. Yes, there were tough days and very tough times and oh, how thankful we were to see the hand of the Lord time and again, but we never wanted to return to those days because each day got better and better.

Why did the children of Israel want to return to Egypt? When we look back, we will never see the next miracle of the working hand of God. Numbers 14:2, "And all the children of Israel murmured against Moses and against Aaron: and the whole congregation said unto them, would God that we had died in the land of Egypt! Or would God we had died in the wilderness!" They did not die, and God provided for them in every way all the way. I looked at some construction on a shop that my son-in-law and grandsons had done. The boards and sheeting that were cut and assembled could never go back to the original trees that they were taken from, so why do God's people, when we get in to tough times, seem to want to turn back? We lose sight of what God has done and is doing. We lose faith in the miracle-working hand of God. What a joy to my heart to read Luke 20:38, "For he is not a God of the dead, but of the living: for all live unto him." The greatest days of our lives are always ahead, having our faith and trust in God grow and seeing His hand work miracles in our lives. Proverbs 28:20, "A faithful man shall abound with blessing." Think with me right now and begin to praise the Lord for all He has done for you in days gone by. Just think of all the prayers that He has answered for you. Think of the miracle of your salvation. Think of the joy of the forgiveness of your sins. Think of the steps of faith that you have taken. Proverbs 29:25, "The fear of man bringeth a snare: but whoso putteth his trust in the LORD shall be safe." The longer we live in Christ, the stronger our faith in Him should be. Psalm 52:8, "But I am like a green olive tree in the house of God: I trust in the mercy of God for ever and ever." Don't look back and wish you could go back. You will miss all that God has for you ahead. Don't stand still in your walk with God because it will only be a short time and you will begin to backslide. Forward, my brother and sister in Christ. Forward in your walk and relationship and growth in Christ. "Whoso putteth his trust in the LORD shall be safe." (Proverbs 29:25). The shop where my son-in-law and grandsons are working is going to be a great place to build beautiful things. So why would anybody want all the wood to return back to the trees that they came from? Keep pressing on and be the miracle in Christ that He is shaping.

The longer we live in Christ, the stronger our faith in Him should be.

February 29

Numbers 15 Psalm 53 Proverbs 29 Luke 21

Ignorance or Disobedience?

Good morning! We have been singing the song, "And The Rain Came Down And The Floods Came Up," here at the Ranch. The heavy rains have caused the creeks all to be out of their banks and water is across the road in many places. Thank the Lord for higher ground. Yes, higher ground for being in a safe place when the rains come and higher ground in our walk with God. I want us to look and consider several words today in our reading. Numbers 15:26, "And it shall be forgiven all the congregation of the children of Israel, and the stranger that sojourneth among them; seeing all the people were in ignorance." Let us look at the definition of the word "ignorance": absence or destitution of knowledge, the negative state of mind which has not been instructed; uninstructed or uniformed. We are speaking of a people that have not been taught. They have not had the guidelines and rules laid out for them and the consequences of disobeying the rules explained. Now let us look at Numbers 15:30, "But the soul that doeth ought presumptuously, whether he be born in the land, or a stranger, the same reproacheth the LORD; and that soul shall be cut off from among his people." First let us look at the word "presumptuously": bold and confident to excess, arrogant, unduly confident, willfully. Simply put, knowing and not caring if they disobey what they know is wrong. Now, one more word for us to consider; "reproacheth": that which is the cause of shame or disgrace.

Just this week, a man was saved. I went and visited him and spent time with him, gave him a Bible and a little pamphlet that I put together on learning what the Bible says about his decision for salvation. He came to church Sunday, and I had another man for him to sit with in Sunday School and church. I took both of them back by the baptistry and the man looked at me and said, "If this is what the Bible teaches I am to do, then this is what I want to do." AMEN!! The action of presumption is knowing what we need to do, such as read our Bibles, be faithful in giving of tithes and offerings and be faithful in church attendance when the doors are open, as well as being a soul winner, etc. We need to ask ourselves this morning where we fit in to these verses. Sin is like a flood when the rains come; nothing stops the path of high flood water. When we allow sin in, and know it is sin, it is like the floods come and the sins grow. Luke 21:33, "Heaven and earth shall pass away: but my words shall not pass away."

We cannot claim ignorance with God when we have His Word, His church, His people to fellowship with, a preacher that loves us and preaches the truth to us, Sunday School classes that are a place to help us grow in our walk with the Lord. Proverbs 30:3, "I neither learned wisdom, nor have the knowledge of the holy." We must not give this excuse because we do have everything we need to grow in our walk with the LORD. Proverbs 30:5, "Every word of God is pure: he is a shield unto them that put their trust in him." Psalm 53:1, "The fool hath said in his heart, There is no God. Corrupt are they and have done abominable iniquity: there is none that doeth good." I am so thankful God forgives us, but may we take these verses and words and consider today where we are spiritually. We cannot claim ignorance. My brother and sister, allow the precious Words of God to instruct and strengthen your daily walk with God. The flood waters in our creeks will soon go down, but the flood waters of sin will rise and rise unless we confess and forsake the sins that are attempting to control us. There is no dam to hold the sin back. Oh, what a joy and comfort when we allow the Words of God to flow freely in our lives. Lord bless you.

We cannot claim ignorance with God when we have His Word,
His church, His people.

March 1

Numbers 16 Psalm 54 Proverbs 1 Luke 22

Who Influences You?

Good morning! Yesterday I worked at the camp for a while before I took some saddles and bridles to the church for our NYFC youth conference. As I was working in the barn, I heard the honking of geese flying over. Oh yes, the sounds of spring. I went out of the barn and looked up and saw that beautiful "V" that they always form. I thought for a moment about leadership in our lives. I wrote in my notes this morning, who is leading you and where are they leading you? Then I wrote, who is influencing you or what is influencing you?

Listen with me to Moses' words concerning Korah and his being critical of leadership and his leading people in the wrong direction and spirit. Numbers 16:26, "And he spake unto the congregation, saying, Depart, I pray you, from the tents of these wicked men, and touch nothing of theirs, lest ye be consumed in all their sins." Who or what is influencing you is who or what you soon shall be. God said you will be "consumed" of them and their attitude. God brought judgment upon Korah, his family and those he had influenced. Numbers 16:32, "And the earth opened her mouth, and swallowed them up, and their houses, and all the men that appertained unto Korah, and all their goods." Please listen again, who or what influences you? There were others who had a wrong attitude and spirit toward the judgment of God and God brought a plague. Numbers 16:49, "Now they that died in the plague were fourteen thousand and seven hundred, beside them that died about the matter of Korah." All because of a wrong influence. We must be alert and very careful of who and what influences us. Jesus gave warning to Simon Peter in Luke 22:31, "And the Lord said, Simon, Simon, behold, Satan hath desired to have you, that he may sift you as wheat." I can only imagine after Peter heard those words, his spirit of pride rose up and then Jesus said in Luke 22:32, "But I have prayed for thee, that thy faith fail not."

Are you being influenced to be in church or have you been influenced that you do not need church? Are you being convicted of the Lord to be faithful in Bible reading and a time of prayer, or has the flesh influenced you and you have weakened? All of us had that first love to be in church, read our Bibles, go soul winning, bring others to church and to Christ, serve in any way we can, and now our influences have almost ruined us spiritually and we have lost our first love. As there is always a goose at the point when the flock of geese fly, may we allow Christ to always be at the greatest point of influence in our lives. Proverbs 1:33, "But whoso hearkeneth unto me shall dwell safely, and shall be quiet from fear of evil." Let us get back in formation with Christ as our point, leading us, guiding us, directing us, loving us, providing for us, being our all. Psalm 54:2, "Hear my prayer, O God; give ear to the words of my mouth." Let us this day and every day be careful who or what is influencing us, because who or what it is, will soon be leading us. Spring is in the air, so notice that every flock flying back north has a point goose that they are following. Let Christ always be the point leading you in every area of your life.

May we allow Christ to always be at the greatest point of influence in our lives.

March 2

Numbers 17 Psalm 55 Proverbs 2 Luke 23

Alive in Christ

Good morning! Spring is in the air and all around us. Trees are starting to bud, grass is starting to green in some areas, and the sound of the frogs in the pond can be heard loud and strong. How are you doing this fine morning? The Lord is still on His throne and our name is still in the Lamb's Book of Life, and we have the promise of eternal life. Sounds perfect to me. Well, I guess we could say that we still are living is this sin cursed world, but there is victory in a walk with Jesus. The ice storm broke off a lot of limbs and Mrs. Smith and I were talking yesterday about how the buds have come out on some of the broken limbs that fell from the trees. It is like there is still life in them as the sun melted the ice and warmed the ground. As I looked at those branches on the ground with the buds coming out on them, and I looked up into the tree where there are limbs still attached to the main branches, I had a thought about our Scripture reading this morning.

If you remember about Korah and the rebellion and God's judgment, we then see God commanding Moses to have dead rods brought into the tabernacle. Aaron's rod was also brought in along with all the other rods. Only Aaron's rod budded, and this is what God said in Numbers 17:10, "And the LORD said unto Moses, Bring Aaron's rod again before the testimony, to be kept for a token against the rebels; and thou shalt quite take away their murmurings from me, that they die not." God gave life to Aaron's rod and it brought forth buds. Only a life in Christ can bring forth a victorious life. We need to quit living in our own strength and stay walking, serving, and yielding to Christ. Those branches that were on the ground and budding will only have those buds on them for a very short time and they will fall off and that branch will die. Just like a Christian does through the storms of life when we try to make it ourselves instead of staying in fellowship with Christ and faithful in every area. As Jesus was judged, He said this in Luke 23:31, "For if they do these things in a green tree, what shall be done in the dry?" Jesus was the Messiah, now rejected. He brought life to a sin sick world. We must stay alive in Christ by staying in constant fellowship with Him. Proverbs 2:20-22, "That thou mayest walk in the way of good men, and keep the paths of the righteous. For the upright shall dwell in the land, and the perfect shall remain in it. But the wicked shall be cut off from the earth, and the transgressors shall be rooted out of it."

The fallen branches will be cleaned up and burned. It is sad that they did not stay attached to the tree to not only bloom, but bring forth beautiful leaves that bring shade, and then in the fall a beautiful color. Many a Christian will fall away from the Lord, which is their strength, and fall so that their life is of no value and use. I was blessed by what the

Psalmist wrote in Psalm 55:16-17, "As for me, I will call upon God; and the LORD shall save me. Evening and morning, and at noon, will I pray, and cry aloud: and he shall hear my voice." Stay walking with the Lord and living and serving Him. Bring forth fruit as you blossom in a life in Christ.

We must stay alive in Christ by staying in constant fellowship with Him.

March 3

Numbers 18 Psalm 56 Proverbs 3 Luke 24

Fulfilling Our Responsibility

Good morning! We need every generation to help another generation to learn, accept and grow in accepting and producing with the responsibility given to them. As I began my reading this morning, I could hear my father say, "Son, I am giving this job to you and I expect you to do it the way that I have told you." One of the many reasons my wife and I love working with the summer staff at camp is watching them grow in the responsibilities that they are given and observing them hunger for more. Nothing is more satisfying than a job given, a job performed, and a job completed. Our world is crying for men to take the full responsibility of a home in partnership with his wife and train another generation.

Numbers 18:3, "And they shall keep thy charge, and the charge of all the tabernacle: only they shall not come nigh the vessels of the sanctuary and the altar, that neither they, nor ye also, die." Can you imagine being given responsibility and if not carried our correctly, people would die? I kept noticing the phrases, "keep the charge" and "given thee the charge." Responsibility given is an opportunity to help develop character in an individual. Yes, the individual must accept the responsibility and carry it out correctly. I am afraid we have given responsibility and then given a reward and missed the fact that the real reward is a person growing because they have fulfilled the responsibility. It is the satisfaction of a job well done instead of always needing a reward. Numbers 18:20, "And the

LORD spake unto Aaron, Thou shalt have no inheritance in their land, neither shalt thou have any part among them: I am thy part and thine inheritance among the children of Israel." Should that not be the goal of all of us, that our part would be God? Look at the phrase again, "I am thy part and thine inheritance." May our goal be to help a generation seek the relationship and blessing of Almighty God. Jesus was walking with two of the disciples and they did not recognize Him and then we read in Luke 24:31, "And their eyes were opened, and they knew him." Luke 24:23, "Did not our heart burn within us, while he talked with us by the way, and while he opened to us the scriptures?" May we all have a burning in our heart to walk with God and to do His work and to accept the responsibility of being faithful to Him.

Proverbs 3:6, "In all thy ways acknowledge him, and he shall direct thy paths." Proverbs 3:7, "Be not wise in thine own eyes: fear the LORD, and depart from evil." I can hear dad say, "David, I am expecting you to . . . ," and he would give me the task. It helped me to grow. I remember the day that I did not fulfill all my responsibilities and it caused a conflict with my dad and me. Oh, how badly I felt. I wanted to run and hide from dad. May we face the task, whatever it is. Psalm 56:10, "In God will I praise his word: in the LORD will I praise his word." Psalm 56:11, "In God have I put my trust." God will never fail us and will only bless us when we live the responsibilities that please Him. I love those words we read in Numbers 18, "I am thy part and thine inheritance." Have a blessed day. Walk with Him and serve Him.

May we all have a burning in our heart to accept
the responsibility of being faithful to Him.

March 4

Numbers 19 Psalm 57 Proverbs 4 John 1

A Straight Path

Good morning! Daily as I drive from the camp to the church, the road takes me across the Kentucky River. As the road heads toward the bridge that crosses the river, you can see the massive rocks that had to be drilled, blasted, and removed to make the passage to which the road and bridge were built for traffic heading both north and south. When we first came to the camp, we began to take time and drive different roads to learn the area. A major highway that we travel on for a short period of time shows on the Kentucky state road map that it crosses the river. Mrs. Smith and I traveled that road, and when we came to the river, there is no way to cross. You can look across the river and see another road that one time connected to the road that we were presently driving on. I talked with some older people about the road stopping at the river and how you can look across and see where the other road was. I asked if there was a bridge there at one time. The answer was no, but you could cross there if you were careful because of the rock structure in the river. I learned that for many years that was where people crossed with horse and buggies and eventually there were bridges built in other locations. Because of dams being built on the river to control flooding and to provide better water supply for growth of population, the crossing place where my wife and I were could no longer be used.

In our reading in Numbers 19 this morning, we read of the sacrifice of the red heifer. We read how this heifer was sacrificed, what they did with the blood, hide, and all other parts and the ashes when the carcass was burned. I want to look at a phrase in Numbers 19:9, "it shall be kept for the congregation of the children of Israel for a water of separation: it is a purification for sin." The road was once used to cross the river, but now a bridge has been built, and that is where we cross. Jesus had not come to earth yet, so there were sacrifices such as the sacrifice of the red heifer to show what the people did to have their sins forgiven, to show separation from sin, and for them to live a life pleasing to the Lord in obedience to the Lord. Just as the bridge was built to cross the river, Jesus came so that you and I do not have to sacrifice animals and all that needed to be done for our forgiveness of sins and to show obedience to Christ. As we read in John 1:34, "And I saw, and bare record that this is the Son of God." John the Baptist was the forerunner of Jesus, which means he was making the path to Christ. When Jesus came to John to be baptized, he knew it was Christ. John 1:36, "And looking upon Jesus as he walked, he saith, Behold the Lamb of God!."

Thousands of people each day cross the Kentucky River going across a beautiful four lane bridge. A bridge was built so that we can better and more safely cross the river. Jesus is the living sacrifice for our sins and shed His blood to make the straight path to God for you and me. Proverbs 4:25-27, “Let thine eyes look right on, and let thine eyelids look straight before thee. Ponder the path of thy feet, and let all thy ways be established. Turn not to the right hand nor to the left: remove thy foot from evil.” We are so thankful for the bridge that we use to cross the river, but greater than any bridge that will ever be built is the perfect path to eternal life through which Jesus Christ made the way for each of us. Instead of coming to a dead end road in life, we need to live and walk in the path that Jesus Christ has made for us. Psalm 57:1, “Be merciful unto me, O God, be merciful unto me: for my soul trusteth in thee.” Psalm 57:7, “My heart is fixed, O God, my heart is fixed: I will sing and give praise.” Psalm 57:11, “Be thou exalted, O God, above the heavens: let thy glory be above all the earth.” Of the thousands that cross that four-lane bridge, I doubt if very many have any idea that there was a time down the river a place where people used to cross the Kentucky river. What a privilege we have now since Christ has come and shed His blood for the forgiveness of our sins, that we can be saved and have a straight path to our eternal home in Heaven. I will head across that bridge in a few minutes, and each time I cross, I am so thankful for the beautiful view I get to see. I do not know when I will cross from this earth to Heaven, but oh, how thankful I am that I know the Way! Have a very blessed day.

What a privilege that we can be saved and have
a straight path to our eternal home in Heaven!

March 5

Numbers 20 Psalm 58 Proverbs 5 John 2

The Blessing of Obedience

Good morning! Follow the instructions or the warranty will be voided. Do it the way the manufacturer says or it will not work. Put it together by the instructions given or there will be pieces left over. Do the job the way I told you. If you had listened and followed what you were told, you would not be in the mess that you are in. Do any of these statements cause you to remember something that you wished you could have changed? Maybe I could say it this way, what will we miss by our disobedience? Who is going to be affected by our disobedience? We must learn to do things God's way.

Numbers 20:7-8, "And the LORD spake unto Moses, saying, Take the rod, and gather thou the assembly together, thou, and Aaron thy brother, and speak ye unto the rock before their eyes; and it shall give forth his water, and thou shalt bring forth to them water out of the rock." Very simple instructions. Moses and Aaron had gone before the Lord to seek His guidance to provide water for the people. The instruction received was very simple; "speak ye unto the rock." Numbers 20:11, "And Moses lifted up his hand, and with his rod he smote the rock twice." Why, Moses, why? All you had to do was speak! Yes, God had put His power before in the rod, but now God was wanting to teach the people His power and His blessing comes from obedience to Him and faith in Him. Look at the results of disobedience in Numbers 20:24, "Aaron shall be gathered unto his people." Now Moses loses his brother. Obedience to God, His Word, and His will is always the right thing to do. At the wedding in John 2 we read these words of Jesus' earthly mother in John 2:5, "His mother saith unto the servants, Whatsoever he saith unto you, do it." Those are some of the greatest words we will ever learn; "do it." Proverbs 5:1-2, "My son, attend unto my wisdom, and bow thine ear to my understanding: That thou mayest regard discretion, and that thy lips may keep knowledge."

We must learn that our excuse why we cannot be obedient and faithful to God will never be blessed by God. Parents and grandparents, we will reap what we sow in our lives. God sees and God knows. Proverbs 5:21, "For the ways of man are before the eyes of the LORD, and he pondereth all his goings." When we do a task correctly, do we not always enjoy the compliment that is received? Let us examine ourselves today and our obedience or lack thereof. Psalm 58:11, "So that a man shall say, Verily there is a reward for the righteous: verily he is a God that judgeth in the earth." All God said was, "speak ye unto the rock." Obedience to the Lord is simple and right and always blessed.

Obedience to God, His Word, and His will is always the right thing to do.

March 6

Numbers 21 Psalm 59 Proverbs 6 John 3

Don't Let the Devil Bite You

Good morning! I can remember as a boy going to several major league ball games with my father and uncle. The men that were put up before us as role images were so different than what is put up before young people today. We live in a time that so many are being offended by some of the most ridiculous things. I am going to just say it plainly. Grow up and get some maturity. Well, I feel better now. Can you imagine how childish the children of Israel were to complain about Moses and God? Just who did they think they were? Yet at the same time, who do we think we are?

God had had enough, and He sent the fiery serpents. Numbers 21:6, "And the LORD sent fiery serpents among the people, and they bit the people; and much people of Israel died." I looked at the little three letter word "bit." I thought how our world today has been "bit" by so many false truths, we have been "bit" by wrong heroes, we have been "bit" by living for things and fame, we have been "bit" by bitterness, we have been "bit" by anger, we have been "bit" by laziness, we have been "bit" by lack of character, and I think you know I could keep going. What brought all of this on? Numbers 21:5, "And the people spake against God, and against Moses." We are no different than the people back then with our lack of putting God where He needs to be in our lives. We need to thank God for His mercy toward us, that we have not been destroyed and His love and patience is still toward us. The people came to the reality that they had sinned, and we read their confession in Numbers 21:7, "We have sinned, for we have spoken against the LORD, and against thee." We read of the same problem in the New Testament as we read the words of Jesus in John 3:12, "If I have told you earthy things and ye believe not, how shall ye believe, if I tell you heavenly things?" We must heed to God and His Word. Proverbs 6:20-21, "My son, keep thy father's commandment, and forsake not the law of thy mother: Bind them continually upon thine heart, and tie them about thy neck."

I can remember going to the ball game with dad. The crowd stood for the national anthem, everybody was quiet, all hats were taken off and there was a focus on principle. Now look how far we have come. We have been "bit" by the devil and all he has, to try to destroy anything that shows love and respect toward a holy God. We must not get our healing and strength from what is raised in this world before us, but we must be a people that bows on our knees before God and seeks His face. Psalm 59:9, "Because of his strength will I wait upon thee: for God is my defense." Psalm 59:17, "Unto thee, O my strength, will I sing: for God is my defense, and the God of my mercy." Please be careful and do not get "bit" by the things of this world. Stay focused on our God who sent His Son for all to be saved. The only image that we need before us is to please Christ and to hold the truths of His Word high.

We must be a people that bows on our knees before God and seeks His face.

March 7

Numbers 22 Psalm 60 Proverbs 7 John 4

God Knows Best

Good morning! Did you ever ask your parent's permission to do something, and they said no? You accepted the answer, but then a little later came back and asked again and the answer was still no. You left, and then came again and your parents said, okay, but if you get hurt, do not come to me crying. I have been there too often. In our reading today, we see Balaam going to the Lord and seeking guidance, and gets a plain "no" from God, but follow along with me and watch what happens. Numbers 22:12, "And God said unto Balaam, Thou shalt not go with them." King Balak wanted Balaam to go with him, and God had already told Balaam no, but Balak put the pressure on. Numbers 22:16-17, "Let nothing, I pray thee, hinder thee from coming unto me: For I will promote thee unto very great honour." The devil will always try to lead us away from the will of God by trying to offer us something better, but know it never is. Balaam responded to Balak again in Numbers 22:18, "I cannot go beyond the word of the LORD my God, to do less or more." That should have been the end. When we have clear direction from God and we know exactly what God wants us to do, we need to never question God about it again. God's will is clear and should never be questioned.

Balaam headed back to God again and follow with me to see what God now says. Numbers 22:20, "If the man come to call thee, rise up, and go with them; but yet the word which I shall say unto thee, that shalt thou do." God had already given Balaam an answer and clear leadership, but that was not good enough. Numbers 22:22, "And God's anger was kindled because he went." We know he got on his ass and the ass saw the angel and tried to go around the angel. God allowed the ass to talk and then Balaam, after he had lost his temper and beat his ass, saw the angel of God and heard these words in Numbers 22:32, "behold I went out to withstand thee, because thy way is perverse before me." We must learn that God always knows what is best, and God will never bless what He does not approve. The woman at the well in John 4 listened to the words of Jesus and said this, "Come, see a man, which told me all things that ever I did: is not this the Christ?" (John 4:29). Listen to the wisdom from our Proverbs reading. Proverbs 7:1, "My son, keep my words." Proverbs 7:2, "Keep my commandments." Proverbs 7:24, "Hearken unto me now therefore, O ye children, and attend to the words of my mouth."

I can hear my parents now as they said to me on several occasions, "I knew you would get hurt," or "I knew things would not work the way that you thought they would." I think we all need to heed to the words of Psalm 60:6, "God hath spoken in his holiness." May we listen and heed to the leadership of the Lord in our daily lives and in all decisions that we make. May we listen and immediately obey. I do not think any of us wants to hear the words Balaam heard, "because thy way is perverse before me." We need to just obey God and His Word.

God always knows what is best, and God will never bless what He does not approve.

March 8

Numbers 23 Psalm 61 Proverbs 8 John 5

Walking With the Lord

Good morning! Can you hear the little boy say to his mother after he has been caught doing wrong, "I promise, mother, I will never do it again?" How many little boys and girls have made that same promise to their parents, and yet we know most of the time that is a promise that is not kept. I often wonder how many times God has heard us say, Lord Jesus, please forgive me, I will never do that sin again, and yet we do. Oh, how thankful I am for the forgiveness of God. Let us ponder for a moment what will help us to not repeat a sin.

Numbers 23:12, "Must I not take heed to speak that which the LORD hath put in my mouth?." It is a question, but it is really a statement made by Balaam to Balak. Balak wanted God to stop Israel from advancing and taking the territory given unto them. Balaam just kept saying and doing what the Lord said. Numbers 23:26, "All that the LORD speaketh, that I must do?" In the first part of verse 26, Balaam says, "told not I thee." If we would just do what God says! If we would just decide to put God first. If the child would just decide to do right. What keeps the child from doing wrong again? It is when the child sees that the punishment is not worth the fun of the wrong. When the Christian sees that, by doing what God says and not giving excuse for not doing right, the very special blessings of the Lord. Then we will see and sense His presence in a closer and more powerful way. As we read on in John 5, we see the man that had laid for thirty-eight years. The words Jesus said to him were very simple, plain, and straightforward. John 5:8, "Jesus saith unto him, Rise, take up thy bed, and walk." We read two more times in verses eleven and twelve the words, "Take up thy bed, and walk." He only said "rise" one time. I thought how we get saved once and then we are supposed to do right. Jesus told this man to rise, get up, stand up, and then Jesus told him to pick up his bed. Is not the bed a picture of our old life? Now look at John 5:14; "Behold, thou are made whole: sin no more, lest a worse thing come unto thee."

So often a new Christian will go through a major trial and testing right after they get saved. We need to realize the test and trial can help us to develop a determination in our walk with the Lord. When we got saved, we got up from our sin and we are to do what God says, and that is to keep moving forward in Christ. Proverbs 8:6, "Hear; for I will speak of excellent things; and the opening of my lips shall be right things." Proverbs 8:10, "Receive my instruction, and not silver; and knowledge rather than choice gold." God's way and will is always the right way. Balak wanted to change what God was doing and God said no. The palsied man had laid for thirty-eight years and God said, "rise." Today we need to "take up" the sins that are keeping us from growing in the Lord and just like the little child, ask God's forgiveness and learn to "walk" with the Lord. When we are walking and serving the Lord, there will be a joy in our hearts. Psalm 61:8, "So will I sing praise unto thy name for ever, that I may daily perform my vows." My brother and sister, "take up thy bed, and walk." Have a blessed day.

When we are walking and serving the Lord,
there will be a joy in our hearts.

March 9

Numbers 24 Psalm 62 Proverbs 9 John 6

God is Working

Good morning! It is so very important for all of us to never lose our faith in what God can do. We too often get discouraged because we only see what we are doing and not what God is doing. When we focus on what we think should be going on and not allowing the Lord in His timing to do His work in us, we can easily lose our joy and become discouraged. Balaam said to Balak in Numbers 24:13, "I cannot go beyond the commandment of the LORD, to do either good or bad of mine own mind; but what the LORD saith, that will I speak?" Going through trials and testings, we must always keep our focus on God. Sometimes during those trying times, we might not even be able to see the hand of the Lord working, but we must not lose our faith in God.

Numbers 24:17, "I shall see him, but not now: I shall behold him, but not nigh: there shall come a Star out of Jacob, and a Sceptre shall rise out of Israel." Look at the capital "S" on Star and Sceptre. That is Jesus and the prophecy of His coming soon.

I unloaded a pile of wood yesterday that was used scrap materials left over from the NYFC. To some the wood is junk, but to me I can use the material for another idea I have for camp. We must live in the Spirit and not in what we just see. We must have faith in what God is doing and not what we want to see happening. John 6:63, "It is the spirit that quickeneth; the flesh profiteth nothing: the words that I speak unto you, they are spirit, and they are life." The attention in John chapter six by the people was on what they saw Jesus was doing and not on who He is. That is why He said what He did in John 6:66-67, "From that time many of his disciples went back, and walked no more with him. Then said Jesus unto the twelve, Will ye also go away?" The Christian life and our walk with the Lord is not about what we see, but what He is doing. The pile of used wood is not about what is seen, but it is about what I can do with that pile of wood. Our lives are not about what we see, but about what God can do in and through our lives. We need to seek the Lord and seek His purpose. Proverbs 9:9, "Give instruction to a wise man, and he will be yet wiser: teach a just man, and he will increase in learning."

Summer staff applications are starting to come in for staff for this summer. This summer is not about what the staff want to do, but it is about what the Lord is going to do in and through each one of them. Proverbs 9:10, "The fear of the LORD is the beginning of wisdom: and the knowledge of the holy is understanding." We need to seek the face of God, trust in Him for His purpose, and fully allow Him to work in every area of our lives. Psalm 62:7-8, "In God is my salvation and my glory: the rock of my strength; and my refuge, is in God. Trust in him at all times; ye people, pour out your heart before him: God is a refuge for us. Selah." God has a purpose for each of us. It is our privilege to give our lives completely to Him.

The Christian life and our walk with the Lord is not about what we see, but what He is doing.

March 10

Numbers 25 Psalm 63 Proverbs 10 John 7

A Renewed Commitment

Good morning to you! You know, as I write each morning, I wish there was a way that I could express the burden I have to help folks grow in their walk with the Lord. I look back over the past several years that I have been sending daily text messages to members of our Sunday School class and begging the Lord for them to have a consistent, daily walk with the Lord. Each of us who have been saved for a while and have fallen in love with the Lord, His Word, and have a desire to live in His will, have seen those who have been excited to be saved and have grown and now fallen away from the Lord. It daily breaks my heart as I not only pray for those who have stayed faithful to the Lord, but I also pray for those who have grown cold toward the Lord. This morning's readings really started out in a way that even brought a heavier burden on my heart to help encourage others to stay faithful to the Lord.

Israel has now fallen to the temptation to worship other gods. Numbers 25:2, "And they called the people unto the sacrifices of their gods: and the people did eat, and bowed down to their gods." All that God has done and is willing to do for us and yet there is a constant drawing away from Him. Numbers 25:3, "And Israel joined himself unto Baalpeor: and the anger of the LORD was kindled against Israel." The world, money, wrong friendships, work, recreation and entertainment, laziness, lack of Godly character, plus a world of other things keep us from God. Yes, the Lord was angry, and He sent a plague where thousands died. Numbers 25:9, "And those that died in the plague were twenty and four thousand." What God is doing in our world today surely does seem to be the judgment of God that we deserve and to some extent I think it is only beginning. As we turn to John 7, Jesus is standing in enemy territory where there were those who wanted Him dead. In His teachings He makes this statement in John 7:37-38, "In the last day, that great day of the feast, Jesus stood and cried, saying, If any man thirst, let him come unto me, and drink. He that believeth on me, as the scripture hath said, out of his belly shall flow rivers of living water."

May I ask, what is flowing out of our lives? What is our focus? What are our priorities? Proverbs 10:11, "The mouth of a righteous man is a well of life." Proverbs 10:13, "In the lips of him that hath understanding wisdom is found." Proverbs 10:29, "The way of the LORD is strength to the upright." Oh, that there would be a renewing in us to live for and to give our lives to serve the Lord at the workplace, in our homes and through our daily lives! Psalm 63:8, "My soul followeth hard after thee: thy right hand upholdeth me." May we not be doing the same as the people of Israel did by bowing to the gods of the world. My prayers are with you today. May we renew our commitment to serve faithfully until He comes or He calls us Home.

There should be a renewing in us to live for and to give our lives to serve the Lord.

March 11

Numbers 26 Psalm 64 Proverbs 11 John 8

Willing to Serve

Good morning! The reading today sent me back in memories quite a long distance. Numbers 26:1-2, "And it came to pass after the plague, that the LORD spake unto Moses and unto Eleazar the son of Aaron the priest, saying, Take the sum of all the congregation of the children of Israel, from twenty years old and upward, throughout their fathers' house, all that are able to go to war in Israel." I want to look at one three letter word, and that is "all." The plague of God is past, and the people of Israel are getting ready to move forward to the land God has promised. Now it is time to get a head count of "all" the people and especially a special group of men, all men "twenty years old and upward." It is time, men, to do your part. It is time, men, for you to step forward in your position for your country. Now, before I go any farther in thought, let me explain what I am focused on today. We as God's people take in a lot more than we give out. May I ask a very simple basic question? What are we doing as far as serving in our local church or even for the cause of Christ? Men were counted from all families, from twenty years old and upward.

I remember the day that I came home from work and there was a letter in the mailbox from the department of Army, letting me know that I was going to be drafted for military service. I had registered when I turned eighteen, like all young men were supposed to do. I had received an exemption because of my attendance in Bible college. Mrs. Smith was expecting our first child and I had not returned for one semester, anticipating the arrival of our little one. When I opened the letter, I read it several times. We looked at each other and I began to receive several calls from the Army recruiters and the Marine recruiters. We decided that I should enlist so that I could have some kind of decision in my service for our country, and the rest is history. Think with me about the little word "all." Every man that was able had a responsibility. What about our service for the Lord? Every man and every woman who is born again should decide to be serving the Lord in any way that we can. Our life as a Christian is not going to grow unless we learn how to serve and seek ways to serve. Learning to serve is growing in the Lord. John 8:12, "Then spake Jesus again unto them, saying, I am the light of the world: he that followeth me shall not walk in darkness, but shall have the light of life." I had an obligation to serve my country, and I was physically and mentally capable of serving. How can I do anything less for my Lord than serve Him with my life?

Not everyone is called to be a preacher, but we are all called to give our life for the Lord to use as He desires. John 8:31-32, "If ye continue in my word, then are ye my disciples indeed; and ye shall know the truth and the truth shall make you free." John 8:47, "He that is of God heareth God's words." What are the deep desires of your heart? Not in things or position, but in living and serving the Lord Jesus who forgave our sins and has given us life eternal. Proverbs 11:28, "He that trusteth in his riches shall fall: but the righteous shall flourish as a branch." Our country has chosen to no longer draft young men for military service and our Lord does not send a letter to require us to serve Him, but there should be a desire in our hearts to live our lives to please our Saviour who has given us life eternal and, without reservation, paid the eternal price for us. Psalm 64:1, "Hear my voice, O God, in my prayer." May that be the cry from all our hearts to please the Lord with our lives. May you have a very blessed day in your living for and serving the Lord.

Learning to serve is growing in the Lord.

March 12

Numbers 27 Psalm 65 Proverbs 12 John 9

A Purpose in Life

Good morning! Could I just ask a quick question as we begin our thoughts this morning? What do you see that God wants you to do with your life? We need to consider the thought that we do have life for a purpose. I am now old enough to know that there are changes in life that sometimes change what the Lord has for us to do, but we must realize that He does have a purpose for each of us. A couple, when they first get married, will focus on each other and that first house so that they may begin having a family. Then the focus changes to do things as a family and watching the children grow. As the children grow and one by one leave home and begin their own lives, there is another change in life to watch our children on their own and beginning to establish their own homes. Then there is another change when the grandchildren arrive and become part of our lives. There is another major change that I have observed in others, and yet I have not experienced yet, and that is when the one that you love and have spent your life with gets a disease or sickness and you might be left alone. All of these changes in life will come, and yet God has a purpose for our life.

As I read this morning about Moses not going into the Promised Land, I thought about what the Lord might have for me, but maybe sin will not allow me to get to do or be what was God's will for me. Numbers 27:12, "And the LORD said unto Moses, Get thee up into this mount

Abarim, and see the land which I have given unto the children of Israel." I underlined the little word "see." How sad that Moses only got to look at a distance. He never even got to set his foot on the Promised Land or drink of the fresh water, eat of the beautiful fruit. All because of sin. Yet Moses does get to give the charge to Joshua, the man God picked to lead the people on. What is it that you and I could miss in the will of God because of sin, lack of obedience, lack of surrender, focusing on something other than God's purpose and will? We turn to John 9 and the disciples ask the question about a blind man. John 9:2, "who did sin, this man, or his parents, that he was born blind?" Jesus answered in verse 3, "Jesus answered, Neither hath this man sinned, nor his parents: but that the works of God should be made manifest in him." Do not miss what God wants to do because you feel you have committed a sin that God is judging you for. Ask God's forgiveness and do the will of God. You and I have life and God has a purpose that is far better for us. I do not want to just see what God could have done. May we press on and live what God wants us to do. Look up this morning. God is not done with us. He has a purpose and we must seek and live God's purpose.

Last night I was on the phone with someone I dearly love. Yesterday they found out they have cancer. I called a distant state this week to talk with someone and pray with them, as their daughter might not live. I looked at a young person who has messed up and I said, God still has a purpose for you, just get right with God and live His purpose in you. Proverbs 12:28, "In the way of righteousness is life; and in the pathway thereof there is no death." I went into a business yesterday and purchased what I needed and then began to talk with the owner. I asked about his son that I knew, and the business owner asked if he could speak with me. Tears began to flow as this man my age began to tell me the story of his son and the addiction of drugs his son has. I went to the car where my wife was and just sat and cried. We must put God first and live His purpose in our lives, because the devil is throwing everything he can at us in these days. Psalm 65:4, "Blessed is the man whom thou choosest, and causest to approach unto thee." If you and I have life, and we do, then live it for God's purpose. May we be parents and grandparents, singles and everything in between living and serving the Lord. May we bring praise to our God. Make a decision and live the decision to put God and His will in first place.

May we press on and live what God wants us to do.

March 13

Numbers 28-29 Psalm 66 Proverbs 13 John 10

Spiritual Cleaning

Good morning! I would like for you to think with me about the things that we do every day without giving much thought about what we are doing. We brush our teeth, eat food, put on our clothes, go to work, pick up around the house, make the bed, take a shower, do the work before us, come home, eat supper, and many more things, without giving a second thought about what we are doing. With spring on its way and summer right behind, we know that mowing season is coming and spring cleanup outside around the house. These things are just part of our everyday life, and we know these things have to be done. When one of our family gets sick, we go to the doctor. When we have a toothache, we go to the dentist. We have our eyes checked annually to see about needing glasses or contacts and we make regular visits to keep up with taking care of being able to see. The list of things we do daily or annually is quite a long list.

May I ask where the Lord fits in? Are we regular or have we established a time daily that we spend in prayer and Bible reading? Is faithful church attendance part of our weekly plans in life? This hit me this morning as I read Numbers 28:2, "Command the children of Israel, and say unto them, My offering, and my bread for my sacrifices made by fire, for a sweet savour unto me, shall ye observe to offer unto me in their due season." I would like us to look at the words "my" and "me," referring to God himself. Here we read this was a command by God to keep regular worship. Numbers 28:4, "The one lamb shalt thou offer in the morning and the other lamb shalt thou offer at even." Numbers 28:24, "After this manner ye shall offer daily."

Did you see the words, "morning," "even," and "daily?" Sounds like the Lord was teaching the people to have regular, consistent times of worship to Him and for Him. We spend time teaching our children things of life that must be done. Do we spend time teaching and helping them and leading them in daily devotions, faithfulness in church and service for the Lord? John 10:27-28, "My sheep hear my voice, and I know them, and they follow me: And I give unto them eternal life; and they shall never perish, neither shall any man pluck them out of my hand." What security we have in being saved! Nothing can take away our gift of salvation. Oh, that our appreciation in part would be our faithful worship to God. Jesus said in John 10:29, "My Father, which gave them me, is greater than all; and no man is able to pluck them out of my Father's hand."

I thought this morning about our determination to be faithful to God. Many do not have the Word of God to hold and read and study as we do. I challenge you, as I was challenged, from Proverbs 13:6, "Righteousness keepeth him that is upright in the way: but wickedness overthroweth the sinner." Spring cleaning will soon begin. May we begin spiritual cleaning in our lives. Psalm 66:8-9, "O bless our God, ye people, and make the voice of his praise to be heard: Which holdeth our soul in life, and suffereth not our feet to be moved." May we build a constant, daily walk with our Lord that is always there with us and for us. Have a blessed day.

Have we established a time daily that we spend in prayer and Bible reading?

March 14

Numbers 30 Psalm 67 Proverbs 14 John 11

A Promise is a Promise

Good morning! I listened as Pastor told us the weddings that are planned for the next couple of months, just at our church. As I was pondering some of the couples, I thought about that day that my wife and I said our wedding vows to each other, and I also thought about how some couples in this day that we live have forgotten the vows that they made to each other and now the lawyers have been hired and the divorce papers are being filled out. What happened? Could they not get counseling and work things out? What was missing that brought this couple to now want to go separate ways and only a few years back they said vows to each other, "until death do we part?" How much greater is our promise to God with our lives to serve Him and for us to break that promise?

Numbers 30:2-3, "If a man vow a vow unto the LORD, or swear an oath to bind his soul with a bond; he shall not break his word, he shall do according to all that proceedeth out of his mouth. If a woman also vow a vow unto the LORD, and bind herself by a bond." Oh, that we would go farther to not only say a vow with our mouth, but to mean it in our hearts and to live it with our lives. I am thankful beyond words how God keeps His promises to us, and He never fails us. I looked at some decision forms that were in a file at the camp. As I read each form, I tried to remember who the campers were, and several names I recognized. I sat there and prayed for each one by name, and my prayer was, "Lord, let them remember what they said and what they gave to you, and what they told a counselor that they believed you wanted them to do with their lives." Let us take time and refresh in our minds things that we have told the Lord we would do for Him, and what sin we would stay away from, and how we committed or vowed our faithfulness to Him. Picture with me the grave of Lazarus and Jesus standing there and calling for Lazarus to come forth. All are silent and they hear Jesus say these words that are recorded in John 11:40-42, "Jesus saith unto her, Said I not unto thee, that, if thou wouldest believe, thou shouldest see the glory of God? Father, I thank thee that thou hast heard me. And I knew that thou hearest me always." Look at those precious words Jesus said to our Heavenly Father, "I knew that thou hearest me always." Glory to our God, He is always there to hear us, and He does hear us.

Proverbs 14:5, "A faithful witness will not lie: but a false witness will utter lies." Proverbs 14:25, "A true witness delivereth souls: but a deceitful witness speaketh lies." We must keep our vows to God, and we must realize our promises are promises. A commitment is a commitment.

Lord, give us men and women of all ages who are faithful to you and to their vows. Psalm 67:5, "Let the people praise thee, O God; let all the people praise thee." What better praise can we give other than faithfully keeping our vows? May God find us faithful today and every day.

We must keep our vows to God,
and we must realize our promises are promises.

March 15

Numbers 31-32 Psalm 68:1-18 Proverbs 15 John 12

An Encourager

Good morning! My wife and I are camping for a few days before the spring and summer push begins. We were sitting by a fire and a car pulled up by a motorhome RV that had a trailer hooked up behind it. A man got out who could barely walk and was all bent over. As I watched him lift some ramps to hook to the back of the trailer that they were using to haul the car, I got up and went toward them and said, "Sir, may I help you?" As I approached the man I thought of my father who could not walk straight because one leg was much shorter than the other, and his leg had a twist in it. The man looked at me and said, "Thank you, but I will be fine. I just move a little slow." I wanted to help but he said, "I will be fine."

When a person gets saved, I want to help them grow in the Lord. I did not always want to help because I thought I did not know what to do. Our lives as Christians should be lived to help others grow, as well as leading new people to Christ. As we read this morning in Numbers 31-32, we saw that the children of Gad and Reuben saw land that was good for their herds, and they wanted to stop there. Moses then said in Numbers 32:6, "Shall your brethren go to war, and shall ye sit here?" The Promised Land still had to be taken and there were battles to be fought. I thought this morning about how we as God's people do not pray for each other and are often not the encouragers that we ought to be. My heart was blessed by the man that said, "I will be fine, I just move a little slow."

He was determined to keep doing what he can. Jesus said in John 12:25-26, "He that loveth his life shall lose it; and he that hateth his life in this world shall keep it unto life eternal. If any man serve me, let him follow me; and where I am, there shall also my servant be: if any man serve me, him will my Father honour."

When we started camping many years back and we would pull by our campsite, there have been many that have come over and said, "Can we help?" It is like there is an understanding by other campers. The Christian life should be lived to encourage others, pray for others, be there for others to encourage them in their walk with the Lord. Proverbs 15:9, "The way of the wicked is an abomination unto the LORD: but he loveth him that followeth after righteousness." Proverbs 15:29, "The LORD is far from the wicked: but he heareth the prayer of the righteous." If you are a new Christian, may I encourage you to keep on? None of us have made it. None of us are perfect. We are all growing in God's grace. We are all learning each day. The family of God is the greatest family on this earth. I love what I read in Psalm 68:5, "A father of the fatherless, and a judge of the widows, is God in his holy habitation." My father was a strong man in many ways, and I watched him and mom reach out to others in so many ways. May our lives be lived to be an encourager to other brothers and sisters in Christ.

The Christian life should be lived to encourage others.

March 16

Numbers 33-34 Psalm 68:19-35 Proverbs 16 John 13

Sin and Cocklebucks

Good morning! I would like for you to take a walk in your mind with me this morning. We are going to walk across a field and down into a place that is by the creek where the water does not really flow off the land well, and there is a weed that grows there. This weed sometimes grows near a pond or wetland. If our dog comes along with us, it will get these football-like stickers stuck in their fur and you will get them all over your clothes. You guessed it right, I am talking about "cockleburs."

As I was reading this morning, God told the children of Israel what to do with different things as they entered the Promised Land. Numbers 33:52, "Then ye shall drive out all the inhabitants of the land before you, and destroy all their pictures, and destroy all their molten images, and quite pluck down all their high places." God was saying to them, get rid of all the sin, and then God tells them what will happen if they do not. Numbers 33:55, "But if ye will not"; "they shall be pricks in your eyes, and thorns in your sides, and shall vex you in the land wherein ye dwell." Did you see the words, "pricks" and "thorns?" Things that will bring constant pain and agony. I began to study about the "cockleburs" and learned a little about a weed that has brought frustration to me often and has caused me to spend a lot of time getting the burrs out of my dog's hair and out of horses' manes and tails. The cocklebur is an extremely toxic plant to mammals and many cattle have been poisoned by them. Now listen to this, they grow their blooms only in the night and they need more darkness than light. Sounds like sin, doesn't it? That is why we do not see the blooms in the summer, but mostly in the late fall when there is more darkness than light and why we begin to see them in early spring before the longer days begin. I remember deer hunting and coming back and finding tears in my clothes just from walking through patches of cockleburs, and seeing a horse's tail and mane full of them and trying to keep them brushed and combed. An older farmer told me one time that cockleburs will destroy a good grazing field. Sin destroys and sin loves darkness better than light. As our reading took us to John 13, I noticed when Jesus told the disciples in verse 21, "Verily, verily; I say unto you, that one of you shall betray me."

Oh, how sad that we would love sin more than being faithful and pleasing the Lord. We love money and things and have idols and images, just like the children of Israel were told to destroy. Now look at when Judas left to betray Jesus. John 13:30, "He then having received the sop went immediately out: and it was night." The sins of this world are great, but we all know that they are greater at night. The cocklebur grows and blooms at night and so does sin. Our forefathers had it right more than we know, about going to bed at dark and getting up when the sun comes up. Proverbs 16:6, "By mercy and truth iniquity is purged: and by the fear of the LORD men depart from evil." "Iniquity" means wickedness and sin. Psalm 68:35, "the God of Israel is he that giveth strength and power unto his people. Blessed be God." I try and try to keep all the "cockleburs" mowed so that they cannot fully develop and spread. They so remind me of sin and how it grows and spreads. May we think about what God told the children of Israel about destroying and plucking down anything that riseth up. Have a blessed day and stay away from sin and cockleburs.

How sad that we would love sin more
han being faithful and pleasing the Lord.

March 17

Numbers 35-36 Psalm 69:1-15 Proverbs 17 John 14

Consistently Christlike

Good morning! I read several quotes yesterday that have stuck with me. These quotes had to do with training another generation with Godly principles that will last more than a generation. I love my children and grandchildren, and I daily check many things out in my life to keep a self- check, if I am holding the line. By holding the line, I mean am I consistently living Biblical principles? It does not matter what I think or feel; it only matters what God's Word says. This is one of the quotes that I thought on for a long time, "The man of God should be sold out, and never a sell out." (Dr. Shelton Smith).

As I read the Scriptures this morning, I kept noticing the importance of men following God, teaching Godly principles, and standing true and unwavering. Numbers 35:1, "And the LORD spake unto Moses in the plains of Moab by Jordan near Jericho, saying." Numbers 35:2, "Command the children of Israel." Numbers 35:10, "Speak unto the children of Israel, and say unto them." God was giving instructions for man to follow and teach. God is still looking for men that will follow Him and live for Him. God is looking for Godly leadership. Numbers 36:5, "And Moses commanded the children of Israel according to the word of the LORD." I wrote this on the top of my notes this morning, "Position does not make a person." We need a generation of leaders who lead from the trenches with those in the trenches. What is happening is that we are living in the times of the followers and not the leadership of the leader, our Lord and Saviour, Jesus. Jesus said these very words in John 14:10-11, "Believest thou not that I am in the Father, and the Father in me? The words that I speak unto you I speak not of myself: but the Father that dwelleth in me, he doeth the works. Believe me that I am in the Father, and the Father in me: or else believe me for the very works sake." We as men need to be established and producing where we are instead of moving like we have no foundation of principle. John 14:23, "If a man love me, he will keep my words."

I was putting fuel in my truck last night and I watched a young couple looking at me. I tipped my head and touched my hat as if to say howdy. I went in and paid for the fuel and when I came out, they were waiting in their car by my truck. The young man said, "Excuse me sir, but were you in the military?" I said yes, and then he stuck his hand out the window and he and his wife both said "thank you for your service." I am not a hero. I just gave some of my life to serve our country, but greater than that is all of us giving our lives to serve the LORD. My children and grandchildren must see me standing firm on Biblical principles. Give us a generation that can lead themselves and teach another generation what they were taught so that they will live for God. Proverbs 17:6, "Children's children are the crown of old men; and the glory of children are their fathers." I am teaching myself this morning and asking the Lord to help somebody else. We must not just live life, but live life with the purpose of living for and serving our Lord. I was humbled that the young couple saw something in me that caused them to think I had been in the military, but as I got into my truck, I thought, why could I not have been recognized as a Christian with Christian character? May our hearts be burning with a desire to show Christ in everything we do. Psalm 69:13, "But as for me, my prayer is unto thee, O LORD, in an acceptable time: O God, in the multitude of thy mercy hear me, in the truth of thy salvation." Christlikeness should be seen in everything we do and say.

Live life with the purpose of living for and serving our Lord.

March 18

Deuteronomy 1 Psalm 69:16-36 Proverbs 18 John 15

Front Porch Wisdom

Good morning! Did you ever notice how older homes have large front porches, or most homes in the country have large front porches? As I began my reading this morning, I went back in time to many front porches that I have sat on listening to older men talk. So many stories have been told on a front porch and only the Lord would know if they are true stories or not. Am I saying that some of my uncles might have exaggerated just a little? That is a possibility. I miss the time sitting in a yard under a big shade tree, sitting on a front or back porch, or sitting on the living room floor and listening and learning from the older men.

As we begin our reading this morning in Deuteronomy 1, I feel as though we are sitting down close to Moses as the review of what God has done, is doing, and will be doing is before us. Deuteronomy is a summary of the wilderness wanderings of Israel. Deuteronomy 1:1, "These be the words which Moses spake unto all Israel on this side Jordan in the wilderness, in the plain over against the Red Sea, between Paran, and Tophel, and Laban, and Hazeroth, and Dizahab." Never lose the wisdom that will be said by a generation that will soon be passing. I have often said, a man that ceases to learn ceases to lead, and there is no better teacher than those who have lived longer than we have lived. Wisdom and knowledge will be lost if we do not seek after it and learn to pass it on. Listen to the words of Jesus as He is giving wisdom and leadership concerning the growth of a Christian. John 15:4, "Abide in me, and I in you. As the branch cannot bear fruit of itself, except it abide in the vine; no more can ye, except ye abide in me." Many today look at the time spent on the front porch with an older person, listening and learning, as a waste of time. That is why a generation that spends so much time in front of a TV or computer and listens to the junk that is pumped into the mind rejects the simple truths of wisdom learned by an older generation. I can remember mom and dad saving to buy their first house and dad saying he never had a car payment because of learning to save for things he needed. Now generations will never be debt free because of greed and not wisdom. Jesus went on to say in John 15:5, "I am the vine, ye are the branches: He that abideth in me, and I in him, the same bringeth forth much fruit: for without me ye can do nothing." You have to be patient and persistent to grow fruit. We are now living in a mobile generation where they are always seeking better things someplace else instead of staying, being faithful, and learning to produce where they are and waiting upon the Lord to lead them. My parents and my wife's parents moved in their years of marriage only twice after they bought their first homes and our fathers worked the same jobs for most of their lives. Now couples move every couple of years or sooner.

There was much wisdom given on the front porch. Check the joy and peace we do not have in the lives of many Christians today. Listen again to the words of Jesus in John 15:11, "These things have I spoken unto you, that my joy might remain in you, and that your joy might be full." Oh, that we would raise a generation to seek Godly mature counsel, seek prayer from our pastors and wait on the plain leadership of the Lord. Drive down a street and look at the missing front porches. Oh, I know there are now large decks being built on the back of many houses, but when was the last time you either sat or observed a younger generation sitting and listening to the wisdom of an older generation telling stories of things they had learned? Proverbs 18:15, "The heart of the prudent getteth knowledge; and the ear of the wise seeketh knowledge." I have not learned all I need to learn and I hunger to have an older generation keep teaching me. So, if you are older than me, please take the challenge to let me spend some time on the front porch with you. Let us take the words to heart of Psalm 69:30; "I will praise the name of God with a song, and will magnify him with thanksgiving." Guard your heart and heed to the teaching of Psalm 69:32, "The humble shall see this, and be glad: and your heart shall live that seek God." It is time we all spend some time on the front porch with God and a generation that stayed faithful to Him and His Word.

There is no better teacher than those who have lived longer than we have lived.

March 19

Deuteronomy 2-3 Psalm 70 Proverbs 19 John 16

Meddle Not

Good morning! Another day is before us and the decision is ours how we will live this day. From the fall of man to the destruction of Satan and his control, temptation of every kind will be thrown at us to distract us from walking with God and living to please God with our lives. The devil's plan from the very beginning is to destroy man's love for God. As I read this morning in Deuteronomy 2:4, "Ye are to pass through the coast of your brethren the children of Esau." Did you see the word "brethren?" Esau was family but the people were warned to keep on moving and not to stop. Then in Deuteronomy 2:5, "Meddle not with them, for I will not give you of their land, no, not so much as a foot breadth." God wants our focus and priorities to be on what He is doing in our lives.

I have seen too many Christians who were growing in the Lord and they let a friendship pull them away from the Lord. Our lives should be lived to strengthen each other, but at the same time our lasting, true strength should be in our walk with the Lord. Let us think about the word "meddle." My Webster 1828 dictionary defines the word "meddle": to mix, to mingle, to act in the affairs of others when not necessary, an intrusion. God said, I do not want you to mix or mingle with the children of Esau even though they are brethren. God gives us good Godly relationships, but we must be very careful that friendships do not pull us away from growing in our walk with God. Jesus was teaching in John 16 and he said in verse 33, "These things I have spoken unto you, that in me ye might have peace. In the world ye shall have tribulation: but be of good cheer; I have overcome the world." Did you see the phrase, "in me ye might have peace?" Our joy, fulfillment comes from that growing relationship with God.

I love my wife more than words can tell, but my relationship with God is where peace, contentment, true joy and fulfillment comes from. Proverbs 19:3, "The foolishness of man perverteth his way: and his heart fretteth against the LORD. Proverbs 19:20-21, "Hear counsel, and receive instruction, that thou mayest be wise in thy latter end. There are many devices in a man's heart; nevertheless the counsel of the LORD, that shall stand." I received several phone calls yesterday asking me questions, and my counsel must always be centered in principles from the Word of God. The devil will continue to have victories and gain ground in destroying lives, marriages and families when we grow in the ways of the world and not in a relationship with the Lord. Psalm 70:4: "Let all those that seek thee rejoice and be glad in thee: and let such as love thy salvation say continually, Let God be magnified." "Meddle not with them." What is influencing you the most? Is the relationship helping you to grow in the Lord or are you losing ground? Be wise and be careful.

Our lasting, true strength should be in our walk with the Lord.

March 20

Deuteronomy 4 Psalm 71:1-16 Proverbs 20 John 17

An Odor of Holiness

Good morning! I am so thankful each day as I open the Word of God, how it is fresh for every day. Last evening, I said to Mrs. Smith, how do you feel about us taking a walk and then sitting by a campfire? She said, that sounds great. I would have a fire every day of the year if I could. I love to hear the wood crackling and just let me get lost in thought by staring into the coals of the fire. Along with a fire comes the smoke, and if you love to sit as close as we do, your clothes are going to smell like smoke. When we came into the house last night, I asked Mrs. Smith if I smelled of smoke, and she said, you better take your clothes to the laundry room.

As I began to read this morning, I thought about us being so filled with the Word of God that it just puts off an odor of holiness. By that I mean we are so saturated with God, His Holy Spirit, His Word that when we talk, where we walk, how we act, is always Christ-like. Deuteronomy 4:6-7, explains what I am trying to say; "Keep therefore and do them; for this is your wisdom and your understanding in the sight of the nations, which shall hear of these statutes, and say, Surely this great nation is a wise and understanding people. For what nation is there so great, who hath God so nigh unto them, as the LORD our God is in all things that we call upon him for?" Oh, that our total being would be so filled with God! Deuteronomy 4:9, "Only take heed to thyself, and keep thy soul diligently, lest thou forget the things which thine eyes have seen, and lest they depart from thy heart all the days of thy life: but teach them thy sons, and thy sons' sons." There is a lot to absorb in those verses and we need to hunger for a likeness of Christ so strong that the world and all others around us can tell that God is present. Jesus spoke in John 17:25-26 these powerful words, "O righteous Father, the world hath not known thee: but I have known thee, and these have known that thou hast sent me. And I have declared unto them thy name, and will declare it: that the love wherewith thou hast loved me may be in them, and I in them."

If I put on the clothes that I wore sitting by the fire last night and went into the store, people around me would know that I had been by a fire. If I wore the same clothes to church, people would know that I had been by the fire. May we live, walk, and serve in such a manner that people know we have been with God. Proverbs 20:27, "The spirit of a man is the candle of the LORD, searching all the inward parts of the belly." Spend time with God and God will spend time with you. Psalm 71:1, "In thee, O LORD, do I put my trust: let me never be put to confusion." Psalm 71:5, "For thou art my hope, O Lord GOD: thou art my trust from my youth." I remember the day I got saved, and I so remember the day I knelt at an altar and gave my life to serve the Lord. I pray the rest of my life will show forth what God is doing so that those

I am around may sense the odor of God. You are welcome any time at my campfire.

May we live, walk, and serve in such a manner that people know we have been with God.

March 21

Deuteronomy 5-6 Psalm 71:17-24 Proverbs 21 John 18

God is Jealous

Good morning! Have you ever been jealous? Think with me about how you had feelings toward someone, and you thought that someone else was trying to take them from you. Think of a best friend that you had growing up and another person came along and took this best friend from you or at least tried to take them from you. You did everything together. You had a bond that you thought could never be broken and now you have lost that friend. At one time they spent most of their time with you, and now you can hardly even get them to say hi to you. All of us have been there.

Let us look this morning at the word "jealous": Suspicious that we do not enjoy the affection or respect of others, or that another is more loved and respected than ourselves. Think how God feels about us when there was a time we rejoiced in our salvation, we wanted to go to church, we wanted to serve Him and we knew that is was important for us to be there, and now something or someone has drawn us away. Deuteronomy 5:9-10, "I the LORD thy God am a jealous God, visiting the iniquity of the fathers upon the children unto the third and fourth generation of them that hate me, And shewing mercy unto thousands of them that love me and keep my commandments." We try to tell ourselves that it is important that we live unto ourselves, but the fact is, we will reap what we sow. Many a parent has asked themselves why their children have no interest in church or the things of God and most always the answer is that there was a time that mom and dad drifted away and began a habit of church not being a priority. Let us go a little deeper and say that mom and dad did not see the importance of having a consistent walk with the

Lord. Read the words of plea by our Lord in Deuteronomy 5:29, "O that there were such an heart in them, that they would fear me, and keep all my commandments always, that it might be well with them, and with their children for ever!" God is jealous of us because He loves us and gave His Son to pay the full debt for us. How can we not give Him our faithful love? We read on and come to the garden where Jesus and the disciples are praying and the soldiers come to take Jesus. Peter now stands, draws his sword and we read in John 18:10, "Then Simon Peter having a sword drew it, and smote the high priest's servant and cut off his right ear." Jesus stops Peter, and they take Jesus away. I have often asked myself, did Peter just run off and why did the soldiers not chase him? Anyway, we now find Peter warming himself by the fire outside where Jesus is being questioned and judged, and Peter now says in John 18:17, and verse 25, when he is asked if he is one of Jesus's disciples and he says those haunting words, "I am not." Peter, just a short time ago, you drew your sword and now you deny Him. John 18:26, "Did not I see thee in the garden with him?" The question was asked and we read Peter's response in John 18:27, "Peter then denied again: and immediately the cock crew."

We need to realize God is jealous for us and our love for Him. We need to be careful and not be drawn away from the one that gave all for all mankind. Let us look how God sees us and quit looking how we see things. Proverbs 21:2, "Every way of man is right in his own eyes: but the LORD pondereth the hearts." What husband is not jealous over his wife, and what wife is not jealous over her husband? What friend would not be jealous over losing a friend because someone took that friend away? May we look and consider our love and actions for and toward our Lord. Psalm 71:23, "My lips shall greatly rejoice when I sing unto thee; and my soul, which thou hast redeemed." I thank the Lord that He is jealous over me.

We need to realize God is jealous for us and our love for Him.

March 22

Deuteronomy 7-8 Psalm 72 Proverbs 22 John 19

He is Our Everything

Good morning! Come to the barn with me and my dog Noelle, and ride with us on the four- wheeler. I want to show you something that I never get tired of seeing. As we head down the road at the ranch, be watching for squirrels and rabbits and watch Noelle's alertness. Yesterday as we passed by this spot, she saw a squirrel and jumped off the four-wheeler to chase it. As we hauled some trash and then headed out to the back of the ranch, she spotted a turkey running. I stopped the four-wheeler and thought for a moment. She is always alert to what is going on around us.

Deuteronomy 7:6 is written to the children of Israel, but there are principles in that verse that can be applied to our lives. "For thou art a holy people unto the LORD thy God: the LORD thy God hath chosen thee to be a special people unto himself, above all people that are upon the face of the earth." To be special to God is beyond what we can understand. We are special in every way to Him. Noelle is always watching and scanning around everywhere we go and whatever we are doing. Just think with me, God loves us so much and He is constantly watching out for us. Deuteronomy 7:9, "Know therefore that the LORD thy God, he is God, the faithful God, which keepeth covenant and mercy with them that love him and keep his commandments to a thousand generations." Noelle would be considered a faithful dog. When we leave, she watches. When we come home, she is there. Wherever I go she wants to be with me. If I am working on a project, she will lay close by and be watching all around and will also be watching me. John 19:17-18, "And he bearing his cross went forth into a place called the place of a skull, which is called in the Hebrew Golgotha: Where they crucified him, and two other with him, on either side one, and Jesus in the midst." He bore the cross and was placed in the very middle of sinners. He was and is everything for us. He is watching and protecting. Proverbs 22:20-21, "Have not I written to thee excellent things in counsels and knowledge, That I might make thee know the certainty of the words of truth." God has given Himself and His Word to comfort us. Oh, that you and I would allow the Lord to be our all, our everything. Psalm 72:18, "Blessed be the LORD God, the God of Israel, who only doeth wondrous things." Let God love you today. Allow the Lord to be everything He wants to be today.

Just as that dog that has no soul and wants to be with me and go everywhere I go, and be constantly watching everything around me; my God is there everywhere, every day for me and you to be everything for us. He promises us, "to a thousand generations." May I just say it as plain as I can? He will be with us forever and ever. Praise His Name.

Oh, that you and I would allow the Lord to be our all, our everything.

March 23

Deuteronomy 9-10 Psalm 73:1-14 Proverbs 23 John 20-21

From the Inside Out

Good morning! An older man many years ago said to me, "Dave, do you know that a tree dies from the inside out?" I looked at him and thought about how many trees I have seen that have fallen and yes, the center of that tree was rotten. Yesterday, two young men from CBC were helping me clean up some limbs from the past storms. Some of the limbs were quite large and I used the chainsaw to cut them up, while others were small branches. As we were loading the cut-up wood and branches, I passed on the statement as it had been passed on to me about trees dying from the inside out. As the day ended, I thought about the big beautiful maple tree that is dying in our front yard. It is dying from the inside out.

How about us? Has your heart drawn cold to the things of God? Is your fire within to serve the Lord dwindling away? In Deuteronomy 9:26-27, Moses is pleading with the Lord for the people, because when he came down from the mount after being with God and fasting for forty days, the people had made the golden calf and had already grown cold toward God. "I prayed therefore unto the LORD, and said, O Lord God, destroy not thy people and thine inheritance, which thou hast redeemed through thy greatness, which thou hast brought forth out of Egypt with a mighty hand. Remember thy servants, Abraham, Isaac, and Jacob; look not unto the stubbornness of this people, nor to their wickedness, nor to their sin." Moses said, "Remember thy servants." God never forgets. He has saved us, but have we let the rotting of sin begin in our hearts? Is our heart getting cold toward the things of God? Deuteronomy 9:28, "Lest the land whence thou broughtest us out say." Moses asks the Lord, what will the world think? The question we need to ask every day is, what will and how will others be affected by backsliding, and what testimony am I giving for the name of God? We read on in John 20, how the tomb is empty because Jesus is risen and we find the disciples looking, and then leaving. John 20:10, "Then the disciples went away again unto their own home." What happened to their faith? What happened to their memory about Jesus teaching them about His resurrection? John 20:11, "But Mary stood without at the sepulchre weeping." Oh, how her heart was filled as she did not leave and she heard the words of the Saviour in verse 16, "Mary."

Do not quit on God. Do not let your faith in God die. Keep looking to Him for daily strength. Proverbs 23:23, "Buy the truth, and sell it not; also wisdom, and instruction, and understanding." We need to stay on our knees and stay in God's Word. The tree rots from the inside out and so do Christians. Psalm 73:2-3, "But as for me, my feet were almost gone; my steps had well nigh slipped. For I was envious at the foolish, when I saw the prosperity of the wicked." Please do not let your heart turn cold. Mrs. Smith and I have planted new trees and we are going to plant more. All of us will pass on, but I do not want to pass on out of this world with a cold, dead heart. Clean the broken branches up and live on for God. Confess the sin, and serve the KING.

We need to stay on our knees and stay in God's Word.

March 24

Deuteronomy 11-12 Psalm 73:15-28 Proverbs 24 Acts 1

Faithful to the End

Good morning! Growing as a Christian is a constant battle between flesh and our spirit wanting to do right. Many have grown in the Lord and now lead a consistent walk with God, but they decided the fight was worth it for all that Christ did for them. To some the fight is not worth it and the flesh of man or the sin of man wins another battle. All of us every day fight the flesh and the sins of the flesh.

The Scripture was so plain for us to see this morning. Deuteronomy 11:26-28, "Behold, I set before you this day a blessing and a curse; A blessing, if ye obey the commandments of the LORD your God, which I command you this day: And a curse, if ye will not obey the commandments of the LORD your God, but turn aside out of the way which I command you this day." That is putting in right down on the lower level for us to understand. "A blessing" and "a curse." We have to decide every moment of every day. God never rejects us, but as the flesh weakens, we have a decision to make. We turn to the book of Acts and we see the last verbal conversation the Saviour has with man, and as they met together, we read their attitude and actions in Acts 1:14, "These all continued with one accord in prayer and supplication, with women, and Mary the mother of Jesus, and with his brethren." See the words, "continued with one accord." They did not stop being sinners, but they realized they had a mission and that was to reach the world for Jesus Christ. Their focus was on what pleased the Lord in their daily lives, and how God wanted to use each of them. We read on down how the betrayal of Judas did not stop them as we see in verse twenty-six how they chose Matthias. May I encourage you to keep on for the Lord? Proverbs 24:5, "A wise man is strong; yea, a man of knowledge increaseth strength." We never arrive at the point of knowing all. That is why we are challenged through the Scriptures to keep growing. I have learned as I have read the Scriptures and watched those much wiser, that a wise man is hungry to grow and gain spiritual strength. The preciousness of a close walk with God is never realized until our life is totally daily given to God. Psalm 73:17, "Until I went into the sanctuary of God; then understood I their end."

We spend too much time searching for happiness instead of yielding to the spirit of God. Many times we do not understand what is going on but Psalm 73:23 should be a comfort to us. "Nevertheless I am continually with thee: thou hast holden me by my right hand." I have watched a person at the last few moments of their life have a smile on their face as they have been faithful to the end, and when that time approaches there is an unmistakable joy that only a walk with Christ can reveal. Let us want it and go after it. I am speaking of having a walk and relationship with Christ that brings a joy and fulfillment to the very end.

A wise man is hungry to grow and gain spiritual strength.

March 25

Deuteronomy 13-14 Psalm 74:1-11 Proverbs 25 Acts 2

Continue Steadfastly

Good morning! I believe if you are reading this simple little devotional, there is a desire in your heart to please the Lord with your life. I also desire from the depths of my heart to please the Lord in everything, every way and every day. Deuteronomy 13:18, "When thou shalt hearken to the voice of the LORD thy God, to keep all his commandments which I command thee this day, to do that which is right in the eyes of the LORD thy God." See the little phrase, "When thou shalt hearken to the voice." On the day of salvation, when we invited the Lord into our hearts, there was for the first time a personal invitation by you and me to ask the Holy Spirit, which is God, to come into our heart. What a day to have God with us all the time! All of us at that moment had an overwhelming desire to please God. Is that desire still there as it was on the day you asked God the Holy Spirit to come into your life?

God says over and again in His Word that we are to be a holy people. Deuteronomy 14:2, "For thou art an holy people unto the LORD thy God, and the LORD hath chosen thee to be a peculiar people unto himself, above all the nations that are upon the earth." Everything about us is to be different from the things of this world. When we accepted Christ, did we accept Him as leading our lives? Did we accept His ways instead of our ways? Acts 2:41-42, "Then they that gladly received his word were baptized: and the same day there were added unto them about three thousand souls. And they continued stedfastly in the apostles' doctrine and fellowship, and in breaking of bread, and in prayers." I am thankful for those words "continued steadfastly." There was a revival spirit and our prayer should be for that same spirit to permeate us today. Where is our heart toward those who seem to be against us and the cause of Christ? Are we praying for the lost as we should? Are we reaching out and living the life of a Christian toward a dying world? Proverbs 25:1, "If thine enemy be hungry, give him bread to eat; and if he be thirsty, give him water to drink."

May I say it again as I have often said, God has not forgotten us. Have we forgotten Him? Is our attitude toward the Lord that He forgot us, where the truth really falls on us? Psalm 74:2, "Remember thy congregation, which thou hast purchased of old." May we be a people that "continued steadfastly." May our prayer be today to see a lost world as Christ sees and to be a holy people unto the Lord.

Are we reaching out and living the life
of a Christian toward a dying world?

March 26

Deuteronomy 15-16 Psalm 74:12-23 Proverbs 26 Acts 3

Remember

Good morning! I love history. I love to try and understand moments in our history, to understand the sacrifice of individuals who were willing to give their lives for a cause. There have been many monuments that I have read in my lifetime and tried to remember that moment in history, and something special of why the monument was erected. It is a sad day that in our country we have had monuments destroyed because of a generation that puts no value on the price that someone paid.

We are challenged today in our reading by three words, "remember the day." Deuteronomy 16:3, "that thou mayest remember the day when thou camest forth out of the land of Egypt all the days of thy life." Notice even those last words, "all the days of thy life." I went to another funeral of a loved man from our church this week, and pastor talked about how the life of this man that we were there to honor, will be remembered. As we read on in our reading today, we came to Deuteronomy 16:17, "Every man shall give as he is able according to the blessing of the LORD thy God which he hath given thee." Are we using what God has given us? Have we given freely of our lives to be used by and for the Lord? We can go around the world and find monuments honoring people and events. I looked up the definition of the word monument: "anything by which a memory is preserved or perpetuated." It might be a pile of rocks, a building, a marker, a statue, or anything. Now let us look at the word "perpetuated": "continued through eternity or for an indefinite time." We are challenged continually throughout the Scriptures to "remember." Acts 3:24, "Yea, and all the prophets from Samuel and those that follow after, as many as have spoken, have likewise foretold of these days." This was another challenge by Peter to "remember." God gives us so much to remember and Proverbs lets us know that we are a fool if we do not. Proverbs 26:7, "The legs of the lame are not equal: so is a parable in the mouth of fools." God gives us wisdom to remember and apply daily in our lives. Remember the words and wisdom of God.

Let us be challenged today to learn to "remember" those things that give us God's blessing in our lives. Never forget, and always remember the sacrifice for us through God's plan of salvation. Psalm 74:12, "For God is my king of old, working salvation in the midst of the earth." The next time you stop and read a monument, take the time to learn why that monument is there. "That thou mayest remember the day." Do not live to be great, but live a life to bring greatness to our Lord. Our lives should live on because of our testimony for Christ, even when we are gone, because we have been given life eternal. Let your life "perpetuate" Christ.

Let us be challenged today to learn to "remember" those things that give us God's blessing.

March 27

Deuteronomy 17-18 Psalm 75 Proverbs 27 Acts 4

What Are You Filled With?

Good morning! I was just asked how I make my dog obey so well. I said, she does not always obey, but I learned a long time ago that most dogs want to please who feeds them, waters them and spends time loving them. I also learned a long time ago that if you want an animal to want to be with you, you have to show them that you want to be with them. I have grown to understand that walking with God as a Christian is a lot like working with animals. God wants to walk with us all the time and our love grows for each other when we do not want anything other than to just spend time together, loving on each other.

The children of Israel came to the land that God had promised, and we have to come to the place of wanting to have a life in Christ. Being saved is just the first step. Having a walk with Christ is to have a life in Christ. Deuteronomy 18:9, "When thou art come into the land which the LORD thy God giveth thee, thou shalt not learn to do after the abominations of those nations." God allowed them to get to the land that He had promised, but He warned them to not do the abominations of the people and the land. A dog is not a bad dog because of its habitat. It is a bad dog because the master of the dog has allowed the dog to take on bad habits. A dog left to himself will act like a wild dog. A Christian that does not grow in Christ will live like a Christian that has no standards or convictions, or will live the same way or worse than before they were saved. Look at the phrase, "thou shalt not learn to do after the abominations of those nations." Many Christians watch and play computer games on their TVs, computers, phones, and tablets that show divination, enchantment, witches, charmers, different ungodly spirits along with ungodly music and language and dress. How can a person want to read the Bible, come to church or walk with God while doing those things? The disciples in Acts 4 were questioned and they showed something that we all should desire to show. Acts 4:13, "Now when they saw the boldness of Peter and John and perceived that they were unlearned and ignorant men, they marveled; and they took knowledge of them, that they had been with Jesus." Can people tell that we have been with Jesus? Is our prayer life that of showing we have been with God? Acts 4:31, "And when they had prayed, the place was shaken where they were assembled together; and they were all filled with the Holy Ghost, and they spake the word of God with boldness." Wow, what a testimony!

My dog knows when I want to be with her, and she responds by wanting to be with me. Wagging her tail, jumping around, she has a little whine, she will rub up against my leg, and I will respond to her. When she does not obey, I do not yell, but I am firm, patient and consistent. I almost lost a dog because the neighbor's dog chased cars and my dog was hit one day. After I brought her home, I often would hear her head toward a car or truck when they came by and I would call her back and be patient in saying, NO, NO, NO. The neighbor's dog was hit one day and died from chasing cars. Proverbs 27:12, "A prudent man foreseeth the evil, and hideth himself; but the simple pass on, and are punished." What do you put in front of you that goes into your mind? What kind of people do you allow to influence you? Proverbs 27:17, "Iron sharpeneth iron, so a man sharpeneth the countenance of his friend." Who I hang around with will influence me. Listen to these words of Psalm 75:9-10, "But I will declare for ever, I will sing praises to the God of Jacob. All the horns of the wicked also will I cut off; but the horns of the righteous shall be exalted." My daughter sent me a text with an attachment that said, "Dad, I think this will be a blessing to you." I opened the text and it was a preacher named Evangelist Lester Roloff preaching a message from 1981 entitled, "And the mule walked on." Praise the Lord! What I am is what I fill myself with. What are you filling your life with?

Can people tell that we have been with Jesus?

March 28

Deuteronomy 19-20 Psalm 76 Proverbs 28 Acts 5

Blessing for Obedience

Good morning! I love watching animals with their young. I have observed a cow calling her young calf to follow her and I have also watched that same cow give a kick to her calf to stop her nursing. I have watched a sow bear knock her cubs around to get them to follow. I have watched as a mother bird had brought worms to a nest and I have watched as a mother bird scolds her birds like she is trying to get them to leave the nest and fly. Nature has a way of teaching their own to grow up and mature. God is always so patient with us. Each of us face battles as we grow in life and especially as we grow in our walk with the Lord. God promises blessing for obedience and He also will bring chastisement for our disobedience. That word "chastisement" is God's love to us and disciplining us for disobedience. God promises blessing and growth for obedience. Deuteronomy 19:9, "If thou shalt keep all these commandments to do them, which I command thee this day, to love the LORD thy God, and to walk in his ways." It is so very simple; "keep," "do them," "love the LORD," and "walk in his ways."

I have read many times the story of Ananias and Sapphira in Acts 5 and the truth is, they kept back from God what was His and the results were death. Acts 5:3, "why hath Satan filled thine heart to lie to the Holy Ghost, and to keep back part." Animals in nature live daily to live. They know they must search for food to stay alive. My question is, why do God's people not search the Scriptures and build a life of faith in prayer to the God who saved them to stay spiritually alive? God gave me the answer to the question in Proverbs 28:5, "Evil men understand not judgment; but they that seek the LORD understand all things." Our flesh will never be satisfied until we have that internal satisfaction that comes from a consistent walk with God and it will overflow to every area of our life. Proverbs 28:14, "Happy is the man that feareth alway: but he that hardeneth his heart shall fall into mischief." A sow bear will fight to death to protect her young. That same sow or mother bear will look, scrap, turn over logs and keep wandering the forest to sustain life for herself and her young. God says what we are when we turn away from God. Proverbs 28:26, "He that trusteth in his own heart is a fool: but whoso walketh wisely, he shall be delivered."

I asked my wife early what was the key in her heart that caused her to begin having a walk with God, and after all these years, what is the key to keep daily searching the Scriptures? She said without reservation, "I was thankful for my sins to be forgiven." A sow bear can get mad at her young when they do not follow, but listen to the words of Psalm 76:7, "Thou, even thou, art to be feared: and who may stand in thy sight when once thou art angry." What keeps us going forward for the Lord are the words from Deuteronomy 19:9, "keep all these commandments," "do them," "to love the LORD thy God," "walk in his ways." Let us decide to do it and never quit.

God promises blessing and growth for obedience.

March 29

Deuteronomy 21-22 Psalm 77 Proverbs 29 Acts 6

The Final Authority

Good morning! Who sets the standards of life that you and I live by? Do I have guidelines that I live by or do I just do what I feel like doing? Life is sure changing fast. Things that used to be wrong, and I saw the wrong when I was a young man, for some reason seem to be okay in this world that we live in. As I read the Scriptures in Deuteronomy this morning, I came across a verse that seems very simple to me but this one verse has been questioned so much. Before I type the verse, let me tell you something I did yesterday. I went to the farm supply store to get some dog food. The lady behind the counter was very nice and helpful as I asked for what kind of dog food they have. She said, "Sir, do you want the orange bag or the yellow bag?" My first thought was to say, I am not feeding the bag. I did not say that, but I asked the difference. The ingredients are different. The purpose of the feed is different. The outcome of the dog eating the feed is different.

As I read Deuteronomy 22:5, "The woman shall not wear that which pertaineth unto man, neither shall a man put on a woman's garment: for all that do so are abomination unto the LORD thy God." It is very simple, but I do not feed my dog chicken starter feed, and I do not feed the horses steak and eggs. God gives us what we need to grow in a life in Christ. Deuteronomy 22:22, "If a man be found lying with a woman married to an husband, then they shall both of them die, both the man that lay with the woman, and the woman, so shalt thou put away evil." We are not to wear things that are an "abomination," and the sin of adultery was to be taken care of by putting both the man and woman to death. How would the world handle that? We now have men's clothes that look like women's clothes and adultery looks okay according to Hollywood and to many Christians. Who decides what is right? The disciples needed help so they looked for more men to spread the gospel and tend to the needs of the people. Acts 6:4-5, "But we will give ourselves continually to prayer, and to the ministry of the word." ." . . and they chose Stephen, a man full of faith and of the Holy Ghost."

So much needs to be said today, but I want to focus on the question, who decides what is right in your life and mine? Do we fear more what man and society might think that what God says? Proverbs 29:25, "The fear of man bringeth a snare: but whoso putteth his trust in the LORD shall be safe." A life in Christ is an abundant life, a life filled with the blessings and peace of God. Oh yes, there are trials and testings but the victory is wonderful, and the trials and testings are to make us stronger in Christ. To see God's hand and provision is more than can be explained. Living a life by the Scriptures and growing in God's grace brings peace of heart. The Psalmist says it this way in Psalm 77:11-12, "I will remember the works of the LORD: surely I will remember thy wonders of old. I will meditate also of all thy work, and talk of thy doings." My flesh can never bring joy and satisfaction. The world and its ways will destroy me. The horse feed given to a dog will never satisfy or meet the needs of the dog. Why do we allow the world and the things of the world to pull us away from the Word of God that has been preserved for us to be a guide for us to live a victorious life? The world will go farther and farther away from God, but walking with God and living to please Him will bring a fulfilled life, blessed marriages, fruit of sharing Christ with others, peace of heart and mind, satisfaction like nothing else in this world. My brother and sister in Christ, let God, His Word and the Holy Spirit be your guide and the Word of God be your final authority. Anything that pulls you away from God will spiritually destroy you. Who decides what is what in your life?

Living a life by the Scriptures and growing in God's grace brings peace of heart.

March 30

Deuteronomy 23-24 Psalm 78:1-20 Proverbs 30 Acts 7

Leaving Good Memories

Good morning! I trust you are having a good morning. There are days when I finish my Bible reading, have written a few notes, and I am ready to begin writing another devotional, that I just wish I could express my heart better than the words that I type. This morning is one of those mornings. At the top of my note paper in red ink this morning is the phrase, "What are you leaving behind?" I hunger for my children and grandchildren to not have bad memories of their Dad and Papa, but memories of a life lived for Christ. Along the way of life, we should be leaving things behind that will strengthen another coming generation. Pick up a picture of someone that was a great part of your life, and begin to think about them. What is it that you remember? I love listening to Mrs. Smith tell me what she got out of her personal devotional time.

This morning we read in Deuteronomy 24:19, "When thou cuttest down thine harvest in thy field, and hast forgot a sheaf in the field, thou shalt not go again to fetch it: it shall be for the stranger, for the fatherless, and for the widow: that the LORD thy God may bless thee in all the work of thine hands." Remember the story of Ruth and her going to the fields of Boaz and picking up the stalks of grain dropped or left behind.

What are you and I leaving behind for God to use and bless? In Acts 7:34, Stephen is giving testimony and he is speaking of God as he saw and heard the suffering of God's people. Stephen is talking about when God called Moses to lead the children of Israel. History was left behind for us to remember God's leading and provision. Acts 7:34, "I have seen, I have seen the affliction of my people which is in Egypt, and I have heard their groaning, and am come down to deliver them. And now come, I will send thee into Egypt." God gives each generation what they need to be faithful and press on for the next generation. Proverbs 30:8-9, "Remove far from me vanity and lies: give me neither poverty nor riches, feed me with food convenient for me: Lest I be full, and deny thee, and say, who is the LORD? Or lest I be poor, and steal, and take the name of my God in vain." What are we leaving behind to strengthen the faith of the coming generation, as well as those watching our lives today? Psalm 78:4, "We will not hide them from their children, shewing to the generation to come the praises of the LORD, and his strength, and his wonderful works that he hath done."

I looked at a picture in my office at the church of my mom and dad. As I was just looking at the picture, my mind went to much they left behind for me. Psalm 78:6, "That the generation to come might know them, even the children which should be born; who should arise and declare them to their children." What are you leaving behind in memories of encouragement for a life in Christ? We all are leaving memories, but may those memories be a strength for the next generation to keep walking with God.

What are you and I leaving behind for God to use and bless?

March 31

Deuteronomy 25-26 Psalm 78:21-33 Proverbs 31 Acts 8

Praise Him!

Good morning! I took a trip in my mind this morning. Please do not think that I am losing my mind. Give me a couple of sentences to explain. Deuteronomy 26:11, "And thou shalt rejoice in every good thing which the LORD thy God hath given unto thee, and unto thine house." Spend a few moments right now with me in your mind to think of all that the Lord has done that you and I should be rejoicing over. Oh, my heart is so full of so many things that God has done. So many prayers that the Lord has answered. So many burdens that the Lord has lifted. So many friends in the family of God that we have. On and on we could all keep going at God's blessing.

I just grabbed a hymnal off of Mrs. Smith's piano and opened the cover to the song, "My Savior's Love." "I stand amazed in the presence Of Jesus the Nazarene, And wonder how He could love me, A sinner condemned, unclean." There will be the day the last verse could be sung in His presence in Heaven. "When with the ransomed in glory His face I at last shall see, 'Twill be my joy through the ages To Sing of His love for me." May our song always be praise to HIM. As we turned to the New Testament this morning and read in Acts 8:1, "And at that time there was a great persecution against the church which was at Jerusalem." Do not stop when trials and testings come. Our Lord and Saviour is still in control, and we need to keep on and be faithful and learn to be stronger in Christ. Acts 8:4, "Therefore they that were scattered abroad went every where preaching the word." As they were scattered and stayed faithful, some great things happened. Acts 8:8, "And there was great joy in the city."

You might be going through some sickness, trial, testing, or you might just be downhearted. Look up, my brother and sister, and heed to the first words of Proverbs 31:8 and 9, "Open thy mouth." "Praise Him, Praise Him! Jesus our blessed Redeemer! Sing, O Earth, His wonderful love proclaim! Hail Him! Hail Him! Highest archangels in glory, Strength and honor give to His holy name! Like a shepherd Jesus will guard His children- In His arms He carries them all day long: Praise Him! Praise Him! Tell of His excellent greatness! Praise Him! Praise Him! Ever in joyful song!" Look around and praise Him. In Psalm 78:29, "So they did eat, and were well filled." Even in the wilderness, God provided. Praise Him today!!!

Our Lord and Saviour is still in control,
and we need to keep on and be faithful.

April 1

Deuteronomy 27-28 Psalm 78:34-55 Proverbs 1 Acts 9

A Stone of Testimony

Good morning! Did you ever think how important rocks are? Rocks of all sizes and all shapes. As we began to build the buildings here at Circle C Baptist Ranch, it seems every time we began to dig a ditch or excavate for digging footings for a building or just moving earth to prepare flat areas to build, we encountered rocks. Even after all these years of clearing rocks, there are more that appear when I mow. It seems like this beautiful ground in Kentucky grows rocks. In our reading in Deuteronomy this morning, God told His people to pick out some very special rocks, or as we read in Deuteronomy 27:2, "And it shall be on the day when ye shall pass over Jordan unto the land which the LORD thy God giveth thee, that thou shalt set thee up great stones, and plaister them with plaister." The people were to select special stones for a very important use. Verse 5 tells us, "thou shalt not lift up any iron tool upon them." Verse 6 tells us, "offer burnt-offerings thereon." Verse 7 tells us, "rejoice before the LORD thy God." Then in verse 8, "And you shalt write upon the stones all the words of this law very plainly." The people of God are to build a monument of special stones, untouched by man, plaister them together so that they cannot be moved and will pass the years of time. Plus the people need them to be in a place they can pass by and "rejoice" to remember what God did for them. Lastly, the people were to record the "law very plainly," so that it would be a reminder of what God told them.

Please think with me this morning and make application with me. You and I are supposed to be special stones shaped by God, living a consistent set apart life for Christ, and be a testimony for all to see a sanctified life in Christ showing forth convictions and standards given by God through His Word. As we turned to Acts 9, we see the great persecutor of the church, Paul, struck with blindness and Ananias is sent to find him and lead him to Christ because God had a special will for him. Acts 9:15, "But the Lord said unto him, Go thy way: for he is a chosen vessel unto me, to bear my name before the Gentiles, and kings, and the children of Israel." See those words, "he is a chosen vessel unto me, to bear my name." You and I are so very special also. Jesus died for us and has given us life to be a living testimony just like those stones that were set up for all to see, and just like Paul was saved to be a "chosen vessel," so are you and me. Proverbs 1:8-9, "My son, hear the instruction of thy father, and forsake not the law of thy mother: For they shall be an ornament of grace unto thy head, and chains about thy neck." We who are born again are to be a living, visual testimony of a new life in Christ.

I looked at a stone wall yesterday and thought that is a marker for a boundary of land. I thought about Mount Rushmore in South Dakota and the thousands or millions that have seen the carvings of past presidents and the testimony of our nation. My brother and sister, our lives being shaped by Christ and being a living testimony for His glory will bring forth a greater reaping in the eyes of God than all the statues that will ever be carved. God showed us again in Psalm 78:35, "And they remembered that God was their rock, and the high God their redeemer." Oh my, my brother and sister, He is our ROCK, our salvation! May we be the stones that we are to be for a testimony of His greatness. Stand as a solid rock in Christ today. Be a testimony all your life of what God has done in and through you. Stand today with and for our ROCK, Jesus.

We who are born again are to be a living,
visual testimony of a new life in Christ.

April 2

Deuteronomy 29-30 Psalm 78:56-72 Proverbs 2 Acts 10

The Choice is Yours

Good morning! There are times that my wife and I just take a drive. We are not going any certain place. We are just driving, talking, and discovering new things, new places and new roads. I was asked the other day how I know how to get around in all these back roads. There are places that we have gone where the road just stops or narrows, or the road turns into an unpaved road. Life is not a road, but life is a path that we all live, and we can very easily head down the wrong path. I guess the best way for me to say it is that life is a series of choices. Is the will of God your first choice? Is to make a good living and have a good retirement your first choice? Is to have things your choice of life? We could go on, but let us ask ourselves the questions, what choices am I making and why am I making them?

Deuteronomy 30:15, "See, I have set before thee this day life and good, and death and evil." God loves us and that can never be questioned, but how about our love for Him? Obedience or disobedience is a decision that is continually made by all of us. God provided everything for the children of Israel and yet there was rebellion. Now we read in Deuteronomy 30:19, "I call heaven and earth to record this day against you, that I have set before you life and death, blessing and cursing: therefore choose life, that both thou and thy seed may live." Every decision we make will affect others. Peter said in Acts 10:34, "Then Peter opened his mouth, and said, Of a truth I perceive that God is no respecter of persons." God is saying through Peter that God does not look at the rich and the poor any differently, nor does He look at the abilities that we have or do not have. It is our decision to obey and follow that determines everything. The Psalmist says very plainly in Psalm 78:56-57 why the judgment of God falls, "Yet they tempted and provoked the most high God, and kept not his testimonies: But turned back, and dealt unfaithfully like their fathers: they were turned aside like a deceitful bow." It is a decision to get up every morning and spend time with God in prayer and Bible reading and study. It is also a decision to sleep in and then have to rush to get the day started without a private time alone with God. It is a decision to work a job or not work a job. It is a decision to be faithful to God or to not be faithful.

As Mrs. Smith and I drive down a new road and we come to an intersection, we often say, which way should we go? I can turn a truck or car around, but when I make a wrong choice or decision in life, the results could be very destructive. May we heed to the words we read in Proverbs 2:3-5, "Yea, if thou criest after knowledge, and liftest up thy voice for understanding; If thou seekest her as silver, and searchest for her as for hid treasures; Then shalt thou understand the fear of the LORD, and find the knowledge of God." Let us go back to the very first verse we looked at in Deuteronomy 30:15, "See, I have set before thee this day life and good, and death and evil." The choice is yours, but make sure you make the right choice.

Obedience or disobedience is a decision that is continually made by all of us.

April 3

Deuteronomy 31-32 Psalm 79 Proverbs 3 Acts 11-12

Pass It On

Good morning! Did you ever feel like you cannot keep up with all the changes and the fast-moving things that it seems we need to learn? I am thankful that I can take a picture with my phone, but I have not learned all the different lighting adjustments, and the things I can do to make the picture look better. If I take a picture and I can post the picture or send the picture and all goes well, I feel like I have made a major accomplishment. Do you have those times that you feel like you just have nothing to pass on to another generation and they are just running far ahead of you? If so, then stop feeling that way. New gadgets and new things that can be done on a computer does not mean that you are out of touch.

In all of my reading in the Bible this morning, I noticed that no matter the age, there is the constant importance of two things: teamwork and passing on wisdom, or maybe a challenge, to those following. A young man who worked on our summer staff for a few years and is now in our college, walked up to me and asked if I could go soul winning with him and teach him how to start discipling a convert. I was honored and yet embarrassed at the same time, because I am trying to grow in my learning every way I can to put tools in the hands of new converts to help them grow in Christ. My point today is that we who are growing older need to see the need to spend time with the coming generation. Not to push ourselves and our ways, but to take time to listen and be observant when they want our input.

Build relationships with the coming generation instead of tearing bridges down and saying, "what is wrong with them?" Deuteronomy 31:2, "I can no more go out and come in: also the LORD hath said unto me, Thou shalt not go over this Jordan." The older we get, the more we see that we cannot do some things that we used to, but are we spending all our time with the "can't anymore's" or are we also spending time with those that do want to learn? Deuteronomy 31:7, "And Moses called unto Joshua." Joshua was right there with Moses waiting to learn all that he could learn. We first read of Joshua back in the book of Exodus. Listen to the words of Deuteronomy 31:8, "And the LORD, he it is that doth go before thee; he will be with thee, he will not fail thee, neither forsake thee: fear not, neither be dismayed." Sounds to me like an older man was preparing a younger man to lead. Even as we look at Acts 11:12, we see Peter with others, "And the Spirit bade me go with them, nothing doubting. Moreover these six brethren accompanied me, and we entered into the man's house." These brethren saw Peter at his spiritual work. Acts 12:25, "And Barnabas and Saul returned from Jerusalem, when they had fulfilled their ministry, and took with them John, whose surname was Mark." Older seasoned men working with younger men, together doing the work of God.

As we get older, do not quit. Keep the young around you and pass on to them when asked. I have learned if we keep our opinions and thoughts to ourselves, we will be asked questions. Proverbs 3:27, "Withhold not good from them to whom it is due, when it is in the power of thine hand to do it." I am learning that growing old is not bad when we still keep a growing relationship with those that are coming behind. It is a blessing to watch when something that you have tried to teach is now passing on to another generation. Psalm 79:13, "So we thy people and sheep of thy pasture will give thee thanks for ever: we will shew forth thy praise to all generations." Reach out a hand to somebody coming behind you, even if you do not think you have anything to give. Let them know that you care about them too.

We who are growing older need to see the need to spend time with the coming generation.

April 4

Deuteronomy 33-34 Psalm 80 Proverbs 4 Acts 13

Sound Off for God

Good morning! Several times during the week mowing and getting ready for the upcoming retreat at the camp, I have encountered a little bird called the killdeer. They make their nests in some of the most peculiar places; beside a road in the gravel, in short grass next to a rocky area, in a gravel parking lot. If you get close to the nest they will make a loud noise, raise one wing and act like they are hurt. Last night after we came home from church, I heard a killdeer sounding off and it was just about dark. Why do they make their nests in places that are really not protected? We as Christians think that we are so unprotected at times and yet this morning we can be encouraged from the Scriptures that God is our "refuge" or abiding place and even though there are times we feel so alone, we can be assured that He is there watching and protecting us.

Deuteronomy 33:27, "The eternal God is thy refuge, and underneath are the everlasting arms: and he shall thrust out the enemy from before thee; and shall say, destroy them." The disciples were bold in their witness for the Lord and the places they ministered were not always a safe place, but praise be to our Lord they were filled with the joy and power of God. Acts 13:49, "And the word of the Lord was published throughout all the region." Acts 13:53, "And the disciples were filled with joy, and with the Holy Ghost." Those little birds do everything they can to sound off so loud to protect those eggs that will soon bring on newborn birds.

Are we sounding off for our Lord with the joy and power of God, realizing that He is there to guide us and to aid us in the proclaiming of the Gospel? Proverbs 4:18, "But the path of the just is as the shining light, that shineth more and more unto the perfect day." May we follow the will of God and be the proclaimers of the greatest gift that has ever been provided, the gift of salvation to all mankind. In Psalm 80, there are three verses exactly the same. It is as though God is wanting us to understand He is asking us to be even greater of a sound for the Gospel story than the clamoring of a little bird. Psalm 80:3, 7, 19, "Turn us again, O God, and cause thy face to shine, and we will be saved." Sound off today for the glory of God, my brother and sister.

Are we sounding off for our Lord with the joy and power of God?

April 5

Joshua 1-2 Psalm 81 Proverbs 5 Acts 14

Observe To Do

Good morning! Did you ever drive down a road and make this statement, "I did not know that was there," or "When did they build that?" Did you ever make a turn at an intersection and think you had turned down the wrong road because things did not look familiar to you? Or your wife said to you, "Honey, I do not think this is the right way." Sometimes we are not very observant of what is going on all around us. Men, can I give you some great advice? Make sure you look at your wife and how she is dressed and ask her to look at you before you walk out the door. There have been a couple of times my wife has said to me, "Honey, how far would I have gone before you would have noticed?" Do not ever get yourself caught in that spot because there is no way to explain yourself clear of not observing.

In Joshua 1:8, Joshua is now in charge, Moses is gone, and God says to Joshua, "This book of the law shall not depart out of thy mouth; but thou shalt meditate therein day and night, that thou mayest observe to do according to all that is written therein: for then thou shalt make thy way prosperous, and then thou shalt have good success." May we focus on the phrase, "observe to do." We must not just read God's Word but observe and learn and do what we read. Observation is the ability to see what is before and around us, to guide us, forewarn us, and lead, to aid us in not falling into the traps of the devil. Observe some phrases set before us in Joshua chapter 2. Joshua 2:1, "Go view the land." Joshua 2:14, "Our life for yours." Joshua 2:16, "hide yourselves there three days." Joshua 2:18, "thou shalt bind this line of scarlet thread in the window." We have in these phrases a picture of God's provision, Jesus' sacrifice for us, Jesus in the grave three days and conquering death, Hell and the grave, and God's forgiveness and the blood price paid and seen by God that gives us forgiveness of sin and eternal life. A lesson could be taught on each phrase but let us just see how the Old Testament saints would be able to see the promise of God in their lives.

There is no victory in our lives until we take the time to observe what God is trying to show us in His Word, and when we spend time with Him in prayer and walk with Him. Acts 14:27, "And when they were come, and had gathered the church together, they rehearsed all that God had done with them, and how he had opened the door of faith unto the Gentiles." Did you see the phrase, "rehearsed all that God had done?" If we do not take the time to praise God in all the blessings He gives, we will soon forget all that He does. Notice in our reading this morning in Proverbs 5:2, "That thou mayest regard discretion, and that thy lips may keep knowledge." "Regard discretion" means to observe what God is teaching us and doing in our lives. When you and I begin to slow down in our fast-paced lives and observe all that God is doing, that is the beginning of building a life-long lasting walk with God. Psalm 81:13, "Oh that my people had hearkened unto me, and Israel had walked in my ways." One who is observant of what God is trying to do is learning and enjoying their walk with God. There is not a greater compliment than observing something a wife or husband have done for each other without them being told to do it. Destruction in a relationship will begin when you begin to take each other for granted. Building a relationship with each other and with Christ is when we begin to observe everything that we can without being forced to. Let us dwell on the phrase, "observe to do."

One who is observant of what God is trying to do is learning and enjoying their walk with God.

April 6

Joshua 3-4 Psalm 82 Proverbs 6 Acts 15

What or Who Leads You?

Good morning! Have you been driving out west across Kansas, Missouri, Nebraska and approaching the Rocky Mountains, and you saw them almost a hundred miles before you actually got there? The size, the majestic height, even as you look to the south and the north. The mountain range is so long, so tall, so indescribable. I remember when Mrs. Smith and I started our journey up Pikes Peak in Colorado. The drive was beautiful and then we were still not to the top and we drove on, even past the tree line. The mountains and their ranges that I am describing often create a feeling in us where words are lost to describe. Those beautiful mountains have no leadership. They have beauty, but they will lead us nowhere.

What do you have standing before you and leading you to follow and serve the Lord? I will show you what I am speaking about. Joshua 3:3, "And they commanded the people, saying, When ye see the ark of the covenant of the LORD your God, and the priests the Levites bearing it, then ye shall remove from your place, and go after it." The ark of God was carried by the priests and the people were instructed to keep their focus on it and to "go after it." Joshua 3:4, "that ye may know the way by which ye must go: for ye have not passed this way heretofore." In our life as a Christian, we must keep our eyes on His Word and follow the leadership of the Holy Spirit. Are we holding the Word of God in such a manner that God can use it to lead us? I am not speaking of physically holding it high, but I am speaking of holding the principles that are contained in such a way that God can use His Word to lead us. May we ask ourselves, what or who is truly leading us in our daily lives, in the decisions that we make and in the priorities that we have? Acts 15:16-17, "After this I will return, and will build again the tabernacle of David, which is fallen down; and I will build again the ruins thereof, and I will set it up: That the residue of men might seek after the Lord." That phrase spoke deeply to me this morning, "That the residue of men might seek after the Lord."

May I ask again, what or who are you following? Proverbs 6:20-22, "My son, keep thy father's commandment, and forsake not the law of thy mother: Bind them continually upon thine heart, and tie them about thy neck. When thou goest, it shall lead thee; when thou sleepest, it shall keep thee; and when thou awakest, it shall talk with thee." I think we need to dwell this morning on the question I keep raising, "who or what are you following?" Let God, His Word, His Spirit, be the guide for your life. Not emotion, not things, not fame, not flesh, not culture, but God. Psalm 82:1, "God standeth in the congregation of the mighty." I have seen many wonderful sights of greatness in my life, but nothing more life changing and motivating than God's Word and following the sweet Holy Spirit. My we stop today and ask ourselves, "who or what am I following?"

We must keep our eyes on His Word and follow the leadership of the Holy Spirit.

April 7

Joshua 5-7 Psalm 83 Proverbs 7 Acts 16

The Accursed Thing

Good morning! Our readings this morning are overflowing with truth, conviction and guidance. We must stay on our Bible reading schedule to not miss one word or one truth that God desires for us to know and apply to our lives. The children of Israel have crossed over on dry ground as we read yesterday, and today we read that they have a seven-day march around the city of Jericho. The first day one time around, and on the seventh day they march seven times. Joshua 6:15, "And it came to pass on the seventh day, that they rose early about the dawning of the day." That one phrase is an admonition for us to rise at the beginning of the day and have our personal time with the Lord. Joshua

6:18, "keep yourselves from the accursed thing, lest ye make yourselves accursed, when ye take of the accursed thing, and make the camp of Israel a curse, and trouble it."

I wish we had time to spend on just studying the word "accursed." Let me define it as anything in our possession or, as we will soon see, our "household" that God says we are not to have because it is not pleasing to the Lord. My heart is convicted today to check my life, my marriage, my home, my dress, my music, my books, what I have in possession, to see if there is anything that is not pleasing to God. Achan "coveted," "took," and "hid," that which was "accursed." It was accursed because God said so!!!!! There is one word that was in our Old Testament, New Testament, Proverbs and Psalms reading this morning, and that word is "house." They had in their possession what God said should not be, and thirty-six men lost their lives because of what one man thought he could hide from God. Acts 16:31, "Believe on the Lord Jesus Christ, and thou shalt be saved, and thy house." The word "house" is mentioned five time in Acts 16, and four times in Proverbs 7. Psalm 83:12, "Who said, Let us take to ourselves the houses of God in possession."

From our personal life to our homes and to our churches, it is important to God that we do not possess the "accursed" thing, and when I speak of the "accursed" thing I am speaking of anything that is not pleasing to God. We must quit seeing only through our eyes and our wants and look through the eyes of what is pleasing to God. Let us stop today and do a thorough examination of the stuff in our lives, our homes, and our churches. Are there things hidden that need to be cleaned out? Something to work on.

It is important to God that we do not possess anything that is not pleasing to God.

April 8

Joshua 8-9 Psalm 84 Proverbs 8 Acts 17

Beware of the Ambush

Good morning! As I was headed out to the back part of the Ranch to do some work, something caught my eye. Hiding in the tall grass was one of the cats that make their home at the camp. I stopped a distance away and watched. Sure enough, a field mouse came running by and the ambush of the cat paid off.

As I was reading this morning, the word "ambush" kept coming to my mind. Joshua 8:2b, "lay thee an ambush for the city behind it." Joshua 8:14b, "but he wist not that there were liers in ambush against him behind the city." God gave Joshua guidance to take the city by setting an "ambush." If we are not walking with the Lord, that is exactly what the devil does to us. He is subtle, and he will tempt us and get us caught in an ambush of sin, but there is victory in Christ and protection from the devil's ambushes. Acts 17:28, "For in him we live, and move, and have our being." We must daily spend time in the Word of God to prepare ourselves with the wisdom of God to stay away from being ambushed by the devil and his demons. Proverbs 8:1, "Doth not wisdom cry? And understanding put forth her voice?" Proverbs 8:12, "I wisdom dwell with prudence, and find out knowledge of witty inventions." See those words, "witty inventions." Those are ambushes that are set to catch us and cause us to sin. God's way is a protective way. Proverbs 8:20, "I lead in the way of righteousness, in the midst of the paths of judgment."

As I watched the cat for a few moments, that cat lay so still and so quiet, so the mouse had little or no warning of the ambush that had been set. My brother and sister, be aware. There are ambushes set to trip us and cause us to sin. Psalm 84:5, "Blessed is the man whose strength is in thee; in whose heart are the ways of them." As you begin your day, be aware of the ambushes and allow the Lord to be your guide and protector. Walk in victory today.

There is victory in Christ and protection from the devil's ambushes.

April 9

Joshua 10-11 Psalm 85 Proverbs 9 Acts 18

Slack Not

Good morning! When I was in Boy Scouts as a young man, we used a lot of ropes for different needs. Securing a pack to be carried, tent guide ropes, lashing logs together, making bridges across creeks, etc. Matter of fact, we made most all our ropes, and that was quite an experience. Homemade ropes with homemade rope-making tools. Oh, those years bring back many memories. When using ropes, you have terms you use as you work together as a team. There are knots that need to be learned to secure the ropes for what use you are to be using them. Often as you will be working as a team with ropes, the term "slack off" or "give me some slack" is used.

In our reading this morning in Joshua 10:6, we read the phrase, "Slack not thy hand from thy servants." There is a battle at Gibeon and the plea is sent out to, "Slack not thy hand." In other words, stay in the battle, keep fighting, do not give up, do not quit. When we keep pressing on even when we are tired, exhausted, and ready to quit, we need to realize that victory is close. Look what the Lord did in Joshua 10:11, "that the LORD cast down great stones from heaven upon them unto Azekah, and they died: they were more which died with hailstones than they whom the children of Israel slew with the sword." These words should challenge us in our battles living for the Lord. Don't quit, don't "slack." Keep on. Joshua 11:6, "And the LORD said unto Joshua, Be not afraid because of them: for to morrow about this time will I deliver them up all slain before Israel."

Keep on, my brother and sister. When Paul was in prison the words in Acts 18:9 rang in the heart and ears of Paul, "Then spake the Lord to Paul in the night by a vision, Be not afraid, but speak, and hold not thy peace." Proverbs 9:6 challenges us to keep our focus and to "Slack not." "Forsake the foolish, and live; and go in the way of understanding." There are those times I would hear the words, hold tight, do not "slack" up, keep the ropes tight. Listen for the voice of the Lord and "slack not." Psalm 85:8, "I will hear what God the LORD will speak: for he will speak peace unto his people and to his saints: but let them not turn again to folly." Stay faithful and focused in your walk and service for the Lord, and "slack not."

When we keep pressing on even when we are tired and ready to quit, victory is close.

April 10

Joshua 12-13 Psalm 86 Proverbs 10 Acts 19

More To Do

Good morning! I would like for you to ride with me in your mind this morning in my truck and imagine that we are going on a vacation. You pick where you would like to go. All expenses are paid, and we are going to stay in the most beautiful place that you can imagine. We have never been there before. The longer we travel the more excited we get because of getting to our beautiful vacation and destination.

As I read Joshua 13:1 this morning, my heart got excited and I thought about a destination that is a perfect place to go. "Now Joshua was old and stricken in years; and the LORD said unto him, Thou art old and stricken in years, and there remaineth yet very much land to be possessed." Do you ever feel tired, worn out, exhausted? The answer to that question is we all feel that way at some time. Let us reread the last part of the verse, "there remaineth yet very much land to be possessed." God was not done with Joshua. He is older and has fought many battles and yet the Lord says there is more that I need you to do. My brother and sister, there is more that the Lord has for us to do. You may not see what it is, and you may not feel like you can do any more, but the Lord sees what we cannot see and knows what the next step is. Acts 19:20, "So mightily grew the word of God and prevailed." Proverbs 10:25, "As the whirlwind passeth, so is the wicked no more: but the righteous is an everlasting foundation." There is still work to be done. God wants to use us all. Psalm 86:7, "In the day of my trouble I will call upon thee: for thou wilt answer me."

There is an excitement as we travel and know that we are getting close to our destination. We think about the time of rest and what we will see and what we will be doing. As a Christian, our place of rest is Heaven, and our hearts should be full of excitement as we draw closer to our place of rest. Let the excitement build as you continue to serve God and get closer to that place for eternity with our KING. Don't quit, don't give up, fire up, keep your eyes looking forward and up, keep seeking to serve Him. Psalm 86:12, "I will praise thee, O Lord my God, with all my heart: and I will glorify thy name for evermore." "There remaineth yet very much land to be possessed." Keep going. Life only gets better as we think on the place of rest and peace.

You may not feel like you can do any more,
but the Lord sees what we cannot see.

April 11

Joshua 14-15 Psalm 87 Proverbs 11 Acts 20

Go For the Mountain

Good morning! How many times and places in our lives have we seen the words, "The End?" It is the end of the trail, the end of a book, the end of a vacation, the end of a family video, the end of a school year, the end of college, the end of a revival, the end of. . . .

As I was reading this morning, I saw several ends, but yet they were the beginnings. In Joshua 14, Caleb is now 85 years of age and he says in verse 11, "As yet I am as strong this day as I was in the day that Moses sent me: as my strength was then, even so is my strength now, for war, both to go out, and to come in." The very first statement in verse 12 is, "Now therefore give me this mountain." At 85, he is still ready to fight, and he wants a mountain. In Acts 20 we read of Paul in verse 20, "And how I kept back nothing that was profitable unto you, but have shewed you, and have taught you publicly, and from house to house." On down in verse 24, "But none of these things move me, neither count I my life dear unto myself, so that I might finish my course with joy." Both of these men are at the end, but their spirit is like it was at the beginning. Paul ends chapter 20 in verse 35 with these words, "It is more blessed to give than to receive." In Proverbs 11:30, "The fruit of the righteous is a tree of life; and he that winneth souls is wise." Caleb wanted a mountain. I hunger to see a tree that is alive and reproducing fruit, and may that fruit be my life, my testimony of not quitting, not giving up, but going, growing, and giving to the end. Our end is really our beginning.

My father-in-law was a great man and had many traits that blessed my heart. He enjoyed going to a cemetery and reading the explanation on a tombstone of a person's life. Many great saints of the past still live and are still producing fruits through their lives given to Christ. Psalm 87:6, "The LORD shall count, when he writeth up the people." What will the LORD be counting about your life? May we ask God for a mountain to use for His glory. May we finish the course with joy, and may we give so that our God can use everything in our lives. Go for the mountain, my brother and sister.

May we ask God for a mountain to use for His glory.

April 12

Joshua 16-17 Psalm 88 Proverbs 12 Acts 21

The Power of Prayer

Good morning. He Is Risen!!!! As I read my Bible this morning and thought of the history of America and the history of the followers of Christ, as well as the faith of the saints in the Old Testament, there is a common factor in all. We constantly read that there were times that all sought the face of God in prayer. Joshua 16:17, "Thou art a great people, and hast great power." As we read in Acts 21:5, "And when we had accomplished those acts, we departed and went our way; and they all brought us on our way, with wives and children, till we were out of the city: and we kneeled down on the shore, and prayed."

We must be a praying people to see the hand of God move. We must be a people that seek the hand of God and His power. We must be a people that plead for the will of God to be accomplished. Selfishness has no place in the heart of a yielded saint. Proverbs 12:7, "The wicked are overthrown, and are not: but the house of the righteous shall stand." We serve a risen Saviour that hungers for a relationship with those that He shed His blood for. That relationship grows its strength through the time we spend in prayer and His Word. May it be said of us today as the Psalmist wrote in Psalm 88:1, "O LORD God of my salvation, I have cried day and night before thee:." Psalm 88:9, "LORD, I have called daily upon thee, I have stretched out my hands unto thee." Psalm 88:13, "But unto thee have I cried, O LORD; and in the morning shall my prayer prevent thee."

As Jesus spent the time in prayer before His betrayal, may we hear those words that He said to His disciples that night in Luke 22:40, "Pray that ye enter not into temptation." May we first of all always seek the face and will of the Father. May we continue and grow in our time of prayer with the Father. The strength of every believer is the strength that they attain through the time they spend in prayer. May our Lord bless you greatly.

Our relationship with God grows through
the time we spend in prayer and His Word.

April 13

Joshua 18-19 Psalm 89:1-18 Proverbs 13 Acts 22

A Godly Inheritance

Good morning! As I read the Word of God this morning, I asked myself about a word that appeared at least sixteen times. That word was "inheritance." When we hear the word "inheritance," we immediately think about money, property, stocks and bonds, possessions. We read in Joshua 18:3, "How long are ye slack to go to possess the land, which the LORD God of your fathers hath given you?" You and I have been given life. What have you done with your life? What will you be remembered by? What does your life today tell people about you?

I often walk through the woods of the camp's property. There are many fence rows that have rocks piled in them. As the ground was cleared for farming, the farmers of the past had to pick up these rocks and get them out of the way so the ground could be plowed and planted. Some of these rocks are gigantic in size. That tells me a lot about the men who in past generations worked this ground. We need to ask ourselves, what is our life leaving behind for others to see? A Christian of faith, compassion, humility, steadfastness, servanthood, etc.; or a self- centered, prideful, selfish, critical, lazy, impatient life? When Paul was giving his testimony in Acts, he shared what the angel told him. Acts 22:14, "The God of our fathers hath chosen thee, that thou shouldest know his will." Paul is most remembered for his zeal and determination to spread the gospel of Christ, his determination to not fear what man can do to him, but for what Christ can do for man. Proverbs 13:22, "A good man leaveth an inheritance to his children's children: and the wealth of the sinner is laid up for the just." Money will be gone, but the testimony of a life lives on.

I do not know the men that piled the rocks in the fence rows, but I know they were men of character and hard work. Psalm 89:15, "Blessed is the people that know the joyful sound: they shall walk, O LORD, in the light of thy countenance." A preacher's character will always live longer than his message. A mother's love will always live longer than the tasks she did. We have an inheritance to leave behind. What kind of inheritance will you leave? All the money in the world will be gone, but the life that worked hard to earn the money will live on. A life given to Christ by daily spending time in a walk with God will live on and on and on. A faithful servant leaves a much stronger testimony than a prideful, self-centered, talented person. What inheritance are you leaving for the generation to come? The rocks of Godly character will always last longer than a flower that only lasts for a season.

What is our life leaving behind for others to see?

April 14

Joshua 20-21 Psalm 89:19-37 Proverbs 14 Acts 23

Seek Him

Good morning! The power of a storm that comes from the heavens or the destruction of a tornado can be far beyond what a man can imagine. A virus unseen, and yet it can bring a world to their knees. The power of God is far beyond what a man can imagine. God is in control and He has never failed. We need to be seeking Him in the storms and in the sunlight. Seek Him when the blessings are there and when you are going through a trial.

Joshua 21:45, "There failed not ought of any good thing which the LORD had spoken unto the house of Israel; all came to pass." When man binds his hate toward God and makes the attack, God is still in control. Acts 23:14, "We have bound ourselves under a great curse, that we will eat nothing until we have slain Paul." The hate of those who know not God or have fallen away from God will be the destruction of their lives, but repentance of sin and a drawing nigh unto God brings peace to the heart and soul. Proverbs 14:6, "A wise man feareth, and departeth from evil: but the fool rageth, and is confident." We must seek Him, listen to Him, and obey Him. Proverbs 14:26, "In the fear of the LORD is strong confidence: and his children shall have a place of refuge." In a time of storm, we seek shelter. Should not we seek God in times of trial and testing? Psalm 89:24, "But my faithfulness and my mercy shall be with him." Psalm 89:36, "His seed shall endure for ever, and his throne as the sun before me."

I have been through many tornados and heard the loudness of the wind and seen the destruction, and yet I have stood in the rubble and felt the calmness of the air and seen the sunshine again. Look to God today. He is there. The peace you seek is waiting. God has not moved; it is we who have left the place we need to be.

We need to be seeking Him in the storms and in the sunlight.

April 15

Joshua 22-24 Psalm 89:38-52 Proverbs 15 Acts 24

Focused on the Saviour

Good morning! Selfishness and self-centeredness have destroyed more lives and relationships than could ever be known. Have you ever tried to communicate with a person that only talks about themselves and what they do and never asks about you? Or that person does ask about you, then before you can answer, they start talking about themselves again.

In Joshua 22:19, "but rebel not against the LORD, nor rebel against us, in building you an altar beside the altar of the LORD our God." I read these chapters in Joshua several times and kept coming back to see that we focus on ourselves and what we do, more than on how God wants to use us in ways that we will never see or know. Our focus should always be on the Lord and what He is doing, not on what we are doing.

In Acts 24:16, "And herein do I exercise myself, to have always a conscience void of offense toward God, and toward men." The focus was not on what he did or who he was, but on God. Proverbs 15:14, "The heart of him that hath understanding seeketh knowledge: but the mouth of fools feedeth on foolishness."

May we be challenged today to realize that a true life in Christ is about Christ and not us. Psalm 89:44, "Thou hast made his glory to cease, and cast his throne down to the ground." The devil lives to have the glory that is to be given to God. Selfishness in our lives does not bring glory to us or God, but to the devil. May we spend our lives focused on Christ working in lives and not what we do, or what we think God needs to help someone else with. May I challenge us today to let Christ be seen in us in everything we do and let HIM receive all the glory. As I read Psalm 89:47, "Remember how short my time is," I thought how our lives are just a passing vapor, but what is done for Christ will last for eternity. Live to honor Christ and to bring Him the glory. Someone is coming your way today who needs to hear about and receive Christ as their Saviour. Be focused on the Saviour today.

A true life in Christ is about Christ and not us.

April 16

Judges 1-2 Psalm 90 Proverbs 16 Acts 25

Dig It Out

Good morning! As spring preparations for camp move forward, the spring rains and wind seem to keep me daily cleaning up branches and limbs. Each year there are older trees along a fence row or by a trail or building that have to be cleaned up. As I was working yesterday, I noticed how I had several stumps that I really needed to get out of the ground, or they could be a hazard when mowing. Even though the stump was cut low to the ground, a mower blade could still hit it and cause damage to the mower blade, and possible damage to the mower.

As we read this morning in Judges chapters one and two and especially in 1:21, "And the children of Benjamin did not drive out the Jebusites that inhabited Jerusalem." We see the two words, "neither did" five more times. Joshua challenged the children of Israel to "drive out" the enemies, but they did not. The people who had seen the hand of God give victory over many enemies are passing on and in Judges 2:10, "there arose another generation after them, which knew not the LORD, nor yet the works which he had done for Israel." We must pull out and dig out the roots of sin in our lives in order for God to bless us as He desires. Paul stood before the accusers and when the king listened to his testimony and saw the life of Paul, king Agrippa said in Acts 25:27, "For it seemeth to me unreasonable to send a prisoner, and not withal to signify the crimes laid against him." Proverbs 16:7, "When a man's ways please the LORD, he maketh even his enemies to be at peace with him."

We must dig out the roots of sin in our lives so that the next generation can see the blessings and power of God in and through our lives. Psalm 90:16, "Let thy work appear unto thy servants, and thy glory unto their children." Dig out the stump and the roots, or the grass will cover what you might hit with the mower. What sin keeps being covered in our lives, and it keeps growing over, but God knows we keep dealing with it? Dig it out!!!

We must pull out and dig out the roots of sin in our lives for God to bless us as He desires.

April 17

Judges 3-4 Psalm 91 Proverbs 17 Acts 26

Nothing Between

Good morning! One day it seems like spring has arrived and then the cold hits again. A couple of days ago I was mowing the camp with my winter jacket and gloves, and it started snowing. One thing for sure as you drive down the country roads, the sign of spring is here with all the newborn calves. You can see two or three new calves running together and then you can hear a cry from their mom, or it is like mom is scolding them and telling them to get by her side. A neighbor went to check his new calves and he left his truck and started walking toward a new calf he was worried about. The mother cow of the new calf started charging him. He fell down and the cow butted him with her head and before he could get up, she had broken several of the neighbor's ribs.

God loves us and He always hears our cry and will come in defense of us. I just do not understand why we want or why we allow the world to get a hold of us. In Judges 3:6, the children of Israel "took" what they should not have taken, and "gave" what they should not have, and "served" what they should not have. Judges 3:7 says they "forgat" and Judges 3:15 said they "cried." When giving his testimony before Agrippa in Acts 26:18, Paul said, "To open their eyes, and to turn them from darkness to light, and from the power of Satan unto God, that they may receive forgiveness of sins, and inheritance among them which are sanctified by faith that is in me." Then we read in Acts 26:28, "Then Agrippa said unto Paul, Almost thou persuadest me to be a Christian." I can only imagine how God aches when we do not turn our backs on sin. The children of Israel went from seeing God's blessing, to sin and had to cry out to God. Proverbs 17:25, "A foolish son is a grief to his father, and bitterness to her that bare him."

That mother cow charged that neighbor when he got between her and her calf. God is there and wants to strengthen us and help us if we would just call upon Him. Psalm 91:1 "He that dwelleth in the secret place of the most High shall abide under the shadow of the Almighty." Psalm 91:15, "He shall call upon me, and I will answer him: I will be with him in trouble, I will deliver him, and honor him." There will come a day when the neighbor farmer will separate the calf from his mother but that calf will be strong and ready to be on his own. There is never a time that we need to be separated from God but be reassured when we do and face our sin and cry unto Him, He will be there for us. Stay close to Him, He is always there.

God loves us and He always hears our cry and will come in defense of us.

April 18

Judges 5-6 Psalm 92 Proverbs 18 Acts 27

Pay Attention to the Signs

Good morning! A man from the church was helping me cut up some downed trees and we loaded the four-wheeler and he said to me, "Are those tracks from a buck or a doe?" As we were working, I had seen the tracks before he asked because I had seen some signs. I will repeat a short statement, "I had seen some signs."

That is exactly what Gideon requested from the angel of the Lord in Judges 6:17, "shew me a sign that thou talkest with me." As Paul was a prisoner and on a ship and they were ready to set sail, we read in Acts 27:9-10, "Now when much time was spent, and when sailing was now dangerous, because the fast was now already past, Paul admonished them, And said unto them, Sirs, I perceive that this voyage will be with hurt and much damage." Paul was seeing "signs" of warning. In Acts 27:23 we read, "For there stood by me this night the angel of God, whose I am, and whom I serve." We must learn to pay attention to the "signs" that God sends us and to the voice of the Holy Spirit that dwells within us and stands there with us. Oh, that we would live in a relationship with God to hear His voice, observe His leading and follow His "signs." Proverbs 18:15, "The heart of the prudent getteth knowledge; and the ear of the wise seeketh knowledge."

There were no alarm clocks in the lives of our forefathers, but they observed the "signs." We live in a world that runs twenty-four hours a day and yet has no time for the Lord and cannot see the signs of His leadership or they must have decided to ignore them. Psalm 92:2, "To shew forth thy lovingkindness in the morning, and thy faithfulness every night." Why not decide to observe and pay attention to the "signs" that God leaves us and leads us by? Learn to praise him in the morning and thank Him in the evening and follow His "signs" throughout the day. He is there in us and with us. Follow His "signs."

We must learn to pay attention to the "signs" that God sends us.

April 19

Judges 7-8 Psalm 93 Proverbs 19 Acts 28

Just Wandering Around

Good morning! The last two days at the ranch we have had a visitor from a neighboring farm. I looked out the window and there was a sow hog. It is a pot belly pig, and she is bound and determined to come over to Circle C Baptist Ranch. The neighbors keep repairing the pen and somehow, they say, she keeps getting out. I asked if they fed and watered her there and they said yes, but she gets out and just wanders around.

The story of Gideon in the book of Judges has many lessons, but the one I would like to focus on today is at the end of Gideon's life. Judges 8:33, "And it came to pass, as soon as Gideon was dead, that the children of Israel turned again." The people turned away from following God and His leadership. The victory that God had brought was now forgotten about. We read today in Acts 28:27, "For the heart of the people is waxed gross, and their ears are dull of hearing, and their eyes have they closed." We read in Proverbs 19:3, "The foolishness of man perverteth his way: and his heart fretteth against the LORD." Too often Christians just wander around with no purpose or direction and that is how we backslide, and sin becomes part of our lives. Is your walk with God dependent on encouragement from someone else or are you attempting to grow in the Lord? I thank God for fellowship, friendship, and encouragement but through these trying times we are going through, have you used this time to spend more time with the Lord? Or has it been a time like what the pot belly pig is doing, just wandering around? God has brought us to a time of evaluation. How strong is your spiritual walk with God? Will you turn away and go backwards or are you using this time to draw close to the Lord and become more dependent on Him? Psalm 93:5, "holiness becometh thine house, O LORD, for ever."

You see, the little hog had a friend, a companion, and it died. It is like the pot belly pig is just wandering around trying to find its lost companion. God has not left us, but the Christian life must be lived with purpose. We must live and reach others for Christ. Do not wander around looking, but be doing. The pot belly pig is pitiful, lonely, and searching. God is there for us, and He desires for us to draw closer to Him so that we can help others grow in the Lord and be the servants that He wants us to be. I do not want to lose what God wants me to be and miss how God wants to use me. Some things to think about.

Are you using this time to draw close to the Lord and become more dependent on Him?

April 20

Judges 9-10 Psalm 94:1-11 Proverbs 20 Romans 1-2

All Are Important

Good morning! I am constantly amazed how people have a temperament similar to animals, or is it the other way? I was going to ride one of the horses, so when I got the saddle, blanket, and tack, all the horses came over. You go to feed them, and you are putting equal amounts of grain in their feed bins, and they all want to eat out of the same one. When you brush down the horse you are going to ride and saddle it up and head down a trail, the others whinny because they all want to go.

How sad and ungodly it is for one brother to have seventy brothers killed just so he could be king. That is exactly what Abimelech did. Judges 9:4, "Abimelech hired vain and light persons, which followed him." Yet one hid himself to tell the story. Judges 9:5, "yet Jonathan the youngest son of Jerubbaal was left; for he hid himself." Oh, the demon of jealousy, covetousness, and envy. They will destroy a life, a home, a friendship, a relationship, and on and on the path of destruction will go. In Judges 9:56 we read that God brought the judgment, "Thus God rendered the wickedness of Abimelech, which he did unto his father, in slaying his seventy brethren." Yet this morning we read in Romans 1:22, "Professing themselves to be wise, they became fools." Romans 1:25, "Who changed the truth of God into a lie, and worshipped and served the creature more than the Creator, who is blessed for ever. Amen." God loves us all the same and we need to be careful of what we let control us. God looks at all of us through His eyes of love for all mankind. Romans 2:11, "For there is no respect of persons with God."

The horses all want the attention. They all want to get out and run, be first, whatever it is. There is always a power struggle. May that not be said of us. May that spirit of "me first" or "me the greatest" not control us. All are of importance in the eyes of God. Proverbs 20:3, "It is an honor for a man to cease from strife: but every fool will be meddling."

Proverbs 20:6, "Most men will proclaim every one his own goodness: but a faithful man who can find?" Parents, beware lest you brag on one child more than the other. Show equal interest and give equal time. God did not make any second-class creations. We all are created in His image. Be careful how highly you look at yourself. Psalm 94:11, "The LORD knoweth the thoughts of man, that they are vanity." I feed and water all the horses the same, and I love both of my dogs the same. God loves us all so much He gave His Son for all. Let us see others through the eyes of God.

God looks at all of us through His eyes of love for all mankind.

April 21

Judges 11-12 Psalm 94:12-23 Proverbs 21 Romans 3-4

Keeping Vows

Good morning! I have seen many a young person and adult kneel at an altar during a week of camp and shed tears. I have seen those tears become a puddle on the floor or in the sawdust. There was a sincerity of heart and a full heart to keep the commitment made. When those buses, cars and vans pull out and go under the camp entrance sign, there is an urgency in my heart to keep praying that those campers and counselors will keep their promises to God. A time away from the world and all its sin and distraction is what brought them to their point of brokenness before the Lord. Bible preaching, right standards, the world shut out and so much more.

We read in Judges 11:30, "Jephtah vowed a vow unto the LORD." He was a "mighty man of valour" (Judges 11:1). He had a sad beginning and was rejected and yet he was brought back to lead the people of Israel to victories in battle. He vowed to the Lord that if the Lord would give them victory, "that whatsoever cometh forth of the doors of my house to meet me, I will offer it up for a burnt offering" (Judges 11:31). It was his daughter. Judges 11:35, "I have opened my mouth unto the LORD, and

I cannot go back." Greater than this is what God did for all mankind. In Romans 3:23, "For all have sinned, and come short of the glory of God." We are all sinners, and in our sin we have no hope and yet look what God promised and did. Romans 3:24, "Being justified freely by his grace through the redemption that is in Christ Jesus." God did so much greater than Jephthah and yet men cannot keep their vow of faithfulness, service, yielded life to God. We read in Proverbs 21:3, "To do justice and judgment is more acceptable to the LORD than sacrifice."

Are you keeping your vows to the Lord? He is always there for us and is always willing to welcome us back to Him in our walk with Him. Psalm 94:22, "But the LORD is my defense; and my God is the rock of my refuge." Oh, that we would be faithful to the Lord to live for Him and to serve Him daily with everything we have. Can you see the tears on the floor or in the sawdust? Can you remember how your heart was brought under great conviction? Remember the words of Jephtah, "I have opened my mouth unto the LORD, and I cannot go back." (Judges 11:35). He kept his vow unto the Lord.

Are you keeping your vows to the Lord?

April 22

Judges 13-14 Psalm 95 Proverbs 22 Romans 5-6

Staying Faithful

Good morning! Things do not always turn out the way you plan or the way you would like, but time marches on. A friend of mine from many years back raises rodeo stock such as bucking bulls and other types of cattle. I had sold him a calf from one of my cows and that little calf grew to be a beautiful looking heifer. He has been sending me pictures and letting me know when the new calf is to come into this world. A couple of days age he called me and said the new calf did not make it. He sent me the picture of the little calf. Everything was right with the mother and the vet said the new calf to be born was doing great.

In delivery some things got turned around that no one could help, and the little calf did not make it. Life must go on.

The judge Samson was raised in a good home by parents who were obedient to the Lord. Listen to their attitude in asking the angel of the Lord how to raise him, in Judges 13:12, "How shall we order the child, and how shall we do unto him?" They did what they were told, and we read the result in Judges 13:24, "the child grew, and the LORD blessed him." Just like Adam and Eve, the flesh grew weak, the lust of the eyes and the pride of life weakened another man. We will read tomorrow the end result of Samson but listen today to Paul's writings in Romans 5:19, "For as by one man's disobedience many were made sinners, so by the obedience of one shall many be made righteous." There is a payment for the sins of man and there is the gift of God. Romans 6:23, "For the wages of sin is death; but the gift of God is eternal life through Jesus Christ our Lord."

Do not give up, parents. Pray, stay faithful, serve the Lord to the end of life's course. Proverbs 22:6, "Train up a child in the way he should go: and when he is old, he will not depart from it." Listen to the Psalmist, my brother and sister. Psalm 95:8, "Harden not your heart." Can I leave you with a thought for the day? Never go against Biblical principles. The result will always be wrong. Thank the Lord for our Lord Jesus Christ and that He loves all of us sinners and picks us up and keeps us going. Do right and be blessed.

Pray, stay faithful, serve the Lord to the end of life's course.

April 23

Judges 15-16 Psalm 96 Proverbs 23 Romans 7

Sin Always Destroys

Good morning! Another day begins and I have not messed it up yet. Do you ever say that to yourself? I hunger to do right in the sight of God and not let my flesh get in the road of being a blessing to others, and the servant that I need to be. I so want to please the Lord in everything I say and do.

As I read Judges chapters 15 and 16, we see deceit, lies, lust, compromise, revenge, repentance and victory, but yet death. As I was reading, I wrote these words at the top of my notes, "sin always destroys." Our fleshly desires cannot be what drives our lives. Judges 15:10, "to do to him as he hath done to us." Judges 15:11, "As they did unto me, so have I done unto them." Samson was in the wrong place, doing the wrong things and compromised his separation unto God, and yet in the end, had a confession of sin and faith in God. Judges 16:28, "And Samson called unto the LORD, and said, O Lord GOD, remember me, I pray thee, only this once, O God, that I may be at once avenged of the Philistines for my two eyes." I am afraid that our lives are so focused on what we want instead of what God wants that the truth is found in Romans 7:19-20, "For the good that I would I do not: but the evil which I would not, that I do. Now if I do that I would not, it is no more I that do it, but sin that dwelleth in me."

What we all need to constantly do is found in Proverbs 23:23, "Buy the truth, and sell it not; also wisdom, and instruction, and understanding." May we learn from the Scriptures today the importance of being truthful with ourselves and know that true happiness and joy comes from what we read in Psalm 96:9, "O worship the LORD in the beauty of holiness: fear before him, all the earth." My brother, my sister, stand true and faithful. The eternal rewards in Heaven are far greater than what the flesh thinks it wants. "Buy the truth, and sell it not."

Our fleshly desires cannot be what drives our lives.

April 24

Judges 17-18 Psalm 97 Proverbs 24 Romans 8

Spiritual Confusion

Good morning! Have you ever woken up during the night and been in confusion as to what day it is or what time it is? I have woken up and got right up and walked into a wall in the dark. Go ahead and laugh, Mrs. Smith did. When our lives are not in order spiritually, we will live in confusion and the devil will mount an attack on us. We must keep our lives in spiritual order even in trials and times of discouragement.

Judges 17:6, "In those days there was no king in Israel, but every man did that which was right in his own eyes." How can anyone try to live for God without God? We cannot make a decision that is right spiritually without the mind of Christ. Judges 17:5, "And the man Micah had an house of gods, and made an ephod, and teraphim, and consecrated one of his sons, who became his priest." Basically, Micah did what he thought and wanted. Romans 8:5-6, "For they that are after the flesh do mind the things of the flesh; but they that are after the Spirit the things of the Spirit. For to be carnally minded is death; but to be spiritually minded is life and peace." We must always do what God wants and in God's way and in God's timing. Confusion spiritually will always come along with sin when we do things our way and just what we want. Consistency in our walk with Christ is a must if we are going to stay in God's will and do God's will. Proverbs 24:21, "My son, fear thou the LORD and the king: and meddle not with them that are given to change." We need to settle down in our walk with God and live one step at a time.

When I have been startled in the night or awakened and jumped right out of bed, I almost always stub my toe or walk into something. That is just what we do in our walk with God when we do not wait on Him and get His guidance in our lives. Living for God is not living in darkness and confusion. Jesus is the light, so why not be led by the light? Jesus is the way, so why not be patient and let Him guide us in the way? Psalm 97:11, "Light is sown for the righteous, and gladness for the upright in heart." It was funny when I have walked into a wall or stubbed my toe, but there was also pain. Let us end with the thought that we read in Judges 18:18, "What do ye?" Live in the light, not in the darkness of confusion.

Consistency in our walk with Christ is a must
if we are going to stay in and do God's will.

April 25

Judges 19-21 Psalm 98 Proverbs 25 Romans 9

Hen Pecked

Good morning! I would like to invite you to go out to the chicken house with me this morning. We are going to observe something about chickens that I have never understood but it is a reality. I remember as a boy asking my mom why a certain chicken had an area on them where all the feathers were gone. Mom just simply said, the other chickens are picking at it, and they will eventually pick all the feathers or maybe even kill that chicken. If a chicken will see what it thinks is a bug on another chicken, it will begin to peck and pick at that spot. That is right, they will peck away at their own kind.

How sad the story that we read in Judges 19-21 this morning. Basically, I can say they killed their own. Judges 19:30, "There was no such deed done nor seen from the day that the children of Israel came up out of the land of Egypt unto this day." How did this happen? Judges 21:25, "In those days there was no king in Israel: every man did that which was right in his own eyes." A chicken will pick at and possibly kill their own because of what they think they see. We must look at all situations of life through the eyes of God and not what we think we see. Romans 9:32, "Because they sought it not by faith but as it were by the works of the law. For they stumbled at that stumblingstone." They could not and would not see the love of Christ and it caused them to miss God's gift to man. Proverbs 25:8, "Go not forth hastily to strive, lest thou know not what to do in the end thereof, when thy neighbor hath put thee to shame." We must not live in the flesh but the spirit. Sin and our emotions will cause us to often react in a way that we will soon regret and even cause us to attack the ones we love the most. Psalm 98:2, "The LORD hath made known his salvation: his righteousness hath he openly shewed in the sight of the heathen."

I used to feel so sorry for the chickens that had been pecked by the others, but it is much worse for us to attack and almost destroy others with our mouth and with our actions. We must pray for others, see this world through the eyes of Christ and be the soul winners we need to be. Be patient with a younger brother in Christ or a brother that might not see things exactly the way that you see them. I remember seeing one chicken get another one down and pick at it, and how it disturbed me. Let us encourage, pray, and lift others up for the glory of Christ.

We must look at all situations of life through the eyes of God and not what we think we see.

April 26

Ruth 1-2 Psalm 99 Proverbs 26 Romans 10

Steadfast in Life

Good morning! Have you ever pushed open a door and the door has swung back and hit you? Open a shed door and the wind catches the door and it comes back to hit you. As I read Proverbs 26:14, "As the door turneth upon his hinges, so doth the slothful upon his bed." I am afraid we are living in a time where people are willing to change almost anything in life just for an easier way.

We begin our walk through the book of Ruth, and we find three wives without their husbands and no way to make it. We see their action in Ruth 1:6, "Then she arose with her daughters in law, that she might return from the country of Moab: for she had heard in the country of Moab how that the LORD had visited his people in giving them bread." In chapter one of Ruth, we read the words, "turn again" twice and "again" another time. I thought this morning about how many I know who have been like a swinging door. They get right with God and disappear from church, and they leave their sin and return to their sin. There are those who get excited about living for God and serving Him, and then their excitement goes away, or they do not keep the fire in them burning from their walk with God. We read in Ruth 1:18, "steadfast minded." Ruth 2:12, "The LORD recompense thy work, and a full reward be given thee of the LORD God of Israel, under whose wings thou art come to trust." It is so very important for us as God's people to be "steadfast" in our lives, consistent in every area. Paul never lost the burden of his heart as he wrote in Romans 10:1, "Brethren, my heart's desire and prayer to God for Israel is, that they might be saved."

Naomi and Ruth returned to where they knew the blessings of God would be, even though they had no idea how God would provide. Our Lord again and again has forgiven His people of their sins. He picks us up every time and washes us clean by His forgiveness. Psalm 99:8, "Thou answeredst them, O LORD our God: thou wast a God that forgavest them, though thou tookest vengeance of their inventions." God is saying to us today, quit being like a swinging door and get "steadfast" in your life. Stay the course, finish the race, be faithful and growing in His grace to the end of the race of life.

It is so important for us as God's people to be "steadfast" in our lives, consistent in every area.

April 27

Ruth 3-4 Psalm 100 Proverbs 27 Romans 11

Grafted by God

Good morning! Each day before I begin to read my Bible, I spend time in prayer with the Lord. I hunger to hear from Him. I fear too many Christians just read their Bibles to mark a chart, feel they are fulfilling an obligation, or please their flesh. Or there might be a true sincerity to grow but do we spend the time to prepare our hearts like we should? As I beg the Lord to speak to me each day, I hunger to learn more about Him. I want you to think about one word today, and that word is "graft." I love apples. I love baked apples, fried apples, apple pie, fried apple pies, apple fritters, apple crisp, apple cobbler. Last night I put apples in my yogurt.

We read today in Ruth 3:10, "thou hast shewed more kindness in the latter end than at the beginning." Naomi and Ruth had no idea what God was going to do. Ruth 4:15, "And he shall be unto thee a restorer of life, and a nourisher of thine old age." If we would learn to grow in God's grace and spend the time each day with Him and in His Word, the results could be greater than we could ever imagine. I know life must go on, but time with God is above all the most important. Proverbs 27:25, "The hay appeareth, and the tender grass sheweth itself, and herbs of the mountains are gathered." Do not look at life as just going on and what will be will be. Romans 11:2, "God hath not cast away his people." Romans 11:23, "And they also, if they abide not still in unbelief, shall be grafted in: for God is able to graft them in again." There are many kinds of apples and there became many kinds because of the grafting process; taking the good and making it better. We are sinners bound for Hell and through accepting Christ by faith, we have been grafted into His grace to become His likeness. Psalm 100:3, "know ye that the LORD he is God: it is he that hath made us, and not we ourselves, we are his people, and the sheep of his pasture."

God used the sadness of Naomi and Ruth to bring about His Son. Listen to the lineage, as Ruth was married and had a child. Ruth 4:17, "and they called his name Obed: he is the father of Jesse, the father of David." Jesus was born of this earthly lineage. The delicious apples that I eat have been grafted from the best, to become even better. We have been grafted into the family of God. May we live for Him even more.

Through accepting Christ by faith, we have been grafted into His grace to become His likeness.

April 28

1 Samuel 1-2 Psalm 101 Proverbs 28 Romans 12-13

One Life to Live

Good morning! Can you hear a child say as they played with their friends, "It is mine?" Can you hear an adult say, "It is mine, I worked for it, I earned it, it is mine?" What is truly ours? Did we provide the air we breathe? Did we make the body that we live in? Do we give ourselves life? I live with the reality that my life can end at any time and in numerous ways.

As we read in the first two chapters of I Samuel, you can feel the heart of Hannah and her desire to have a child, but more than that, a man child. Her purpose is what always draws me to study thoroughly this passage. From the very beginning we read in I Samuel 1:11, "I will give him unto the LORD all the days of his life." I Samuel 1:22, "that he may appear before the LORD, and there abide for ever." I Samuel 1:28, "Therefore also I have lent him to the LORD; as long as he liveth he shall be lent to the LORD."

I was loading straw yesterday and I received a text message from a pastor that has a young man in his church who wants to work on summer staff. We received a letter yesterday in the mail from a young lady who wants to come to camp early and help work. Two opposing attitudes: "it is mine" and "the child did minister." God says in Proverbs 28:20a, "A faithful man shall abound with blessings." Psalm 101:6b, "he that walketh in a perfect way, he shall serve me." Does God have your all? Do you think about what you can do for God, or is your focus on what you want? Do you spend time doing everything else and spend little or no time with God? Do we only call on God when we need Him or is there a desire and discipline to daily spend time with Him and His Word? I Samuel 2:30b, "for them that honour me I will honour, and they that despise me shall be lightly esteemed." We only have one life to live. How are you living it? Hannah received the young man she prayed, fasted, and daily pleaded with God for, and she gave Samuel to the Lord to serve Him, and the results are there. I Samuel 2:26, "And the child Samuel grew on, and was in favour both with the LORD, and also with men." We only have one life to live. May I suggest you give the rest of your life to living and serving God? The blessings are eternal.

Do you think about what you can do for God,
or is your focus on what you want?

April 29

1 Samuel 3-4 Psalm 102:1-17 Proverbs 29 Romans 14

The Value of a Sparrow

Good morning! What is of absolute importance in life to you? I am constantly amazed at our God and how His Word can teach us so very much if we just stop, listen, meditate and apply. In I Samuel 3-4 we see sadness all around. I Samuel 3:1, "there was no open vision." I Samuel 3:3, "And ere the lamp of God went out in the temple of the LORD, where the ark of God was." I Samuel 4, the children of Israel are in battle, and they think bringing the ark of the LORD to the battlefield will help. I Samuel 4:4, "So the people sent to Shiloh, that they might bring thence the ark of the covenant of the LORD of hosts, which dwelleth between the cherubims." This is a perfect example of bringing God down to the people instead of bringing the people to God.

Then we read four different times in I Samuel 4, "the ark of God was taken." Eli receives word and dies. His sons are killed and his daughter in law has a child and names him I-chabod. I Samuel 4:21, "And she named the child I-chabod, saying, The glory is departed from Israel." How sad and heartbreaking this chain of events was! Romans 14:13, "Let us not therefore judge one another any more: but judge this rather, that no man put a stumbling block or occasion to fall in his brother"s way." That is what happened in Israel as the ungodly sons of Eli did not set and lead by a spiritual example. Rebellion all the way, and so is this generation we live in today. Proverbs 29:1, "He that being often reproved hardeneth his neck, shall suddenly be destroyed, and that without remedy."

Now to the real point of our thought for the day. Psalm 102:7, "I watch, and am as a sparrow alone upon the house top." Samuel had to feel all alone as he was listening and walking with God. The sparrow, little, not pretty, seemingly alone and a pest. Not so. The sparrow is one of the most valuable birds in eating seeds from plants and trees and spreading them through the forest. If all the trees and grasses just dropped their seeds, there would not be the beauty we see in forests and fields. I thought how we often feel alone and of little effect in this wicked world and yet God says, look, "a sparrow alone upon the house top." The beauty we see all around us of flowers, bushes, trees, and a multitude of plants could have been started because God gave us the little, ugly sparrow. Just think what God could do with us if we just kept spreading His Word and sowing the seeds of salvation right in the middle of a lost and doomed world. Let God use you today, just as a little sparrow that has no beauty but does a tremendous job for the Lord's creation.

God and His Word can teach us so much if we just stop, listen, meditate and apply.

April 30

1 Samuel 5-6 Psalm 102:18-28 Proverbs 30-31 Romans 15

Wake, Walk, and Work

Good morning! Every parent has had to say those same words, "good morning," to their children to get them up and get them ready for school. I can hear those words, "it is time to get up and get ready for school." I can remember these words, "David, it is time to get up, the papers are here." Oh, what a nightmare in the wintertime when the wind was blowing at one hundred miles per hour, and it was at least fifty degrees below zero and I had to get up and deliver papers and get my chores done. Now, you know that is not the truth but just an exaggeration by me. We as God's people must wake up and realize God has a purpose in every day that we live, and nothing can stop His purpose and control.

We read this morning in I Samuel 5 how the Philistines had taken the ark of God and God's judgment fell on them. I Samuel 5:3, "And when they of Ashdod arose early on the morrow, behold, Dagon was fallen upon his face to the earth before the ark of the LORD." We must keep our faith in God because He is always in control and trying to teach and show us something. We must learn from God's Word and listen to God's leadership. Romans 15:4, "For whatsoever things were written aforetime were written for our learning, that we through patience and comfort of the scriptures might have hope." We must let the hope of God and love of God be our strength. Romans 15:13, "Now the God of hope fill you with all joy and peace in believing, that ye may abound in hope, through the power of the Holy Ghost." Little did I understand that when I was awakened to do chores and deliver papers early in the morning, I was being prepared to have a habit built into my life to help me get up and be in my Bible and time of prayer with the Lord. Our trust cannot be in man or this world, but in God and His Word. Proverbs 30:5, "Every word of God is pure: he is a shield unto them that put their trust in him." God knows what we need, and we need to take it from Him. Proverbs 30:7, "Two things have I required of thee; deny me them not before I die." Proverbs 30:8, "Remove far from me vanity and lies: give me neither poverty nor riches; feed me with food convenient for me."

We who are saved are writing another chapter in God's timetable for the generation to come. Psalm 102:18, "This shall be written for the generation to come." God laid the foundation, and each generation is to build through God's strength on that foundation. Psalm 102:25, "Of old hast thou laid the foundation of the earth: and the heavens are the work of thy hands." Psalm 102:26a, "They shall perish, but thou shalt endure." It is time for us as God's people to wake up, walk daily and do the work that He has called each of us to do. God does not have a beginning and He has no ending. We must wake, walk, and work until He calls us Home. Psalm 102:27, "But thou art the same, and thy years shall have no end." Let us commit ourselves afresh to wake, walk, and work until the eastern skies part and we go Home.

We must let the hope of God and love of God be our strength.

May 1

1 Samuel 7-8 Psalm 103 Proverbs 1 Romans 16

The Deceiver

Good morning! One evening this week a couple of men helped me to move some things and clean up, preparing the camp for another summer. I used the tractor and moved several bales of hay and as I was moving the bales, I was watching for something that often lives under those bales. When we got the area cleaned, I moved over to a large pile of rocks and made a statement, "That is a good place for snakes to live." The temperature is getting warmer, and it is time for some snakes to be coming out and finding a place to warm themselves.

As we know, the devil took the form of a serpent in the Garden of Eden, and he has continually been a deceiver. The children of Israel were deceived as we read in I Samuel 8:7, "for they have not rejected thee, but they have rejected me, that I should not reign over them." The devil is hiding just like a snake. He hides in the tall grass (when we get too busy to read our Bibles), under some dead leaves (when other things seem more important than praying), in the middle of a pile of rocks (when we mechanically serve God instead of by His power), or under a large bale of hay. He is a deceiver. I Samuel 8:19, "Nevertheless the people refused to obey the voice of Samuel; and they said, Nay; but we will have a king over us." We must pay attention to false doctrine and worldly, ungodly ways of religion that are not of God. Romans 16:17, "Now I beseech you, brethren, mark them which cause divisions and offences contrary to the doctrine which ye have learned; and avoid them." Proverbs 1:10, "My son, if sinners entice thee, consent thou not." Proverbs 1:15, "My son, walk not thou in the way with them; refrain thy foot from their path."

The devil's goal is to use anything he can to draw us away from right Bible doctrine and to turn our worship of God to some false doctrine. Stay true, stay faithful, stay the right path, finish God's course for your life. Psalm 103:17, "But the mercy of the LORD is from everlasting to everlasting upon them that fear him, and his righteousness unto children's children." God's way is always the right way, the safe way, the true way.

The devil's goal is to use anything he can
to draw us away from right Bible doctrine.

May 2

1 Samuel 9-10 Psalm 104:1-17 Proverbs 2 1 Corinthians 1-2

Biblical Leadership

Good morning! Life seems to be changing so very fast all around us. I left the ranch early yesterday morning and had several appointments and the day seemed to explode with everything going different directions. I was saying yesterday that I rode motorcycles when you did not need a helmet, and I was driving before there were seatbelts. Boy, has time changed! We find ourselves in a time of life when things are different and not making any sense. I thank the Lord that His Word is unchanging. I am thankful for helmets, as I have had motorcycle accidents and I am thankful for seatbelts even though I do not like them.

My heart is burning for us not to lose or try to change the importance of spiritual leadership from God in our lives. We have plenty of leadership in our lives today, but I am speaking of Biblical, spiritual, God-anointed leadership. I Samuel 9:9, "let us go to the seer." The children of Israel were calling for a king and God told Samuel about Saul coming and looking for his father's mules that were lost. The word "seer" is used five times, speaking of a man that was before called a prophet. This man had a special anointing of God. I Samuel 9:17, "And when Samuel saw Saul, the LORD said unto him, Behold the man whom I spake to thee of!" He was to be trained, called out and filled with God's powers. I Samuel 9:27,

"Samuel said to Saul, stand thou still a while, that I may shew thee the word of God." I Samuel 10:6, "And the Spirit of the LORD will come upon thee, and thou shalt prophesy with them, and shalt be turned into another man." I Samuel 10:9, "God gave him another heart." I Samuel 10:10, "the Spirit of God came upon him." I Samuel 10:24, "See ye him whom the LORD hath chosen." We need to follow a man of God who is filled with the power of God, and we need men of God who have had their hearts set afire by God to lead the people of God. We go to I Corinthians 1 and we see the words, "call," "called," "calling," used five different times. Listen to Paul speak about himself and his calling in I Corinthians 2:4, "And my speech and my preaching was not with enticing words of man's wisdom, but in demonstration of the Spirit and of power."

God gives us men called of Him and filled with Him, who are to be used of Him. Proverbs 2:7, "He layeth up sound wisdom for the righteous: he is a buckler to them that walk uprightly." Pray for your pastor to be filled with God's power. Listen to your pastor, seek His counsel and guidance. We are living in a time that is full of emotion and we need to be listening to God, His Word and His man as God's Word is taught and preached. Psalm 104:4, "Who maketh his angels spirits; his ministers a flaming fire." We need preachers today set on fire by God to preach God's truth to a dying, doomed world that is lost. Pray for your preacher, his family, his staff who love the flock of God and want to be filled and used by the power of God.

We need men of God who have had their hearts set afire by God to lead the people of God.

May 3

1 Samuel 11-12 Psalm 104:18-35 Proverbs 3 1 Corinthians 3-4

How Great Thou Art

Good morning! I looked at a hole where a rabbit runs in and out. I looked at a nest where a bird had picked up each dead branch and each blade of grass to build a nest. I watched as a squirrel jumped from limb to limb. I watched as the cows and horses ate the grass of the field. I listened as the creek below sang its song as it flowed over the rocks the Lord had made. I saw the sun as it broke the barrier of night's darkness and my heart was filled with how great our God is.

Sing with me this morning. "O Lord my God! When I in awesome wonder Consider all the worlds Thy hands have made, I see the stars, I hear the rolling thunder, Thy power through out the universe displayed, Then sings my soul, my Savior God, to Thee; How great Thou art, how great Thou art!" I Samuel 12:24, "Only fear the LORD, and serve him in truth with all your heart: for consider how great things he hath done for you." I Corinthians 3:16, "Know ye not that ye are the temple of God, and that the Spirit of God dwelleth in you?" Proverbs 3:1, "My son, forget not my law; but let thine heart keep my commandments." Psalm 104:31, "The glory of the LORD shall endure for ever."

"When Christ shall come with shout of acclamation And take me home, what joy shall fill my heart! Then I shall bow in humble adoration And there proclaim, My God, how great Thou art!" PRAISE HIM TODAY! Praise Him for who He is, for all He is, and for what He is! Praise Him!! Have a blessed day!

"Then sings my soul, my Savior God, to Thee;
How great Thou art, how great Thou art!"

May 4

1 Samuel 13-14 Psalm 105:1-15 Proverbs 4 1 Corinthians 5-6

The Heart of God

Good morning! Each morning I go and check on the animals to make sure they are alright, are where they need to be and to make sure they are not out. In just a short while there will be two dogs sitting at the door waiting for me to come out. They both want me to pet them and when I go to check the rest of the camp, they will go wherever I go. We have a pony that was purchased for my granddaughter when she was around one or two years old, and at that time that pony was over ten years old. Now our granddaughter will be twenty this August and that pony is still just as gentle as ever and she just keeps on going. I asked myself this morning, is it our heart or our mind that keeps all of us going? I know it is a balance of both but I asked God to come into my heart and my heart should help me control my mind.

Saul sinned when he saw the enemy and did not wait on Samuel the prophet in I Samuel 13:8. I Samuel 13:14, "The LORD hath sought him a man after his own heart, and the LORD hath commanded him to be captain over his people, because thou hast not kept that which the LORD commanded thee." The dogs and the horses seem to want to be with me and go where I go because of their hearts, because I really do nothing for them except give them time. Yes, I provide feed and water, but when they are not eating, they want to be by my side. Is that what is missing in the lives of many Christians? We are living and serving with our minds only and not our hearts. I Corinthians 6:12, "All things are lawful unto me, but all things are not expedient: all things are lawful for me, but I will not be brought under the power of any." Solomon teaching his son in Proverbs 4:4 said, "He taught me also, and said unto me, Let thine heart retain my words: keep my commandments, and live." Proverbs 4:23, "keep thy heart with all diligence; for out of it are the issues of life."

That old little pony will look and her ears will stand tall when I call her name and as I approach her, she will come to me and let me pet her. It is not because of a treat. Do we only come to God because of our want or is there a heart that yearns for fellowship with God? From the very beginning of creation God just wanted the heart of man because a right heart will bring obedience. Psalm 105:3, "Glory ye in his holy name: let the heart of them rejoice that seek the LORD." Who or what has your heart today? Do you have a heart for God? Can you pray without asking for things and just pray because you love Him and want to be with Him? It is not wrong to ask, but that should not be our motive to pray. May our hearts be in tune with the heart of God because we have allowed our hearts to be stirred for the things of God's heart. Have a blessed day.

Do we have a heart that yearns for fellowship with God?

May 5

1 Samuel 15-16 Psalm 105:16-45 Proverbs 5 1 Corinthians 7

Stay Faithful

Good morning! As I was reading this morning, a phrase kept coming to me, "God never forgets." So much in God's creation has the character of God and yet man was the only one created "in our image, after our likeness" (Genesis 1:26). Psalm 105:42, "For he remembered his holy promise, and Abraham his servant." God does not forget. Saul is king and is given very clear instructions on what to do. I Samuel 15:1, "now therefore hearken thou unto the voice of the words of the LORD." I Samuel 15:3, "Now go and smite Amalek, and utterly destroy all that they have, and spare them not." The battle began, victory came, and yet obedience failed. All was not destroyed as God said, "he is turned back from following me, and hath not performed my commandments" (I Samuel 15:11). The prophet Samuel arrives and says, "to obey is better than sacrifice, and to hearken than the fat of rams, for rebellion is as the sin of witchcraft, and stubbornness is as iniquity and idolatry" (I Samuel 15:22-23).

A couple of days ago, Mrs. Smith and I were at the kitchen table having our devotions and prayer time together and she said, "Look, they are back." She had not put out her hummingbird feeder but the hanger was still there and the little birds had returned from their long journey to the same place. This morning, as every morning, the dogs will be waiting at the same place as they do every day waiting for me to come and feed them and give fresh water. Why do we, who are created greater than any of God's creation, not stay faithful and obedient? We fail to obey and seemingly go on with life and wonder why God is not blessing like He promised. God convicts us of some sin and we leave it for a while and return to the slop. We say we are and we don't. I Corinthians 7:20, "Let every man abide in the same calling wherein he was called." I Corinthians 7:12-13, "How have I hated instruction, and my heart despised reproof; and have not obeyed the voice of my teachers, nor inclined mine ear to them that instructed me!" Is a dog, a cat, a horse, a hummingbird, more faithful and true to man than a saved person is to their Redeemer? Our life is before the Lord and He is our God. Be faithful, loyal, consistent to Him and for Him. Proverbs 5:21, "For the ways of man are before the eyes of the LORD, and he pondereth all his goings."

Yesterday as I was eating my noon meal on the front porch, both of my dogs were laying close by and a neighbor drove into the lane who always has his dog with him, and my dogs love to run after his truck and bark at his dog. I saw the truck turn in and I said, "Stay, Tipper stay. Noelle, stay." They both looked at their master with those brown eyes and I said, STAY! Both dogs just lay there. Stay with God and be a faithful servant of the LORD. He is faithful and He is watching. He is our LORD.

Be faithful, loyal, consistent to Him and for Him.

May 6

1 Samuel 17-18 Psalm 106:1-15 Proverbs 6 1 Corinthians 8-9

A Hunger for Wisdom

Good morning! As I read my Bible this morning, I asked myself, where is my focus in serving the Lord? In life we have things we would like to accomplish, we have responsibilities that we have to do, and all of us have distractions that pull us many different directions. Our world is changing so fast and the coming of the Lord draws closer each day and each moment of each day.

We find ourselves this morning in the middle of a battlefield, with David obeying his father and his heart being convicted by a giant defying the armies of God. A challenge is brought forth by the giant to give him one man to fight. No one steps forth and then David's heart is stirred, but he is just a lad. As we read, David stepped forth and defeated the giant. How did this come about? It was not ability, it was not human strength, it was not equipment that he used, it was not counsel that he had received, it was not anything less than what all of us need to gain daily from the Lord. David gave testimony to king Saul about his fighting a lion and a bear, and defeating them and we read in I Samuel 17:36, "this uncircumcised Philistine shall be as one of them, seeing he hath defied the armies of the living God." The giant was defeated, and now in I Samuel 18 we see the jealousy of Saul's rage, and we also see the key to David's walk, growth, and development of a man with God. I Samuel 18:5, "behaved himself wisely." I Samuel 18:14, "And David behaved himself wisely in all his ways; and the LORD was with him." I Samuel 18:15, "Wherefore when Saul saw that he behaved himself very wisely, he was afraid of him." I Samuel 18:30, "David behaved himself more wisely than all the servants of Saul; so that his name was much set by." David hungered for and lived by the wisdom of God. David learned that being a servant of God and using wisdom from God is the key to life. I Corinthians 8:1, "knowledge puffeth up, but charity edifieth." I Corinthians 8:3, "But if any man love God, the same is known of him."

I love hunting, and I have learned you have to use wisdom greater than the animal you are hunting. The rifle is not the key, the camouflage is not the key, other equipment that we think will help the hunt is not the key, but being wiser than the animal you are hunting. Proverbs 6:5, "Deliver thyself as the roe from the hand of the hunter, and as a bird from the hand of the fowler." May we hunger and live for knowing the wisdom of God. God has a purpose for us, just as he had a purpose for David in the battle against Goliath, but it took the wisdom of God to attain the victory for the glory of God. Psalm 106:8, "Nevertheless he saved them for his name's sake, that he might make his mighty power to be known." May I encourage us not to live in our own strength, but in the wisdom of God in every area of our lives so that we can do God's calling.

Being a servant of God and using wisdom from God is the key to life.

May 7

1 Samuel 19-20 Psalm 106:16-33 Proverbs 7 1 Corinthians 10

Rottenness of Jealousy

Good morning! The trees are starting to have their leaves come out and the beauty of a big tree with full branches moving in the breeze is so relaxing. As I was working and checking some fences that need repairing, I came upon another tree that had split and fallen. I looked and thought how sad it is that a beautiful mature tree can die on the inside and split and fall. I read this morning about the jealousy of Saul against David and how Saul became so bitter, he sought David's life. I Samuel 20:1, "What have I done? What is mine iniquity? And what is my sin before thy father, that he seeketh my life?" The decaying process that a jealous heart can bring will cause one to even attack his very own. Jonathan asked his father Saul what David had done and Jonathan caught his father's wrath. I Samuel 20:33, "And Saul cast a javelin at him to smite him: whereby Jonathan knew that it was determined of his father to slay David."

I got off my side by side and looked at this beautiful tree now laying on the ground and the center was hollow and rotten. I read this morning in I Corinthians 10 about temptation and how God provides a way of escape, because that temptation will lead us to sin and sin will destroy even a strong mature Christian. I Corinthians 10:13, "There hath no temptation taken you but such as is common to man: but God is faithful, who will not suffer you to be tempted above that ye are able, but will with the temptation also make a way to escape, that ye may be able to bear it." We face temptation daily in multiple areas of our lives and we can have victory. Proverbs 7:2, "keep my commandments, and live; and my law as the apple of thine eye." Don't forget what God has done for you. That large tree started as a little sapling or a bird dropped a seed from a bud. That little sapling grew into a young tree, developing a solid root base but something caused the rot, and the tree began to die. The Psalmist wrote about how the children of Israel forgot God and all that He had done. Psalm 106:21, "They forgat God their Saviour, which had done great things in Egypt." We must stay strong in the Lord and not let any sin destroy us.

That large tree now lays on the ground and I will cut it up and burn it all in a bonfire or wood stove. Are we growing in the Lord or is there a sin that is destroying us? As I am writing, the sun is just starting to break its way through the darkness. We see jealousy all around us. The jealousy of Saul destroyed what God could have done in his life. He let it eat and grow so that he tried to kill his very own son. Let the ill feelings that you have toward another die or it will destroy you. We live in a world where it seems everybody is attacking everybody, and hatred and anger is running out of control. Walk with God today and see a lost world that needs Christ. Let the love for sinners grow and a jealous heart die. Reach out to a sinner today and let an envious, jealous, attacking heart die. Confess the sin that controls you and live for the glory of God.

We must stay strong in the Lord and not let any sin destroy us.

May 8

1 Samuel 21-22 Psalm 106:34-48 Proverbs 8 1 Corinthians 11

Strength in Fellowship

Good morning! Mrs. Smith and I enjoy driving the back roads that wind through the hills and along the creeks. During a rain storm, the water runs off the hills and down into the creeks and as the different creeks join together to eventually flow into the river, those creeks get larger and it makes the river more powerful. As I read this morning in I Samuel 22:2, "And every one that was in distress, and every one that was in debt, and every one that was discontented, gathered themselves unto him; and he became a captain over them." The small creeks gather into the river and the river will feed a beautiful lake.

As David felt rejection, so did others and they joined together and found strength. First of all, it is so important for us to have a personal walk with the Lord, but add to that the fellowship, prayers and worshipping together with others and it will add strength to each of us who are part of the family of God. Paul wrote in I Corinthians 11:1, "Be ye followers of me, even as I also am of Christ." When we are praying for each other, it draws us closer in our hearts to each other. As we read Proverbs 8 this morning, we read in verse 17, " I love them that love me; and those that seek me early shall find me." This is wisdom from God available for us if we seek it. We read on in Proverbs 8:21, "That I may cause those that love me to inherit substance; and I will fill their treasures."

As the many creeks flow together, the river grows and the lakes provide a reservoir for so much more. Reach out today to someone and be a blessing to them. Let your prayer list grow for others. Put a smile on your face and a happy gleam in your eyes. God is always there for us as we read in Psalm 106:43a, "Many times did he deliver them." Decide today to reach out and share Christ. Be a special blessing or encouragement; a smile is known in every language of the world. You might think you have nothing to add, but you and I are just like the little creek that flows into the river and becomes the great mighty ocean. Give God what you have and watch Him bless it today.

Reach out today to someone and be a blessing to them.

May 9

1 Samuel 23-24 Psalm 107:1-22 Proverbs 9 1 Corinthians 12-13

A Special Purpose

Good morning! The wood stove is going and somehow, I missed the warm spring mornings and the beautiful relaxing summer evenings. As I began to fill the wood stove this morning and prepare to start the fire, I did not put in a big log; I put smaller pieces in that would be easier to start the fire with. This is not a class on fire building; please read on. As I brought in wood last night, I stopped and looked at the wood I have in the pile. I am often teased about saving every piece of wood I can even though there are some that burn better than others. As God has created all trees, all trees are not the same. Some are for fruit, some for furniture, some for construction, some are hard wood and some soft wood. Some produce a sap that can be cooked to make a delicious syrup, some with delicious fruit to eat, some with a beautiful smell, some so hard they are perfect for a strong fence post that will last a life time.

Saul needed David and yet he spent so much time trying to kill him. David was in the same cave as Saul and yet David had a respect and love for the one trying to destroy him. I Samuel 24:10, "I will not put forth mine hand against my lord; for he is the LORD's anointed." This earth is covered with different people that one God has created, and yet the flesh is so weak we spend more time fighting than building. The trees of the forest are not all the same because each has a different purpose. Oh, that we would have a heart for others so great as to see a lost world come to Christ and that we would reach the multitudes with the Gospel and see that God has a purpose for all. I Corinthians 12:11, "But all these worketh that one and the selfsame Spirit, dividing to every man severally as he will." Proverbs 9:1, "Wisdom hath builded her house, she hath hewn out her seven pillars." All of us were created for a purpose by God. The problem is that we are living to ourselves instead of focusing on building for the kingdom of God by reaching a lost world to Christ. Psalm 107:15 and 21, "Oh that men would praise the LORD for his goodness, and for his wonderful works to the children of men!"

Don't be critical of those who are not like you, but realize they need to be saved and grow in the Lord for God's purpose for their lives. The forest is not just filled with one kind of wood or tree. Those trees bring glory to their Creator as they grow and are used for the purpose He intended. May we live and reach people for His glory and may we be surrendered to His purpose for our lives. I enjoy an apple, as well as I enjoy sitting on a good chair made of a beautiful wood, as well as I enjoy the warmth of a fire where a hard wood is burned and sitting and enjoying the comfort of a home built out of lumber grown so straight. We all have a purpose for God. May we allow Him to use us His way.

May we reach people for His glory and
may we be surrendered to His purpose for our lives.

May 10

1 Samuel 25-26 Psalm 107:23-43 Proverbs 10 1 Corinthians 14

Watch Your Attitude

Good morning! I am so thankful that the Lord knows exactly what I need, when I need it and how I get it. There are things in life that we cannot stop. Try to hold the wind back, try to hold and stop a rain cloud, a rain storm. Try to hold back the winter from coming in the fall. So why do we try to control so much in life instead of just submitting and living to and for the LORD? Frustration can ruin a perfectly wonderful day.

Nabal, in I Samuel 25, was selfish, proud, impatient, unkind, would not listen and had no understanding, and no one could change his spirit or attitude. I Samuel 25:17b, "that a man cannot speak to him." Do you know anybody like Nabal? Just try and fix them. You cannot and yet we allow a person like Nabal to destroy or affect our attitude and our spirit. God took care of Nabal. I Samuel 25:39, "And when David heard that Nabal was dead, he said, Blessed be the LORD, that hath pleaded the cause of my reproach from the hand of Nabal, and hath kept his servant from evil: For the LORD hath returned the wickedness of Nabal upon his own head." Then we read on in I Samuel 26 and David goes into the camp of Saul at night and takes a spear and a cruse of water. The next morning David lets Saul know that he could have killed him, and David says in I Samuel 26:23, "The LORD render to every man his righteousness and his faithfulness: for the LORD delivered thee into my hand to day, but I would not stretch forth mine hand against the LORD's anointed." What a lesson Saul learned! I Corinthians 14:1, "Follow after charity, and desire spiritual gifts." Proverbs 10:29, "The way of the LORD is strength to the upright: but destruction shall be to the workers of iniquity."

Yesterday at a store a man lost his temper because of long line and his impatience. The lady worker said, "Sir, I am doing the best I can." My heart was so convicted at what I allow myself to get so frustrated at that I cannot fix or change. We cannot hold the wind back or stop a storm that is coming or the snow in winter, but I can have a spiritual, Christ honoring attitude. Psalm 107:25, "For he commandeth, and raiseth the stormy wind, which lifteth up the waves thereof." Our God is in control and we need to walk, work and serve in the strength and guidance of His Holy Spirit's leading. Stand for God and His principles in His Spirit and in a way that will glorify Him. As my mom used to say, "watch your attitude."

Frustration can ruin a perfectly wonderful day.

May 11

1 Samuel 27-28 Psalm 108 Proverbs 11 1 Corinthians 15

The Mud Hike

Good morning! Don't get stuck in the mud! There is something special about a mud hole to a boy. I can hear all moms say, "Stay out of the mud!" or "Stay away from that mud hole!" To a boy, a mud hole is an adventure, it is exploring, it is a magnet that somehow brings out the best in a man. The deeper the mud, the greater the challenge, the more joy in the victory. All boys need to learn the joy and experience of going through a mud hole. For many years I led what was called nothing more than the mud hike. I have no idea how many shoes were lost during the mud hike at a week of camp. I have been asked hundreds if not thousands of times, "Bro Dave, are we having the mud hike this week?" Now let us hold our thoughts about mud.

I Samuel 27:1, "And David said in his heart, I shall now perish one day by the hand of Saul: there is nothing better for me than that I should escape into the land of the Philistines." What did we just read? That is right, David is discouraged and depressed and he is going to the enemy to find safety. King Saul said in I Samuel 28:15, "I am sore distressed," so he went to a witch because he was so far from God, he could not hear God or get him to answer. Both of these men went to the mud hole and let it suck them in. I have told many a boy and man to keep moving in the mud hole or it will suck you in and when you stop you will sink. KEEP MOVING!!! When trials come, when things get tough in our walk with Christ, KEEP MOVING! Paul said in I Corinthians 15:58, "Therefore, my beloved brethren, be ye steadfast, unmovable, always abounding in the work of the Lord, forasmuch as ye know that your labour is not in vain in the Lord." Paul KEPT MOVING! Proverbs 11:29, "He that troubleth his own house shall inherit the wind: and the fool shall be servant to the wise of heart." This verse teaches us that if we allow trials to stop us, it is like life goes into the wind and that goes nowhere.

The reason many activities at camp are like a mud hole is because the older I get the more I see "quit" and "I can't" in the lives of young people who turn into adults and accomplish so little for Christ in their life. That mud hole can build determination, drive, push, I can make it, I am not quitting, etc. Psalm 108:1, "O God, my heart is fixed; I will sing, and give praise, even with my glory." You know, the girls used to beg for the mud hike because they saw how the boys enjoyed their time and how it did something to them. I am often asked, "Bro Dave, do you still have a mud hike?" I smile and say, come and see. KEEP GOING, my brother and sister in Christ. Let the mud of life teach you lessons on victory and not lessons of defeat. There are always going to be the mud holes, so KEEP GOING!

When trials come, when things get tough in our walk with Christ,
KEEP MOVING!

May 12

1 Samuel 29-31 Psalm 109:1-13 Proverbs 12 1 Cor. 16 & 2 Cor. 1

What Name Are You Known By?

Good morning! What name are you known by? I am not speaking about your name that your parents gave you, but the name that people know you by because of your spirit, your attitude, your actions, your reactions, etc. I Samuel 29:5, "Is not this David." Let us stop there a moment and ponder the name David. What comes to your mind? What age are you thinking about? What action that he did comes to your mind? What do you see him doing? Now let us go back and relook at I Samuel 29:5, "Is not this David, of whom they sang one to another in dances, saying, Saul slew his thousands, and David his ten thousands?" One man looks at David as a great warrior and in the very next verse we read a different spirit about the same man. I Samuel 29:6, "for I have not found evil in thee since the day of thy coming unto me unto this day." One man had a fear what David might be and what he might do, and the other man says that he has done nothing to be afraid of. What name are you known by?

Paul wrote in I Corinthians 16:14, "Let all your things be done with charity." In the very next verse we see the action of people, "they have addicted themselves to the ministry of the saints." We have found ourselves in a time of asking the question, who do we believe and who do we trust? That should never be said about a Christian who has been born again by the blood of Jesus Christ. Our lives should show forth to a saved and to a lost world a new life in Christ. II Corinthians 1:4, "that we may be able to comfort them which are in any trouble, by the comfort wherewith we ourselves are comforted of God." If we live in and by the Bible, we will walk and talk as a result of the Bible. We must not let the news media, the opinion of others, the circumstances of what we think we are seeing affect us in such a way that the Spirit of God is not seen in our lives, words and actions. Proverbs 12:14, "A man shall be satisfied with good by the fruit of his mouth: and the recompense of a man's hands shall be rendered unto him."

How we handle ourselves is what people will know us by. There were teachers I had in school who could have been very wonderful people, but their attitude and spirit gave me a fear of them and a fear that caused me to not be the student I could have been. Are you approachable by others? Can you be talked to and the person talking to you knows that you are listening? Do you have time for others, or is what you are doing the most important thing in the world? Does my spirit repel or draw others to Christ? Psalm 109:4, "For my love they are my adversaries: but I give myself unto prayer." We can tell if a person walks with God or not. What name are you known by?

How we handle ourselves is what people will know us by.

May 13

2 Samuel 1-2 Psalm 109:14-31 Proverbs 13 2 Corinthians 2-3

Our Life Lives On

Good morning! We have before us another day to make history. You might say, I am not living my life to make history. I am not either but as I worked all day yesterday with a granddaughter and grandson, I realized I am making history. Our lives will soon pass but what counts for Christ will last. I had those words on my mind as I read and wrote notes this morning. Many of the books in my library are biographies of men that I enjoy reading about. Their life on this earth is gone, but their life continues to live on through the pages of the books. Whether we realize it or not, our lives will live on through our children, grandchildren, friendships, etc.

Today I read these words, "how are the mighty fallen" in three different verses in II Samuel chapter one. Saul and Jonathan have now died, and word gets to David. He says in II Samuel 1:19, "how are the mighty fallen!," II Samuel 1:25, "How are the mighty fallen in the midst of battle!," II Samuel 1:27, "How are the mighty fallen." The great king Saul, who stood head and shoulders above his men, is gone. David's friend, Jonathan, who was like a brother to him, is gone, but their life lives on in David. I ask us this morning, how will our life live on? What will we be remembered by? I am not talking of worldly greatness. I am not speaking of trying to make a name for ourselves. What I am asking is, has your life been lived for Christ and His glory? II Corinthians 2:15, "For we are unto God a sweet savour of Christ, in them that are saved, and in them that perish." Proverbs 13:22, "A good man leaveth an inheritance to his children's children: and the wealth of the sinner is laid up for the just." What I am and how I live for Christ will last. Life is not about us, but about what Christ does through us. Psalm 109:27, "That they may know that this is thy hand; that thou, LORD, hast done it." The things of this world will pass, rot, turn to dust; but what has been done for Christ lives on and on.

I read a book about a missionary who took the gospel of Christ to a lost people, how a man by faith went to a town to win that town to Christ, the testimony of a man and his answers to prayer because of his faith in God and His Word. Yes, the mighty have fallen and they will continue to fall, but what we do for Christ will live on. May our life be filled with faithfulness to Christ and His work because it will last for generations and generations. Our small baby boys and girls will grow into men and women. What are we living before them now? Will they see us reading and living the Word of God? Will they see us on our knees and living a life as though we have been on our knees? Will they see a love for God in our lives? Will they see and learn from us the importance of faithfulness? Will they have the love of God in them because they saw that love in us? Yes, they will choose how to live their lives, but may we leave a Godly inheritance for them. Yes, the mighty have fallen, but the work of Christ and for Christ lives on. Be faithful.

Our lives will live on through our children, grandchildren, friendships.

May 14

2 Samuel 3-4 Psalm 110 Proverbs 14 2 Corinthians 4-5

Attitude Check

Good morning! I was working on a piece of equipment at the barn and the dogs were just lying there and watching as cars and trucks came in and out of the lane. Then I heard both of the dogs growl, their ears perked up, they stood up and took off barking. I looked and a neighbor was coming down the lane, and in his truck was his dog. How did they know? What has that dog done to them? Why is there anger in them toward what they think is there, but they do not know? I called them back, but it took two or three times for me to call. There is an anger that has no justification, but it is sure there and it possesses them. They have never been in a fight with that dog. It does not come and bother them. That dog has never eaten their food or drank their water, but there is something in the heart of my dogs that is wrong or seemingly wrong.

Such is the story between Joab and Abner, faithful men to their leaders and yet there was anger. David reached out to Abner, and we read in II Samuel 3:24, "Then Joab came to the king, and said, What hast thou done? Behold Abner came unto thee; why is it that thou hast sent him away, and he is quite gone?" Is there forgiveness in our hearts toward those who have wronged us? Can we love a wicked world as much as Christ does, who is willing to forgive all men their sins who confess and repent? Is there a love of Christ within us that allows us to look past the sins of others? II Corinthians 4:5, "For we preach not ourselves, but Christ Jesus the Lord; and ourselves your servants for Jesus sake." In this world full of hate, envy, and strife, we as the redeemed of God must get past personal feelings that will destroy what God wants to do in and through us. We will stand before God for our actions, attitudes, and feelings. II Corinthians 5:10, "For we must all appear before the judgment seat of Christ; that every one may receive the things done in his body, according to that he hath done, whether it be good or bad."

Do we need an attitude check? Is our heart burdened for the lost in this time we live in, or is there a built up feeling of attack, just like my dogs that want to attack a dog that has never done anything to them, but it is another dog? II Corinthians 5:17, "Therefore if any man be in Christ, he is a new creature: old things are passed away; behold, all things are become new." The attitude of the dogs is that some other dog invaded their area. We are to reach the world for Christ, the whole world. Proverbs 14:21, "He that despiseth his neighbor sinneth: but he that hath mercy on the poor, happy is he." I know the strength we need is not in us, but it is there for us. Psalm 110:3, "Thy people shall be willing in the day of thy power." As I called the dogs back, the neighbor's truck passed and the dogs looked at me as if to say, I was just protecting our area. The world must hear about Jesus. Let us reach beyond our area and be the disciples that we are to be. Remember, Jesus died for all men because He loved them.

We must get past personal feelings that will destroy what God wants to do in and through us.

May 15

2 Samuel 5-6 Psalm 111 Proverbs 15 2 Corinthians 6-7

The Right Path

Good morning! So often in life we come to a "Y" in the road. We ask ourselves which way should I go? Do I go to the left or do I go to the right? Have you ever taken the direction you thought was right and you said, this is not the right way? This road does not look familiar. Mrs. Smith and I love to take new roads when we just go for a drive, but the roads sometimes end up at someone's farm or at the river, or we end up where the road narrows to a simple path. If we, in our walk with God, could learn how to listen to His voice, follow the right path He has laid out, and be obedient to do what is right, the blessings would come. Sounds simple, but it is so difficult for most of us.

David has become the king and the Philistines show up for another battle. David asks the Lord what he should do. Now follow the path with me. "Go up," II Samuel 5:19; "Thou shalt not go up," II Samuel 5:23; "And David did so, as the LORD had commanded him, II Samuel 5:25; "And they set the ark of God upon a new cart," II Samuel 6:3; "Uzzah put forth his hand to the ark of God, and took hold of it," II Samuel 6:6; "God smote him there for his error," II Samuel 6:7. I read this and thought how we have drifted so far from what God wants. The church is full of Philistine ways of doing service to Christ. II Corinthians 6:14a, "Be not unequally yoked together with unbelievers." II Corinthians 6:17a, "Wherefore come out from among them, and be ye separate." Are we heading down the wrong path in life? Did we take the wrong turn, and we are going away from God instead of being more like He wants us to be? II Corinthians 7:1, "Having therefore these promises, dearly beloved, let us cleanse ourselves from all filthiness of the flesh and spirit, perfecting holiness in the fear of God."

Just because my flesh wants to do it does not make it right in God's eyes. Just because everybody is doing it does not make it right in God's eyes. Proverbs 15:9, "The way of the wicked is an abomination unto the LORD: but he loveth him that followeth after righteousness." Psalm 111:10, "The fear of the LORD is the beginning of wisdom: a good understanding have all they that do his commandments: his praise endureth for ever." Every day and many times a day we stand at a "Y" in our walk with God. Take the right path and be blessed by God.

If we follow the right path and are obedient to do what is right, the blessings will come.

May 16

2 Samuel 7-8 Psalm 112 Proverbs 16 2 Corinthians 8-9

Go Do It

Good morning! Well, the mailbox has been full of graduation announcements and wedding invitations. With great excitement and yet great disappointment, graduation time has arrived. The year 2020 will be remembered as a year of rollercoaster emotions. High school students have waited twelve years and college students have worked, studied, completed exams, and fulfilled all the requirements, only to not have a graduation exercise in most places of this country of ours. The year 2020 is the year of our granddaughter's college graduation and I have watched her work very hard to get the best grades she could, striving for those A's and yet no graduation. To parents, grandparents, students, friends, and relatives, do not be disappointed. Look to what is in your heart to do and do it. That is what truly matters.

David is now king in II Samuel 7:3, and he has spoken his heart to the prophet Nathan and Nathan makes this statement, "And Nathan said to the king, Go, do all that is in thine heart; for the LORD is with thee." Every student made it to graduation because of hard work and a desire to make it. David desired to build a house for the ark and the presence of the Lord. I love the words of Nathan, "Go do all that is in thine heart; for the LORD is with thee." That statement is for all of us. What are we doing for the Lord? The apostle Paul challenged the rich worldly churches at Corinth to look at the churches of Macedonia in II Corinthians 8:2, "How that in a great trial of affliction the abundance of their joy and their deep poverty abounded unto the riches of their liberality." We need to quit looking at the confusion in the world and "Go, do all that is in thine heart." Paul wrote on in II Corinthians 8:3, "For to their power, I bear record, yea, and beyond their power they were willing of themselves." We need to get our wanters to become the doers, and get a work done for God. II Corinthians 8:11, "Now therefore perform the doing of it; that as there was a readiness to will, so there may be a performance also out of that which ye have."

We as adults need to be the encouragers of this generation to reach out and do what is in their heart for the Lord. Set the example, my brother and sister, and get busy being a doer and not just a sitter. Proverbs 16:3, "Commit thy works unto the LORD, and thy thoughts shall be established." Proverbs 16:9, "A man's heart deviseth his way: but the LORD directeth his steps." The world is getting darker by the day; confusion, frustration, lack of desire, lack of direction. I believe there is still vision in the hearts of God's people and we need to "Go, do all that is in thine heart." If you need to get things right with God, then go do it. I want to keep burning for the Lord, not doing nothing. Psalm 112:4 "Unto the upright there ariseth light in the darkness." There is time and we need to "Go, do all that is in thine heart; for the LORD is with thee." Go do it today!

Set the example and get busy being a doer and not just a sitter.

May 17

2 Samuel 9-10 Psalm 113 Proverbs 17 2 Corinthians 10

Love the Unlovely

Good morning! Do you remember the quote that we learned when we were little, or we should have learned it? "Do unto others, as you would have them do unto you." Or the quote, "When you show kindness to others, that kindness will someday be returned to you." I can hear my mom say, "share and share alike," and then your toy gets broken. They are good quotes and great examples of what Christians should do and be for others.

In our readings today we see David reaching out to be kind to king Saul's family and he hears about Jonathan's son, Mephibosheth. II Samuel 9:1, "And David said, Is there yet any that is left of the house of Saul, that I may shew him kindness for Jonathan's sake?" In II Samuel 9 and 10 we see the word "kindness" used four times. This is a perfect picture of God's salvation by grace. The kindness was accepted by Mephibosheth but then we read on and find that King Ammon dies and David reaches out to show kindness to his son Hanun, and David's servants are humiliated and a battle begins. What can we learn and how can we apply this to our lives? II Corinthians 10:3, "For though we walk in the flesh, we do not war after the flesh." II Corinthians 10:4, "For the weapons of our warfare are not carnal, but mighty through God to the pulling down of strongholds." Kindness should always come from the heart and never expect anything in return. Christ gives us the perfect example of always reaching out. The devil would love us to not show the love of Christ to others. We have to realize our lives on the earth are to be lived for Christ, and that is to be reaching out to others. We must not let the devil tell us any reason not to reach out to those hurting and in need, and especially reaching out with the love of Christ's salvation to all mankind. II Corinthians 10:5, "Casting down imaginations, and every high thing that exalteth itself against the knowledge of God, and bringing into captivity every thought to the obedience of Christ." Do not believe the lie of the devil. Proverbs 17:4, "A wicked doer giveth heed to false lips; and a liar giveth ear to a naughty tongue."

God blessed David for his kindness to others and He will bless us even in those times we are not treated kindly, or our kindness is taken in the wrong way. The example is set by Christ. Psalm 113:7, He raiseth up the poor out of the dust, and lifteth the needy out of the dunghill." Psalm 113:8, "That he may set him with princes, even with the princes of his people." David loved Saul even though he treated him terribly. David's love for Jonathan and his family, and especially his son Mephibosheth, is a great example for us to love the unlovely for Christ's sake. Show kindness today.

Kindness should always come from the heart
and never expect anything in return.

May 18

2 Samuel 11-12 Psalm 114 Proverbs 18 2 Corinthians 11

Fight On

Good morning! Our Old Testament reading today is from II Samuel 11 and 12 and as I turned there, I stopped and just sat and thought, how many regrets of life do we carry? "I wish I had, I wish I had not, if I only would have, if I only had not, if I had only known, if I had only listened, if I had not let my flesh. . ." We cannot live in regret. Is your heart heavy today? Why do you choose to live in regret when you can live in victory? I have read and preached from II Samuel 11 and 12 many times, and each time I read this passage, my heart breaks because of how sin destroys. Let us decide to go beyond this morning and look at II Samuel 12:13, "The LORD also hath put away thy sin; thou shalt not die." Learn from your mistakes, rejoice in the forgiveness of God, be thankful God loves us so much the He chastises us or, can I say, spanks us when we as His children do wrong.

Paul wrote in II Corinthians 11:3, "But I fear, lest by any means, as the serpent beguiled Eve through his subtilty, so your minds should be corrupted from the simplicity that is in Christ." Picture a dog that you have to scold. What does it do? Puts its tail between its legs, comes creeping back to the master who loves it, feeds it and gives it treats and fresh cool water. That dog loves the affection and approval of the master. Admit it, so do we. We must face sin, face defeat, face discouragement, face disappointment and come back to our Master, our Lord, our Saviour, our Redeemer. Psalm 114:7, "Tremble, thou earth, at the presence of the Lord, at the presence of the God of Jacob." Do what is right and pleasing to the Lord. II Samuel 12:13, "The LORD also hath put away thy sin; thou shalt not die." We are still alive and breathing because God has a plan for our lives.

Yes, we might have scars and regrets, but we still have life, and we can live in victory. You might be knocked down, but you are not knocked out, so get up. You might be tired and have lost a lot of your fight. Take a breath and fight on. As has been said before, "Grab your bootstraps and pull them up." Proverbs 18:14, "The spirit of a man will sustain his infirmity; but a wounded spirit who can bear?" If you feel you are at the end of the rope, tie another knot in it and just hang on. Keep on, my brother and sister, keep on. The trump of God has not sounded yet. This is another day. Live in victory today.

We are still alive and breathing because God has a plan for our lives.

May 19

2 Samuel 13-14 Psalm 115 Proverbs 19 2 Corinthians 12-13

Grow in Grace

Good morning! Last evening Mrs. Smith and I were relaxing and sitting by a campfire, and as we sat there it began to sprinkle. Not a heavy sprinkle, just enough that we thought we should probably go in for the night. I put away the chairs and said, "It has stopped raining," and I set the chairs back out. We no sooner sat down and the rain came. For a brief moment, I did not like the rain, then my heart was convicted, and I thought about rivers, lakes, streams, water wells, fresh cool water. How foolish it is to hate something that you need or love. There is no better sleep than in a light rain, and yet the same rain can cause a flood and bring great destruction.

As we read in II Samuel 13:15, "so that the hatred wherewith he hated her was greater than the love wherewith he had loved her." Amnon's lust grew greater than his love for his sister and brought destruction to his life, shame to her life, and hatred in his brothers. Our desire for things or importance must never be greater than being in the will of God. Position must never get stronger than a heart to serve. Paul wrote in II Corinthians 12:10b, "for when I am weak, then am I strong." Paul went on to say in II Corinthians 12:15, "And I will very gladly spend and be spent for you; though the more abundantly I love you, the less I be loved." The lust overcame the love. A gentle sprinkle can turn into a great flood. I remember being told, "David, are you getting too big for your pants?" Mom and dad were not talking about the pants being too tight to wear, but my attitude was getting bad. Proverbs 19:11, "The discretion of a man deferreth his anger; and it is his glory to pass over a transgression."

Do not let the same rain that brings a sprinkle turn into a rainstorm that brings a flood. Give life's situations to God and trust in Him. Have patience and grow in God's grace. Tamar tried to stop Amnon, and his flesh brought about hatred by Absalom which brought death and the splintering of family. Psalm 115:11, "Ye that fear the LORD, trust in the LORD: he is their help and their shield." You cannot stop a gentle sprinkle, so why fuss over the rain? Grow in God's grace.

Give life's situations to God and trust in Him.

May 20

2 Samuel 15-16 Psalm 116 Proverbs 20 Galatians 1-2

Stay on Course

Good morning! May I say this morning and every morning, our God is there. Psalm 116:1, "I love the LORD, because he hath heard my voice and my supplications." Psalm 116:2, "Because he hath inclined his ear unto me, therefore will I call upon him as long as I live." As we read in II Samuel 15-16, David's very own son Absalom has started a conspiracy. To type that word in the times we are in brings a sick feeling in the pit of my stomach. Yes, Absalom started a conspiracy toward his own father. David takes off, but where he goes is my focus for today. II Samuel 15:30, "And David went up by the ascent of mount Olivet, and wept as he went up, and had his head covered, and he went barefoot: and all the people that was with him covered every man his head, and they went up, weeping as they went up."

Now let us see the right picture. This is not a picture of weakness but a humble heart that is broken over sin, showing reverence toward a holy God. The bare feet brought to my attention God telling Moses to take off his shoes. David is desiring to draw close to God. This passage is a perfect picture of how our Saviour was broken, humbled for our sins as He provides salvation for all men, and how His heart aches as man rejects the sweet perfect gift of God. Galatians 2:20, "I am crucified with Christ: nevertheless I live; yet not I, but Christ liveth in me: and the life which I now live in the flesh I live by the faith of the Son of God, who loved me and gave himself for me." Absalom thought he had it going in the right direction. This world thinks it is in control and the devil thinks he is going to win. Proverbs 20:17, "Bread of deceit is sweet to a man; but afterwards his mouth shall be filled with gravel." Absalom will soon meet his destruction and David will be in the place God has for him. Stay faithful, my friend. Stay on course. Stay in the battle. Stay humble before God. Proverbs 20:27, "The spirit of man is the candle of the LORD, searching all the inward parts of the belly."

We were sitting in our camper last night and we heard some children yelling, so I looked out and a bear walked through our campsite. That bear does not go to a store to find his food, he does not have a bank account, he does not have to do maintenance on any vehicle. He is not being possessed by politics. As a matter of fact, that bear just keeps on looking until he finds food, water, and all he needs in life. As I watched him walk along the creek and wander on in the darkness, I thought if only we, as man created by God, could just keep on as the old bear and be faithful to be what we are supposed to be. You can sure learn from an old bear walking through your campsite. Have a blessed day serving the LORD.

Stay faithful, my friend. Stay on course. Stay in the battle.
Stay humble before God.

May 21

2 Samuel 17-18 Psalm 117 Proverbs 21 Galatians 3-4

God Knows

Good morning! I stood by a mountain creek and watched the water flow so very fast over the different sizes of rocks, and as I looked, I thought about how life passes by us all and some are seen, and some are not. By "seen," I mean we only see the rocks that the water is flowing over; we do not see the rocks underneath that are really holding the ground where the creek flows. Those rocks not seen could be the biggest because they hold the direction that the creek or river flows.

Such is a phrase that caught my eye in the battle between Absalom and David's men. II Samuel 18:10, "And a certain man saw it, and told Joab, and said, Behold, I saw Absalom hanged in an oak." II Samuel 18:11, Joab said to this "certain man," "why didst thou not smite him there to the ground? And I would have given thee ten shekels of silver, and a girdle." The "certain man" said in II Samuel 18:12, "yet would I not put forth mine hand against the king's son: for in our hearing the king charged thee and Abishai and Ittai, saying, Beware that none touch the young man Absalom." God sees all and we must remember what God sees that no one else sees is usually the most important thing to see. II Samuel 18:13, "there is no matter hid from the king." Absalom is killed, word gets to the king, and the king goes into grief. Proverbs 21:2, Every way of man is right in his own eyes: but the LORD pondereth the hearts." Proverbs 21:3, "To do justice and judgment is more acceptable to the LORD than sacrifice." Oh, that we would be more interested in pleasing the Lord than our flesh. We are God's sons, and we should live as sons of God. Galatians 4:6, "And because ye are sons, God hath sent forth the Spirit of his Son into your hearts, crying, Abba, Father."

A "certain man" did right, and we will never know his name, but God does. Most of what we do in life, no one will ever know, but God does. The burdens we carry, the heartache we feel, is little known by others, but God knows. The rocks that hold the direction of the creeks, streams, and rivers are little seen but God knows which ones they are. As we close our thoughts for this morning, may we dwell on the words of Psalm 117:2, "the truth of the LORD endureth for ever." Remember, God knows, God hears, God sees, and God cares.

The burdens we carry, the heartache we feel,
is little known by others, but God knows.

May 22

2 Samuel 19-20 Psalm 118:1-14 Proverbs 22 Galatians 5-6

A Daily Walk with God

Good morning! Lessons learned the hard way seem to be the best learned lessons. II Samuel 19:2, "And the victory that day was turned into mourning." There are times in life for all of us that we look back over our shoulders and wish we could do something over again, so that those words we said, the hurt we caused, the heart that was broken, the mistake we made, would have never happened. David is mourning the loss of his son Absalom and he has shut the people out of his life that brought the victory of battle to him. II Samuel 19:5, "Thou hast shamed this day the faces of all thy servants, which this day have saved thy life, and the lives of thy sons and of thy daughters, and the lives of thy wives, and the lives of thy concubines." II Samuel 19:6, "In that thou lovest thine enemies, and hatest thy friends." Those two words, "In that," press a point to me.

Today, Mrs. Smith and I have been married 49 years. There are mistakes that I have made that I cannot correct, but I cannot look back or it will destroy the future. I sat at a meal last night with some of my grandchildren and our daughter and son-in-law. We talked and enjoyed the fellowship and yet as we pulled away, I thought about how fast life is going, and I only have one life to live. We must each day walk in the Spirit. Galatians 5:16, "This I say then, walk in the Spirit, and ye shall not fulfil the lust of the flesh." Galatians 5:25, "If we live in the Spirit, let us also walk in the Spirit." Let the words, "I am sorry, will you forgive me?" be ready at all times. Let the words, "I should have not said that, or I should not have done that, would you forgive me?" be ready at all times. Proverbs 22:21a, "That I might make thee know the certainty of the words of truth." Our daily walk with God is so vitally important. We can never return to correct mistakes, but we can walk in God's wisdom in the future. God is for us. Psalm 118:6, "The LORD is on my side; I will not fear: what can man do unto me?" As David mourned the loss of his son, he shut out those that loved him, served him, and were willing to give their lives for him.

Do not live to self and miss the real important things of life. Do not live with regrets of not doing something you should have done. Do it now. Forget it if you have been offended, just do not be the offense. Press on for the days and years ahead. Be the husband, wife, friend, brother, or sister that you should be. Get the chip off your shoulder, forgive, and forget. I cannot change one thing yesterday, but I sure can walk with God today, tomorrow and the rest of my life. When I have my eyes on myself, I cannot see the love, kindness, and sacrifice of others toward me. It is Christ in us that the world needs to see. He saved us to walk in newness of life for Him and His glory. Have a blessed day.

We can never return to correct mistakes,
but we can walk in God's wisdom in the future.

May 23

2 Samuel 21-22 Psalm 118:15-29 Proverbs 23 Ephesians 1-2

The Light of Christ

Good morning! There is a great hunger in my heart to see people walk in the light of the Lord and not in darkness. The ways of this world do not bring us the light that is in Christ. For people to be saved and still walk in darkness is not of God. My heart breaks as I see, talk, and try to be an encouragement to Christians who still walk in darkness under the control of sin. They have trusted Christ, asked forgiveness of sin, and still walk in darkness. We do not have to walk in darkness. We have God's Word, we can take our burdens to Him in prayer, we can listen to great preaching and read tremendous books. We do not have to walk and live in darkness. II Samuel 22:29, "For thou art my lamp, O LORD: and the LORD will lighten my darkness." A walk with Christ is not walking a path in darkness. Ephesians 2:10, "For we are his workmanship, created in Christ Jesus unto good works, which God hath before ordained that we should walk in them."

I have been in many caves and walked the narrow paths and gone into the great openings, heard the water deep underground, felt the coolness of the cave, seen the beautiful formations, and especially been standing there when they said, "Do not move, we are going to turn off all the lights." Total dark, a deep blackness in which you cannot even see the hand in front of you if you hold your hand right next to your face. If they did not turn the lights back on, we would probably not find our way out of the depth of the cave. We must see the importance of God's Word lighting our path of life and guiding us. Proverbs 23:19, "Hear thou, my son, and be wise, and guide thine heart in the way." Psalm 118:27a, "God is the LORD, which hath shewed us light." Spend time with God and His Word each day and He and His Word will guide you through a darkened world.

Mrs. Smith and I went to the Mark Twain cave in Hannibal, Missouri for part of our honeymoon when we were married. We walked the paths and heard the stories of people being lost in the dark caves. We enjoyed that cave and many others. Even though you enjoy the journey through the caves and hearing the stories of all that was found and discovered, there is nothing more pleasing to the eye than when you see the glimmer of the outside light, knowing that you have made it through the darkness of the cave. Walk in the light of Christ and His Word today. "For thou art my lamp, O LORD: and the LORD will lighten my darkness." II Samuel 22:29. Have a blessed day.

We must see the importance of God's Word
lighting our path of life and guiding us.

May 24

2 Samuel 23-24 Psalm 119:1-16 Proverbs 24 Ephesians 3-4

A Controlled Spirit

Good morning! As I read this morning, my heart was immediately spoken to and I had to ask myself a question that I ask often. We get so busy with our schedule, our goals, our tasks, our responsibilities, our everything's that I think we need to learn to stop, regroup and face something about ourselves daily, and many times a day. What kind of example for the cause of Christ are we setting in our homes, our marriages, our relationships, at work, in our ministries, with those we love and even with those that we do not know but observe our actions at the store, at work, as we go about our day?

King David was a great leader, a man after God's own heart, and yet he was not perfect, and I notice in the life of David that he did a lot of self-evaluation. II Samuel 23:3, "The God of Israel said, the Rock of Israel spake to me, He that ruleth over men must be just, ruling in the fear of God." David was evaluating his leadership. II Samuel 23:4, "And he shall be as the light of the morning, when the sun riseth, even a morning without clouds; as the tender grass springing out of the earth by clear shining after rain." The word "he" starting out the verse is speaking of David himself. I know we are not all morning people, and some take a little time to wake up, but there is no excuse for us not to try to set a good spirit, not only in the morning but throughout the day. Problems of life will always be there. Flat tires, dead batteries in our vehicles, neighbors' dogs digging in the flower beds, the neighbor's trash spilling and blowing all over your yard, a shoe lace breaking, a zipper not working, etc. Do we let things that happen control our spirit, or do we let our walk with the Lord control our spirit? Ephesians 4:1, "I therefore, the prisoner of the Lord, beseech you that ye walk worthy of the vocation wherewith ye are called." Ephesians 4:3, "Endeavouring to keep the unity of the Spirit in the bond of peace."

Sitting at the grocery store with my wife, a car pulled up next to us. You could tell they were having an attitude problem and a teen girl jumped out of the back seat of the car and with her door hit our car so hard that our car shook. My wife only said one word to me as I got out, "HONEY!" I walked around and the adults in the front seat of the car looked at me and I said, "She hit our car so hard that it shook our car." The woman behind the wheel said, "I don't think she hit your car." Scripture flowed through my mind and a spirit flowed in my veins that I am not proud of. I said no more and looked at where the door hit our car and got back in. I am embarrassed to say, but I did not give them a gospel tract. We just pulled away and went on down the road. The Lord has not left me alone about that situation. Ephesians 4:24, "And that ye put on the new man, which after God is created in righteousness and true holiness." Oh, the Scripture that we have this morning to help us have the right spirit in times of frustrating things that could ruin our testimonies. Proverbs 24:13, "My son, eat thou honey, because it is good; and the honeycomb, which is sweet to thy taste." Psalm 119:2, "Blessed are they that keep his testimonies, and that seek him with the whole heart." We must walk continually with the Lord and our walk must be enforced with His Word. Have a blessed day and watch where you park at the store. It could test your testimony.

Do we let things that happen control our spirit,
or do we let our walk with the Lord control our spirit?

May 25

1 Kings 1-2 Psalm 119:17-32 Proverbs 25 Ephesians 5

A Strong Corner Post

Good morning! I would like you to take a short walk with me this morning and I want you to see an old post in the ground. This post has different chunks of old wire in it because the fence has had to be repaired many times. The wire rusted or broke somehow, but the corner post is still strong and in its place.

King David is old, about to die, has fought well and Adonijah wants to be king, but from the onset Solomon was to be king. Listen to David's words in I Kings 1:30, "Even as I sware unto thee by the LORD God of Israel, saying, Assuredly Solomon thy son shall reign after me, and he shall sit upon my throne in my stead; even so will I certainly do this day." Solomon is anointed king, and he has some clean-up work to do, and we read in I Kings 2:24a, "Now therefore, as the LORD liveth, which hath established me, and set me on the throne of David my father." Look at the words, "established me" and "set me." A corner post is the correct starting point. It is a boundary mark, a definite point that is not to be moved or changed. Paul wrote in Ephesians 5:15, "See then that ye walk circumspectly, not as fools, but as wise." Paul said walk cautiously, watchfully in every way. We must have corner posts of Biblical principles set in our life from the Word of God, and never allow them to be moved or changed. Many change and in Proverbs 25:19 we read, "Confidence in an unfaithful man in time of trouble is like a broken tooth, and a foot out of joint." We need to be established in doctrine, in practice and in principle. The devil is going to do everything he can to get us to move established Biblical principles and we must not move them from the truth that they were established in. Live by the truth of the Word of God that was established before the foundations of this earth. Psalm 119:30, "I have chosen the way of truth: thy judgments have I laid before me." Psalm 119:31a, "I have stuck unto thy testimonies."

Dig your corner post deep in the ground, pack the dirt hard around it and do not let it ever get moved. The old corner post is weathered but still standing strong. Thank the Lord His Word has not and will not ever change. Let us build some fence (lives), and may they stand true and strong, attached to the unmovable corner post (Christ Jesus and His Word).

We must have corner posts of Biblical principles set in our life from the Word of God.

May 26

1 Kings 3-4 Psalm 119:33-48 Proverbs 26 Eph. 6 - Philippians 1

See You in Church

Good morning! It has been often said, "You did not know what you had until you lost it." It is said in several different ways, but we can get the point. The children grow up and get married and leave home. You go to their bedroom and look around. No one is there but you hear their voices, see them playing, watch them grow up and then, like flipping a light switch, they are gone.

My brother and sister, we must never lose the joy and purpose of going to church. As I read in I Kings this morning and observed what the people and king Solomon did, my heart was challenged to share some words that spoke to me. I Kings 3:2, "Only the people sacrificed in high places, because there was no house built unto the name of the LORD, until those days." We realize that Jesus had not yet been the sacrifice for our sins, but we do see the gathering together to a "high place," a set aside place, a specific place, an important place, a gathering together to worship the LORD. I Kings 3:4, "And the king went to Gibeon to sacrifice there; for that was the great high place: a thousand burnt-offerings did Solomon offer upon the altar." Did you see the words "great high place?" King Solomon set the example for having a place to worship the LORD. I Kings 3:15a, "And he came to Jerusalem, and stood before the ark of the covenant of the LORD." Look at those words, "came to." A specific place, an important place, a specified place, a set apart place. That is not our living room, our car, or any other place. We must all make sure we see the importance of being in church together and worshipping the Lord. Philippians 1:1, "to all the saints in Christ Jesus which are at Philippi, with the bishops and deacons." This is a prison epistle written to a specific church that is organized, meeting together in a specific place with bishops and deacons who are serving. We must always realize that church and meeting together as a body of believers is important, and it is all through the Scriptures. Proverbs 26:26, "Whose hatred is covered by deceit, his wickedness shall be shewed before the whole congregation." The word "congregation" is again showing us a group of believers together.

Do not ever take church for granted. Could there come a day that we might be told we can never meet together? There are places like that in this world and we have just about seen it happen here in America. What if we did not have the ability to have electronic communication and media? Psalm 119:38, "Stablish thy word unto thy servant, who is devoted to thy fear." Church is important for all of us. It is established by the Lord. It is a constitutional right here in America, and we just about lost it. It is shown throughout the Word of God. Several books in the New Testament were written to specific churches. The book of Revelation talks of the seven churches. Please do not lose what you might not want to lose when you need it the most. Thank the Lord for a place to meet as the Church, the called-out assembly. See you in church.

We must never lose the joy and purpose of going to church.

May 27

1 Kings 5-6 Psalm 119:49-64 Proverbs 27 Philippians 2-3

More Than Ourselves

Good morning! I am so very thankful for the brothers and sisters that I have in Christ. Across this land and around the world there are people that we all know who are serving the Lord. Missionaries in foreign lands, evangelists that travel this country and around the world, telling others about Christ. I thank the Lord for the many avenues that we have to get the gospel to a lost world. Let us stop this morning and go on a walk to a small pond where the water is so still that it looks like glass. Step with me to the edge of the pond and look down. What do you see? I am not going to push you in the water. Proverbs 27:19, "As in water face answereth to face, so the heart of man to man." As we look into the pond, we see ourselves, but life is just not all about us. The Christian's life is about reaching others with the Gospel.

Psalm 119:59, "I thought on my ways, and turned my feet unto thy testimonies." We need Christ, and we need to not just see ourselves, but see His purpose and plan for us. Solomon focused on his purpose and God promised if Solomon walked with Him and did what was right in God's eyes, he would do God's purpose. I Kings 5:5a, "And, behold, I purpose to build an house unto the name of the LORD my God." God said to Solomon in I Kings 5:12, "if thou wilt walk in my statutes, and execute my judgments, and keep all my commandments to walk in them; then will I perform my word with thee." The apostle Paul wrote, "Brethren, I count not myself to have apprehended: but this one thing I do, forgetting those things which are behind, and reaching forth unto those things which are before." (Philippians 3:13).

When we look into the water and see our reflection, we should see what Christ is doing in and through us, and not just see a reflection of ourselves. Paul wrote in Philippians 3:14, "I press toward the mark for the prize of the high calling of God in Christ Jesus." Facing myself should cause me to see the need I have for Christ and draw me closer to Him to be more like Him and to be able to do His work through me. When the breeze blows, the water will ripple and we cannot see the reflection of ourselves very well. Do not let the things of this world and selfishness distract you from God's purpose for your life. Something to think about today.

We need to not just see ourselves, but see His purpose and plan for us.

May 28

1 Kings 7-8 Psalm 119:65-80 Proverbs 28 Phil. 4-Colossians 1

The Unknown Encourager

Good morning! Take a moment and think of someone who was a spiritual influence on you, an encourager, a strong person who was there for you; and yet this person is little known to people. You could mention their name and very few people would know them, but they were a great help to you. I Kings 7:13, "And king Solomon sent and fetched Hiram out of Tyre." We are not going to look at the king but at who had an influence in his life. There is always someone behind someone. Someone had an influence in your life who taught you, encouraged you, believed in you and helped you. Do not forget them but be challenged by what they did for you so that you can be that person in other's lives.

I Kings 7:14, "He was a widow's son of the tribe of Naphtali, and his father was a man of Tyre, a worker in brass: and he was filled with wisdom, and understanding, and cunning to work all works in brass. And he came to king Solomon, and wrought all his work." Wow! Go back and reread the verse and see who really did all the work of plaiting for Solomon. There are people in our lives who have encouraged us to stay faithful and keep going and most of the time they will remain unknown. Philippians 4:3b, "with other my fellowlabourers, whose names are in the book of life." Paul said there are other faithful labourers who are known to God but not known to others. Colossians 1:2a, "To the saints and faithful brethren in Christ which are at Colosse." Did you see it, "faithful brethren?" They were unknown, but faithful to God and His work. Colossians 1:4, "Since we heard of your faith in Christ Jesus, and of the love which ye have to all the saints." God wants to use all of us and for most of us, it will never be known how God uses us except to God and the people we try to be a blessing to. Be faithful! Proverbs 28:20, "A faithful man shall abound with blessings."

Let God use you in unknown places by doing unknown things and enjoy the blessings of God and forget about the recognition of men.

Recognition of men has destroyed many. Psalm 119:73, "Thy hands have made me and fashioned me: give me understanding, that I may learn thy commandments." God is looking for workers that He can use and bless. Let us focus on being what God would have us to be in the place that God would have us, doing what God has us to do. It is time we go to the "Tomb of the Unknown Soldier," known but unknown, and yet gave all. Someday, we will meet in Heaven some of the greatest unknown servants of God and yet they are known by God. Some things to consider.

Let God use you in unknown places by doing unknown things and enjoy the blessings of God.

May 29

1 Kings 9-10 Psalm 119:81-96 Proverbs 29 Colossians 2-3

Keep the Brush Cut

Good morning! The simplicity of things around us each day can teach us so very much. As I was mowing on the tractor, I looked over at the valley next to where I was mowing. I remembered when that area was full of brush of all kinds, weeds, small trees that would never really grow to be very much. Each year, for the last fifteen years, I have mowed that area with a brush mower. I sat upon the tractor and noticed how the brush and worthless plants and bushes are almost gone and the area has beautiful grasses growing in it. That is just like our lives. When we keep cutting the junk out, the good grows stronger.

King Solomon enjoyed God's blessings, but we read the caution of God in I Kings 9:6, "But if ye shall at all turn from following me, ye or your children, and will not keep my commandments and my statutes which I have set before you, but go and serve other gods, and worship them." I Kings 9:7, "Then will I cut off Israel out of the land which I have given them." The area that I was looking at while out on the tractor is where we now are able to cut and bale hay. God will always send blessings to our lives when we do right in His eyes. Colossians 2:6-

7, "As ye have therefore received Christ Jesus the Lord, so walk ye in him. Rooted and built up in him, and stablished in the faith, as ye have been taught, abounding therein with thanksgiving." When I first started trying to clear the area, there was not very much grass to bale, but as I have kept mowing down the bad, the good grass has grown stronger and stronger. Colossians 3:16, "Let the word of Christ dwell in you richly in all wisdom, teaching and admonishing one another in psalms and hymns and spiritual songs, singing with grace in your hearts to the Lord." As we grow in the Lord, we must be very careful not to let the pride destroy us. Proverbs 29:23a, "A man's pride shall bring him low."

If I do not keep cutting that area the brush will come back. We must keep dealing with sin in our lives to have a victorious Christian life. Psalm 119:104, "Through thy precepts I get understanding: therefore I hate every false way." I am so thankful that we will be able to cut, rake and bale hay in the next few days. We will enjoy our walk with God when we work to keep the sin out. It takes work to keep the brush cleared out, and it takes work to keep sin cleaned out. The results are a beautiful victorious life.

God will always send blessings to our lives when we do right in His eyes.

May 30

1 Kings 11-12 Psalm 119:97-112 Proverbs 30 Col. 4-1 Thess. 1

Godly Guidelines

Good morning! As we daily read the Word of God, we read about how God gave specific rules to follow. His blessing was there for obedience and His judgment was there for disobedience. His love, grace and mercy are there daily for us. To kneel in prayer and to ask God to reveal sin that we can confess and for Him to forgive us, is beyond human understanding, but I am so thankful He does forgive and forget.

I Kings 11:1a, "But king Solomon loved many strange women." My heart breaks each time I read this. I Kings 11:2b, "Ye shall not go in to them, neither shall they come in unto you: for surely they will turn away your heart after their gods," and they did. I Kings 11:6, "And Solomon did evil in the sight of the LORD, and went not fully after the LORD, as did David his father." In the very next chapter, we read how the counsel of the older men was forsaken. In I Kings 12:13, Rehoboam "forsook the old men's counsel." In everything in life and in every area of life we must live by God's principles. The water company has guidelines for purity of water, the gas company, the doctor, the hospital, the auto manufacture, the clothing manufacture, the state we each live in has guidelines and principles, but why do we as born again believers not live by principles of God? Colossians 4:17, "Take heed to the ministry which thou hast received in the Lord, that thou fulfil it."

In our ministries for the Lord, we must live by guidelines and principles given us by God. Have we forgotten what we were saved from and how sin was destroying our lives? I Thessalonians 1:9b "how ye turned to God from idols to serve the living and true God." Stay in God's Word, hide it in your heart, live God's principles in every area of your life. Proverbs 30:5, "Every word of God is pure: he is a shield unto them that put their trust in him." Psalm 119:105, "Thy word is a lamp unto my feet, and a light unto my path." Psalm 119:112, "I have inclined mine heart to perform thy statutes alway, even unto the end." Thank the Lord that we have His Word to guide us in every area of our lives and in every decision that we make. Have a blessed day in the LORD.

In our ministries for the Lord, we must live by
guidelines and principles given us by God.

May 31

1 Kings 13-14 Psalm 119:113-128 Proverbs 31 1 Thess. 2-3

Lessons From a Killdeer

Good morning! We live in a day and time that the drawing nigh of the Lord's return is ever so close. We ask ourselves often, what or who do we believe? Is that true what I heard? Did they tell the whole truth? Such was our reading in I Kings 13:18b, "But he lied unto him." An old prophet came to a man of God and told him a lie and the man of God died because of disobedience. I Kings 12:26, "It is the man of God, who was disobedient unto the word of the LORD." The devil loves nothing more than when he can lead us away from the Lord. I love the words of the apostle Paul in I Thessalonians 2:13, "For this cause also thank we God without ceasing, because, when ye received the word of God which ye heard of us, ye received it not as the word of men, but as it is in truth, the Word of God, which effectually worketh also in you that believe."

I came out of the barn with some tools and there was a bird called a killdeer. I did a short study on them and found out they are also called the Chattering Plover or the Noisy Plover. When anything comes near to their young, they act like they have a broken wing and try to lead the predator away from the nest. This has happened to me often. I stopped as I came out of the barn and thought, that killdeer is faking just like the devil, and trying to lead me another direction. Proverbs 31:3, "Give not thy strength unto women, nor thy ways to that which destroyeth kings." Do you know that a killdeer will also fluff itself up, put its tail over its head and run directly toward the oncoming person or animal? The devil wants to put every fear in us he can. Our attitude toward the devil and his ways should be what we read in Psalm 119:115, "Depart from me, ye evildoers: for I will keep the commandments of my God." When temptation comes, cry out as the Psalmist did in Psalm 119:117, "Hold thou me up, and I shall be safe: and I will have respect unto thy statutes continually."

I stood still and did not move, and three little killdeer babies came running by. I can also look at the killdeer bird as protecting her young, as God desires for us to learn His Word and stay so close to Him in all His ways. Psalm 119:124-125, "Deal with thy servant according unto thy mercy, and teach me thy statutes. I am thy servant; give me understanding, that I may know thy testimonies." God sends so much of His creation into our lives to teach us His ways. Have a blessed day.

God desires for us to learn His Word and stay close to Him in all His ways.

June 1

1 Kings 15-16 Psalm 119:129-144 Proverbs 1 1 Thess. 4-5

Watch Dogs or Wild Dogs?

Good morning! I am awakened again from the bark of the dogs. I get up, get the flashlight, open the door, step out into the darkness and the dogs come running. Why the barking? Why again tonight? In the distance is the barking, the howling of the coyotes as they run in their pack. Other dogs begin to bark. I watch as the ears of my dogs go up because of the howl of the coyotes and the other dogs. It is just like sin. It is contagious, it grows and distracts and eventually destroys.

I Kings 15:13, "And he walked in all the sins of his father, which he had done before him." Over and over in I Kings 15 and 16, we see the phrase, "walked in the way." Sin is a magnet; it is a deceiver. A dog will hear a bark, and bark, and then another, and another, and another. As sin goes on in our lives, it just gets worse and worse. I Kings 16:33, "And Ahab made a grove; and Ahab did more to provoke the LORD God of Israel to anger than all the kings of Israel that were before him." We must quit being followers and become leaders for the sake of Christ. Stand and live what is right. I Thessalonians 4:7, "For God hath not called us unto uncleannness, but unto holiness." Proverbs 1:8, "My son, hear the instruction of thy father, and forsake not the law of thy mother." A riot in a city most always starts from a peaceful march of a group of followers that will eventually get out of control. Sin destroys! Confess and forsake, or reap and watch the cancer of sin destroy. Proverbs 1:23, "Turn you at my reproof: behold, I will pour out my spirit unto you, I will make known my words unto you." Read the Word of God, live the Word of God, teach the Word of God. Psalm 119:133, "Order my steps in thy word: and let not any iniquity have dominion over me." Psalm

119:144, "The righteousness of thy testimonies is everlasting: give me understanding, and I shall live."

Oh, that we would purpose to not live as a pack of wild dogs. We need the dogs to bark at an intruder. We need to stand against sin and cry out for holiness. Live for Christ today. Let us focus on training another generation to live a life holy unto God.

Sin is contagious – it grows, distracts, and eventually destroys.

June 2

1 Kings 17-18 Psalm 119:145-160 Proverbs 2 2 Thess. 1-2

Look and Listen

Good morning! In I Kings 17:2, 8, and 18:1 we read, "the word of the LORD came." We should live in a relationship with the Lord so that He can speak with us at any time. In times of joy, sorrow, peace or trial, we should maintain a relationship of oneness with Christ. As we read on, we see Elijah lived his faith, obedience, service and testimony to God. When he faces the prophets of Baal, we can hear Elijah pray in I Kings 18:36-37, "LORD God of Abraham, Isaac, and of Israel, let it be known this day that thou art God in Israel, and that I am thy servant, and that I have done all these things at thy word. Hear me, O LORD, hear me, that this people may know that thou art the LORD God." Verse 38 says, "Then the fire of the LORD fell, and consumed the burnt sacrifice, and the wood, and the stones, and the dust, and licked up the water that was in the trench." PRAISE THE LORD! May we live in such a way that our faith, obedience, service and testimony would bring glory and honor to our Lord.

As I was working yesterday, I noticed something moving in the grass by me. I stood still and watched as two snakes crawled by my boots. As I have listened and learned from men that have wisdom which I hunger for, I was told not to kill a black snake because they keep the poisonous snakes away. I stood very still and watched as not one, but two, snakes crawled right past me. There was a time in my life that I would have run, killed the snakes, or yelled at someone. I was by myself and I just stood still and watched.

It seems that we are living in a time that God's people are not looking to God and His Word. It is time that we look to God, stand fast in His Word, walk in prayer with Him and listen for His voice and return. Be faithful in soul winning. Paul wrote in II Thessalonians 2:1-2, "Now we beseech you, brethren, by the coming of our Lord Jesus Christ, and by our gathering together unto him, That ye be not soon shaken in mind, or be troubled, neither by spirit, nor by word, nor by letter as from us, as that the day of Christ is at hand." Christ Jesus' return is getting closer every moment. Proverbs 2:11, "Discretion shall preserve thee, understanding shall keep thee." Look to the Lord today, not the news media, not the crime, not the virus. Psalm 119:145-146, "I cried with my whole heart, hear me, O LORD: I will keep thy statutes. I cried unto thee, save me, and I shall keep thy testimonies." Stop and regroup. It is time for each of us to live in faith, be obedient, serve and be a testimony to others that the answer is Christ and Him alone.

It is time that we look to God, walk with Him, and listen for His return.

June 3

1 Kings 19-20 Psalm 119:161-176 Proverbs 3 2 Thes. 3-1 Timothy 1

Stay Spiritually Strong

Good morning! Have you ever said to yourself, "It is enough?" The great man of God, Elijah, did. I Kings. 19:4b "It is enough; now O LORD, take away my life; for I am not better than my fathers." The pressures and trials of life can wear us down to the point of just saying, "it is enough." We try and try and try, and yet the fight brings us to the point of saying, "it is enough." When we get tired physically, we often get tired emotionally. I am not a physician. I am just a man closing in on seventy years of age and realize I have to keep myself spiritually, emotionally and, as best I can, physically strong. God has a work for us to do and we must keep our eyes on what we are doing and not look at what we think others are not doing. Elijah said in I Kings 19:14, "I, even I only, am left." That was not true, because down in I Kings 19:18, God said, "I have left me seven thousand in Israel."

Life is battle, victory, trial, learning, encouragement, defeat, etc. It is so vitally important that we keep our eyes on what we are doing, and what God is doing in our lives personally. Paul challenges us as he ends the book of II Thessalonians in verse 13, "But ye brethren, be not weary in well doing." We read Paul's charge to Timothy and to us in I Timothy 1:18, "This charge I commit unto thee, son Timothy." Verse 19, "Holding faith, and a good conscience." We read of wisdom in Proverbs 3:21, "keep sound wisdom and discretion." Proverbs 3:22, "So shall they be life unto thy soul, and grace to thy neck."

I stopped the tractor yesterday in the heat, let it idle and went and sat under a shade tree, and just spent time with the Lord. Sure, I pray while I am working, but I did not want my attention distracted by watching what I was doing. Start this day with the most important thing all of us need to do, and that is cry out to the Lord. Take time during the day and spend time in prayer. Psalm 119:169, "Let my cry come near before thee, O LORD: give me understanding according to thy word." Psalm 119:173, "Let thine hand help me; for I have chosen thy precepts." We serve a wonderful Saviour. Enjoy Him today and every day. He is always there. He is never too busy. He will always listen. Have a very blessed day.

God has a work for us to do and we must
keep our eyes on what we are doing.

June 4

1 Kings 21-22   Psalm 120   Proverbs 4   1 Timothy 2-3

Stay and Serve

Good morning! Yesterday afternoon I was working on an electrical project and I received a text message. I looked at my phone and it was from a missionary couple on deputation. They thanked Mrs. Smith and I and went on to say how they both had been saved at camp. Tears of joy came to my heart, knowing that we were in God's place and doing God's will when these young people were saved. Now they are adults with a family, on their way to the mission field. Do not give up serving God, living for God, and walking with God. What is more wonderful than God working in the heart of someone else where you are doing the will of God?

King Ahab wanted a vineyard while Naboth wanted to keep what was his inheritance. I Kings 21:4, "I will not give thee the inheritance of my fathers." Stay and serve in the place of God, the perfect will of God, doing the complete will of God. Notice one word in I Kings 22:43, "nevertheless." He did less than what was right to do. King Jehoshaphat "walked in all the ways of Asa his father," but he did not remove the "high places" of false worship (I Kings 22:43). Do not let the devil cause you to be satisfied with less than what is best. I Timothy 2:5, "For there is one God, and one mediator between God and men, the man Christ Jesus." Proverbs 4:26, "Ponder the path of thy feet, and let all thy ways be established." Do not let the world, the devil or the flesh draw you away from the perfect will of God. None of us know what God is doing in or through us in the lives of others. Psalm 120:2, "Deliver my soul, O LORD, from lying lips, and from a deceitful tongue."

Let God be God in and through you, in the way He chooses. Just stay in His will and do it. We would have a big problem with pride if we saw what God was doing in and through us. That is why it is so very important to focus on the will of God and just be doing it. He is God, and He loves us to be satisfied, serving, in His will, His way. Keep on being faithful where God has planted you and let Him show you the next step. Do not give up your inheritance.

Stay and serve in the place of God, the perfect will of God, doing the complete will of God.

June 5

2 Kings 1-2 Psalm 121 Proverbs 5 1 Timothy 4-5

Can You Hear Him?

Good morning! As the workday was ending, I was hurrying to get things put away and cleaned up before the rain began. I noticed the dogs acting very nervously, the horses were heading from grazing in the field to the tree line and the sky was darkening fast. I heard an alert go off on my phone. I looked and it was a weather warning for bad storms. Those dogs and horses knew a storm was coming because God created them to listen to His signs and voice, even though they do not have a soul to receive God's gift of salvation.

In II Kings 1:3, 6, 16, we read the phrase, "Is it not because there is not a God in Israel." Ahaziah had fallen and sent a messenger to enquire of Baal-zebub, the god of Ekron. There was a rejection of the voice of God and the seeking of false gods. Elijah lets the messenger know that Ahaziah is going to die and fifty soldiers are sent. The first two sets of fifty are consumed by fire. The captain of the third group of fifty "came and fell on his knees before Elijah, and besought him, and said unto him, O man of God" (II Kings 1:13). This captain humbled himself and recognized the power and presence of God. I sometimes wonder if animals with no souls have more of a sense of God and His presence than humans who are created in the image of God. I Timothy 4:1, "Now the Spirit speaketh expressly, that in the latter times some shall depart from the faith, giving heed to seducing spirits, and doctrines of devils." It cannot be expressed enough about staying daily in the Word of God and learning how to seek, listen to, and follow the voice of God. I Timothy 4:13, "Till I come, give attendance to reading, to exhortation to doctrine." God is watching us to see who and what we will follow and listen to. Proverbs 5:21, "For the ways of man are before the eyes of the LORD, and he pondereth all his goings." God is still on His throne and He is and will always be in charge. Take time this morning to let God have full control, listen to His voice, follow His Word and fellowship continually with the Holy Spirit.

Psalm 121:5, "The LORD is thy keeper: the LORD is thy shade upon thy right hand."

As the horses headed to the safety of the timber and the dogs headed for shelter, I stood there as a man with the Holy Spirit in my heart and the preserved Word of God to teach, guide and instruct me. The animals will be gone some day and I will live for eternity in Heaven. Let us always be sensitive to the voice of the LORD. Some things to think about.

Stay daily in the Word of God and learn to seek,
listen to, and follow the voice of God.

June 6

2 Kings 3-4 Psalm 122 Proverbs 6 1 Tim. 6 - 2 Tim. 1

Strengthen Your Faith

Good morning! As we open the pages of Scripture each day and spend time reading, we must be aware that the Word of God is a living Book for our every need. It is important to understand what we are reading, but it is of vital importance to allow the words of God to speak in a personal way for our every need and guidance. The faith we read that another person had, can strengthen our faith. Godly music is so important. We read this morning of the prophet Elisha calling for a minstrel (musician). II Kings 3:15, "But now bring me a minstrel. And it came to pass, when the minstrel played, that the hand of the LORD came upon him." Godly, Christ honoring music can strengthen us and meet a spiritual need.

The Shunamite woman had faith. Her son died and she went to the man of God. When Gehazi, who was sent by Elisha, came to her, Elisha said in II Kings 4:26, "Run now, I pray thee, to meet her, and say unto her, Is it well with thee? Is it well with thy husband? Is it well with the child? And she answered, It is well." It is well?? Her son was dead! (II Kings 4:20). Her faith in what God could do should strengthen our faith, not in man but in God. God has a plan or will for each of us, and this must be in the forefront of our service for God. I Timothy 6:20, "keep that which is committed to thy trust." II Timothy 1:6, "Wherefore I put thee in remembrance that thou stir up the gift of God, which is in thee by the putting on of my hands." II Timothy 1:12, "for I know whom I have believed, and am persuaded that he is able to keep that which I have committed unto him against that day." We need to keep our faith, commitment and trust strong in the Lord and His will for our lives. We get so caught up in things that really do not matter and we need to heed the words of Proverbs 6:5, "Deliver thyself as a roe from the hand of the hunter, and as a bird from the hand of the fowler."

Somehow the animals get away from the hunter, and we need to stay away from the devil and his wicked ways that will rob us of the joy and peace of the Lord and serving in God's way, in God's place, in God's time. Psalm 122:7a, "Peace be within thy walls." Psalm 122:8b, "Peace be within thee." Meditate on God's Word today, and let it bring a peace. Spend some special time of extra prayer with the Lord today. He loves you and desires to be with you and comfort you.

We need to keep our faith, commitment and trust strong in the Lord.

June 7

2 Kings 5-6 Psalm 123,124 Proverbs 7 2 Timothy 2-3

A Humble Servant

Good morning! II Kings 5:13, "if the prophet had bid thee do some great thing, wouldest thou not have done it?" That is what the servant asked his leader, Naaman, the captain with leprosy. We are to be servants of the Lord. All that Naaman had to do was what he was told to do. Dip in the water seven times. That is not hard, but it is humbling. It is not a great feat of a warrior, not a great action in front of other soldiers. He is not commanding, but submitting to a humble act. Elisha refused any payment for what he told Naaman to do but Elisha's servant, Gehazi, thought only of gain. II Kings 5:20, "I will run after him, and take somewhat of him." Look at what happened because of selfish greed, self-centeredness, and a "me first, me feeling sorrow for myself" spirit. II Kings 5:26, "Is it a time to receive money, and to receive garments, and oliveyards, and vineyards, and sheep, and oxen, and menservents, and maidservants?" Gehazi was struck with leprosy. II Kings 5:27, "And he went out from his presence a leper as white as snow."

We are to be servants of the Lord, no matter the task, no matter the recognition. II Timothy 2:24-25, "And the servant of the Lord must not strive; but be gentle unto all men, apt to teach, patient, In meekness instructing those that oppose themselves; if God peradventure will give them repentance to the acknowledging of the truth." Solomon, in the wisdom of God, wrote in Proverbs 7:24, "Hearken unto me now therefore, O ye children, and attend to the word of my mouth." Generations past were generations of serving people. Some of the greatest people that we will read about were first great servants. Psalm 123:2, "Behold, as the eyes of servants look unto the hand of their masters, and as the eyes of a maiden unto the hand of her mistress; so our eyes wait upon the LORD our God, until that he have mercy upon us."

I stepped out into the darkness this morning after I had spent some time in prayer and reading my Bible. As I stood there in the quietness, I heard the chirping of the frogs in the pond and then, out of the stillness of the morning, came the crow of the rooster. I took my phone and looked up why a rooster crows before the sun comes up in the morning. It was very interesting reading. The rooster is created with an internal clock to sound off one-half hour before day light. You and I know that internal clock was a creation of God for a humble purpose, to be an alarm to begin the day. What purpose have you and I been created for as a servant of the Lord? If it is something as humble as the crow of a rooster, may we give out the loudest crow of all. Serve Him today with all you have.

Some of the greatest people that we will read about were first great servants.

June 8

2 Kings 7-8 Psalm 125,126 Proverbs 8 2 Tim. 4 – Titus 1

God of the Impossible

Good morning! Have you ever challenged somebody to do something? You thought you could do it better or just as well as they could. Let us look at the other side. Have you ever been given a challenge? Someone thought they could do something better than you and they wanted to prove that to you and to themselves. Let us face it; the challenge is because of pride. Pride out of control can ruin us. Pride is not bad when it comes to doing something the best you can, such as pride in accomplishing something that was very difficult or hard to do. There is the pride from completion. For example, doing some landscaping that was a vision, but after time and hard work it became a reality.

II Kings 7:2, "if the LORD would make windows in heaven, might this thing be? That is a question to put God to the test. That is a challenge to see if God can. That is an attack on God's character. There was a fear of the Syrian army and its power. It is night, the great Syrian army is at rest in preparation for the battle the next day. II Kings 7:6-7, "For the Lord had made the host of the Syrians to hear a noise of chariots, and a noise of horses, even the noise of a great host: and they said one to another, Lo, the king of Israel hath hired against us the kings of the Hittites, and the kings of the Egyptians, to come upon us. Wherefore they arose and fled in the twilight, and left their tents, and their horses, and their asses, even the camp as it was, and fled for their life." Yes, the man that challenged what God could do then died (II Kings 7:19).

Stay with God, have faith in God, believe Him that He is and that He can do the impossible. If you're weak in spirit today, let Him strengthen you. If you're discouraged, let Him encourage you. II Timothy 4:17, "Notwithstanding the Lord stood with me, and strengthened me." Proverbs 8:17, "I love them that love me; and those that seek me early shall find me." Take time and be refreshed with God. Read and meditate on the Word of God. Fellowship with God in prayer. Let God lead in every area of your life. Proverbs 8:20-21, "I lead in the way of righteousness, in the midst of the paths of judgment: That I may cause those that love me to inherit substance; and I will fill their treasures." The older I get, the more I notice that my eyesight is going, my physical strength weakening, my endurance slowing. However, my spirit and faith in God is strengthening, my prayer life advancing and my desire to finish right is more of a priority than anything in my life. Psalm 125:1-2, "They that trust in the LORD shall be as mount Zion, which cannot be removed, but abideth for ever. As the mountains are round about Jerusalem, so the LORD is round about his people from henceforth even for ever." When I am weak, He is strong. Human strength will soon fail but Godly strength will prevail. The greatness of man will soon fade, but the greatness of God will always prevail. Live for God today.

Have faith in God and believe that He can do the impossible.

June 9

2 Kings 9-10 Psalm 127 Proverbs 9 Titus 2-3

Lesson from a Rooster

Good morning! As I read from the Old Testament reading this morning in II Kings 9 and 10, I wrote in my notes, "The sin that we fight the most, if not conquered through Christ, will be the sin that destroys us." My heart breaks as I have seen so many that have started right in their hearts, desire right, and hunger for right, but the sin, if not conquered through the Word of God, prayer, confession, and forsaking will eventually destroy what God is trying to build. Judgment fell to Ahab's house by the killing of all, including his wife Jezebel. Let this verse penetrate deep in the hearts of all of us. II Kings 10:10, "know now that there shall fall unto the earth nothing of the word of the LORD, which the LORD spake concerning the house of Ahab: for the LORD hath done that which he spake by his servant Elijah." God means what He says, and God will always have His day against sin.

Let us sit and listen to the old man of God, Paul, as he writes under the direction of the Holy Spirit to Titus in Titus 2:1, "But speak thou the things which become sound doctrine." Titus 2:7, "In all things shewing thyself a pattern of good works." Titus 2:12, "Teaching us that denying ungodliness and worldly lusts, we should live soberly, righteously, and godly, in this present world." Man constantly tries new ways and new methods, but true victory only comes God's way. Psalm 127:1, "Except the LORD build the house, they labour in vain that build it."

My dad told me one day, as we were out by the barn and the chicken house, that if I did not quit bothering the old rooster, it was one day going to flog me good and spur me. That day came. I did not realize the old rooster was trying to protect his brood of hens. I would go into the chicken house and move the hens to get the eggs, but instead of taking my time, I would just rush in and they would go crazy clucking. Sure enough, one day the old rooster met me as I left the chicken house and jumped on my back and began flogging me with his wings and spurring me. I ran to the gate trying to keep the eggs from breaking and trying to get him off my back. From that day forward, until that rooster met the end of his life, every time I came to gather eggs, he watched how I treated his hens. Brother and sister, sin destroys and sin is never satisfied. Proverbs 9:6, "Forsake the foolish, and live; and go in the way of understanding." Walk with God in a way that, when in temptation, you flee to God and His Word. Learn to leave sin alone and forsake it. I took care of the old rooster one day, and dad looked at me and said, if you had just left him alone when I told you. Dad was right and God is even more right. Forsake sin and live for Christ.

Learn to leave sin alone and forsake it.

June 10

2 Kings 11-12 Psalm 128 Proverbs 10 Philemon 1- Hebrew 1

Deal with the Thistles

Good morning! Do you have any thistles in your life? It is something that keeps coming up in your life, that you wish you could get rid of and yet it keeps coming back. We try our best to do right and stay right, and yet a sin keeps coming back. It is like a prickly thistle that come from nowhere. Joash was hidden as a child and protected as his family was destroyed, and he became king by the providence of God at the age of seven (II Kings 11:21). He reigned forty years in Jerusalem (II Kings 12:1). II Kings 12:2, "And Jehoash did that which was right in the sight of the LORD all his days wherein Jehoiada the priest instructed him." In the very next verse, we read one word that brings an alarm, "but." II Kings 12:3, "But the high places were not taken away: the people still sacrificed and burnt incense in the high places." Whatever sin we have that we do not completely deal with will keep coming back.

As I was mowing and string trimming yesterday, I got into a batch of milk thistles. They need to be dug out, and I have dug out many, but they keep coming back. I have to dig them out before they go to seed. I stopped yesterday as I got pricked several times from the points on the leaves and praised the Lord for the Holy Spirit that pricks us of sin that needs to be confessed and forsaken in our lives. If we do not deal with sin, it will grow and become worse. If we do not deal with sin, it will overtake our joy and our service for the Lord and can eventually take us completely away from the Lord. Philemon 21, "Having confidence in thy obedience I wrote unto thee, knowing that thou wilt also do more than I say." We must go beyond just going to church. We must go beyond just being saved. We must go on and grow in the Lord to be able to recognize and deal with sin that can keep us from the Lord. Proverbs 10:29, "The way of the LORD is strength to the upright: but destruction shall be to the workers of iniquity."

Each milk thistle bloom produces over 200 seeds. The average plant, if not dug up, can produce 6,350 seeds per year. Psalm 128:1, "Blessed is every one that feareth the LORD; that walketh in his ways." Psalm 128:4, "Behold, that thus shall the man be blessed that feareth the LORD." There are several healthful uses for the milk thistle plant, but out of control it can destroy an area where people walk. Natural gas is a wonderful tool to heat a home and cook our food, but out of control, natural gas can take lives. Sin has no place in the life of a Christian. Deal with it today or it will grow and grow and destroy a victorious life in Christ.

Whatever sin we have that we do not completely deal with will keep coming back.

June 11

2 Kings 13-14 Psalm 129 Proverbs 11 Hebrews 2-3

Let the Sun Shine Again

Good morning! As I finished reading this morning, a song came to my mind entitled, "Let the Sun Shine Again." The first verse goes like this, "I remembered the time when I first knew the Savior, When the sunlight of blessing so flooded my heart. Oh the sweetness of "first love," with Jesus so near me, and I thought such devotion would never depart." And the chorus goes like this, "Let the sun-shine again, Let the flowers bloom again; Stir the embers of love in my heart! Holy Spirit re-prove, then embrace me again; Let the sun shine a-gain in my heart!"

Do not live your life to say the words that we found in II Kings 13:19, "Thou shouldest have." What sad words of not doing everything that should have been done to receive the Lord's blessing. "Let the Sun Shine Again!" Hebrews 2:1, "Therefore we ought to give the more earnest heed to the things which we have heard, lest at any time we should let them slip." Do not let yourself drift from the Lord. Hebrews 3:12, "Take heed, brethren, lest there be in any of you an evil heart of unbelief, in departing from the living God." We need to often confirm in our minds and hearts that God is still on the throne, and He is still aware of everything that is going on. This world needs to see those who are saved by the blood of the Lamb on the top side. Hebrews 3:13, "But exhort one another daily, while it is called To day; lest any of you be hardened through the deceitfulness of sin." Sin and this world is still the destroyer. Stay away from sin and "Let the Sun Shine Again!" Proverbs 11:3, "The integrity of the upright shall guide them: but the perverseness of transgressors shall destroy them." We ought to shut out the sounds and actions of this world and what we think we need of this world and "Let the Sun Shine Again." Psalm 129:2, "Many a time have they afflicted me from my youth: yet they have not prevailed against me."

Look up today and allow the Lord, His Word, and the precious Holy Spirit to encourage and strengthen you. I wish we could sing together "Let the Sun Shine Again." It is time to let the SON have total control of our lives and all of our situations and circumstances. Lord Bless you today.

The world needs to see those who are saved by the blood of the Lamb on the top side.

June 12

2 Kings 15-16 Psalm 130-131 Proverbs 12 Hebrews 4-5

Producing for God

Good morning! This morning as the sun is just starting to come up, I am standing at the end of a field of corn. As I look down the rows, they seem to go on forever and they are as straight as can be. A farmer took pride in what he planted even before one seed began to germinate. He looked ahead and planted toward the day of harvest. In II Kings 15 and 16, we read five times the statement, "And he did that which was evil in the sight of the LORD." Twice we read, "And he did that which was right in the sight of the LORD." We live in a world where it seems more are trying to do wrong than are trying to do right. We also read that for the kings that started right, they did not stay right.

I stood and looked down the long rows of corn and thought about what I read this morning. The Christian life is a choice. Proverbs 12:11, "He that tilleth his land shall be satisfied with bread: but he that followeth vain persons is void of understanding." Before these rows of corn came up, the ground had to be prepared and planted. This fall the combine will head down these rows of corn because there was a decision made to plow, prepare, and plant. Hebrews 4:2, "For unto us was the gospel preached, as well as unto them: but the word preached did not profit them, not being mixed with faith in them that heard it." Just down the road from where I stood and looked at the rows of corn is a field that has not been plowed, prepared, and planted, and it is all grown up in weeds and will produce nothing for the farmer. Psalm 130:5, "I wait for the LORD, my soul doth wait, and in his word do I hope." The sun has come up over the horizon and it is revealing row after row of corn growing as far as you can see.

May I ask us a question? What is your life producing or is it just growing up in weeds of sin as a field that was not planted? The kings could have been kings that did right and had a full blessing of the Lord, but they chose not. What kind of life will you choose today? The life of victory in Christ is a life of constantly making the right decisions. Did the farmer that planted his field make a better choice than the farmer that let his field grow up in weeds? Do we as the children of God look to the end of being a producer for God, or do we just let our lives grow up in sin, and do nothing for God? The day of harvest will reveal who made the right decision. The day of God's judgment will reveal who made the right decision.

The life of victory in Christ is a life of constantly making the right decisions.

June 13

2 Kings 17-18 Psalm 132 Proverbs 13 Hebrews 6-7

Preserving a Heritage

Good morning! Mrs. Smith and I are visiting her mother and sister. My brother-in-law is a farmer and yesterday was hauling grain with his semi, so I spent some time with him. As we rode together, we began to talk about farms that were once part of a family farm and how when the parents died, the children did not want the farm and they sold the farm ground. They had lost what their families had owned and farmed for generations.

We as God's people must learn from this picture or we have already and will continue to lose a heritage that generations before us have stood, fought, and died for. II Kings 17:19, "And the children of Israel did secretly those things that were not right against the LORD their God." II Kings 17:17, "And they caused their sons and their daughters to pass through the fire, and used divination and enchantments, and sold themselves to do evil in the sight of the LORD, to provoke him to anger." As my brother-in-law and I talked, it was so sad to hear how family farms that were owned by generations are now sold because money was the most important thing in their eyes. What is important to you in your Christian life? To have that wonderful peace with God and enjoy a relationship with God? Or is your joy when God gives things and does things? We must keep reminding ourselves of the words in Proverbs 13:15, "Good understanding giveth favour: but the way of transgressors is hard." Abraham learned to be obedient to God and wait on God. Hebrews 6:15, "And so, after he had patiently endured, he obtained the promise."

Stay faithful to God and His Word. Live and teach the principles of God from His Word. Psalm 132:12, "If thy children will keep my covenant and my testimony that I shall teach them, their children shall also sit upon thy throne for evermore." I hunger for God to bless the next generation, but this generation must stand fast on the principles of God and not lose them. One generation lost will destroy all future generations. Some things to think about.

Live and teach the principles of God to the next generation.

June 14

2 Kings 19-20 Psalm 133-134 Proverbs 14 Hebrews 8-9

Preparation Mode

Good morning! I love watching, reading about, and studying the lives of animals that are all around us. They are at work to provide for their own, building a place to live, protecting the young, using God-given wisdom to prepare for each season, watching constantly to be on guard for predators that might bring harm. The animal world created by God lives in a constant preparation mode. Should not we be in a preparation mode to be ready to meet the Lord?

We read this morning in II Kings 20:1, "Set thine house in order." Hezekiah was sick and the prophet Isaiah told him to get prepared. In verse 2 we read, "Then he turned his face to the wall, and prayed unto the LORD." In II Kings 20:5, "I have heard thy prayer, I have seen thy tears." Oh, that our hearts would be tuned to the return of the Lord Jesus. The times are showing that the time is short. There needs to be an urgency to be right with God and ready for God. Proverbs 14:12, "There is a way which seemeth right unto a man, but the end thereof are the ways of death." In II Kings 20:3, we read the prayer of Hezekiah, "I beseech thee, O LORD, remember now how I have walked before thee in truth and with a perfect heart, and have done that which is good in thy sight."

May our lives set the example of urgency that the animal kingdom lives. They are constantly working to keep their house in order. Proverbs 14:34, "Righteousness exalteth a nation: but sin is a reproach to any people." Psalm 134:1a, "Behold, bless ye the LORD, all ye servants of the LORD." May our lives each day be challenged to "Set thine house in order." Have a blessed day.

There needs to be an urgency to be right with God and ready for God.

June 15

2 Kings 21-22 Psalm 135 Proverbs 15 Hebrews 10

Without Wavering

Good morning! Mrs. Smith and I are with our son and his family in Iowa as I am writing this morning. We went to a restaurant in a little town not far away from where our son lives and got to see the owners that we had not seen for many years. The owner said as we greeted each other, you folks have not changed a bit. I thought about that statement as we drove back to where we were staying in our travel trailer. "You have not changed a bit."

God had given king Hezekiah another fifteen years of his life and yet his son Manasseh, after seeing the hand of God in his father's life, "built up again the high places which Hezekiah his father had destroyed" (II Kings 21:3). II Kings 21:6b "he wrought much wickedness in the sight of the LORD, to provoke him to anger." Why, why, why can we not maintain a walk with God and a constant relationship that draws us closer to Him? Manasseh dies and the next king Amon only reigns two years and his own servants kill him, and we read that the people slew all those that conspired against king Amon (II Kings 21:24). Josiah, an 8-year-old young man, comes in to reign and the Word of God is found, read and delivered to the king. II Kings 22:11, "And it came to pass, when the king had heard the words of the book of the law, that he rent his clothes." Please read II Kings 22:11-20. When the Bible was read, it brought conviction, created a stable walk and brought encouragement and direction for life. PRAISE THE LORD!!

Hebrews 10:23, "Let us hold fast the profession of our faith without wavering." God's will and His direction and blessing is plain when we spend time in God's Word and prayer, let the Holy Spirit do a work in our lives, and when conviction of sin comes, we allow that conviction to change us. Proverbs 15:9, "The way of the slothful man is as an hedge of thorns: but the way of the righteous is made plain." Oh, that we would give our lives unto the Lord that He may make us as is His perfect will.

Psalm 135:6, "Whatsoever the LORD pleased, that did he in heaven, and in earth, in the seas, and all deep places." God will do His will in all of creation. May we allow and do His will in our lives. Please think about it.

When the Bible is read, it creates a stable walk and direction for life.

June 16

2 Kings 23-25 Psalm 136 Proverbs 16 Hebrews 11

How is Your Faith?

Good morning! As the time draws closer to the return of the Lord and the signs are all around us, we need to stop and ask ourselves, where is our faith or what is our faith in? We read this morning in II Kings 25:9, "And he burnt the house of the LORD, and the king's house, and all the houses of Jerusalem, and every great man's house burnt he with fire." II Kings 25:14, "took they away." II Kings 25:15, "took away." One thing that can never be destroyed or taken away in a Christian's life who walks with God is their faith.

We need to ask ourselves, what or who is my faith in? Hebrews 11:6, "But without faith it is impossible to please him: for he that cometh to God must believe that he is, and that he is a rewarder of them that diligently seek him." I asked myself as I read God's Word this morning, how is my faith? Faith is mentioned 25 times in Hebrews 11. Our faith should grow stronger in the Lord the more we serve Him and the longer we live for Him. Hebrews 11:34, "out of weakness were made strong." Do not let the media, the market, or the frustration of the times control you. May our faith in God and His soon return be strengthened because our faith in Him is where our strength is. Proverbs 16:3, "Commit thy works unto the LORD, and thy thoughts shall be established."

I would encourage you to take the time today and reread Hebrews 11. As we read this morning in Psalm 136, we saw every verse contained the phrase, "for his mercy endureth for ever." It is as if the Lord is trying to say to us this morning that our faith in Him can grow when we trust in His mercy. What a Saviour, what a KING, what a LORD! His name is Jesus. He is our Redeemer. May I conclude our time this morning with a phrase from Hebrew 11:3, "Through faith we understand." God is in control. Have faith in Him. Lord bless you today.

Our faith should grow stronger in the Lord the more we serve Him.

June 17

1 Chronicles 1-2 Psalm 137 Proverbs 17 Hebrews 12-13

Be the Encourager

Good morning! Being with our son and his family the last couple of days and getting to see Mrs. Smith's mother and sister has brought back a lot of memories. As I read this morning in I Chronicles 1-2, I noticed two phrases that I want to bring to our attention, "The sons of," and "These are their generations." All of us realize life is so short and the older we get, the shorter life seems to be. We as born-again believers have a lineage and a heritage that needs to be known and remembered. The more time ticks on, the more real the loss of those we love; but with Christ the more time passes the closer we get to really being with family.

The last phrase of Hebrews 13:5 says, "I will never leave thee, nor forsake thee." In the hours of loneliness, weariness, discouragement, defeat, and weakness, He is there. He never leaves and we can always talk to Him. Hebrews 13:8, "The Lord is my helper, and I will not fear what man shall do unto me." Our Lord is always the same. Hebrews 13:8, "Jesus Christ the same yesterday, and today, and for ever." We need to be thankful for the true friendships that we have. Proverbs 17:17, "A friend loveth at all times, and a brother is born for adversity."

As you go throughout this day, ask the Lord to use you to be a blessing to someone else. Let us look beyond ourselves. Reach out to someone that is hurting. Send a note to someone that you have not heard from in a long time. Take time to pray for others. Psalms 137:6, "If I do not remember thee, let my tongue cleave to the roof of my mouth." All of us need to be encouraged, but let us be the encourager today. We have an heritage that is Heavenly. We read of the generations, so let us live for the generations of believers in Christ. Make a list of those that you can call, send a note to and pray for. I promise that reaching out to others will bring a bundle of blessings to yourself today.

Ask the Lord to use you to be a blessing to someone today.

June 18

1 Chronicles 3-4 Psalm 138 Proverbs 18 James 1-2

What are Your Hands Producing?

Good morning! As we begin this morning, I would like you to take a look at your hands and ask yourself this question, what are my hands producing? As I was growing up, my dad encouraged me, and others also, to be looking at a trade or a craft. I heard said, God gave you a brain and hands to use, so use them together. As I read this morning in I Chronicles 4:14, "for they were craftsmen." I Chronicles 4:21, "and the families of the house of them that wrought fine linen." I Chronicles 4:23, "These were the potters, and those that dwelt among plants and hedges: there they dwelt with the king for his work."

Not everyone can be a preacher or a preacher's wife, missionary or evangelist. I believe with all my heart a minister of the Word of God is a divine calling of God. All of us who are saved are called to sow the seed of the Word of God, to win and disciple souls for Christ. All of us are to live holy, separated lives unto the Lord. My heart this morning is to ask again the question, what are you doing with your hands? We have raised an unproductive generation. Many are now rioting in the streets, rebelling against authority, rejecting history that made our nation and world, and yet with their hands and head they are producing nothing. I remember when my son asked if he could have a couple of boards, nails and paint to build his sister a little table for a Christmas gift. What do we do with our hands other than play? Do we have goals other than to make money to buy things and live for retirement, and then when retirement comes, there is nothing to do other than continue to play? Are we taking the time to teach our children and grandchildren to produce something from their lives? My father made a cedar chest for his mother, which was passed to my mother and on down the line and now my daughter has it in her home.

James 1:22, 23 and 25 have one word that jumped out at me this morning, "doer." James 1:25b, "this man shall be blessed in his deed." I watched as one of my grandsons worked on a dining room table, another on a leather belt, another learning an instrument, another working on an engine of a motorcycle, and I watched as a granddaughter worked in a kitchen. I am thankful and proud that they all are learning to produce with their hands. Yes, daily I ask for their heart to be tender to the voice of God, the leadership of God; but I hunger for them to be God-called and not Papa-called. Proverbs 18:9, "He also that is slothful in his work is brother to him that is a great waster." Psalm 138:8, "The LORD will perfect that which concerneth me: thy mercy, O LORD, endureth forever: forsake not the works of thine own hands." As I look at my hands this morning, I am asking the Lord to not only let me win and disciple souls, but Lord Jesus, please let me keep using these hands to work. I am praying for you.

God gave you a brain and hands to use, so use them together.

June 19

1 Chronicles 5-6 Psalm 139 Proverbs 19 James 3-4

The Lazy Carp

Good morning! You are important in the eyes of God. He sent His Son to pay the price for our sins. Just think about that. We get so lost in the business of life, but we are the most important in the eyes of God. Even if no one else in the world knows us, God does. For those of us who have accepted, trusted, asked Christ to forgive us of our sins and asked Him by faith to be our Saviour, He has also written our names down in the "Lamb's Book of Life." We must be important to God. Are you serving the Lord? Are you being faithful to the Lord's house? Are you seeking ways to serve God? Are you asking God to use you to win others to Christ? Are you telling the Gospel story? Are you willing to do anything to serve in the house of God? I Chronicles 6:32b, "they waited on their office according to their order." I Chronicles 6:48b, "were appointed unto all manner of service of the tabernacle of the house of God." I Chronicles 6:49, "were appointed for all the work of the place most holy." Sounds like there were jobs to do and people were appointed to do their job. We as humans are such a jealous creation. "Me first, that's mine, not fair, nobody sees what I do," and so on. James 3:16, "For where envying and strife is, there is confusion and every evil work." James 4:7 "Submit yourselves to God. Resist the devil, and he will flee from you."

I stood at the edge of a pond fishing with one of my grandsons, and I looked at the moss all around the edge of the pond and the moss growing in the pond. Then we saw two or three great big buffalo carp, made by God to clean up moss and other weeds in the water. They have a purpose created by God. The owner of the pond said that those big carp have gotten lazy and they are not doing their job. He wants them caught and out of the pond. He has thrown several new smaller carp in the pond. I thought as I watched and we tried to catch those big, lazy, "not doing what they were created to do," huge carp. We tried and tried, but never did catch those huge carp. They are like many Christians who have become lazy in Christ and are doing nothing for the Lord. God has a purpose for us and that should be at the forefront of our hearts, minds and souls to be in the perfect will of God, doing the will of God. Psalm 139:14, "I will praise thee; for I am fearfully and wonderfully made: marvelous are thy works; and that my soul knoweth right well." Proverbs 19:23, "The fear of the LORD tendeth to life: and he that hath it shall abide satisfied; he shall not be visited with evil."

May we be actively doing the will of God or we will get lazy in the service of our King, just like the big lazy carp not doing what God created it to do. There will be that day when the devil will catch us and destroy us because we were not busy doing the service God has for us.

God has a purpose for us and that should be at the forefront of our heart and mind.

June 20

1 Chronicles 7-8 Psalm 140 Proverbs 20 James 5 - 1 Pet. 1

A Call for Godly Men

Good morning! As I read the Word of God today, my heart was challenged to do a self-evaluation about the man God wants me to be. "Father's Day" is upon us and as we approach that day, it is time for all men to take a look at what God would have them to be. It is also time for moms and children to look at the place where they have put the man in their lives. Manhood is changing and it must be kept in place by the focus and principles established from the Word of God. I Chronicles 7:2, "they were valiant men of might in their generation." I Chronicles 7:3, I noticed the phrase, "chief men." I Chronicles 7:5, "valiant men of might, reckoned in all by their genealogies." I Chronicles 7:9, 11, "mighty men of valor." I Chronicles 7:40, "choice and mighty men of valour, chief of the princes." As we read on to chapter 8, we read four different times, "heads of the fathers."

Where are the Godly men? Men that live by biblical principles, men that serve God, have a heart for souls, stand as leaders, are compassionate and yet firm and loving. I Peter 1:13, "Wherefore gird up the loins of your mind, be sober, and hope to the end for the grace that is to be brought unto you at the revelation of Jesus Christ." We need a revival amongst men today. Men that will lead spiritually in their homes, places of work, in their communities. Proverbs 20:6-7, "Most men will proclaim every one his own goodness: but a faithful man who can find? The just man walketh in his integrity: his children are blessed after him."

Yes, I said the Lord convicted me as I read His Word today. May we cry out to God and be the men God needs for this time and this generation. Psalm 140:6, "I said unto the LORD, Thou art my God: hear the voice of my supplications, O LORD." Give us men that love God, love family, love their children and grandchildren and stand firm on the truths of God.

Manhood must be kept in place by the
focus and principles of the Word of God.

June 21

1 Chronicles 9-10   Psalm 141   Proverbs 21   1 Peter 2-3

A Chosen Generation

Good morning! My father and grandfathers have gone to Heaven many years ago. I remember spending time with all of them personally, asking them about when they trusted Christ as their Saviour. I now see my children and grandchildren looking at me and asking questions about when I was a boy. As we read in I Chronicles 9:27, "the charge was upon them." A charge of holiness, a charge of standing for truth, a charge of living by Biblical principle. We need another generation to step up.

My heart is breaking as city after city is having our history destroyed and it seems that everyone is just turning away. We must realize that I Peter 2:9 is still in the Scriptures, "But ye are a chosen generation, a royal priesthood, an holy nation, a peculiar people; that ye should shew forth the praises of him who hath called you out of darkness into his marvelous light." The example has been set before us that we should pattern after. I Peter 2:21, "For even hereunto were ye called: because Christ also suffered for us, leaving us an example, that ye should follow his steps."

I looked up into the sky this morning and saw another day dawning. May we be challenged to live this day for Christ, follow Him, live for Him. Proverbs 21:21, "He that followeth after righteousness and mercy findeth life, righteousness, and honor." The Psalmist wrote in Psalm

141:8, "But mine eyes are unto thee, O GOD the Lord: in thee is my trust; leave not my soul destitute." May our God find us faithful. Stand today, serve today, surrender today to God and His will. May God use us all to be faithful to HIM until He returns.

The example has been set before us that we should pattern after.

June 22

1 Chronicles 11-12 Psalm 142 Proverbs 22 1 Peter 4-5

Keep Rank

Good morning! I am so very thankful that God is still on the throne. It seems as though God has been or is being removed from everything. He is NOT! God is still in control of a world that is fulfilling His Word. But what a time for us as believers in Christ to stand and be busy! As I read this morning in I Chronicles 12:38, "that could keep rank, came with a perfect heart." God seeks for men and woman in every generation that can stay in fellowship, service, and devotion to Christ. As I read on down in verse 38, "were of one heart," they were like minded." They had the same goal, same desires. My brother and sister, it is not time to live in fear, but in victory with faith in the Lord Jesus. We often ask ourselves, what can we do? I believe the answer is always in the Word of God and as we read this morning in I Peter 4:17, "For the time is come that judgment must begin at the house of God: and if it first begin at us, what shall the end be of them that obey not the gospel of God?"

We go to the grocery store and the gas station. We do things like go to a park, and yet we do not go to church. May the Lord help us to be faithful to the house of God. I am afraid we put everything first except God. I Peter 5:6, "Humble yourselves therefore under the mighty hand of God, that he may exalt you in due time:." God is watching us. What is He seeing? Proverbs 22:29, "Seest thou a man diligent in his business? he shall stand before kings; he shall not stand before mean men." The word "business" means this man is a diligent man, hard-working, disciplined.

Is there a priority to be a hard worker to earn money, and not be as diligent at being in church and serving God? That is why judgment must begin at the house of God.

May we get on our knees this morning before God, as the Psalmist did, and cry out as we read in Psalm 142:5, "I cried unto thee, O LORD: I said, Thou art my refuge and my portion in the land of the living." Yes, we need men and woman to "keep rank with a perfect heart." The "time is come that judgment must begin at the house of God." May we stop this morning and "humble yourselves therefore under the mighty hand of God." Oh, that today we would look to Heaven and rededicate our lives, families, and service to the Lord. May He find us faithful. Have a blessed day in the LORD.

We need men and women to keep rank with a perfect heart.

June 23

1 Chronicles 13-14   Psalm 143   Proverbs 23   2 Peter 1-2

Hungering for His Voice

Good morning! Mrs. Smith and I were awakened out of a sound sleep to the howling and barking of our dogs as well as attacking sounds of some unknown animal. I ran to the door, grabbed my flashlight, and went outside to find both dogs and some animal laying there growling. The dogs were running around me, and I settled them down and approached the animal. Laying there in a pile, growling at me, was a large black cat. I thought to myself after the fight was over and things settled down, how my wife and I woke up from a sound sleep.

Can the Lord wake us out of a sound sleep? Am I sensitive to the voice of God as I was sensitive to the sound of the fighting of the animals? Do I hunger to hear the voice of God? I Chronicles 14:10, "And David enquired of God"; "And the LORD said unto him." I Chronicles 14:14, "Therefore David enquired again of God; and God said unto him." I Chronicles 14:16, "David therefore did as God commanded him." Can we hear the voice of God? Do we hunger and desire to hear the voice of God? I am not speaking of an audible voice, but a voice that speaks to your heart. II Peter 2:19, "We have also a more sure word of prophecy; whereunto ye do well that ye take heed, as unto a light that shineth in a dark place, until the day dawn, and the day star arise in your hearts." God's Word is living and He wants to speak through it, but we have to read it patiently and listen to hear His voice. Proverbs 23:19, "Hear thou, my son, and be wise, and guide thine heart in the way." As king David called to the Lord for guidance, so can we.

What is your burden today? Call upon the Lord, search His Word, listen for His voice. Psalm 143:8, "Cause me to hear thy lovingkindness in the morning; for in thee do I trust: cause me to know the way wherein I should walk; for I lift up my soul unto thee." When my wife and I were awakened we had to go see what made the sound. We cannot hear the voice of God unless we spend time in His Word and in prayer with Him. He desires to speak to us and guide us. Call out to Him today, search His voice for guidance as you spend time in His Word. God is waiting to hear from us.

We cannot hear the voice of God unless
we spend time in His Word and prayer.

June 24

1 Chronicles 15-16 Psalm 144 Proverbs 24 2 Pet. 3 – 1 John 1

Even Nature Praises Him

Good morning! Did you ever notice that the devil knows where to hit us to try to discourage us? He hits an area of our life that is weak. With me, one of the areas is something that I do almost every day --working with a piece of equipment such as a mower, the tractor and some of the equipment, the truck, or our car. What I mean is, did you ever notice that when you live by a budget, there is always something that breaks down and blows your budget? You then ask yourself, how am I going to pay for that? Yesterday, something broke that I cannot fix myself and it is going to be very expensive to fix. I stopped and headed out to a corn field of a neighbor's to just spend some time alone and pray. While I was walking down the rows, I stopped, looked at the corn that is just about knee high and noticed the leaves of the corn. It is as if they are all raised in praise to God. Picture us lifting our arms and hands up to the Lord. It was like the Lord said all plant life knows that I sustain them and they praise me!

I went to the house to clean up for supper and I received a phone call. During that phone call, a prayer that was a heavy burden to me was answered. Glory to the KING! As I read this morning, I kept noticing verse after verse of praise to our God. Whatever burden you are carrying today, take it to the Lord in prayer. I Chronicles 16:11, "Seek the LORD and his strength, seek his face continually." I Chronicles 16:34, "O give thanks unto the LORD; for his is good; for his mercy endureth for ever." As I turned to my reading in the New Testament, the strength from God's Word kept coming. II Peter 3:14, "Wherefore, beloved, seeing that ye look for such things, be diligent that ye may be found of him in peace, without spot, and blameless." II Peter 3:18, "But grow in grace, and in the knowledge of our Lord and Saviour Jesus Christ."

As I stood and looked at each stalk of corn lifting itself up in praise to where the sun and rain will come to nourish the ground it grows in, I felt a strength to know that even the plants know how to praise the Creator of all. We need to stand fast in the Lord in a world that is drifting farther from Him. Proverbs 24:21, "My son, fear thou the LORD and the king: and meddle not with them that are given to change." God has a plan for each of us, and we just need to stay in that plan where our true joy will be. Psalm 144:15, "Happy is that people, that is in such a case: yea, happy is that people, whose God is the LORD." Take some time today to look how plants lift their branches, leaves and buds to the LORD.

Our true joy comes from staying in the plan God has for us.

June 25

1 Chronicles 17-18 Psalm 145 Proverbs 25 1 John 2-3

Don't Forget

Good morning! Another beautiful day is before us. I remember being told many years ago, never forget where you came from. I would think about that. What are they saying? What does that statement mean? Do not forget who loved you, fed you, provided for you, and took care of you. As I read this morning in I Chronicles 17:7, "I took thee from the sheepcote, even from following the sheep." God reminded king David how God took him from being a shepherd boy and now he is king. I Chronicles 17:8, "And I have been with thee whithersoever thou hast walked." God said, David, wherever you went and whatever you went through, I was there with you. When dad said, "Do not forget where you came from," he was telling me or reminding me to not forget what I have been taught.

I John 2:6, "He that saith he abideth in him ought himself also so to walk, even as he walked." Don't forget spiritually where you have come from. How we were lost in sin, doomed for Hell and God loved us, saved us, gave us a new life in Christ. Psalm 145:2, "Every day will I bless thee; and I will praise thy name for ever and ever." Psalm 145:3, "Great is the LORD, and greatly to be praised; and his greatness is unsearchable." Has our country forgotten God? Have we learned how to live without God? Have we turned to church on a computer, phone, or TV instead of being faithful to His house? We see destruction of history, that if forgotten, will be repeated. Proverbs 25:28, "He that hath no rule over his own spirit is like a city that is broken down, and without walls." We need to stop and remember where we came from. Psalm 145:18, "The LORD is nigh unto all them that call upon him, to all that call upon him in truth."

I can hear those words, "Do not forget where you came from." We need to drop on our knees right now and say God, I have not forgotten how you saved my soul, forgave all my sins, and gave me a new life. Do not forget how God gave you hope. My brother and sister, please do not forget where you came from. God is where He has always been. Reach out to Him today, walk with Him today. Get back in church, spend time with Him in prayer, read His Word, forget the excuses. What a joy to be with the family of God, singing hymns, being there hearing the preaching of the Word of God, seeing brothers and sisters in Christ. Enjoy being with the family that we will spend eternity with. I challenge you today, "don't forget where you came from."

Never forget how God saved your soul,
forgave your sins, and gave you new life.

June 26

1 Chronicles 19-20 Psalm 146 Proverbs 26 1 John 4-5

Keep on Loving

Good morning! What another beautiful morning to live for and serve the Lord! I am so very thankful for the Word of God and for the relationship we can have with our Lord through prayer. Have you ever tried to do something kind for someone else and it was taken in the wrong way? You loved and gave and it was thrown back in your face. I Chronicles 19:2, "And David said, I will shew kindness unto Hanun the son of Hahash, because his father shewed kindness to me. And David sent messengers to comfort him concerning his father."

You took the time to go buy a nice sympathy card, wrote a note, and maybe even purchased a little gift, and yet it made somebody mad. Or you did some act of kindness and it was taken wrong. Do not find yourself saying, well, I will never try to help them again. I Chronicles 19:3, "Thinkest thou that David doth honour thy father, that he hath sent comforters unto thee? are not his servants come unto thee for to search, and to overthrow, and to spy out the land?" To share the gift of salvation with a lost person is because of a love for their soul, and yet sometimes we try to share the simple plan of salvation and it is rejected, or there is even an attacking rejection. Don't quit! Kindness to others is because of the love of Christ in our hearts. Do not let the devil tell you a lie. Do not let the devil distract you from loving a lost sinner or a brother or sister in need. I John 4:7-8, "Beloved, let us love one another: for love is of God; and every one that loveth is born of God, and knoweth God. He that loveth not knoweth not God; for God is love." Some people will reject a sincere love for them because they are not honest with themselves, and they only see themselves. Proverbs 26:1, "As snow in summer, and as rain in harvest, so honour is not seemly for a fool." Psalm 146:3, "Put not your trust in princes, nor in the son of man, in whom there is no help."

Do not quit loving people and reaching out to help others because you got hurt or your love and compassion was taken wrong. There is a world of hurting people just waiting for somebody to reach out, check on them, do special something for them. That is what Jesus did. Reach out to someone today and watch your heart be blessed. Love a sinner and tell them the greatest story that will ever be told, God's plan of salvation.

Do not let the devil distract you from loving a lost sinner or a brother or sister in need.

June 27

1 Chronicles 21-22 Psalm 147 Proverbs 27 2-3 John

Stay in the Nest

Good morning! What does it take to cause you to lose your temper? What does it take to get you distracted from a walk with God? I walked into the back of the barn and on the ground was a baby bird that had fallen out of its nest. I looked up in the barn and I could not see a nest. I picked up the little bird and thought to myself, why did you not stay where you should have been until you could fly? The little bird had no hope of being able to live. I tried but failed to help.

I Chronicles 21:1, "And Satan stood up against Israel, and provoked David to number Israel." The word "provoked" means to incite, a reaction of emotion, an arousing of anger. The devil and our flesh work overtime to have us fall out of the safety of the hands of God. The mother bird was a protector, a provider, but the little bird decided it knew best and wanted out of the nest before its time and fell to the ground. Joab looked at king David and said in I Chronicles 21:3, "why then doth my lord require this thing?" I Chronicles 21:6, "the king's word was abominable to Joab." More than Joab knowing this was wrong for David, listen to what God said in I Chronicles 21:7, "And God was displeased with this thing." We are in trouble when we think we can make it spiritually without God or do things our way. Be careful, you are about to fall out of the nest. III John 11, "Beloved, follow not that which is evil, but that which is good, He that doeth good is of God: but he that doeth evil hath not seen God." I held the little bird and knew that even if I found the nest, more than likely the mother would reject taking care of the bird because of my human smell on the little bird. Proverbs 27:8, "As a bird that wandereth from her nest, so is a man that wandereth from his place." God means for His people to fellowship with Him and to fellowship with His people. Be in church, be in your Bible daily, spend time in prayer, grow daily in your walk with God. Proverbs 27:12, "A prudent man foreseeth the evil, and hideth himself; but the simple pass on, and are punished."

One of the greatest steps I learned early in my Christian growth was that I need church, a daily time with God, fellowship with His people, singing of the hymns, giving of tithes and offerings. We need to understand the importance of being in our place as God's people. The little bird thought it could make it on its own. Psalm 147:11, "The LORD taketh pleasure in them that fear him, in those that hope in his mercy." Don't let the devil provoke you and weaken your flesh. Stay where you can grow in the LORD.

We are in trouble when we think we can
make it spiritually without God or do things our way.

June 28

1 Chronicles 23-24 Psalm 148 Proverbs 28 Jude-Rev. 1

Earnestly Contend

Good morning! Picture with me this morning a game of "tug of war." Two teams, a strong rope, and a mud hole. The rope has a mark in the very center and when the whistle blows, each team will pull as hard as they can to pull the other team through the mud. The team that pulls together and does not give up will be the team that wins.

Life is like a "tug of war." Our flesh and the devil pull against what God's will is for our lives. We must decide first thing every day to be with God, in His Word and in prayer. I Chronicles 23:30, "And to stand every morning to thank and praise the LORD, and likewise at even." We must, we must, we must do as Jude 3 says, "Beloved, when I gave all diligence to write unto you of the common salvation, it was needful for me to write unto you, and exhort you that ye should earnestly contend for the faith which was once delivered unto the saints." "Earnestly contend" means to stick with it, give it everything you have. It is a fight and God is on our side. Quit looking at the mud hole and pull to win the fight. Proverbs 28:14, "Happy is the man that feareth alway: but he that hardeneth his heart shall fall into mischief."

I have seen many a little, smaller team outpull a seemingly larger group, because they pulled together and did not quit until they won. God is on our team so let us pull together with HIM. Psalm 148:14a, "He also exalteth the horn of his people, the praise of all his saints." We must "earnestly contend" for the victorious life in Christ. Sin will never satisfy; it only brings sorrow and defeat. I love it when a team loses and they scream out, "Can we try again?." My brother and sister in Christ, "earnestly contend." Don't quit. Get up and try again. The victory is ours because Christ is for us and pulling with us. A team will not win unless they pull together. Keep pulling, keep pulling, "earnestly contend for the faith." The victory is ours through Christ. May you have a blessed day.

The victory is ours because Christ is for us and pulling with us.

June 29

1 Chronicles 25-26 Psalm 149 Proverbs 29 Revelation 2-3

Our First Love

Good morning! Each day I am amazed at the Lord's love for me and patience with me. I hunger, and I pray that you hunger, to please the Lord with your life. All of us fight our flesh daily and the sins of the flesh. God is desiring to give us victory in each step of our life, but we must arrive at a point of understanding that we cannot make it without Him. It is one thing to agree with that statement, and another thing to live that statement. I Chronicles 26:8, "they and their sons and their brethren, able men for strength for the service." Daily as I kneel and pray for my wife, children, grandchildren, and a list of people that grows daily, I hunger to be what the Lord would have me to be, an "able" man "for strength for the service."

Six times in Revelation chapters two and three we read, "I know thy works." God knows our every thought, our every action, our every intent. Do we live for His glory, or do we live in embarrassment of not being what we know He would be pleased in? I realized a long time ago that I cannot live the Christian life for anybody else. I can pray for others, but I cannot correct another person's sins. It must be each individual. I cannot let the sins of others destroy the relationship with God that He wants me to have. We might not have another day to live, so why not live each day for the Lord? Revelation 3:11, "Behold, I come quickly: hold that fast which thou hast." As I read in Revelation 2:4, "Nevertheless I have somewhat against thee, because thou hast left thy first love." God is not against us, but against our actions that do not please Him. He is standing there at our heart's door this morning. He is desiring to walk with us today.

Does your sin keep Him from being the Lord He wants to be in your life? Has God showed you sin in your life before? Proverbs 29:1, "He that being often reproved hardeneth his neck, shall suddenly be destroyed, and that without remedy." God is always ready to hear our plea, and He is always ready to forgive and help us get back up and do right. Psalm 149:4, "For the LORD taketh pleasure in his people: he will beautify the meek with salvation." Have you left your first love of being thankful for salvation and putting God first in every area of your life? God is for us, but He cannot give us victory and blessing if we do not put Him first. Let Revelation 2:4 ring over and over in your heart and mind today. "Nevertheless I have somewhat against thee, because thou hast left thy first love." Put God in first place and enjoy the sweet peace throughout the day. We cannot erase the past, but we can return to our "first love."

We might not have another day to live,
so why not live each day for the Lord?

June 30

1 Chronicles 27-29 Psalm 150 Proverbs 30-31 Revelation 4-5

Maintenance Check

Good morning! I am constantly evaluating my walk with God. How can I make it stronger, how can I learn more from my Bible reading, how can my prayer time be strengthened, how can I get more of the heart of God? Maintenance is a very important part in many areas of our lives. We must maintain or we will be destroyed. Too many Christians get in a rut in their walk with God and lose their joy, strength and zeal for the Lord. In our reading today in I Chronicles 27, I saw the phrase, "in his course" many times. I also saw the phrase, "over the." Men were selected for a very specific place of service and given specific instruction for this service. I Chronicles 28:7, "Moreover I will establish his kingdom for ever, if he be constant to do my commandments and my judgments, as at this day." The phrase, "if he be constant," must be studied. The Christian life must stay alive and growing. It cannot be purchased. We must daily grow in our walk with God. Our walk cannot stay the same, it must grow more intimate with God. I Chronicles 29:3, "I have set my affection to the house of my God."

My marriage is not the same as it was when it began in 1971. My love and my affections for my wife have grown. My understanding and desire to understand my wife has grown. A verse that God has used much in my life is Proverbs 30:25, "The ants are a people not strong, yet they prepare." Ants are constantly working and preparing to live. Storing food, searching for food, building their homes. I am afraid we as humans want to be satisfied with accomplishments and do not focus on growth when it comes to a walk with God. Proverbs 31:15 teaches us that a virtuous woman "riseth also while it is yet night." She is working and preparing for her family. Our walk with God should be a work in progress. We read in Revelation 4:8 about the four beasts in Heaven "that rest not day and night, saying, Holy, holy, holy, Lord God Almighty, which was, and is, and is to come." Our lives must be focused around our Redeemer and growing in a walk with Him.

Do you need to do some maintenance on your walk with God today? Psalm 150:6, "Let every thing that hath breath praise the LORD. Praise ye the LORD." I recently greased the axles on a trailer here at the ranch. The trailer was pulling just fine as we used it, but I knew I needed to do some simple maintenance. I just heard about a trailer that had the bearings burn up. I was thankful that I spent the time to do a little maintenance. My heart breaks for the Christian that gets in a rut spiritually and does not spend the time daily in maintaining a walk with God. There will soon be a causality of a life that could have been but became satisfied with where they were. Let us take some time today and do a spiritual maintenance check. This could keep us going for the Lord.

Our lives must be focused around our Redeemer and growing in a walk with Him.

July 1

2 Chronicles 1-2 Psalm 1 Proverbs 1 Revelation 6-7

Wisdom Applied

Good morning! As I walked out into the darkness of the morning, just to enjoy the freshness of the air before I started reading my Bible, I noticed the darkness of the hour, and yet there was the noise of some birds, a chirping, and the howl of some coyotes in the distance. I came back in the house and began reading in II Chronicles 1:10, "Give me now wisdom and knowledge." Those words "give me now" really began speaking to me this morning. An urgency, a hunger for it now. II Chronicles 2:1, "And Solomon determined." Just these two phrases brings the thought of an urgency to get wisdom and knowledge because he knew this was the most important thing he needed as the new king. Proverbs 1:4, "To give subtility to the simple, to the young man knowledge and discretion." I looked up the word "subtility," and found it means to make fine and to give understanding. It means to break things down in a simple fashion; to not only be understood but to be able to apply to life. I then looked up the word "knowledge" and found it means a clear and certain perception of that which exists, or of truth and fact. I read on in Proverbs 1:7, "The fear of the LORD is the beginning of knowledge: but fools despise wisdom and instruction." Solomon was asking God to help Him understand everything that he needed to know and give him direction in a proper way to apply it to his life and to the kingdom that he was about to lead.

A person who is born again and rejects what is right is a fool. A person who rejects the teachings of the Bible is a fool. It is not according to me, but God. Proverbs 1:22, "How long, ye simple ones, will ye love simplicity? And the scorners delight in their scorning, and fools hate knowledge?" The Word of God has been given to us, preserved for us, in print for us and yet we so often neglect to read it and when we read it, we so often fail to apply it. Let us stop and think for a moment. Do we know the truth and yet reject it or fail to apply it? Do we know what to do to have victory in the Christian life and fail to do it? When I went outside in the dark, both dogs came to my side. One on the left side and one on the right. They both leaned into me and I felt their bodies move with the wagging of their tails. After I read this morning, I went back outside to pray and think on what I read. I thought I would go ahead and feed the dogs. As I turned on the light, both dogs came running, and I looked and both of them were sitting down right in front of me. Before I feed a dog that cannot speak the English language, they were sitting down and ready to receive the food I had for them. How can a dog learn obedience and not a human being?

Psalm 1:6, "For the LORD knoweth the way of the righteous: but the way of the ungodly shall perish." As I read this morning in Revelation 7:17, "God shall wipe away all tears from their eyes," I thought of how many Christians live in sorrow of heart instead of the joy of the Lord. If a dog can anticipate being fed, can we not anticipate the strength and feeding that we will receive from a feeding on the Word of God and fellowship with the Holy Spirit of God? My heart rejoiced as I took a long time to study the word "subtility." God puts things so simply that even a simple person, a young person, an intelligent person can understand the principles that we need from the Word of God. Take time today with God and His Word. Write down some special verses to memorize. Solomon was "determined" to get "wisdom and knowledge" from the Lord. Should not we do the same?

Do we know the truth and yet reject it or fail to apply it?

July 2

2 Chronicles 3-4 Psalm 2 Proverbs 2 Revelation 8-9

Overlaid with Christ

Good morning! I stood in the Main Street of Cowboy Town and was telling about the beginning of Circle C Baptist Ranch, and as I was talking, I said to those listening that they were actually standing in the middle of a field that once was planted and grew crops. As we stood on a gravel Main Street and looked at buildings, it was a little difficult to picture a plowed field with crops growing in it. The property of the camp has changed so much from the beginning days of bulldozing, removing trees, digging water lines, building power lines and construction of buildings.

In our reading this morning in II Chronicles chapter 3, we see a phrase several times, "overlaid with gold." In the construction of the temple, there were several things that the Scriptures mentioned were "overlaid with gold." What they saw as a finished item was not really the way it was in its original state. As I read on in II Chronicles 4:9, "overlaid the doors of them with brass." The doors were very large and strong, but they were not of solid brass; they were "overlaid." You and I who have trusted Christ as our Saviour should be showing a change in our lives because we have been forgiven and have been "overlaid" with a newness in Christ. The word "overlaid" means to completely cover and to be pressed upon. Did we only get saved to be changed a little or did we ask God to forgive us of all our sins and to completely come into our heart? We read in Revelation 8 and 9 how six angels "sounded." The word "sounded," means announced judgments of God. Revelation 9:20, "yet repented not of the works of their hands." Why do we not want a complete covering of Christ in every area of our lives? We cannot have a walk with Him as He desires if we only allow the Lord to have part of our life. Christ loves us and gave everything in His payment for our sins. Proverbs 2:8, "He keepeth the paths of judgment, and preserveth the way of his saints." As I read this verse in Proverbs, I asked the Lord to show me any area of my life that I have not given to Him. I hunger to be completely "overlaid" with and in Christ. Stop today and do a self-evaluation. Ask yourself what area of your life you have not let Christ completely have. Let me encourage you to give Him everything. Psalm 2:12b, "blessed are all they that put their trust in him."

At one time the camp property was a farm, growing crops, and now this same ground is used by God to see souls saved and lives changed for His glory and His use. This ground that once grew crops is now "overlaid" for the sole use of seeing lives changed. Have you been "overlaid" for the Master's use?

We should hunger to be completely overlaid with and in Christ.

July 3

2 Chronicles 5-6 Psalm 3 Proverbs 3 Revelation 10-11

One with God

Good morning! It was early in the morning, way before daylight. It was our first time to go on a real hunt together. We had the license, the guns, the ammunition, the proper clothing. We were ready to go on our first deer hunt together. It was so cold and the snow was deep as we made our way to where we were going to sit and wait on the biggest deer that the Lord ever created. We did not talk. We moved slowly. The morning light had not begun to show itself, so we moved by the light of the stars and what little light was from the moon. We arrived at the place where we had scouted many times. It was time now to become one with nature. We did not move, we did not talk, we had taken every precaution of our scent not to be detected. We waited, waited, and waited some more. I know it is in the beginning heat of summer, but as I read my Bible this morning, my mind went to the first time my son and I went deer hunting together.

As I read II Chronicles 5:13, "It came even to pass, as the trumpeters and singers were as one, to make one sound to be heard in praising and thanking the LORD; and when they lifted up their voice with the trumpets and cymbals and instruments of musick, and praised the LORD, saying, For he is good; for his mercy endureth for ever: that then the house was filled with a cloud, even the house of the LORD." Let us take a look this morning at the three words, "were as one." I have tried to imagine how beautiful that sound must have been that day in bringing praise to the Lord. Every instrument and every singer "were as one." They were together, they were united, they were blending, they were praising, they were bringing glory to the Lord; "they were as one." My heart hungers to be one with God. Our personal lives, our families, our service for the Lord should bring us in oneness with God. Revelation 11:15b, "The kingdoms of this world are become the kingdoms of our Lord, and of his Christ; and he shall reign for ever and ever." Our lives should be lived "as one" with Christ. We should be in tune, in harmony, in likeness with Christ. Our will should be His will. Our focus of the Christian walk should be "as one" with Christ. Proverbs 3:10, "So shall thy barns be filled with plenty, and thy presses shall burst out with new wine." We get in trouble every time we fight the will of God and try to go on our own. Why not decide today and every day to be "as one" with Christ? Psalm 3:3-4, "But thou, O LORD, art a shield for me; my glory, and the lifter up of mine head. I cried unto the LORD with my voice, and he heard me out of his holy hill. Selah."

My son and I have walked into the woods together to hunt deer, squirrels, rabbits, etc. and we always tried to be "as one" with nature. I am not on a hunt today, but I do hunger to have God's blessing, so I give myself so that He and I "were as one." Are you living in harmony with Christ today? If not, you are missing the true joy of the Christian life. It should be the goal of every Christian to live every day with Christ so that it can be said you and He "were as one."

Our focus of the Christian walk should be "as one" with Christ.

July 4

2 Chronicles 7-8 Psalm 4 Proverbs 4 Revelation 12-13

Keep on Learning

Good morning! It was a very hot day. The humidity was very high and I was fishing with four of my five grandsons and my son-in-law. We do not get to be together very much and this day was very special to my wife and I. The youngest grandson and I went and looked for another place to fish, and I saw a place of shade on the side of a hill. After fishing for a while, I sat down in that place of shade and my grandson came and sat beside me. I said, a fellow could lay down and go to sleep here. He looked at me and said, you sure could. I then looked at him and said, that other spot over there is not the place to sit down and rest. He asked, how come? We got up and I went and pointed out some poison ivy that was growing in that spot. He looked and said to me, "I see." Earlier that day one of my grandsons had caught a pretty good size cat fish. He yelled at me and I went over to see, and he was trying to get a hold and get the hook out. I said, let me show you how to hold the fish so it will not horn you. As I did, he said, "I see." Both of my grandsons said, "I see."

I was reading in II Chronicles 7:3, "And when all the children of Israel saw how the fire came down, and the glory of the LORD upon the house, they bowed themselves with their faces to the ground upon the pavement, and worshipped, and praised the LORD, saying, For he is good; for his mercy endureth for ever." The one word "saw" spoke to me this morning. The children of Israel "saw" and understood. In II Chronicles 7:14, we read those powerful words, "If my people." If we see, if we listen, if we understand, if we obey. II Chronicles 7:17, "if thou wilt walk, do, observe." Then as we read on, the words of warning come in II Chronicles 7:19, "turn away, forsake my statutes, shall go and serve other gods." As I get older, I am still hungering to learn everything I can. To sit beside or stand beside a grandson and hear them say, "I see"; those were very powerful words to me. Words of encouragement that they want to learn, they want to understand, they want to grow in their knowledge.

They are young men in the making. We live in a time of know-it-all's, "my way," and "I know." Everybody throws a fit until they get their way, just like a little child throwing a fit.

Can I throw a challenge out to all of us? Never stop learning and growing in life and in your walk with the Lord. Do not let the devil and pride keep you from growing. The devil will not have the victory, as we read this morning in Revelation 12:10, "Now is come salvation, and strength, and the kingdom of our God, and the power of his Christ: for the accuser of our brethren is cast down, which accused them before our God day and night." We have more casualties in the Christian life when we think that we have made it or that we know how to handle things. Always be growing in your walk with God. None of us have made it. Psalm 4:3, "But know that the LORD hath set apart him that is godly for himself: the LORD will hear when I call unto him." God is waiting to hear our cry unto Him to walk with Him and grow in Him. Proverbs 4:10, "Hear, O my son, and receive my sayings; and the years of thy life shall be many." The thing that so blessed my heart about both grandsons is they never said, "I know that." My prayer for myself and all of us is that we keep a humble, open heart to learn and grow as men and women of God. Have a blessed learning day.

Never stop learning and growing in life and in your walk with the Lord.

July 5

2 Chronicles 9-10 Psalm 5 Proverbs 5 Revelation 14-15

A Christian's Apparel

Good morning! This time of the year the mornings are so humid and hot even before the sun begins to rise. I told my son the other day in a phone call about how hot the temperature is and we talked about how hard it is to breathe when the humidity is so high, and I said, the corn in the fields love this humidity. It is true that the high humidity helps our gardens to grow but it also causes man to have lack of dress. Yes, I said it right, lack of dress. I found it interesting in II Chronicles 9 when the Queen of Sheba came to see for herself all the riches of Solomon, his wisdom and greatness; that she also observed something I would like to point out for us today. II Chronicles 9:4, "And the meat of his table, and the sitting of his servants, and the attendance of his ministers, and their apparel; his cupbearers also, and their apparel; and his ascent by which he went up into the house of the LORD; there was no more spirit in her." Twice in one verse we read that she observed, "their apparel."

You can sure get the fur raised on the back of a person when you decide to talk about clothes. Yes, the word "apparel" means clothing. We read in Revelation 15:6, And the seven angels came out of the temple, having the seven plagues, clothed in pure and white linen, and having their breasts girded with golden girdles." When God gave us His Word, He felt it very important for us to know that these angels were "clothed in pure and white linen." I am not the Holy Spirit, but we have a generation of God's people that have arrived at the point of saying it does not matter what a person wears or does not wear. Yesterday, I worked and came to the house to go to town and do some grocery shopping with my wife. She knew, and I knew, that my clothes would be all covered in grass and dirt from the work that I was doing. I have heard my mother say many a times even though she has been in Heaven for well over twenty years, "You are not leaving this house dressed like that." When will we realize that "apparel" does make a statement? Does our "apparel" give a testimony of holiness and separation unto God? Does our "apparel" give a statement of righteousness? Clothes do not make the man or woman, but it does tell a lot about them and makes a strong statement about their heart. In Proverbs 5, Solomon is talking to his son about the "strange woman." She is identified in part by her "apparel." Proverbs 7:10, "And, behold, there met him a woman with the attire of an harlot." "Apparel" is our outward testimony even before we say one word. There is a plea in Proverbs 5:1, "My son, attend unto my wisdom, and bow thine ear to my understanding." Proverbs 5:2a, "That thou mayest regard discretion."

We all have different tastes and likes, but what about the testimony for Christ when it comes to our "apparel?" "Apparel" does not make the Christian, but it makes a statement about the heart of a Christian. Let us take a long look at how we dress. I have always lived and taught that there are clothes for work, going to town, and Sunday clothes; but no matter the occasion, my "apparel" makes a statement. Psalm 5:8a, "Lead me, O LORD, in thy righteousness." Psalm 5:12, "For thou, LORD, wilt bless the righteous; with favour wilt thou compass him as with a shield." It is summer and we as God's people should be so very careful that our "apparel" brings glory to our Lord.

Does our apparel give a testimony of holiness and separation unto God?

July 6

2 Chronicles 11-12 Psalm 6 Proverbs 6 Revelation 16-17

How Cautious Are You?

Good morning! I pulled the Ranch truck out of the barn and raised the hood to check some things, and it was like something tapped me on the shoulder, and I turned around. Less than twenty-five yards away, standing there looking at me, was a deer. I was still and a neighbor started a mower and the deer turned away from me and looked toward the sound. I just stood very still and observed the deer looking around. Why are animals that live in the wild more cautious about their lives than we as humans are about our spiritual lives?

II Chronicles 12:1, "And it came to pass, when Rehoboam had established the kingdom, and had strengthened himself, he forsook the law of the LORD, and all Israel with him." I know too many that have thought they had it all together spiritually, and they quit daily reading their Bibles, quit faithfully praying, quit coming to church, quit tithing. Now those same and once faithful people that hungered to serve the Lord are gone. We can return, we can get the relationship back, the fire can come back, the dedication can come back. II Chronicles 12:7, "And when the LORD saw that they humbled themselves, the word of the LORD came to Shemaiah, saying, They have humbled themselves; therefore I will not destroy them, but I will grant them some deliverance." Our flesh gets weak, the temptations are great, but humility in facing our wrongs is the first step in coming back to God. Revelation 17:14, "the Lamb shall overcome them: for he is Lord of Lord's, and King of kings: and they that are with him are called, and chosen, and faithful."

The deer was constantly observing everything. May we be cautious in our walk with God and not drift into a state of confidence that nothing will happen to us spiritually. We need to stay faithful in the Word of God, in prayer, in church attendance, in our tithes and offerings, in our service for the Lord. Psalm 6:8-9. "Depart from me, all ye workers of iniquity; for the LORD hath heard the voice of my weeping. The LORD hath heard my supplication; the LORD will receive my prayer." I have seen that same deer several times this spring and summer. It is very cautious, very alert. Proverbs 6:5, "Deliver thyself as a roe from the hand of the hunter, and as a bird from the hand of the fowler." Be careful, stay faithful, always keep a humble heart, repent of sin and keep a clean heart. The deer and I looked eye to eye, and it saw no harm in me because I stood as still as I could. Look straight into the eyes and heart of God and you will see safety from sin. Do not take your eyes off of what Christ would have you to be. That doe turned and walked away into the safety of the forest. Live in the arms of God and walk with Christ.

May we be cautious in our walk with God and not drift into a state of confidence that nothing will happen to us spiritually.

July 7

2 Chronicles 13-14 Psalm 7 Proverbs 7 Revelation 18-19

On Fire for God

Good morning! Life is a battle and the victory is ours in Christ, but the battle must be fought with His strength. We grow through battles if we fight in His strength. Anybody can quit, but it takes a walk with the Lord and a continual looking to Him for strength to get the victory. II Chronicles 13:10, "But as for us, the LORD is our God, and we have not forsaken him." As I read, "we have not forsaken him," I thought, there were those that did forsake Him.

Last night during the rain storm, there was some powerful lightning. I read a little bit about lightning this morning. Hot air from the earth rises and creates a water vapor, and as the warm air continues to rise, a cloud is formed. At the top of the cloud is cooler air, and that cooler air gets below freezing to form ice particles. These ice particles bump into each other and cause electrical charges. This is just like the static electric charge a person can get walking on carpet. Lighter, positively charged particles on top of a cloud bump into negatively charged particles on the bottom of a cloud and create a spark. When the particles get bigger and bump into each other more, we see the lightning.

I stopped and thought. Hot and cold bumping into each other causes a spark. That is what happens in our lives when we are not hot and right with God and we turn cold on hearing and listening to Him. There is a battle. Revelation 19:10b, "I am thy fellow servant, and of thy brethren that have the testimony of Jesus: worship God." Our lives should be a challenge to each other to "worship God." Proverbs 7:2, "Keep my commandments, and live, and my law as the apple of thine eye." It is no wonder when we are walking with God and on fire for God reading His Word, faithful in church, etc., and then we begin to backslide, that there is a battle. It is just like when you mix cold air and warm air, you have a storm brewing. Psalm 7:11, "God judgeth the righteous, and God is angry with the wicked every day." That lightning in the sky can strike and burn a barn or house. I have seen great and mighty trees struck by lightning and split in the middle. May we take this simple illustration of lightning and stay on fire for God. When the storms of life come, check where the cold might be coming from in your life. Weather the storm and live for God.

It takes a walk with the Lord and a continual looking to Him for strength to get victory.

July 8

2 Chronicles 15-16 Psalm 8 Proverbs 8 Revelation 20-21

Joy in Serving Christ

Good morning! Quit looking and listening to all the bad. It is about time that we as God's people quit looking and listening to all the negatives and realize there is joy in living and serving Christ. I had a flat tire on the batwing mower. It is a fifteen-foot mower that I pull behind the tractor. That mower has twelve tires on it. As I was greasing the mower and checking all the tires, I came to one that was low in air. I put some air in it and when I did, I heard the air coming out of a very small hole. Well, I took the tire off and headed to the shop to have it repaired. While I was standing and waiting outside the repair shop, two people drove up and told me what they needed fixed. I smiled and said, I am sorry but I do not work here. A man then pulled up right in front of me with a truck and trailer with three riding mowers on it. He got out, came over and got in my face and began hollering at me for not properly fixing his front tire on his mower. I tried to tell the man that I did not work here and he kept hollering and said, I recognize your face and you are the one that worked on my mower. The owner then came out and stopped the man. I just smiled and thought, I am not going to stand here anymore, and just chuckled. As I drove home, I called my wife and said, "What a day I am having!" and explained all that had happened and we laughed together.

II Chronicles 15:2b, "The LORD is with you, while ye be with him; and if ye seek him, he will be found of you; but if ye forsake him, he will forsake you." I was falsely identified. I am so very thankful that the Lord knows me and never mistakes me for anyone else. II Chronicles 16:9, "For the eyes of the LORD run to and fro throughout the whole earth, to shew himself strong in the behalf of them whose heart is perfect toward him." God has always and will always know who I am and what I am doing or not doing. We need to quit letting circumstances control us and quit letting fear destroy us. Enjoy the end promise that is coming.

Revelation 21:4, "And God shall wipe away all tears from their eyes; and there shall be no more death, neither sorrow, nor crying, neither shall there be any more pain: for the former things are passed away."

We may get accused of something we are not or never did. We may be persecuted or we may go through difficult trials, but hang on to God's words. Proverbs 8:8-9, "All the words of my mouth are in righteousness; there is nothing froward or perverse in them. They are all plain to him that understandeth, and right to them that find knowledge." Focus on God, His Word and His promises. Psalm 8:1, "O LORD our Lord, how excellent is thy name in all the earth!" I drove away from the tire shop and had a good old laugh. How else to look at things! God knows!

We need to quit looking at all the negatives
and realize there is joy in serving Christ.

July 9

2 Chronicles 17-18 Psalm 9 Proverbs 9 Revelation 22

Making Right Decisions

Good morning! Each day that we live on this earth is full of making decisions. Decisions are as various as our lives. The most important area is that of our walk with Christ. It is the decision to get up early enough in the morning to read the Word of God, spend time in prayer, a time in meditation about what we read. It seems that we put God off first. I want you to think with me for a moment about a decision that you made and after you made this decision, you said to yourself, I should have stuck with my first decision. In other words, you talked yourself out of what was right to do.

II Chronicles 17:3, "And the LORD was with Jehoshaphat, because he walked in the first ways of his father David, and sought not unto Baalim." Let us this morning look at the phrase, "he walked in the first ways." As we walk and grow in the Lord, we will be more sensitive to the voice and leadership of the Holy Spirit's speaking in a still small voice. Jehoshaphat was listening and following his heart as he allowed his love for God to lead him. II Chronicles 17:6, "And his heart was lifted up in the ways of the LORD." Doing right is not hard when we let the ways of the Lord dominate our decision-making process. God never goes against His principles. Tithing, church attendance, service, faithfulness, separation, etc. will all be very clear to us when we follow the guidelines given us in the Bible. Christ will return and it can be today so we need to heed the words of Revelation 22:12, "And, behold, I come quickly; and my reward is with me, to give every man according as his work shall be." Revelation 22:14a, "Blessed are they that do his commandments." Making right spiritual decisions is not hard when those decisions are made in the light, understanding and obedience of the Scriptures. Proverbs 9:6, "Forsake the foolish, and live; and go in the way of understanding."

You say that you are going through a tough time? Then apply Psalm 9:9, "The LORD also will be a refuge for the oppressed, a refuge in times of trouble." God is always there for us to seek and follow. We need to learn to put our trust in God and His Word. Psalm 9:10, "And they that know thy name will put their trust in thee: for thou, LORD, hast not forsaken them that seek thee." Decisions of life made in consistency with the Scriptures will always be right decisions. God never asks us to compromise His principles. If you are going through some tough times and you do not know what to do, I suggest the same path that Jehoshaphat took, "he walked in the first ways of his father David."

Doing right is not hard when we let
the Lord dominate our decision-making process.

July 10

2 Chronicles 19-20   Psalm 10   Proverbs 10   Matthew 1-2

God's GPS

Good morning! Are you old enough to remember going on a trip and following a map? I remember stopping at gas stations and having to buy maps of different states that we were going through. I remember keeping a road atlas in the car. Now we take our cell phones and put in an address or we have a GPS in our vehicles and we put in an address. I was recently scheduled to go preach in a revival meeting. My wife and I had checked the mileage from my phone and we looked at the three different suggested routes and we chose one. As it came that day to travel, we had picked the route and my wife entered it in the phone. Well, I thought I would also enter it in the car's GPS. Our car is a 2014 and we are so thankful for it. I entered the address and off we went. As we got to a part of the trip where there had been some major construction and road changes, the car GPS and the phone GPS did not agree on where to turn and what road to follow. I, as the leader of our home, chose the car's GPS and to make a long story short, we had to turn back and follow the phone's GPS. Pride swallowed once again.

Many Christians often struggle on who and what to follow instead of maintaining a focus on the Word of God and spiritual leadership in our lives. We often think we know what is best and we head down the wrong road of life. II Chronicles 20:15 caught my attention this morning, as the Lord was giving king Jehoshaphat direction before what he thought was going to be a destructive battle, "for the battle is not yours, but God's." As the people were preparing to face the enemy, Jehoshaphat said in II Chronicles 20:20b, "Believe in the LORD your God, so shall ye be established; believe his prophets, so shall ye prosper." As we read on in Matthew this morning, we read in Matthew 1 and 2, five different times statements are used like, "the angel of the Lord appeared unto him," "being warned of God." Too many of us are trying to follow what we think instead of following what God says and shows us through spiritual God-called leaders. Proverbs 10:29, "The way of the LORD is strength to the upright." God is not like a GPS leading us in the wrong direction because it has not been updated. Directions from God are always the right direction. Psalm 10:17, "LORD, thou hast heard the desire of the humble: thou wilt prepare their heart, thou wilt cause thine ear to hear."

Mrs. Smith said, you have to decide which GPS you are going to listen to. You are getting lost. I stopped the vehicle, looked at her, looked at both GPS's and said, you are right, what I am following is wrong. You know what? When I followed the right path, we arrived at our destination at the right time and had a great service. Who or what are you following today? May I suggest that you stop, humble yourself before God and give Him full leadership of your life.

Directions from God are always the right directions.

July 11

2 Chronicles 21-22 Psalm 11 Proverbs 11 Matthew 3-4

Who Influences You?

Good morning! I remember a preacher whom I have the highest respect for, one day said, "I might not know very much, but what I know, I know very well." I have used that quote a lot throughout the years. All around us are people that are saying and doing things and I really do not think they know what they are doing. We have a generation that does not know their history, and they are destroying what will really help them to appreciate what they have if they would only study about it before they destroy it. They make accusations without knowing the facts. There is hatred toward authority that has been established to protect, not bring harm. Wrong associations will bring wrong results.

King Jehoshaphat had an association with wicked king Ahab and it not only affected his life but, when Jehoshaphat was gone and his son Jehoram began to reign, we see wickedness from the very beginning. II Chronicles 21:6, "And he walked in the way of the kings of Israel, like as did the house of Ahab: for he had the daughter of Ahab to wife: and he wrought that which was evil in the eyes of the LORD." Can you picture the wickedness? When he died, the Scriptures record in II Chronicles 21:20, "he reigned in Jerusalem eight years, and departed without being desired." Those words "without being desired," should ring in our ears. Living a life without honors, no respect shown. Now his son Ahaziah reigns, and as father, so as son. II Chronicles 22:3, "He also walked in the ways of the house of Ahab: for his mother was his counsellor to do wickedly." Mom and dad, what guidance and counsel are you giving your children? Young person, what counsel and guidance are you following? II Chronicles 22:9b, "So the house of Ahaziah had no power to keep still the kingdom." We turn this morning to the book of Matthew and find the devil tempting our Lord Jesus, and saying to Him in Matthew 4:9, "And saith unto him, All these things will I give thee, if thou wilt fall down and worship me." The devil is a liar and deceiver, and most of all a destroyer. Listen to the words of Jesus in Matthew 4:10, "Then saith Jesus unto him, Get thee hence, Satan: for it is written, Thou shalt worship the Lord thy God, and him only shalt thou serve."

My friend, please pay attention to who is influencing you. Our pride will destroy us and keep us from heeding proper counsel. Proverbs 11:2, "When pride cometh, then cometh shame: but with the lowly is wisdom." We must build solid foundations of understanding and Bible principles. Psalm 11:3, "If the foundations be destroyed, what can the righteous do?" Our world is filled with a lot of wrong information and it is destroying the very foundations that teach us to do right. Stand strong, stand for truth only. Listen to the quote that I began with, "I do not know very much, but what I know, I know very well." Psalm 11:7, "For the righteous LORD loveth righteousness; his countenance doth behold the upright." Be around the right friends and know the right information.

We must build solid foundations of understanding and Bible principles.

July 12

2 Chronicles 23-24 Psalm 12 Proverbs 12 Matthew 5

Unity with God

Good morning! To decide to live for and to serve the Lord is not a difficult decision. The part that is hard is to face every day and to make every decision according to God's Word and according to what is right in the sight of the Lord. Many have started and had a great desire to live for the Lord but have dropped off, stopped, quit during a difficult time. I would like us to focus for a moment on a phrase in II Chronicles 23:6, "but all the people shall keep the watch of the LORD." It is up to all of us who are saved to build unity in the family of God. We are all different but all loved by the Lord. God did not make one mold, and yet we are all created in His image and after His likeness. We need to be faithful to God, patient with others, loving as brethren and understanding when people are growing in the Lord.

In II Chronicles 23, we see the Priest Jehoiada spiritually leading the people to turn to God. II Chronicles 23:16, "And Jehoiada made a covenant between him, and between all the people, and between the king, that they should be the LORD's people." And yet after his death the people turned. II Chronicles 24:19, "but they would not give ear." Our challenge today from the Bible is to build unity with God, and to take a stand for God even when others do not, but do not be on the attack when others do not do exactly like you do. Matthew 5:44, "But I say unto you, Love your enemies, bless them that curse you, do good to them that hate you, and pray for them which despitefully use you, and persecute you." Do not let the devil or your flesh have the victory when you are hurt by the words of someone else. Matthew 5:45, "That ye may be the children of your Father which is in heaven." Matthew 5:48, "Be ye therefore perfect, even as your Father which is in heaven is perfect." The word "perfect" means growth in maturity. Sometimes the words of others hurt and the hurt is deep. Proverbs 12:18, "There is that speaketh like the piercings of a sword: but the tongue of the wise is health."

Let God's Word be the comfort and teaching tool to do right when you go through a trial. Let His Word be the tool, bandage, healing that it is meant to be. Psalm 12:6, "The words of the LORD are pure words: as silver tried in a furnace of earth, purified seven times." Hold your head high, be mature, do right, hold your tongue, and go forward for the Lord.

Build unity with God and take a stand for God even when others do not.

July 13

2 Chronicles 25-26 Psalm 13 Proverbs 13 Matthew 6-7

Let the SON Shine

Good morning! Because of the rain last evening and the change in temperature, the ground is covered this morning with a heavy ground fog. You cannot see very far ahead of you but as the sun comes up, the light lets you see just a little bit further. I stopped and thought that is just like the Christian life. We cannot always see as far as we want to see. Some days life seems so clear and other days we can hardly see twenty feet in front of us. The most important step forward in the Christian life is to do what is right in the eyes of God.

II Chronicles 25:2, "And he did that which was right in the sight of the LORD, but not with a perfect heart." Doing right but not with a right heart can and will get us in trouble. Let us back up and ask ourselves why we do not always do things with a right heart. We will fail when we think we know better than God knows. II Chronicles 26:16, "But when he was strong, his heart was lifted up to his destruction: for he transgressed against the LORD his God." When excuse becomes the reason for lack of obedience, excuse is the step toward destruction. As I look into the heavy mist, I cannot see, but as the sun comes up higher, the way is clearer to walk. May we let the SON come to a higher place in our lives that we may see the right way more clearly. Matthew 6:33, "But seek ye first the kingdom of God, and his righteousness; and all these things shall be added unto you."

Many Christians desire a walk with God, but they walk in a mist of excuses. Proverbs 13:4, "The soul of the sluggard desireth, and hath nothing: but the soul of the diligent shall be made fat." The key word is "sluggard," which means idle, inactive, having no power to move self. Press on, my brother and sister. The more we grow in our relationship with the SON, the more we understand how to grow in a world of sin. Psalm 13:6, "I will sing unto the LORD, because he hath dealt bountifully with me." Walk in the light of the LORD. He will always make the path clear. When I let the SON shine in my life, the sun always seems brighter each day.

The most important step forward in the Christian life
is to do right in the eyes of God.

July 14

2 Chronicles 27-28 Psalm 14 Proverbs 14 Matthew 8-9

A Prepared Heart

Good morning! When someone else says they believe in you, they see more than you see in yourself. They say those words to be of an encouragement. Yesterday, I found myself making mistake after mistake. I felt like quitting several times and just calling it a day, and yet I needed to get work done at the ranch. So, I pressed on and did accomplish several goals. We will never reach our ultimate potential for Christ if we do not press on. God believes in what He can do through us, but we must give ourselves to Him.

II Chronicles 27:6, "So Jotham became mighty, because he prepared his ways before the LORD his God." The three words, "because he prepared" spoke to me this morning. What are we preparing for? Are we preparing? It is fine for someone to see something in us, but unless we are preparing ourselves to do more and come closer to the Lord, we will not grow in our walk with God. Follow along as I show you what happens to king Ahaz in II Chronicles 28:23, "Because the gods of the kings of Syria help them, therefore will I sacrifice to them, that they may help me. But they were the ruin of him, and of all Israel." We let the world be a priority in our lives because we think that is where our help is, instead of preparing ourselves in and for that relationship with the Lord. We read this morning of many that Jesus came to and healed in Matthew 8 and 9, but I love what we read about the woman with the issue of blood. Matthew 9:21, "For she said within herself, If I may but touch his garment, I shall be whole." She "prepared" herself with a strong faith in what Jesus could do even before she got to Him. Read with me what Jesus did in Matthew 9:22, "But Jesus turned him about, and when he saw her, he said, Daughter, be of good comfort; thy faith hath made thee whole. And the woman was made whole from that hour."

Keep your heart "prepared" for God to do great things in you, through you, and for you. Proverbs 14:12, "There is a way which seemeth right unto a man, but the end thereof are the ways of death." Just believe God can and quit feeling God can't unless you look to the world. "Prepare" your heart to be faithful to God in every area of your life. Psalm 14:2, "The LORD looked down from heaven upon the children of men, to see if there were any that did understand, and seek God." God is looking. Let us be the ones that, when He sees us, have "prepared" our ways to serve Him.

Keep your heart "prepared" for God to do great things in you, through you, and for you.

July 15

2 Chronicles 29-30 Psalm 15 Proverbs 15 Matthew 10

Let God Prepare You

Good morning! There is something special about working in the soil, preparing the ground, planting a seed or plant and watching things grow. This morning we read in II Chronicles 29:19, "we prepared." It is as though the ground of a life is being prepared to serve the Lord. God has a work for each of us who give our lives fully to the Lord. Some will preach, some will clean a building, some will drive a bus, some will teach a class, some will visit the sick, encourage the downhearted or those going through a trial. There is a place for all to serve. The happiest people in the Lord are the serving people. The most unhappy people are those expecting others to serve them and those that do nothing for others. II Chronicles 29:36, "And Hezekiah rejoiced, and all the people, that God had prepared the people." Too many do nothing for the Lord; it is all about themselves.

Many weeks ago, my wife had eyed an old bird bath at a junk store. She had looked at it several times. The day came that we went by, bought this bird bath and my wife cleaned it up and painted it. She had a vision of building a little garden area with this bird bath sitting in the center. To make a long story short, we watched as miracle after miracle happened with the provision of the bird bath, plants, potting soil, mulch and a stone border. What was left was to prepare the ground. We marked the area, dug and tilled, and removed the sod. As we finished and stepped back to look, we rejoiced in the blessing of the Lord's provision. I listened as my wife explained to me what she could see. As we finished last night, I thought of what the Lord can see in our life, but we do not let Him "prepare" us for His plan.

Lose yourself and let God fulfill His plan in your life. Matthew 10:39, "He that findeth his life shall lose it: and he that loseth his life for my sake shall find it." Why do we fight what God sees could be in and through us? Proverbs 15:32, "He that refuseth instruction despiseth his own soul: but he that heareth reproof getteth understanding." I watered the holes that I had dug for the plants, and as I put them in the ground and brought the fresh soil around them and watered them again, they seemed to perk up and stand a little taller. We went to the house and cleaned up and came back out and just stood and enjoyed what God had prepared to happen. All that was needed was someone to do the work. Psalm 15:4, "he honoureth them that fear the LORD." Are you "prepared" to give God your all? Have you "prepared" your heart to say, Lord thy will be done? I love those words in II Chronicles 29:19, "we prepared." Have a very blessed day.

The happiest people in the Lord are the serving people.

July 16

2 Chronicles 31-32 Psalm 16 Proverbs 16 Matthew 11

All Your Heart

Good morning! As pastor welcomed some visitors that were in attendance at church, I looked over and saw the missionary couple that pastor brought to our attention. I told my wife, I think we know that lady. After the service the missionary family came over toward us and before I could speak, the lady said, "Bro. Dave, it is good to see you," and she thanked me for the years that she had attended camp. I met her husband and son and we caught up on the past years. She attended camp for several years and her last year to attend, she surrendered her life to missions and now they have been in the ministry for many years. Our hearts were blessed as we heard the words, "thank you for having camp and not quitting." They are serving on an island many thousands of miles away where they have to take a boat or an airplane to reach this island. I do not know why, but a summer back in 1970, a couple of thousand miles away from where I lived, the Lord did a work in my heart for the camping ministry. It has never left my heart, and the seeds that were planted that year just keep growing and growing.

What have you given your life to do for the Lord? Have you given your life for whatever His will is? King Hezekiah did some things that we need to consider as we begin our journey this morning. II Chronicles 31:21, "And in every work that he began in the service of the house of God, and in the law, and in the commandments, to seek his God, he did it with all his heart, and prospered." We need a fresh commitment of giving the Lord "all" of our hearts. II Chronicles 32:26, "Hezekiah humbled himself for the pride of his heart." Pride will keep us from just about everything that God would like for us to give Him. We live in frustration, envy, jealousy, and selfishness. Matthew 11:28-29, "Come unto me, all ye that labour and are heavy laden, and I will give you rest. Take my yoke upon you, and learn of me; for I am meek and lowly in heart: and ye shall find rest unto your souls." The Lord is looking for us to give "all" of our hearts to Him. Proverbs 16:9, "A man's heart deviseth his way: but the LORD directeth his steps."

Little did I know in the mountains of Colorado, as I knelt by myself and gave my heart to the Lord for whatever His will was, that it was a beginning of seeing lives changed, not through me but through God using His ways in His time to fulfill His work. Psalm 16:8, "I have set the LORD always before me: because he is at my right hand, I shall not be moved." We got in the car and sat there and for a few brief moments, time passed and we thanked the Lord for His love and grace to allow us to serve Him. Please give Him "all" your heart today, tomorrow and the rest of your life. He will direct your steps.

We need a fresh commitment of giving the Lord "all" of our hearts.

July 17

2 Chronicles 33-34 Psalm 17 Proverbs 17 Matthew 12

Pull the Weeds

Good morning! As I was mowing, I stopped and looked at a flower garden that has been so beautiful so many times. I shut the tractor off and just sat there looking at the weeds that have now grown right next to beautiful bushes and flowers. The weeds have been pulled many times and mulch has been spread time and again, and yet the weeds continue to come back. When the weeds first begin to grow in the mulch, they are easy to pull up and get rid of, but when they are not pulled and their roots grow so deep, they are hard to remove. I thought, this flower garden is just like our lives.

As long as we keep the sin confessed and forsaken, our relationship and walk with Christ is so rewarding. But when we let the roots of sin sink deep into our lives, it is harder to get the sin out. II Chronicles 34:27, "Because thine heart was tender, and thou didst humble thyself before God, when thou heardest his words against this place, and against the inhabitants thereof, and humbledst thyself before me, and didst rend thy clothes, and weep before me; I have even heard thee also, saith the

LORD." When the ground is hard, it is harder to pull the weeds out. When there is no mulch to keep the ground fertile, it is harder to pull the weeds out. When our lives become hardened to the things of God, it is harder for us to be tender to the voice of the Lord and the conviction of the Holy Spirit. A garden must be maintained and a life must be constantly cleansed from sin. Matthew 12:37, "For by thy words thou shalt be justified, and by thy words thou shalt be condemned." The weeds will grow freely if we do not keep pulling them.

What joy it is to look at blooming flowers and bushes when there are no weeds in them and beautiful mulch around everything. Proverbs 17:22, "A merry heart doeth good like a medicine: but a broken spirit drieth the bones. Psalm 17:6, "I have called upon thee, for thou wilt hear me, O God: incline thine ear unto me, and hear my speech." Do we need to pull some weeds and face some sin in our lives? A weed-free garden is so much more beautiful to enjoy than a garden grown over with weeds. What joy there is in walking with Jesus when we are right with Him and not trying to cover sin in our lives. Psalm 17:15, "As for me, I will behold thy face in righteousness: I shall be satisfied, when I awake, with thy likeness." Let us get down on our knees this morning and get some weeds (sin) out of our lives.

There is joy in walking with Jesus
when we are right with Him and not covering sin.

July 18

2 Chronicles 35-36 Psalm 18:1-15 Proverbs 18 Matthew 13

No Remedy

Good morning! After I had my devotions this morning, I went to get my cell phone. May I interject a thought? Never begin your day by looking at your phone. Always start your day with a time with the Lord in prayer and in His Word. When I got my phone to send this morning's devotional, there were two text messages with pictures. One was of a stack of blocks that were saved by a camper from the Thursday night bonfires of decisions made at camp, and another picture was of a fire and the pastor sending me kind remarks of memories of camp. These pictures were a great blessing to me because of the memories people share from camp.

As we close the book of II Chronicles, there is sadness of rejection. II Chronicles 36:16, "But they mocked the messengers of God, and despised his words, and misused his prophets, until the wrath of the LORD arose against his people, till there was no remedy." How sad and how terrible, that there was "no remedy." They rejected all God was trying to do. That is the way with so many people who reject what God is trying to do in their lives. It is not God rejecting us, but us rejecting God. We see in Matthew 13 Jesus using parables to get a Biblical truth across. Matthew 13:10, "And the disciples came, and said unto him, Why speakest thou unto them in parables?" As we read down in two different verses Jesus gives the answer. Matthew 13:13, "Therefore speak I to them in parables: because they seeing see not; and hearing they hear not, neither do they understand." Matthew 13:49, "So shall it be at the end of the world: the angels shall come forth, and sever the wicked from among the just." I am so thankful for decisions made for Christ and yet we see so many that have rejected what Christ is desiring to do in their lives. Proverbs 18:2, "A fool hath no delight in understanding, but that his heart may discover itself." Proverbs 18:15, "The heart of the prudent getteth knowledge; and the ear of the wise seeketh knowledge." There are those who hunger to grow in the Lord and have a tender heart to the things of the Lord. Then there are those who have salvation and think they have enough or they have never been saved and think that they have life figured out.

As parents, we should have a priority to have our children in church even when perhaps they do not understand, because we are helping them understand the importance to always be in church and to be tender to the obedience of the Lord. I love what the Psalmist wrote for us to read this morning. Psalm 18:1-2, "I will love thee, O LORD my strength. The LORD is my rock, and my fortress, and my deliverer; my God, my strength, in whom I will trust; my buckler, and the horn of my salvation, and my high tower." God is there for us all the time. Call upon Him today. Psalm 18:3, "I will call upon the LORD." I looked at the picture of the pile of blocks from camp with decisions written on them, made by a camper who had a tender heart toward the Lord, and I looked at the picture of a family around a campfire and was so thankful that it brought memories of what the Lord did in their lives. Do not arrive at a point in your life that there is "no remedy."

We must keep a tender heart and not reject what God is trying to do in our life.

July 19

Ezra 1-2 Psalm 18:16-36 Proverbs 19 Matthew 14

Go to the Source

Good morning! I watched as a hummingbird, a wasp, and a yellow jacket came to the same feeder. The feeder is a hummingbird feeder that my wife keeps sugar water in for the hummingbirds. Three different creations of God, and yet all three know where to go to get strength to maintain their life.

This morning we open the book of Ezra in the Old Testament and we read in Ezra 1:1, "the LORD stirred up the spirit of Cyrus king of Persia." Ezra 1:2, "he hath charged me to build him an house at Jerusalem, which is in Judah." Now in verse 5 we read, "all them whose spirit God had raised, to go up to build the house of the LORD." No one forced the hummingbird, wasp or the yellow jacket to come to the feeder; they just knew where to go to get their strength. Can I say it another way? They had a desire to live so they went to the source. We read in Matthew 14:14, "And Jesus went forth, and saw a great multitude, and was moved with compassion toward them, and he healed the sick." Jesus was stirred with the multitudes that He saw. Many a Christian are falling because they do not go to the Source for their strength and when they see the multitudes, their heart is not stirred because they only see themselves. It is as if we are seeing a generation of Christians starving spiritually because they are doing everything the world offers, yet they have not gone to the Source to give them the spiritual strength they need. Proverbs 19:23, "The fear of the LORD tendeth to life: and he that hath it shall abide satisfied; he shall not be visited with evil."

I moved the hummingbird feeder earlier in the week to allow me to do some work, and the birds kept flying by and it was as if they were dive bombing me. I had moved their source and they were searching for it so they can sustain their life. Psalm 18:30, "As for God, his way is perfect: the word of the LORD is tried: he is a buckler to all those that trust in him." Jesus met with the multitudes most of the time in the open, in the heat, without a place to sit, without a nursery, with no drinking fountain and so restroom. The multitude hungered to get to the Source that would heal them, teach them, give comfort, give guidance. May we go to the Source of our strength today. May we go to Jesus and His Word today. The Spirit of the LORD stirred in the heart of king Cyrus and the stirring was felt for a remnant to return to build the temple. May it be said as we read in Psalm 18:21, "For I have kept the ways of the LORD, and have not wickedly departed from my God." Go to and stay with God, our Source, for everything you need.

Many Christians are falling because they do not go to the Source for their strength.

July 20

Ezra 3-4 Psalm 18:37-50 Proverbs 20 Matthew 15

Press On

Good morning! I am writing this morning from the state of Indiana. We are here to help with a week of camp and are excited to see how the Lord is going to bless. How I know He is going to bless is because the devil always fights the work of the Lord when it is going forward.

Just as we read this morning in Ezra 3:3, the people of God were offering offerings morning and evening. They were having a time with God twice a day, and the people were so excited to be rebuilding the temple of God. Just as you and I desire to go forward and serve the

Lord, the devil tries to stop the work. We read in Ezra 4:4-5, "Then the people of the land weakened the hands of the people of Judah, and hired counselors against them, to frustrate their purpose." It did not stop there. They called them a rebellious city in Ezra 4:15. We even read in Matthew 15:2, when Jesus is ministering and doing great miracles, the scribes and Pharisees show up, "why do thy disciples transgress the tradition of the elders?." I love how Jesus tells them like it is in Matthew 15:7-8, "Ye hypocrites, well did Esaias prophesy of you, saying, this people draweth nigh unto me with their mouth, and honoureth me with their lips; but their heart is far from me."

It is just like the time that you and I live in. They say church is not essential, but it is, and we must press on and be faithful to our Lord. The world would love to silence the voice of the Christian, but we must press on as the people of God did in Ezra 3, "morning and evening." Wake up and spend time with God. End each day with a time with God. Proverbs 20:13, "Love not sleep, lest thou come to poverty; open thine eyes, and thou shalt be satisfied with bread." Let the Word of God be your source of strength and encouragement. Psalm 18:46-47, "The LORD liveth; and blessed be my rock; and let the God of my salvation be exalted. It is God that avengeth me, and subdueth the people under me." Hold your head high in a humble walk with God and stand for truth. God is our strength. He is our Lord, our King. Have a blessed day.

We must press on and be faithful to our Lord.

July 21

Ezra 5-6 Psalm 19 Proverbs 21 Matthew 16-17

Purpose of Life

Good morning! As we read this morning starting in Ezra 5, I asked myself as a reminder, what is my purpose of life in the Lord? We all live a very busy life. Ask yourself this morning, what is my purpose of life? There was a group of people in Ezra's day, as there will always be, that wanted to criticize the work of the Lord. Those who are critical are usually those who are doing nothing and only see themselves. The question was asked in Ezra 5:3, "Who hath commanded you to build this house, and to make up this wall?" You see, the walls of the temple were beginning to rise. I love the people's answer in Ezra 5:11, "We are the servants of the God of heaven and earth." Those who were criticizing thought they could get the work of the Lord stopped so they wrote a letter to king Cyrus and his response was perfect in Ezra 6:7, "Let the work of this house of God alone."

God has a work for all of us to do and we must focus on the work that we are doing and not be distracted by the attacks or distractions of others and other things. May I ask the question again, what is your purpose for the Lord? As I look at the campers this week, I know God has a purpose for each of their lives and I am praying that they will come closer to what God has for them through the preaching and teaching. Matthew 16:13, "Whom do men say that I the Son of man am?" Jesus asked his disciples this question to check where their attention to their calling was, and then he asked them personally in Matthew 16:15, "But whom say ye that I am?" Life is more than just having a job and making some money, owning a car, getting an education, buying a house, building a retirement. Life's purpose for us as a Christian is to be actively serving in the perfect will of God. Matthew 16:24, "If any man will come after me, let him deny himself, and take up his cross, and follow me."

Things are not wrong to have in this world, but our priority should not be things, but the will of God. God had the heart of king Cyrus, and God has a purpose in the heart of every king. Proverbs 21:1, "The king's heart is in the hand of the LORD, as the rivers of water: he turnereth it whithersoever he will." Proverbs 21:2, "Every way of man is right in his own eyes: but the LORD pondereth the hearts." God is asking us to check our hearts this morning. Who or what has your heart? May our words be those of Psalm 19:14, "Let the words of my mouth, and the meditation of my heart, be acceptable in thy sight, O LORD, my strength, and my redeemer." God's will and way is the best will and way to have. Have a very blessed day.

Life's purpose for us as a Christian is to be actively serving in the perfect will of God.

July 22

Ezra 7-8 Psalm 20 Proverbs 22 Matthew 18

Fellowship with God

Good morning! Nothing is more comforting than to know that the Lord is with you. To know that when we pray the Lord is hearing, to know He understands the hurt in our hearts. To know He understands the burden we are carrying is a comfort and peace beyond words. We must keep our heart prepared and right before the Lord so that our relationship is in tune and we have a oneness with God.

Ezra 7:10, "For Ezra had prepared his heart to seek the law of the LORD, and to do it, and to teach in Israel statutes and judgments." Ezra had "prepared his heart." He focused on being right with God, having confessed sin, and having a willing obedience to follow God. We read the result of what happens in Ezra 8:22, "The hand of our God is upon all them for good that seek him; but his power and his wrath is against all them that forsake him." It is so important to stay right with God daily and every moment of the day. We must keep ourselves humble before God. When the Holy Spirit convicts us of sin, we must immediately deal with the sin and confess it and forsake it. Matthew 18:3, "Except ye be converted, and become as little children, ye shall not enter into the kingdom of heaven." God will not bless a Christian's life who knows they are living in sin and not getting the sin confessed and forsaken. Matthew 18:4, "Whosoever therefore shall humble himself as this little child, the same is the greatest in the kingdom of heaven." It is a wise person who confesses their sin and deals with it immediately. Proverbs 22:3, "A prudent man foreseeth the evil, and hideth himself: but the simple pass on, and are punished."

Listen and observe these words in Psalm 20, "Now know." Psalm 20:6, "Now know I that the LORD saveth his anointed: he will hear him from his holy heaven with the saving strength of his right hand." "Now know," God will bless a life when we humble ourselves before God, keep all sin confessed, and obediently follow Him in every area of our life. Let us keep our hearts "prepared" as Ezra did. Do it now and keep it all the time in fellowship with our LORD.

When the Holy Spirit convicts us of sin,
we must immediately confess it and forsake it.

July 23

Ezra 9-10 Psalm 21 Proverbs 23 Matthew 19

Set Apart

Good morning! As I was working at the ranch, I went by a field of the neighbor's and noticed an area he had set aside to grow pumpkins. It was far away from the other rows. In the last few weeks, the seeds have germinated and beautiful plants have come up. There is a lot of space, not only from the other parts of the garden but the hills of pumpkin seeds are far from each other. I do not know if you have ever grown pumpkins but they will branch out in all directions.

We as God's people must understand the importance of separation from the world and its sins. Follow with me in Ezra 9:1-2, "The people of Israel, and the priests, and the Levites, have not separated themselves from the people of the lands... so that the holy seed have mingled themselves with the people of those lands." What a mess when plants cross pollinate. There are many vegetables that will cross over and, instead of you having what you thought you planted, you have a vegetable or fruit that really is no good because it was affected by another plant. Ezra wrote in Ezra 10:11, "Now therefore make confession unto the LORD God of your fathers, and do his pleasure: and separate yourselves." At the end of a week of camp the campers have heard many a Bible message and lesson. The influences of the world have been kept away and separation from sin has given the Word of God and the Holy Spirit a time of cleansing and separation. What a blessed time when you see the altars full of tears and campers getting right with God. It is like a fresh start again with God because their heart was given afresh to HIM. Proverbs 23:26, "My son, give me thine heart, and let thine eyes observe my ways." The Heavenly

Father draws us close to Him. To some it seems impossible, but not with God. Matthew 19:26, "With men this is impossible; but with God all things are possible.

As a camper goes to an altar with a heavy, broken heart, I see them one by one get up with another step of victory over sin. As the pumpkin plant grows, the blossoms bloom and soon a bright orange pumpkin will grow from that little hill of separation. Give your heart afresh to God this morning. Psalm 21:2, "Thou hast given him his heart's desire, and hast not withholden the request of his lips. Selah." Oh, the joy to come to God and be loved, forgiven and set anew unto Him as we have separated ourselves unto Him.

We as God's people must understand the importance of separation from the world and its sins.

July 24

Nehemiah 1-2 Psalm 22:1-21 Proverbs 24 Matthew 20

Look Around You

Good morning! I wrote these words at the top of my notes this morning as I was reading my Bible these words, "Is your heart tender to hear and see the needs around you?" We spend most of our life focused on us and not others. Someone might say, if I do not take care of me, then who will? I think the right answer is God, when we do His will, His way. As we begin reading in the book of Nehemiah this morning, we read in Nehemiah 1:4, "And it came to pass, when I heard these words." All Nehemiah heard was the words concerning the remnant left at Jerusalem. The result of his hearing is, "I sat down and wept, and mourned certain days, and fasted, and prayed before the God of heaven."

When is the last time the needs of someone else brought you to your knees before God with a broken heart and such an urgency that you stopped everything, fasted, mourned and wept before God? Nehemiah was so moved by the words that he heard that we read in Nehemiah 1:6, "that thou mayest hear the prayer of thy servant, which I pray before thee now, day and night, for the children of Israel thy servants." We need to look around us and hear the cry, and be brought to our knees in prayer. This is why Jesus came. He came for all mankind. Matthew 20:28, "Even as the Son of man came not to be ministered unto, but to minister, and to give his life a ransom for many."

I sat reading my Bible this morning and heard a very unusual sound and jumped up and ran outside. It was a larger than usual pack of coyotes that made a sound like I had not heard before. Is the cry of this world bringing us to our knees or have we learned to ignore it? Can you hear the plea of a lost and dying world without Christ? Matthew 20:34, "So Jesus had compassion on them." The path of life today will bring us by those whom we should reach out to and give them the true answer to their burdens. Proverbs 24:30, "I went by the field of the slothful, and by the vineyard of the man void of understanding." Let us look today at the needs of others instead of just our needs. Let God move your heart in a way like never before. Carrying the burden of others makes the load we are carrying much lighter. Psalm 22:19, "Be not far from me, O LORD: O my strength, haste thee to help me." There is a joy unspeakable when we allow our hearts to be moved by God for others and our lives are put into action to share the Gospel of Christ with a lost and dying world. Let us keep our ears tuned to the needs of others and watch the urgency of our needs be answered by God in a way we never dreamed. Have a blessed day for the cause of Christ.

Can you hear the plea of a lost and dying world without Christ?

July 25

Nehemiah 3-4 Psalm 22:22-31 Proverbs 25 Matthew 21

A Team Effort

Good morning! I watched a couple of young men as they were playing catch with a baseball. When I was a boy, I lived for baseball season. I practiced almost the year round. On the back of one of our buildings where I was raised, I nailed a bushel basket and when there was time, I would practice throwing balls into that basket. Baseball is a team sport; there is not one position. Every team member is of utmost importance.

In Nehemiah 3 there are some phrases I want to look at this morning; "they builded," "next unto him," "next unto them," "earnestly repaired," "after him repaired." The work of rebuilding the wall around Jerusalem took everyone working as a team, together. Nehemiah 4:6, "So built we the wall; and all the wall was joined together unto the half thereof: for the people had a mind to work." "So built we" means it was not about one person, it was a team effort. Everyone has a part in the work of God. We need a team effort to win the lost to Christ. There is not one person more important than another. Nehemiah 4:17, "They which builded on the wall, and they that bare burdens, with those that laded, every one with one of his hands wrought in the work, and with the other hand held a weapon." Please, never think that you are not important. It takes everyone in their place, doing what they can to make the team. Some will be seen and some will not be seen. The foundation of every building that stands cannot be seen and there is no building that would stand without a foundation. Usually, the most important part of something is what is not seen. Jesus was getting ready to enter Jerusalem and He sent His disciples to get an ass, but watch with me at what they brought. Matthew 21:2, "Go into the village over against you, and straitway ye shall find an ass tied, and a colt with her: loose them, and bring them unto me." How many could Jesus ride upon? Only one, but He said, "loose them, and bring them unto me." All pictures painted by artists only show one, but there were two.

You are important. You are always missed when you are not in your place. You might not feel you are important, but you are. Proverbs 25:13, "As the cold of snow in the time of harvest, so is a faithful messenger to them that send him: for he refresheth the soul of his masters." This verse in Proverbs lets us know when there is a great need in harvest time and winter is coming, it is of great encouragement when the "faithful messenger" shows up to help. Psalm 22:30, "A seed shall serve him; it shall be accounted to the Lord for a generation." Every seed counts just like every person counts. You are of most importance. Always be in your place. The team needs you and wants you. See you in church.

Usually, the most important part of something is what is not seen.

July 26

Nehemiah 5-6 Psalm 23 Proverbs 26 Matthew 22

Press On

Good morning! I have heard it often said, "we are only as strong as what it takes to stop us." I love reading about those missionaries that kept going when the times were tough and it seemed as though everything was against them. Missionaries who never quit, but pressed on because of a burden that was given them to carry for the Lord, will have a very special place in Heaven. I remember the story of a missionary that had given their life to the mission field and was old, tired and had to come home because of failing health. When the ship docked and they walked down the ramp to shore, there was no one there to meet them. The missionary thought how they had given their entire life to serve the Lord and there was no fan fair at the end. They were just lonely and by themselves. The missionary stopped, asked the Lord to forgive them as they thought of the hundreds and, yea, thousands that they will one day meet who were saved on the mission field where the missionary gave them the gospel of Christ.

Are you going through a battle? Does it seem like at every turn you take, there is something or someone standing in the way? Nehemiah 6:2, "That Sanballat and Geshem sent unto me, saying, Come, let us meet together in some one of the villages in the plain of Ono. But they thought to do me mischief." There will always be distractions and discouragements. Nehemiah and the people pressed on and we read in Nehemiah 6:15, "So the wall was finished." The enemies of the work of God and the temptations of the flesh can be defeated. Nehemiah 6:16, "they were much cast down in their own eyes: for they perceived that this work was wrought of our God." The work of God presses on even when the devil and his crowd do everything they can to stop it. Jesus faced the same thing in Matthew 22:15, "Then went the Pharisees, and took counsel how they might entangle him in his talk."

Press on, my brother and sister, press on. Proverbs 26:4, "Answer not a fool according to his folly, lest thou also be like unto him." Proverbs 26:11, "As a dog returneth to his vomit, so a fool returneth to his folly." The world will always return to their sin. Forward for Christ, my brother and sister! Our Shepherd is there with us every step of the way. Psalm 23:4-5, "Yea, though I walk through the valley of the shadows of death, I will fear no evil: for thou art with me; thy rod and thy staff they comfort me. Thou preparest a table before me in the presence of mine enemies: thou anointest my head with oil; my cup runneth over." Our KING is with us as we walk with Him today. Five times they tried to distract, discourage, and get Nehemiah and the people to stop and they pressed on. Press on!!

Forward for Christ! Our Shepherd is with us every step of the way.

July 27

Nehemiah 7-8 Psalm 24 Proverbs 27 Matthew 23

A Light for Christ

Good morning! I stood and looked at the ground where all of the grass is brown from people walking on it and right in the middle there is a weed growing as green as can be. To the world and its ways, it seems that you and I are often looked at as weeds. We do not go with the crowd, we have different principles that come from the word of God, we do not go along with the culture but the truths taught from the Bible. I guess to the world and its ways, we stand out like a weed, but we have the gift of life that the world needs to hear about.

In Nehemiah 7 this morning I kept reading the phrase, "the children of." I then asked myself, what am I reproducing in my life? As the wall was finished and the people gathered together and a count was made, we read in Nehemiah 8:1, "And all the people gathered themselves together as one man." They were unified because of what God had done through them. At one time they were a scattered people, and now God had done a work through them and we read how their focus was now on the Word of God. Nehemiah 8:3, "the ears of all the people were attentive unto the book of the law." We sometimes feel all alone like that weed I looked at, but we are not. In Matthew 23, Jesus is letting the Pharisees have it in 23:28, "Even so ye also outwardly appear righteous unto men, but within ye are full of hypocrisy and iniquity." Basically, they are not what they appear to be. We are not a weed in the middle of some dead grass! We must carry the light of salvation into a darkened world. As the people drew together toward the Word of God in Nehemiah, we must be about seeing the lost world come to Christ. Proverbs 27:23, "Be thou diligent to know the state of thy flocks, and look well to thy herds."

Today we will walk among the world and we must see them as lost and going to a devil's Hell. The world is destroying itself and they know not what they are seeking. Listen to those who claim to be the leaders and you will find that what they are saying is really bringing more hate, confusion and empty hope. I want to say again that we often look like a weed in the middle of dry grass, but truly we have the truth that this world needs. As I read this morning in Psalms, my heart was so stirred to realize how badly this world is seeking something and we know what will meet that emptiness. Psalm 24:6, "This is the generation of them that seek him, that seek thy face, O Jacob. Selah." The weed that caught my eye was green and thriving. We have life in Christ that will be life for this dead, darkened world. Be a bright shining light for Christ today. Be the green life in the middle of deadness.

We must carry the light of salvation into a darkened world.

July 28

Nehemiah 9-10 Psalm 25 Proverbs 28 Matthew 24

Are You Bearing Fruit?

Good morning! As a Boy Scout I earned patches called merit badges. These badges were awarded after I completed the requirements set down by scouting leadership. I love the outdoors, and I remember learning to identify different trees. There are different ways to identify a tree, such as by their leaves, by their bark, by their fruit, by their structure, etc. It is easier to identify the type of tree when there are leaves on the limbs, but there are still ways even when there are no leaves. I asked myself this morning, could we be identified as a Christian?

Nehemiah 9:10, "So didst thou get thee a name." The name "Christian" is more than just a name, it has characteristics. "By their fruits ye shall know them." You can identify a tree by its fruit. The children of Israel paid a price for their sins of hardness toward God. Nehemiah 9:16, "But they and our fathers dealt proudly, and hardened their necks, and hearkened not to thy commandments." Even though they paid a great price for their hardness, God was forgiving. Nehemiah 9:17, "but thou art a God ready to pardon, gracious and merciful, slow to anger, and of great kindness, and forsookest them not." How are you identified today? By your lifestyle, by your dress, by your speech, by the places you go, by the friends that you keep, by your faithfulness to witness, by your faithfulness to church, by your faithfulness to stand for Biblical principles, by your fruit? Jesus is coming again! Will you be ready? Will you be found faithful? Matthew 24:42, "Watch therefore: for ye know not what hour your Lord doth come." Matthew 24:44, "Therefore be ye also ready: for in such an hour as ye think not the Son of man cometh." If you would come and look at the wood pile I have for bonfires, cookouts, campfires, and burning in our wood stove, you would see many different kinds of wood, but one thing for sure, it is all wood. When Jesus comes, He is coming to get His own and they can only be identified by one way, and that is the only way. Those that have personally by faith trusted Him as their Saviour, He will take with Him. Many have heard but have not yet trusted Christ.

Could our life and its actions be giving a false impression of Christianity to a lost and dying world? Proverbs 28:9, "He that turneth away his ear from hearing the law, even his prayer shall be abomination." It does not matter what name I give a tree, for it is a tree. It does matter if you and I know for sure if we are saved. Psalm 25:14, "The secret of the LORD is with them that fear him; and he will shew them his covenant." To the world it is a secret that needs to be told, to us who are saved it is a story that needs to be told. I looked at a beautiful tall, straight, and fruit-bearing walnut tree. When there were no leaves on the tree and the cold of winter had come, you could look on the ground and see the walnuts that had not been picked up and say, this is a walnut tree, because of the fruit that you saw. What kind of fruit is your life bringing forth? Think about it today.

Could our life and its actions be giving a false impression of Christianity to a lost and dying world?

July 29

Nehemiah 11-13 Psalm 26 Proverbs 29 Matthew 25

A Blessing to Others

Good morning! When life is over on this earth, what will really count? It is not how many hours we have worked, how much is in investments and savings, it is not even in what positions we have held. What counts for eternity is what we have done for Christ because that is what will last. Nehemiah 11:2, "And the people blessed all the men, that willingly offered themselves." I am thankful for the Sunday School teachers that not only prepared a lesson, presented a lesson, and sent a card when I missed a class, but I now know they prayed for me. I am thankful for the men that drove the bus, those that helped in the VBS's that I attended, those ushers that smiled when they passed an offering plate, a greeter that welcomed me to church. I could go on and on and give praise and honor to those who have no idea they affected my life for Christ.

As I read on this morning in Matthew 25:21 and 23, "His lord said unto him, Well done, thou good and faithful servant; thou hast been faithful over a few things, I will make thee ruler over many things: enter thou into the joy of thy lord." Have you yielded, are you serving, have you offered yourself to do for others? All of us have had others that have greatly affected our lives. What are you doing for the cause of Christ? Proverbs 29:7, "The righteous consideth the cause of the poor: but the wicked regardeth not to know it." Look at the space in your car or truck or van. If there is space, fill it with a person that needs a ride to church. Go to the Dollar Store and purchase a card and send it to someone that the Lord brings to your mind. We have phones that can reach around the world and yet we do not send a text or make a call to someone that we have not seen in church for a long time. Do we only see ourselves? Proverbs 29:23, "A man's pride shall bring him low: but honour shall uphold the humble in spirit."

My wife and I were coming home from town and we got behind a group of cars. You could look ahead and see it was a line of cars going to a cemetery because of the police escort. Many were impatient and yet on the other side of the road there were cars pulling over to show respect for the deceased. I thought as we drove on, if people will not show respect for the living, they will never show honor for the deceased. Ask the Lord to show you those that you should thank and give honor to today. Psalm 26:12, "My foot standeth in an even place: in the congregations will I bless the LORD." I stopped reading and thought about standing on the side of a hill and then standing on level ground. We are always more stable when standing on level ground, so bring yourself down and reach out to others. What do I mean by "bring yourself down?" We need to quit putting ourselves, our needs, our wants, our desires in first place and see who we can reach out to and be a blessing to. There will be that day when we are all alone, and yet we will not be alone if we have spent our lives for others. Look around and see the needs of others and offer yourself. "And the people blessed all the men, that willingly offered themselves."

Have you offered yourself to do for others?

July 30

Esther 1-2 Psalm 27 Proverbs 30 Matthew 26

The Fruit is Coming

Good morning! Do you remember hearing the statement, "The truth is yet to be told?" Who or what do you believe? We know that the Bible is the perfectly preserved Word of God. It has been preserved through the ages and yet it is not believed. Esther 2:15, "And Esther obtained favour in the sight of all them that looked upon her." Esther 2:17, "she obtained grace and favour in his sight more than all the virgins." Esther is in a prime position, and yet something is still hidden. She is observed, she is separated, she is exalted, she is in position and yet she is not revealed. A sapling of a young fruit tree is planted, and we wait for the growth. Several years pass until we can enjoy the fruit. Seasons will come and go, wind, rain, snow, heat, and drought, and yet the little fruit tree continues to grow until it produces the fruit that it was designed to produce. God had a plan for Esther, and He has a plan for you and me. Let God work His plan and be patient.

In Matthew 26:34, Jesus told Peter, "thou shalt deny me thrice." In Matthew 26:35, we read Peter and the other disciples responded by saying, "Peter said unto him, Though I should die with thee, yet will I not deny thee. Likewise also said all the disciples." As they went to the garden together and the soldiers and Judas showed up, we read in Matthew 26:56, "Then all the disciples forsook him, and fled." How many of us have regrets? Probably all of us. The little sapling will not produce fruit for several years. Many a Christian gives up and quits before they really begin to see and understand the hand of God. The disciples all left Jesus, and yet thankfully they regrouped and God used them again. Do not lose your love and trust in the Word of God. Proverbs 30:5, "Every word of God is pure: he is a shield unto them that put their trust in him."

Okay, you may have quit, you may have given up. Restart, and get going again for the Lord. Be patient in seeing His hand and answering your prayers. God has never left us or forsaken us. Psalm 27:14, "Wait on the LORD: be of good courage, and he shall strengthen thine heart: wait, I say, on the LORD." I looked at a counter full of vegetables as Mrs. Smith was preparing them for the freezer. It took time for those to grow and ripen for picking and for eating. Don't quit. Don't give up, "wait on the LORD." There is fruit that will come if we just wait on the Lord.

Many Christians give up and quit before they begin to see and understand the hand of God.

July 31

Esther 3-4 Psalm 28 Proverbs 31 Matthew 27

God Hears Our Cry

Good morning! Picture in your mind this morning a large barn, and as we approach the barn we hear a mother cat crying for her young. Mrs. Smith had a cat that I think she (the cat) believed it was the will of the Lord to have more kittens than any other cat we ever had. Mrs. Smith called her Calley. I would often hear her crying and I would go to where the cry was and Calley would be calling her kittens to her.

As I read this morning, the word "cry" kept appearing in my reading, and I wrote on the top of my notes this question, "What cry is Heaven hearing?" Wicked, self- righteous, full-of-pride Haman has been promoted. He is parading around enjoying all the glamour of his position in politics. All are to bow to him as he passes but there is a man that is not bowing, and his name is Mordecai. As I often say, his grits got cooked because Mordecai would not bow. Haman was full of anger. Esther 3:5, "And when Haman saw that Mordecai bowed not, nor did him reverence, then was Haman full of wrath." I am thankful and understanding that we can show respect and honor to our elected officials, and we should, but we are not to bow and reverence them like God. I wholly believe in giving honor to whom honor is due, but not reverence. Haman went to the king. Esther 3:8, "And Haman said unto king Ahasuerus, There is a certain people scattered abroad and dispersed among the people in all the provinces of thy kingdom; and their laws are diverse from all people; neither keep they the king's laws." A law was written to destroy this people and it was the Jewish people, of which Mordecai was one. Now observe Mordecai's response and the people's response. Esther 4:3, "there was great mourning among the Jews, and fasting, and weeping, and wailing, and many lay in sackcloth and ashes." There was a "cry" heard in Heaven from the people of God.

God has heard many a "cry" and He needs to hear our "cry" for the condition of our world today. When His Son was being judged, God heard a cry. Matthew 27:23, "And the governor said, why, what evil hath he done? But they *cried* out the more, saying, Let him be crucified." God heard another "cry" in Matthew 27:46, "And about the ninth hour Jesus *cried* with a loud voice, saying, Eli, Eli, lama sabachthani? that is to say, My God, my God, why hast thou forsaken me?" Then God hears His Son "cry" out again in Matthew 27:50, "Jesus, when he had *cried* again with a loud voice, yielded up the ghost." I ask the question again, what "cry" is Heaven hearing from us today? Are we "crying" out for the salvation of lost souls, revival in our lives, revival in our world? Is Heaven hearing a "cry" from us? A mother hears the "cry" of her children. Proverbs 31:2, "What, my son? And what, the son of my womb? And what, the son of my vows?" May Heaven hear today and every day the "cry" from Christians to a wholly righteous God. Psalm 28:2, "Hear the voice of my supplications, when I *cry* unto thee, when I lift up my hands toward thy holy oracle." As a mother cat calls her kittens, they hear the plea of love, compassion, security and, in essence, the "cry" of "come to me." May Heaven be ringing with the "cries" of God's people "crying" out for forgiveness and a healing of our land. Spend extra time today "crying" out to our Redeemer, our Lord, our KING.

Are we crying out for the salvation of lost souls,
revival in our lives and revival in our world?

Esther 5-6 Psalm 29 Proverbs 1 Matthew 28

What is Your Petition?

Good morning! Can you hear with me a little child as they come running to their parents saying, "Mommy, Mommy!" or "Daddy, Daddy!." They come running to the arms of their parents and the parents say, what is the matter, what do you need, what do you want, what is going on? The child comes to the parent to fix or take care of the situation or to help with a need and, most of the time, an urgent need. Are you with me? Picture the child making the plea for help and then the parent saying, "What is it that you want?"

In Esther 5:3, we read the phrase, "What is thy request?." In Esther 5:6, we read, "What is thy petition?" Then we read in Esther 5:7, "Then answered Esther, and said, My petition and my request is." Stay with me and listen to the words of Esther 5:8, "If I have found favour in the sight of the king, and if it please the king to grant my petition, and to perform my request." A child will come pleading to their parent for help and that is the "petition." A good parent will stop and listen to the child's "request," and that will bring action to fix the situation by the parent. When we come to God in prayer seeking Him, that is our "petition," and when we get specific with God in what our need is, that is our "request." Esther went to the king as the authority and let him know what she needed. Oh, that this truth would help us with our prayer life. In Matthew 28:19, Jesus had gone to the cross and these are his words to the disciples after he had conquered death, "Go (plea, petition) ye therefore, and teach (request, action) all nations, baptizing them in the name of the Father, and of the Son, and of the Holy Ghost." Proverbs 1:8, "My son hear (petition, plea) the instruction (request, action) of thy father, and forsake not the law of thy mother." We read on in Psalm 29 and we see the phrase, "The voice (petition, plea) of the LORD," six times. As we read in Psalm 29:11, "The LORD will give strength (request, action) unto his people; the LORD will bless his people with peace (request, action)."

Oh, that as Esther came to the king in a time of critical need because he was her earthly authority, and made a specific request, may we see the important Biblical principle to come to a closer walk with our Lord in our time of prayer with Him. A praying people are a serving people, and a serving people are a happy people. How is your joy today? How is your prayer life today? Take time to go to God, and when you go, let Him hear how you need Him to help you. May God meet with us like He desires to meet with us. The child loves the parent and knows the parent loves them. Does God know you love Him and look to Him?

A praying people are a serving people, and serving people are happy people.

August 2

Esther 7-8 Psalm 30 Proverbs 2 Mark 1

Pray for Missionaries

Good morning! I love reading biographies and listening to people, especially the older generation, tell stories and teach me as I listen. I miss the days of being able to sit with my grandparents and parents and listen to their stories and learn and grow in understanding of life. I have to remind myself often that I am the grandparent now, and I catch myself talking and then I look how they are listening and wanting to know.

Esther comes before the king, Haman gets his judgment, Mordecai is put in a royal position and now the decree of the king is proclaimed throughout the land. I thought this morning how we can hold the unchanging, perfectly preserved Word of God in our hands and how it is to be proclaimed throughout the world. Esther 8:13, "The copy of the writing for a commandment to be given in every province was published unto all people." It was copied and distributed throughout the land. Is that not what we are to be doing with the Word of God, taking it and proclaiming the truths to all people throughout all the world? Thank God for those that surrender their lives to take the gospel throughout the world. Do you have a list of missionaries your church supports, so that you can pray for them as they take the Word of God to the people they are called to? Esther 8:17, "And in every province, and in every city, whithersoever the king's commandment and his decree came, the Jews had joy and gladness, a feast and a good day. And many of the people of the land became Jews; for the fear of the Jews fell upon them." The gospel is life changing to all lands and all people. My heart stirred as I read the words of Jesus in Mark 1:38, "Let us go into the next towns, that I may preach there also: for therefore came I forth." We may not be called to a people of faraway places, but we should hold those up in prayer and give financially to those who do go to take the Gospel of Christ. Proverbs 2:20, "That thou mayest walk in the way of good men, and keep the paths of the righteous."

As the times are showing forth the closer return of our Lord, and as the wickedness of this world grows, we must put a stronger focus on getting the gospel to a world that is lost and without Christ. Psalm 30:12, "to the end that my glory may sing praise to thee, and not be silent. O LORD my God, I will give thanks uno thee for ever." The prayers and fasting, the boldness, the stand that Esther and Mordecai took, and those who prayed and fasted, brought a great victory in the lives of many. May we put our focus on spending time in prayer, fasting and surrendering to take the Gospel of Christ to all people of the world. Pray for your missionaries and do what you can to spread the Gospel.

We should hold missionaries up in prayer
and give financially as they spread the Gospel.

August 3

Esther 9-10 Psalm 31 Proverbs 3 Mark 2

A Binding Relationship

Good morning! My heart is so blessed when I observe a couple in their senior years and their relationship is approaching sixty years of marriage. Some will never be able to see those years because of sickness and disease. For those who have been together so long, there is much to learn. There is something binding between them. That binding is not something you can buy. It is not something that you can get through a book or on the internet. The miracle of almost sixty years of marriage is a constant building of a relationship.

As we read this morning in Esther 9, we see a great victory of relief for Esther, Mordecai and all the Jewish people, but I think we can see much more with them and the reality that God brought the miracle. Esther 9:15, "but on the prey they laid not their hand." Esther 9:16, "but they laid not their hands on the prey." Esther 9:10, "but on the spoil laid they not their hand." The words "prey" and "spoil," caught my eye this morning. Those that hated the Jewish people were killed under the king's authority, but the Jewish people did not take the spoil or belongings of those that they killed. Follow me please. Too many of us have relationships with people for what other people have or can give us. We live in a very political world in many areas of our lives. Some people like you for what they can get out of the relationship, but once they get what they want, they are gone. Many do not have a walk with the Lord because the only time they need the Lord is when they want something. Esther and these others did not want things, position, or anything other than freedom. Sin binds us, sin destroys us, sin captures us, and most of all sin controls us. A true walk with Jesus is a desire to know Him, fellowship with Him, honor Him, live for Him, and please Him. A walk with Jesus is not about getting what we want, but about growing in a relationship with Him.

Many things I have learned from being around those my senior, but one of the most important lessons is that of relationship. It is not about getting, but giving. Let us look at the call of Matthew in Mark 2:14, "And as he passed by, he saw Levi the son of Alphaeus sitting at the receipt of custom, and said unto him, Follow me. And he arose and followed him." Mark 2:15, "for there were many, and they followed him." What did they follow Him for? Yes, some turned back, and some did not. We must soon arrive at a point of building a relationship for a relationship and not just things or needs. Proverbs 3:6, "In all thy ways acknowledge him, and he shall direct thy paths." "All thy ways," every day and every hour and in every situation; "acknowledge him." Psalm 31:3, "For thou art my rock and my fortress; therefore for thy name's sake lead me, and guide me." In every area of our life Jesus must be the reason. Let Him have your heart, let Him be the focus of your life. Psalm 31:23, "O love the LORD, all ye his saints: for the LORD preserveth the faithful, and plentifully rewardeth the proud doer." How my heart is blessed to watch senior saints whot love each other and are still in love with serving the Lord together.

In every area of our life Jesus must be the reason.

August 4

Job 1-2 Psalm 32 Proverbs 4 Mark 3

Compassion for Others

Good morning! Never quit believing in what God can do in the lives of others. We all sin and we all make mistakes, and by the help of Christ we can all get up. In Job 1:4, we read that Job's family sinned, but let us look at verse 5 and Job's response. Job 1:5, "And it was so, when the days of their feasting were gone about, that Job sent and sanctified them, and rose up early in the morning, and offered burnt offerings according to the number of them all: for Job said, It may be that my sons have sinned, and cursed God in their hearts. Thus did Job continually." Please listen to the words, "the number of them all." Our prayer lives are the true strength of our lives. I believe what made Job the man that he was, was his prayer life. Don't give up praying for others. Pray daily for each one of your family members.

When our children started their own home, my time for praying for them increased because they were not under our authority anymore. Do you pray for your loved ones? Do you pray for others? Hurting people need our compassion. When Job lost everything except his life and his wife, he sat down and three of his friends came and said or did nothing for seven days. Job 2:13, "So they sat down with him upon the ground seven days and seven nights, and none spake a word unto him: for they saw that his grief was very great." Oh, that our compassion for others would grow. We read in Mark 3 how others watched with a critical spirit and not a heart of compassion. Mark 3:5, "And when he had looked round about on them with anger, being grieved for the hardness of their hearts, he saith unto the man. Stretch forth thine hand." The ways of this world do not permanently help the hurting because we know that Christ is the answer. Proverbs 4:19, "The way of the wicked is as darkness: they know not at what they stumble." Look at your path of life. Is it a path of compassion? Proverbs 4:26, "Ponder the path of thy feet, and let all thy ways be established." The blessings of God are there, but our stubbornness keeps us from following the path Christ has for us. Psalm 32:9, "Be ye not as the horse, or as the mule, which have no understanding: whose mouth must be held in with bit and bridle, lest they come near unto thee."

The victorious life is a life of compassion for others, to take the gospel story and to be of an encouragement through prayer and reaching out to help others instead of just being focused on ourselves. I have often said, a horse that is not broken is a horse of little or no value. A Christian that constantly focuses on themselves is a Christian that misses the true blessings of the Lord. There is something all of us can do, but we must get our eyes off of ourselves to see it. Some things to think about today.

The victorious life is a life of compassion for others.

August 5

Job 3-4 Psalm 33 Proverbs 5 Mark 4

Drive Defensively

Good morning! God is so good to us. May I start off by saying, "Behold, the eye of the LORD is upon them that fear him, upon them that hope in his mercy;" Psalm 33:18. Who are you serving and why are you serving? As I read the words of God this morning about Job, I had to stop and try to place myself as best I could next to Job. "For the thing which I greatly feared is come upon me, and that which I was afraid of is come unto me." Job 3:25. We think there is a safe territory in life and there is not. We think we have everything under control with our goals, our abilities, our insurance, and so on, but this is not peace and safety. Job 3:26, "I was not in safety, neither had I rest, neither was I quiet; yet trouble came."

I was driving down the road with Mrs. Smith on our way to the grocery store, and we were just talking and enjoying the time together. We were going around the corner and as we entered the curve, there was a truck that had crossed the line going at a very fast speed and cutting the corner. We just missed a head on collision. Our seat belts were on, I was in my lane, going the speed limit and yet we almost had an accident. We are never in total control of our life and we need to realize this every day. Mark 4:19, "And the cares of this world, and the deceitfulness of riches, and the lusts of other things entering in, choke the word, and it becometh unfruitful." God's Word must stay alive within us. We must daily read it, meditate upon it, and apply it. Mark 4:24, "And he said unto them, Take heed what ye hear: with what measure ye mete, it shall be measured to you: and unto you that hear shall more be given." God is so good to us and yet there is a constant battle in our flesh to let the Lord have control of every area of our lives. God knows and nothing can be hidden from Him. Proverbs 5:21, "For the ways of man are before the eyes of the LORD, and he pondereth all his goings." May our focus be on God because His focus is on us. Psalm 33:18, "Behold, the eye of the LORD is upon them that fear him, upon them that hope in his mercy."

As we traveled on (and thankfully swerved safely out of the way of the oncoming vehicle) I said to Mrs. Smith, "What did they teach us long ago in Drivers Ed class?" She looked at me and said, "Always drive defensively." That is also tremendous advice for us daily to live defensively in our daily walk with the Lord. Can I give you a verse for memory today? Psalm 33:20, "Our soul waiteth for the LORD: he is our help and our shield." Drive and walk in Christ defensively. Let Christ have the controls and follow Him.

Our focus should be on God because His focus is on us.

August 6

Job 5-6 Psalm 34 Proverbs 6 Mark 5

Enjoy His Presence

Good morning! I am so very thankful that each day I awake, the Lord is there to hear me. Psalm 34:17, "The righteous cry, and the LORD heareth, and delivereth them out of all their troubles." My heart hungers to be right and stay right with the LORD. I learned a long time ago that my most precious times with the Lord are when I say almost nothing and just enjoy His presence and comfort. I often say to Mrs. Smith, "What are you thinking?." We can be riding in a vehicle, sitting on the deck or front porch, taking a walk and saying nothing to each other. Sometimes she says, "I am just enjoying being with you. Do we have to say anything?." My challenge this morning to all of us is to just enjoy the presence of the Lord.

Job 5:7, "Yet man is born unto trouble, as the sparks fly upward." Our Lord knows that life is full of ups and downs, trials and victories. Job 5:8, "I would seek unto God, and unto God would I commit my cause." I went to feed the horses, and before I got to the fence where the feeders hang, the horses had already started toward me. There was no calling, no conversation, no coaxing, no pleading, they just came. Why? Because they knew I was bringing some grain and would spend some brief moments with them. In Mark 5:18, Legion desired to be with the Lord, "And when he was come into the ship, he that had been possessed with the devil prayed him that he might be with him." There was a hunger to be with the Lord. Oh, that we would have a hunger just to be with Him and feel His closeness, His comfort, His love. Many do not enjoy the Christian life because they are always wanting something from God instead of just enjoying His fellowship. Just wanting things from God will never bring a blessed relationship with God and peace in our hearts. Proverbs 6:35, "He will not regard any ransom; neither will he rest content, though thou givest many gifts." Learn to enjoy time with the Lord. Praise Him for who He is. Thank Him for His love for us. Exalt Him for being the KING of kings. Rejoice with Him for His salvation for all. Yes, He is there for our needs and troubles. Psalm 34:17, "The righteous cry, and the LORD heareth, and delivereth them out of all their troubles." Yes, when we have battles, He is there. Psalm 34:19, "Many are the afflictions of the righteous: but the LORD delivereth him out of them all."

See if you can just enjoy some quiet time with the Lord today. It is not wrong to ask for things and for help, but let us try to just have some time of quiet fellowship with Him. Reach out to Him today and enjoy that quiet time of His presence. The burdens will not seem as great and the needs will be taken care of in a surprising way. Psalm 34:9, "O fear the LORD, ye his saints: for there is no want to them that fear him." The word "fear" is to please and honor him. There is no greater way to please a person than to just enjoy their presence. "Honey, what are you thinking? I am just enjoying being with you." Wow!! I am blessed.

Reach out to God today and enjoy that quiet time of His presence.

August 7

Job 7-8 Psalm 35:1-16 Proverbs 7 Mark 6

Keep Climbing

Good morning! Have you ever played the game, "King of the Mountain?" One person is on top of the hill and the rest of us try to get that person down and we try to get on top and stay there. I have two grandsons that have purchased motorcycles and they enjoy climbing hills with them. They sent me some videos of them in a distant state attempting to climb some very high hills with their motorcycles. I remember those days on my own motorcycle and attempting a bigger and taller hill and not having enough tire grip or power to make it, but I was determined, as my grandsons, to make it to the top. Playing King of the Mountain and having a determination to be the king of the mountain; these pictures came to my mind this morning as I read the Scriptures.

We work to overcome sin and we work to have victory in the Christian life. We work to serve the Lord, to live a righteous life, and to win souls for Christ. Yet it seems as we are trying to climb a mountain, we lose strength and slide back or get pushed back. Job 7:9, "As the cloud is consumed and vanished away: so he that goeth down to the grave shall come up no more." Please do not quit! I know life is sometimes so difficult and unfair. Keep on climbing for the glory of God. When I read Job 7:18, it was like Job is telling us, I met with God each morning and still faced trial after trial. "And that thou shouldest visit him every morning, and try him every moment?" (Job 7:18). We read how Jesus himself was not even given honor by his own earthly family in Mark 6, but He gave us the example of pressing on. Mark 6:7, "And he called unto him the twelve, and began to send them forth by two and two." Mark 6:34, "And Jesus, when he came out, saw much people, and was moved with compassion toward them, because they were as sheep not having a shepherd." Keep climbing and keep looking up. Proverbs 7:1, "My son, keep my words, and lay up my commandments with thee." Proverbs 7:2, "Keep my commandments, and live; and my law as the apple of thine eye." When king David was constantly attacked, he wrote these words in Psalm 35:13, "But as for me, when they were sick, my clothing was sackcloth: I humbled my soul with fasting; and my prayer returned into mine own bosom."

I have stood at the bottom of the hill and said I am going to keep climbing until I make it to the top. May we realize that the climbs of life bring us closer to those crowns that will be given to KING Jesus when we get to Heaven. Keep climbing, my brother and sister. You can get to the top. By the way, can a Papa brag a little bit? My grandsons made it to the top of the big hill. I just wish I could have ridden with them. Have a great day, and I will see you at the top for Jesus.

Keep on climbing for the glory of God.

August 8

Job 9-10 Psalm 35:17-38 Proverbs 8 Mark 7

Who is Your Master?

Good morning! Each evening before we call it a day, Mrs. Smith and I go out and water some new flowers and shrubs that we have planted this summer. We constructed a little flower garden and in the middle is a concrete bird bath that Mrs. Smith found at a junk store. Now, do not let that word *junk* offend you. Have you not heard the statement, what is one man's junk is another's treasures? Well, we have this little flower garden and one of our dogs decided last night while I was watering to take her path right through the middle of the garden. I scolded her with a gruff voice and she took off. In a matter of minutes, she came back to me with her tail between her legs and almost creeping back. My wife said, someone is seeking forgiveness. In Job 9:2, "how should man be just with God?" The dog cannot understand the words I say, but the tone of voice let her know that I was upset and after she took off, she came back to seek a rebuilding of our relationship. Why??? That dog has no soul, no reality of Heaven, no life ever after, no Bible to read, no Saviour to pray to, no Holy Spirit to work in her heart, and yet she seeks a rebuilding of a relationship with her master.

Brother and sister in Christ, are we just giving up, or are we trying to build a relationship with God stronger each day and confessing our sins to be right with God? Job 9:20, "If I justify myself, mine own mouth shall condemn me: if I say, I am perfect, it shall also prove me perverse." I was not unkind to my dog, but firm, and trying to teach boundaries of obedience. We must stop justifying sin and confess it and forsake it and come back to a right relationship with Him. Mark 7:20, "That which cometh out of the man, that defileth the man." Mark 7:23, "All these evil things come from within, and defile the man." We are sinners and we that know Christ have an open door to God to repent and grow in the Lord, but I am afraid the biggest problem that we all have is pride. We only see the problems of others and we do not look deeply enough inside ourselves. Proverbs 8:17, "I love them that love me; and those that seek me early shall find me." I have loved my dog from the day she was given to me as a pup. I have fed her, brought fresh water, combed her, petted her, played with her, given her special treats. I am her master. Who is the master of your life? Proverbs 8:32, "blessed are they that keep my ways." Proverbs 8:34, "Blessed is the man that heareth me, watching daily at my gates, waiting at the posts of my doors."

In just a few moments I will go to the door, and guess who will be waiting to be fed and watered and petted? Are you at the door of God, waiting to spend time with Him? Proverbs 8:35, "For whoso findeth me findeth life, and shall obtain favour of the LORD." Psalm 35:22, "Keep not silence: O LORD, be not far from me." I think I will open the door and see if Tipper is there along with Noelle. My friend, God is waiting for you and me to spend time with Him. We are not anything less than a creation of God after His image and His likeness. How can we do less than walk with Him and please Him? He sent His Son to carry the full load of our sin. Walk with Him.

God is waiting for us to spend time with Him.

August 9

Job 11-12 Psalm 36 Proverbs 9 Mark 8

Even Nature Knows

Good morning! The wisdom of God's creation is a constant amazement to me. It was time for dinner. Now, that is the noon meal to me. As I sat outside and waited for Mrs. Smith to come and eat with me, I just sat and watched the business of birds, bees, wasps, hornets and the such. At the hummingbird feeder, there were four birds fighting for a space at the feeder as well as a wasp and bumble bee. They knew where their source of strength would come from and they were doing everything they could to feed off of the sugar water in the hummingbird feeder. How did they know where this source of food was? How did they know what was inside of the feeder? Why are they working so hard to keep feeding? One simple answer, God. They do not fight how God made them. They do not fight their Creator. They are what they are and they know what they need to exist. It is not just a matter of them eating for today but they are all feeding for the time when fall and winter will arrive. The hummingbirds will have a long flight south. The bees, wasps and hornets will go into hibernation. I learned the other day that a certain kind of wasp feeds on the larvae of wood bees. Mrs. Smith had read this and told me.

How about we as men and women created in the image and after the likeness of God? Man is working overtime to learn to live without being submissive to God. I thought about the words of Job 11:7, "Canst thou by searching find out God? Canst thou find out the Almighty unto perfection?" Job 12:16, "With him is strength and wisdom: the deceived and the deceiver are his." Over ten times we read the word "He," referring to the fact that God is in control. As we read on in Mark 8:18, "Having eyes, see ye not? And having ears, hear ye not? And do ye not remember?" Mark 8:21, "How is it that ye do not understand?" Jesus was doing miracle after miracle, and quoting the Words of God out of the Old Testament writings, and yet man refused to acknowledge Him as who He was. Mark 8:27, "Whom do men say that I am?" Mark 8:29,

"But whom say ye that I am?" "Thou art the Christ." As they truly saw who He was and acknowledged who He was, we read these words in Mark 8:31, "And he began to teach them."

Where are we this morning? Open the Scriptures to learn and obey, as well as follow. Mark 8:34, "Whosoever will come after me, let him deny himself, and take up his cross, and follow me." Mark 8:35, "For whosoever will save his life shall lose it; but whosoever shall lose his life for my sake and the gospel's, the same shall save it." I am afraid we live in self-pity and self-justification and truly it all amounts to self-destruction in a walk with God. Proverbs 9:10, "The fear of the LORD is the beginning of wisdom: and the knowledge of the holy is understanding." All of nature seems to never forget God and all that they do truly reveals God. May we humbly come to Him today and be as He has created us to be, to glorify Him in everything. Psalm 36:10, "O continue thy lovingkindness unto them that know thee; and thy righteousness to the upright in heart." Take some time and observe God, our Creator and Redeemer, in His creation and let it speak to you.

May we come to Him today and be as He created us to be,
to glorify Him in everything.

August 10

Job 13-14 Psalm 37:1-22 Proverbs 10 Mark 9

In God's Hands

Good morning! Picture with me this morning a little child that has been hurt and a decision to take them to the doctor has been made. On the way to the doctor, you do your best to comfort your child and say, it is going to be alright, the doctor is going to make it better. Yet as the parent of the child you love so dearly, there is going to be pain to do what must be done to make it better.

As I read Job 13:13, "let come on me what will"; I thought of how it is necessary for us to turn our lives completely over to the Lord continually. And then as we read on down to Job 13:15, "Though he slay me, yet will I trust in him." The little child grips your hand and snuggles so close, and you want to do anything you can, but we must wait for the physician to do what he or she was trained to do. A parent does not try to do anything but bring comfort. It is not time to blame or ask a question that I have too often asked, "What were you thinking?," or ask an older brother or sister, "Where were you?." Our focus needs to be on the child and getting the child to the doctor where there will be the needed help. God has a plan and we do not always see or understand what God is doing, but when we put everything in God's hands, He will guide us to where He wants. He will take us through what we need to go through to learn and be more like Him in every way. I have often wondered why Jesus chose twelve disciples and yet only took three, Peter, James and John, alone with Him. John 9:2, "And after six days Jesus taketh with him Peter, and James, and John, and leadeth them up into an high mountain apart by themselves: and he was transfigured before them." It seems as though they needed to have something done in their lives that maybe the others did not and yet we read in John 9:35, "And he sat down, and called the twelve, and saith unto them, If any man desire to be first, the same shall be last of all, and servant of all." Life is a continual learning process, and the lessons are different for all of us. The most important thing for all of us to do is to learn and keep learning or to grow and keep growing. Proverbs 10:17, "He is in the way of life that keepeth instruction: but he that refuseth reproof erreth."

I do not know why some get sick from a disease and others do not. I do not know why same have an accident and others do not. I do not know why some seem to have all the breaks of good things and others do not. I do know that our lives are to be given to God and He is the great Physician. Psalm 37:7, "Rest in the LORD, and wait patiently for him: fret not thyself because of him who prospereth in his way." Whatever you are going through, whatever trial you are facing, whatever need you have, wait and rest in the LORD. I have sat next to my son and daughter when they were hurt and said, it is going to be alright. Now, on some occasions my children have sat next to me and said, dad, it is going to be alright. Just think, we can put our hands totally in the hands of the Lord. Do it right now and let Him be your comfort.

When we put everything in God's hands,
He will guide us to be more like Him in every way.

August 11

Job 15-16 Psalm 37:23-40 Proverbs 11 Mark 10

God's Bountiful Crop

Good morning! I believe all of us could say that we so desire for life to go smoothly. The reality is that is not going to happen. As a baby learns to walk, they are going to fall. A child learning to ride a bicycle is going to fall and want to quit. Troubles are going to come, and if we allow them, the troubles will help us to learn and to grow. Job 16:12, "I was at ease, but he hath broken me asunder: he hath also taken me by my neck, and shaken me to pieces, and set me up for his mark." God has a purpose in everything He does and everything that He allows. Job 16:19, "Also now, behold, my witness is in heaven, and my record is on high."

Mrs. Smith and I went to the garden to dig some potatoes. As I stood there in a row of dead plants and hard ground, I thought how that is just like our lives in walking with God. When we learn to die to self and all that we think we are or want, then God can really bring forth the fruit. I gently shoved the potato fork into the ground and lifted the soil at the same time I pulled the dead plant up. There they were. Coming forth where no one could have seen them are fresh potatoes. As I reached down into the soil, one potato after another appeared. Out of sight and yet the fruit was there. Mark 10:43, "whosoever will be great among you, shall be your minister." Mark 10:44, "And whosoever of you will be the chiefest, shall be servant of all." A few weeks ago, the plants in the rows and hills of potatoes were tall and green and bushy, but now what seems to be dead has brought forth a great harvest. Proverbs 11:28, "He that trusteth in his riches shall fall: but the righteous shall flourish as a branch." Let us go back several weeks earlier, and picture sitting down with a bucket of potatoes that have eyes sprouting from them and we cut them up and plant those hills with several cut up potatoes with sprouting eyes. The ground was broken up and tilled. The potatoes were cut up and planted. The plant grew tall and green, and then died. All of that to produce a wonderful crop of potatoes. Psalm 37:25, "I have been young, and now am old; yet have I not seen the righteous forsaken, nor his seed begging bread."

Think about that potato fork going into the ground and bringing forth new, fresh, delicious potatoes. As you look at the rows and the hills, everything seems dead and yet it is alive and ready. Psalm 37:28, "For the LORD loveth judgment, and forsaketh not his saints; they are preserved for ever: but the seed of the wicked shall be cut off." Let God bring forth new life in you. He has a plan beyond what you and I can see or even understand. You might feel buried in a hole or deserted. God is going to bring forth something that none of us can see. Let God dig some potatoes in your life.

God has a purpose in everything He does and everything that He allows.

August 12

Job 17-19 Psalm 38 Proverbs 12 Mark 11

Importance of Prayer

Good morning! I listened on my phone, I looked at the pictures as they came to my phone, and I heard the voice of my son. "Dad, please pray. I cannot get home to the boys and Steph because of the destruction of a storm." I am almost 700 miles away and I can pray but do nothing else. As we prayed and prayed, I realized the storm happened because of God. The trees that were uprooted grew because of God. The wind and rain that came was because of God. The safety of our family was because God protected them.

As I have been praying and as I read this morning, I wonder what will it take to turn people to Christ. Job 19:25, "For I know that my redeemer liveth, and that he shall stand at the latter day upon the earth." God is always in control and we need that confirmed in our hearts. I kept hearing those words, "Dad, please pray." What greater words could a father hear than words that you have tried to live and teach all your life? Mark 11:24, "Therefore I say unto you, what things soever ye desire, when ye pray, believe that ye receive them, and ye shall have them." I was not asked for money and I was not asked for things. I was asked to pray. Oh, that our lives would be lived so that there is always an open door to Heaven because He knows we love Him. We pray not just to ask but to enjoy the time in fellowship with Him because we love Him. Proverbs 12:28, "In the way of righteousness is life; and in the pathway thereof there is no death." Do you spend time in prayer because you love Him? Do you pray because you want to grow in Him? Do you pray because you want to exalt Him as your Saviour? Do you go to Him only in a time of need? Psalm 38:9, "Lord, all my desire is before thee; and my groaning is not hid from thee." Psalm 38:15, "For in thee, O LORD, do I hope: thou wilt hear, O Lord my God." How is your prayer life? Do you have a prayer life? He is there and is waiting to hear from us, spend time with us, and lead us in every situation.

How blessed I was when I said, "Son, what can I do?," and the answer was, "Dad, please pray." More than anything in this world, we need to be people of prayer to see the hand of God in everything in life. Our country needs us to pray. Our leaders need us to pray. Our families need us to pray. Missionaries need us to pray. We need to pray for our pastor. Pray, pray, pray is the foundation of getting and using the power of God. Pray, my brother and sister, PRAY!!

Prayer is the foundation of getting and using the power of God.

August 13

Job 20-21 Psalm 39 Proverbs 13 Mark 12

A Joyful Life of Service

Good morning! Why does a fisherman fish? Why does a hunter hunt? Why does a hiker hike to the top of the mountain? I know it sounds crazy for me to ask questions like I have, but please just stop and think with me. I started fishing and hunting and hiking as a young boy. I have gone fishing many times and not caught fish, as well as gone hunting and come home with no game. I have hiked many trails and I still have many more that I want to hike. I want to ask again, why does a man go fishing, and why does a hunter hunt and why do hikers keep hiking? Answer, because they love to do what they do.

Why do some folks quit on God? As I read this morning in Job 20:5, "That the triumphing of the wicked is short, and the joy of the hypocrite but for a moment?" Sin is never the victory, nor is the big fish, the massive buck, the most beautiful picture at the end of the trail. Sin destroys, does not satisfy, does not build, accomplishes nothing. The widow approached the place to bring her offering and it was so small, but in the eyes of the Lord it was the greatest. Mark 12:44, "For all they did cast in of their abundance; but she of her want did cast in all that she had, even all her living." A life yielded to Christ is an abundant life. A life devoted to please the Lord is a blessed life. A faithful life to Christ is a rejoicing life. A life separated from sin is a victorious life. Proverbs 13:6, "Righteousness keepeth him that is upright in the way: but wickedness overthroweth the sinner." Proverbs 13:13, "Whoso despiseth the word shall be destroyed: but he that feareth the commandment shall be rewarded." Sin brings no reward. Who are your friends? Proverbs 13:20, "He that walketh with wise men shall be wise: but a companion of fools shall be destroyed."

A fisherman keeps going to catch that trophy fish and because he likes to fish. A hunter will keep looking for that spot in the woods, prepare to be camouflaged and have the patience to wait because of the joy of hunting. A hiker never tires of the beauty of the trail. A soul winner rejoices each time to hear that sinner trust in Christ and it drives us to the next door because we know it is God's will for all to be saved. Look beyond where you are today and look for the blessings of a walk with God. Psalm 39:4, "LORD, make me to know my end, and the measure of my days, what it is; that I may know how frail I am." Psalm 39:7, "And now, Lord, what wait I for? My hope is in thee." Wait on HIM, Walk with HIM, and Work (serve) for HIM. Can I testify? My heart is overflowing at the joy of serving Jesus.

Look beyond where you are today and look for the blessings of a walk with God.

August 14

Job 22-23 Psalm 40 Proverbs 14 Mark 13

Faithful and Focused

Good morning! I stood in the middle of a flowing trout stream. I watched as the water flowed over the rocks and through the grassy growth that had grown around some of the rocks. In the blink of an eye, a small trout came from being hidden in the flowing grass out into the open where it could be seen. As I read this morning in Job 23:10, "But he knoweth the way that I take: when he hath tried me, I shall come forth as gold." I kept still in the water, thinking if there is one, there will be more. And then a thought hit me. I am to always be one with God. My path of life is not the same path as others, and He is always with me when I walk with Him. Job 23:11, "My foot hath held his steps, his way have I kept, and not declined." Job 23:12, "Neither have I gone back from the commandment of his lips; I have esteemed the words of his mouth more than my necessary food." Our lives should be challenged from these words of Job to stay faithful and stay firmly attached to the hand of God.

As the straight winds that went across Iowa and left destruction a few days ago, there was little or no advance notice of these winds coming and there will be no announcement of the Lord's return. That is why we must stay ready. Mark 13:33. "Take ye heed, watch and pray: for ye know not when the time is." To stay prepared for the return of the Lord is to stay faithful and watching. Proverbs 14:33, "Wisdom resteth in the heart of him that hath understanding." Oh, that we would focus on staying in the will of God, doing the will of God, being faithful to do the will of God. Psalm 40:8 "I delight to do thy will, O my God: yea, thy law is within my heart." Psalm 40:1, "I waited patiently for the LORD; and he inclined unto me, and heard my cry."

A trout fisherman will patiently stand in the stream and keep working the fly across the water, patiently waiting for that trout to take the bait. As the storm of destruction came and properties were destroyed, the teamwork of neighbors worked together, and many praised the Lord for their preservation of life. More fish will come down stream and more storms will come. Will we be ready? Fish bring joy to a fisherman. A storm often brings sorrow to those in its path. We must stay faithful, whether we go through the victories or the storms. Our God is true and faithful. May we be that to HIM. "He knoweth the way that I take." He will be returning soon, are you ready?

We need to focus on staying in the will of God
and be faithful to do the will of God.

August 15

Job 24-25 Psalm 41 Proverbs 15 Mark 14

Keep the Landmarks

Good morning! Starting down the trail, I begin to mark in my mind trail signs or landmarks to remember. I remember as a young man being taught how to observe landmarks on the trail to keep myself from getting lost in the woods. "Landmarks" are something that is supposed to be unmovable, something that is permanent. Job 24:1, "times are not hidden from the Almighty, do they that know him not see his days?" As we read these words in Job, it is as though the Lord is telling us to focus on His return as we are seeing the attempt to remove "landmarks" before our eyes. Job 24:2, "some remove the landmarks." Going down the trail of life as a Christian, we must not remove landmarks that are there for the purpose of maintaining a walk with God. Job 25:4, "How then can man be justified with God? Or how can he be clean that is born of a woman?" On a trail, "landmarks" build a security so that we can know where we are, where we have been, and how we can safely return.

In Mark chapter fourteen this morning we read of the time of prayer with Jesus and His disciples before His betrayal. Jesus told them that they would deny Him and yet they said, no, they would not, and we read in Mark 14:31, "I will not deny thee in any wise, likewise also said they all." And we know what happened. May we establish "landmarks" in our lives, so that we will be faithful to the end. Landmarks keep us on the right trail, landmarks keep us going in the right direction, landmarks will keep us on a safe path, and landmarks will help us to reach our destination. Proverbs 15:14, "The heart of him that hath understanding seeketh knowledge: but the mouth of fools feedeth on foolishness." There are landmarks of daily reading the Word of God, spending time in prayer, being sensitive to win souls, faithfulness in church, obedience in giving tithes and offerings, offering self for service to the Lord. Psalm 41:12, "And as for me, thou upholdest me in mine integrity, and settest me before thy face for ever."

It seems that the "landmark" of marriage, home, children is being attacked from every side. May we make today a fresh commitment to keep our "landmarks" in place. Years ago, I hiked a thirty-five-mile trail that had been made by some early settlers. As I hiked the trail and saw the landmarks, my heart was filled to think I have walked the same path that my forefathers walked. If you look behind you, you will see others coming down the same path you are on. Do not remove the "landmarks." They need them to stay on the right path.

Make a fresh commitment today to keep the landmarks in place.

August 16

Job 26-27 Psalm 42 Proverbs 16 Mark 15

Fruit Bearing Life

Good morning! I stood in the garden and looked at the labor of hands, thought of the rain that had fallen, the sun that warmed the ground and sent strength through the bright rays, and now I stand and pick the bounty. All that man did was take what God gave, prepared it, planted what God provided and truly watched as God brought the bounty. I picked tomato after tomato, dug more potatoes, thought about the corn on the cob covered in real melted butter, delicious green beans. Man did so little, compared to all that the Lord did! How can we complain?

Stand strong in the Lord. Please stand strong, consistent, and do not waver. God is so good to us. God never fails us. Job 27:4, "My lips shall not speak wickedness, nor my tongue utter deceit." Job 27:6, "My righteousness I hold fast, and will not let it go: my heart shall not reproach me so long as I live." We have nothing to complain about. We have nothing to say that God has not done for us. Picture with me that day when all turned their back on Jesus. Mark 15:3, "And the chief priests accused him of many things: but he answered nothing." Mark 15:4, "And Pilate asked him again, saying, Answerest thou nothing? Behold how many things they witness against thee." He was alone, He was scourged, He was humiliated, He was mocked, He was crucified, and He did it all for us. As I read on in Mark 15:43, "Joseph of Arimathaea came, and went boldly unto Pilate, and craved the body of Jesus."

As I stood in the garden and picked its fruit, and thought of the blessings of God, I wondered how often we crave, long for, live for, determine to have a true relationship with our KING. Proverbs 16:20, "He that handleth a matter wisely shall find good: and whoso trusteth in the LORD, happy is he." Psalm 42:1, "As the hart panteth after the water brooks, so panteth my soul after thee, O God." Psalm 42:2, "My soul thirsteth for God, for the living God." I asked myself this morning, do I thirst more for things of this world than for God? As I took the fruit of the garden to the house, I thought about my life bearing fruit for the only true source of life. Some things to think about.

How often do we long for and determine to have a true relationship with our KING?

August 17

Job 28-29 Psalm 43 Proverbs 17 Mark 16

Keep Your Faith Growing

Good morning! As you and I walk daily upon this earth, did you ever think what we are really walking on? As I read in Job 28:11, "the thing that is hid bringeth he forth to light." The rocks bring forth minerals, the gold dust is in the waters, and the water flows deep below the surface of the earth. God sees what we cannot see, not only in this earth, but in every area of our life. Oh, that we would walk with Him and face all that He wants to take us through and teach us. Listen to Job as he looks back in Job 29:2, "Oh that I were as in months past, as in the days when God preserved me." Think of the questions that we ask God when He already has the answer, the fret that we have even though He has already taken care of a situation, the excuses we give because of our lack of faith and disobedience.

In Mark 16, two ladies go to the tomb of Jesus, and on their way they ask in Mark 16:3, "Who shall roll us away the stone from the door of the sepulchre?" Some of us would have stopped because we saw no way to move that heavy stone. Mark 16:4, "And when they looked, they saw that the stone was rolled away." If we could just learn that the Lord is in control. They saw the tomb was empty. They communicated with an angel of the Lord and the disciples who had walked and been taught and saw miracle after miracle of Jesus, yet they did not believe the testimony of others. I think Jesus would tell us all today the same thing He told the disciples when He appeared to the eleven. Mark 16:14, "Afterward he appeared unto the eleven as they sat at meat, and upbraided them with their unbelief and hardness of heart, because they believed not them which had seen him after he was risen." God sees far greater than we will ever be able to see and knows far more than we could ever desire to know. Proverbs 17:24, "Wisdom is before him that hath understanding; but the eyes of a fool are in the ends of the earth." Psalm 43:3, "O send out thy light and thy truth: let them lead me; let them bring me unto thy holy hill, and to thy tabernacles."

Pick up a rock or a handful of dirt. God filled it with minerals. Look at the water that flows; God uses it for so many purposes beyond our understanding. As a boy I remember standing and watching a windmill turn to pump water from a well, and yet I could not see the wind that God sent. To have a walk with and faith in God is to see what He desires for us to see. May our faith in Him continually be growing through His Word and time we spend with Him in prayer.

God sees what we cannot see, not only in this earth,
but in every area of our life.

August 18

Job 30-31 Psalm 44:1-8 Proverbs 18 Luke 1

Urgently Seeking

Good morning! I opened the door and they were not there. I stepped outside with the treats in my hand, and they were not there. I called their names, and they were not there. I got the keys to the four-wheeler and drove and I could not find them. Then out of the corner of my eye, I saw them digging. Their focus was on getting to the animal that had gone deep into a hole in the ground. I stopped and thought how foolish I was to get so worried that something had happened to my dogs. Do I work that hard to get ahold of the Lord? Is there that urgency in my life to reach God and communicate with Him?

Job 31:35, "my desire is, that the Almighty would answer me." During Job's trials He hungered for the communication with God that He had known, to feel the Lord's presence and to have the comfort of His nearness. As it was recorded concerning Zacharias and Elisabeth in Luke 1:6, "And they were both righteous before God, walking in all the commandments and ordinances of the Lord blameless." Then Elisabeth heard the angel in Luke 1:28, "Hail, thou that art highly favored, the Lord is with thee: blessed art thou among women." The angel of the Lord also came to Mary and said in Luke 1:30, "thou hast found favour with God." To communicate with the Lord and to have the Lord respond should be the greatest desire of our hearts. Are we walking with God in a way that He would find favour in our lives? Are we pleasing to the Lord in the actions of our lives? Are we hungering to have God's blessings on our walk, our marriage, our children, our grandchildren, and all that we do and try to accomplish in life? Luke 1:50, "And his mercy is on them that fear him from generation to generation." Proverbs 18:15, "The heart of the prudent getteth knowledge; and the ear of the wise seeketh knowledge."

The dogs heard my voice and they came running. Listen for Him and may He hear us seeking Him. Psalm 44:8, "In God we boast all the day long, and praise thy name for ever. Selah." God is calling and I am afraid many are not listening to His voice. May our ears be in tune with the voice of God and may He hear us seeking Him.

To communicate with the Lord and to have Him respond should be our greatest desire.

August 19

Job 32-33 Psalm 44:9-26 Proverbs 19 Luke 2

Yearning to Please Him

Good morning! As the storm was approaching, the cool breeze began to pick up speed. I hurried to finish the section I was mowing. The sky was darkening and as I pulled into the barn, the sprinkles of rain began to hit the metal roof. As I headed toward the house, so came the dogs. Those brown eyes looked at me as if to say, the storm is coming, will you let us come in? The creations of God that seem to understand God, continually amaze me. There were no news announcements that the dogs would understand, no forewarning of the storms that were coming, just a created awareness of the acts of God.

We were created by God and have a living soul that dwells within us and we fail to hear and understand the voice and leading of God. Job 32:8, "But there is a spirit in man: and the inspiration of the Almighty giveth them understanding." Job 33:13, "Why dost thou strive against him? for he giveth not account of any of his matters." As I read on this morning in Luke chapter two, we read the testimony of the shepherds and of Simeon and Anna. Luke 2:17, "And when they had seen it, they made known abroad the saying which was told them concerning this child." Luke 2:26, "And it was revealed unto him by the Holy Ghost." Luke 2:38, "And she coming in that instant gave thanks likewise unto the Lord, and spake of him to all them that looked for redemption in Jerusalem." We have a God-consciousness, we have seen the hand of God work, we hold the Words of God in the Bible and yet we fight against the leading and promises of God. Proverbs 19:3, "The foolishness of man perverteth his way: and his heart fretteth against the LORD." May we slow down and learn better each day to hear, obey and follow the voice of God.

As I get older, I hunger more than ever to hear and obey the voice of God. Proverbs 19:20, "Hear counsel, and receive instruction, that thou mayest be wise in thy latter end." I trust your heart is yearning, as mine, to please God even more in these last days. Soon we will face our Saviour and hear Him say well done, or what will He say? Psalm 44:21, "for he knoweth the secrets of the heart." I looked at the dog I call Tipper and said, I cannot let you in, you need to go to the barn. She turned and went to the barn. How is your obedience to God?

May we slow down and learn to hear, obey, and follow the voice of God.

August 20

Job 34-35 Psalm 45 Proverbs 20 Luke 3

There is a Reason

Good morning! What a tremendous comfort it is to read verses such as Job 34:21, "For his eyes are upon the ways of man, and he seeth all his goings." God always knows what is going on in our lives. Nothing can be hidden from Him and nothing is a surprise to Him. I was trying to get some mowing done before church and I fueled, greased, checked fluid levels, checked the tires and headed out to get some mowing done. As I was mowing, the mower began to lose power. It almost died, or should I say it this way, the engine almost stopped. I sat there and said, "Father, let me see what you see that I cannot see." Job 34:32, "That which I see not teach thou me: if I have done iniquity, I will do no more."

We do not always know what the Lord is trying to teach us, but I have learned to always allow Him to show me and teach me. I made it back to the barn and got out the tools. Sure enough, when I began to check things out, one of the fuel filters had some crud in it. I have no idea why the timing of the filter plugging had to be when it was, but God does. I am not sure what lesson I am to learn, but God does. I do know that life is a continual learning process and a process of growing in a stronger relationship with the Lord. Job 35:11, "Who teacheth us more than the beasts of the earth, and maketh us wiser than the fowls of heaven?" As I read on this morning in Luke 3, the last of the chapter keeps having the phrase, "which was the son of." It is the lineage of Jesus all the way from the beginning to His birth and now earthly ministry. God knew all the time the path that would be taken to bring His Son into this world, and God knows His plan for us. It is our responsibility and privilege to go through that perfect plan. Proverbs 20:24, "Man's goings are of the LORD, how can a man then understand his own way?"

We might not understand the whys but be reassured with God that those "whys" are for a reason. Just know for sure that Psalm 45:7 is true, "Thou lovest righteousness, and hatest wickedness." When going through a trial or a testing, keep going. The reason is not important but for sure there is a reason. Just be thankful that our Lord loves us and has a reason for everything. You can make it, in His strength. Keep going and grow in the path that He has for you.

Life is a continual learning process of growing in a stronger relationship with the Lord.

August 21

Job 36-37 Psalm 46 Proverbs 21 Luke 4

What are Your Eyes On?

Good morning! The air was cooler and a little breezy, so Mrs. Smith and I sat by a fire last evening. It was a joy to have our granddaughter sit there with us, along with Miss Ruth Brenner, who has served many years with us in the camping ministry. As we began to eat supper while sitting around the little fire, there were two others that joined us. Two dogs that did everything they could to get a small bite. We told them to go lay down and they did, but something caught my eye. As I read in Job

36:7, "He withdraweth not his eyes from the righteous." As we enjoyed our evening meal and time of fellowship, both dogs laid within eyesight of us. I would look over at them and even though it looked like they were sleeping, if I made the slightest move, their eyes were open and attentive. I read on in Job 36:11, "If they obey and serve him, they shall spend their days in prosperity, and their years in pleasures."

Before supper my granddaughter had some dog treats, and she was having both dogs do several tricks. As each dog was obedient, they would receive a small treat. We are not animals and we should not be obedient just to receive from the Lord, but it is a tremendous principle to understand that our Lord does bless us in many ways for our obedience to Him. Those dogs' eyes were fastened on every move we made. In Luke 4, we read about Jesus being in the temple and He reads Isaiah 61:1-2, and we read in verse 20, "And the eyes of all them that were in the synagogue were fastened on him." Proverbs 21:2, "Every way of a man is right in his own eyes: but the LORD pondereth the hearts."

The fire was slowing down to just coals and it was time to go inside. As we stood to go in the house, both dogs got up and watched us. The entire evening, they never took their eyes off us. What could happen if we never took our eyes off Jesus? Oh, that our lives could stay so close to Him that we would know every move He made so we could be in total obedience to Him. As I read in Psalm 46:8, "Come, behold the works of the LORD." The word "behold" spoke to me as the Lord was saying, always be watching and keeping your eyes on ME. The evening finished, but my thoughts about those two dogs watching every move we made, sure made a convicting impression on me. What are your eyes on?

What could happen if we never took our eyes off Jesus?

August 22

Job 38-39 Psalm 47 Proverbs 22 Luke 5

Time to Stand

Good morning! There is nothing more beautiful than nature, or should I say, God's creation!! Who made the mountains, the valleys, the rivers that flow so freely, the eagles that soar so high, the sounds of the nights that bring such a calm, the clouds in the sky, the winds that cool the air and yet can turn so destructive? Who gave the little ant its wisdom? I read Job 38:25, "Who hath divided the watercourse for the overflowing of waters."

I have stood at the mouth of the great Mississippi River, where it is nothing more than a little brook, and yet I have stood where it is so powerful and wide as it dumps into the vast ocean in Louisiana. I have watched the muddy Missouri River and watched the power of the great Colorado River. As I read Job chapters 38 and 39, I kept seeing, "Who hath," "Who can," "Canst thou," "Hast thou," and many other questions that God asked when He conversed with Job. We need to acknowledge God in every area of our life and live our life to please Him in every area. Simon the fisherman was told to "Launch out into the deep, and let down your nets for a draught" (Luke 5:4). And then he said, as if Jesus did not know, "we have toiled all the night, and have taken nothing: nevertheless at thy word I will let down the net" (Luke 5:5). The fish filled the nets, and the response of Simon Peter should be our daily continual response to our Lord and Saviour, "he fell down at Jesus' knees, saying, Depart from me; for I am a sinful man, O Lord" (Luke 5:8). Simon humbled himself, faced himself and acknowledged the need of the Saviour by calling Him "Lord." Proverbs 22:20-21, "Have not I written to thee excellent things in counsels and knowledge. that I might make thee know the certainty of the words of truth; that thou mightest answer the words of truth to them that send unto thee?"

It is time for us to stand up for God, stand true to God's Word, stand faithful, stand full of praise, stand true in trials and testings, stand as a humble servant of the King of kings. Psalm 47:7, "For God is the King of all the earth: sing ye praises with understanding." He is GOD and He is my GOD. Take time and look at what the hands of God have created. Praise Him with all you have and keep praising Him by living fully for Him. Take your hand and put it over your heart. When that beating stops, it is eternity. Are you ready? Let us live our lives in praise and honor to the "thou hast and thou canst." He is GOD!

Praise Him with all you have and keep praising Him by living fully for Him.

August 23

Job 40-42 Psalm 48 Proverbs 23 Luke 6

Spiritual Cataracts

Good morning! How do we explain the colors of a sunset? How do we express the beauty of a sunrise? When the fall arrives and we drive down the country road and see the multitude of deep colors of the leaves painting the landscape, how do we explain that beauty? Several people that I know, love, and pray for have had to have cataract eye surgery. The doctor had to remove a film that was developing in the eye. Each time we go to the eye doctor, they will test to see if cataracts are developing. I thought about those I have recently been praying for that the cataract surgery would be of help to them.

Job 42:3, "I understood not; things too wonderful for me, which I knew not." Job could not understand or see the reason why he was going through what he was going through. His friends were spoken to by God as we read in Job 42:7, "My wrath is kindled against thee, and against thy two friends: for ye have not spoken of me the thing that is right, as my servant Job hath." What did Job say that got God's approval? Job 42:5, "I have heard of thee by the hearing of the ear: but now mine eye seeth thee." God wants us to see. The will of God is not meant to blind us. A walk with God is not a walk in darkness. Obedience to God brings light on the ways of God. Luke 6:49, "But he that heareth, and doeth not, is like a man that without a foundation built an house upon the earth; against which the stream did beat vehemently, and immediately it fell; and the ruin of that house was great." The simple truth of walking with God is to see what we need to do and to do it. Psalm 48:14, "For this God is our God for ever and ever: he will be our guide even unto death."

What are your eyes upon today? What do you have in your sights as goals for your life, your marriage, your children, and grandchildren? Make sure what you see is what God wants you to see. Proverbs 23:5, "Wilt thou set thine eyes upon that which is not? For riches certainly make themselves wings; they fly away as an eagle toward heaven." The word "eye" or "eyes" are mentioned four times in Proverbs 23. As I have prayed and spoken to folks who have had cataract surgery, they all have said, "The colors I now see are so beautiful." They saw what they were seeing, but not with the clearness and beauty that they could have seen. Can I challenge us all today to make sure we have spiritually clear eyesight? We need to ask the Lord to let us see as He sees, and for us to rejoice at what He wants us to truly see. As Job said, "but now mine eye seeth thee." Make sure sin has not caused a development of sinful cataracts, so that you cannot clearly see the will of God for your life.

We need to ask the Lord to let us see as He sees.

August 24

Ecclesiastes 1-2 Psalm 49 Proverbs 24 Luke 7

How Bright is Your Light?

Good morning! I stepped outside in the darkness of the early morning hours and took two flashlights and pointed them up into the darkness. Both lights worked and both lights had a very powerful beam. As the beam of the flashlights shown up into the darkened sky, I could easily see the difference in the power of each light. The lights shown very brightly into the sky and each light faded off to nothing at the end of the beam. What got me to thinking about what I did this morning with the lights is Ecclesiastes 1:13, "And I gave my heart to seek and search out wisdom concerning all things." Throughout chapters one and two of Ecclesiastes are the words, "I gave" and "I saw."

To what or whom have we given our heart? That is what we will see and, most of the time, only see. I have seen many a Christian have great intentions and then they drift away because their heart was given to something else. They were a bright light at one time and then they faded away. They were on fire for the Lord, serving and faithful, and then they were doing nothing and hardly even attending church anymore. Their light faded away into darkness. Ecclesiastes 2:13, "Then I saw that wisdom excelleth folly, as far as light excelleth darkness." The source of the light was the power that gave the light the brightness. Our power to shine or serve God comes from our relationship, surrender and dedication to God. How is your source of strength today? Both flashlights had good batteries and good bulbs, but the bigger source of power shone brighter and farther in the darkness. In Luke 7:25, the question is asked by Jesus, "But what went ye out for to see?" Many have a desire to live for God, but do not get their strength from the right source and their brightness soon fades out. Proverbs 24:30-31, "I went by the field of the slothful, and by the vineyard of the man void of understanding; and, lo, it was all grown over with thorns, and nettles had covered the face thereof, and the stone wall thereof was broken down." What was at one time a great producing vineyard was now not producing anything. Then we read in Proverbs 24:32, "Then I saw, and considered it well: I looked upon it, and received instruction."

How is your light shining for Christ today? How is your vineyard producing for Christ today? What I am asking is, are you living a life for Christ and seeing others strengthened in the Lord because of your walk and service for the Lord? There is a day we will truly meet our Saviour and we will see Him face to face. May we search our hearts this morning and be strengthened to shine brighter and longer for Christ. Psalm 49:15, "But God will redeem my soul from the power of the grave: for he shall receive me. Selah." Let us decide we are going to shine for God and shine as far as we can for His glory. Christ redeemed us by His shed blood, so let us be a shining beam of light for Him today.

Our power to shine comes from our relationship,
surrender and dedication to God.

August 25

Ecclesiastes 3-4 Psalm 50 Proverbs 25 Luke 8

Redeem the Time

Good morning! It is time for us who are God's people to stand up, sit up, and look at what is happening. Every generation has had their "time." My mind and heart have been touched and stirred this morning with the words we read over and over in Ecclesiastes chapter 3, "a time." Ecclesiastes 3:17, "I said in my heart, God shall judge the righteous and the wicked: for there is a time there for every purpose and for every work." It is not "time" to quit, to tire, to back off, to give up. What are we doing with the "time" God has given us? We are the generation that is before the next generation, our children, our grandchildren and possibly our great grandchildren. Luke 8:18, "Take heed therefore how ye hear: for whosoever hath, to him shall be given; and whosoever hath not, from shall be taken even that which he seemeth to have."

During our "time," we are allowing freedoms to be taken, churches to be closed, missionaries are not getting their support to go to the field that the Lord has called them to. We are acting like we have more "time" and we do not. The "time" that we live is the "time" we should be serving God. Did you ever think how many teenagers did not get saved, called to preach, get their hearts right with God these past few months because we allowed the "time" to shut things down? Proverbs 25:16, "Hast thou found honey? Eat so much as is sufficient for thee, lest thou be filled therewith, and vomit it." Have we taken church for granted and now we have learned to live without it? Have we taken for granted the coming together as believers and singing the hymns, fellowshipping as brothers and sisters in Christ? Do we now stay home from church, but go to the store, or do we watch church on a phone or computer and yet go to work and go on vacation, and yet the "time" in church is gone? Our Lord knows the "time" He has given us, and He is watching how we use it.

Psalm 50:10, "For every beast of the forest is mine, and the cattle upon a thousand hills." Our God owns it all. Psalm 50:11, "I know all the fowls of the mountains: and the wild beasts of the field are mine." He knows every animal, fowl, fish, mountain and stream and He has given us "time" to do with what we have been given. How are you using the "time" you have been given? Have we gotten used to the "time" out of church, the "time" the buses are not running, the "time" the choir is not singing? Let us redeem the "time" and get busy for God like never before. The "time" is short, and the "time" for His return is soon. May we use this "time" to press forward for our God. Some things to ponder about "time."

Our Lord knows the "time" He has given us,
and He is watching how we use it.

August 26

Ecclesiastes 5-6 Psalm 51 Proverbs 26 Luke 9

Fulfill Your Purpose

Good morning! I looked at an older car that had been restored. It was sparkling and an older couple were riding in it. I also saw an older truck setting alongside of an old barn, rusted, weeds growing all around it. As I thought about both vehicles, I thought how one person thought what could be and the other person just let it decay more and let the weeds grow around it. I wondered if one man worked toward what could be and the other man had lost a vision of what could be.

In Ecclesiastes 6:9, "Better is the sight of the eyes than the wandering of the desire: this is also vanity and vexation of spirit." God can see in us what we cannot see ourselves. God sees what He can do with us sinners and yet we so often do not allow Him to be our God that He is. The multitude that listened and followed Jesus needed to be fed, so the disciples told Jesus they needed to be sent home, and Jesus said in Luke 9:13, "But he said unto them, Give ye them to eat. And they said, We have no more but five loaves and two fishes." Jesus saw what could be and the disciples only saw what they saw. Luke 9:23, "If any man will come after me, let him deny himself, and take up his cross daily, and follow me." Luke 9:25, "whosoever will lose his life for my sake, the same shall save it." Too many quit, get discouraged and fall away, because they only see what they see instead of just staying faithful, believing God can, and pressing on by faith in God. A door just swings back and forth and yet the door can be closed and it gives this door purpose. If it is never used, it seems useless, but when it is closed it creates a room and that swinging door is given purpose. Proverbs 26:14, "As the door turneth upon his hinges, so doth the slothful upon his bed." Are we just going back and forth like a swinging door and doing nothing for the Lord? Psalm 51:10, "Create in me a clean heart, O God; and renew a right spirit within me. Psalm 51:12, "Restore unto me the joy of thy salvation; and uphold me with thy free spirit."

I looked at a beautifully restored car and I also looked at an old truck just setting there with weeds almost covering it. We have life because God has a purpose for us. Get busy, pull the weeds of sin, fall on your face before God and beg Him for the forgiveness of letting the weeds of slothfulness, laziness, selfishness, self-pity, and ungratefulness grow up all around you. Quit just swinging back and forth and get purpose for your life. God has given us life, so let us use it for Him.

We have life because God has a purpose for us.

August 27

Ecclesiastes 7-8 Psalm 52 Proverbs 27 Luke 10

Don't Lose It

Good morning! The Lord has given us another day to serve Him. I am so very thankful that as I begin each day, I have the Word of God that I can hold in my hands, read with my eyes, meditate upon the teachings and apply these to my daily life. We must daily feed ourselves on the seeds of the Word of God. We see a world that is getting farther from God, and to the human eye it seems as though nothing will stop the wickedness, but as I read this morning in Ecclesiastes 8:12, "Though a sinner do evil an hundred times, and his days be prolonged, yet surely I know that it shall be well with them that fear God, which fear before him." The very next verse lets us know that God sees and there will be that day that God says, judgment has come. Ecclesiastes 8:13, "But it shall not be well with the wicked, neither shall he prolong his days, which are as a shadow; because he feareth not before God."

I wrote in my notes this morning in bright red ink, "Don't forget what God has done for you!" God has blessed us so much and has been so longsuffering to each of us. May I encourage you to be faithful. Keep looking up. He never leaves us and He is always there for us if we call upon Him. As I read in Luke 10:13, "Woe unto thee, Chorazin! Woe unto thee, Bethsaida! For if the mighty works had been done in Tyre and Sidon, which have been done in you, they had a great while ago repented, sitting in sackcloth and ashes." Do not lose what you had or have. Do not lose the desire to serve that you once had. Please do not get used to not coming to church and singing the hymns and seeing and fellowshipping with other brothers and sisters in Christ. Please do not lose what you have or once had. As a farmer watches and takes care of his livestock, we need to be careful not to lose what God has done for us. Proverbs 27:23, "Be thou diligent to know the state of thy flocks, and look well to thy herds." King David said in Psalm 52:7, "Lo, this is the man that made not God his strength; but trusted in the abundance of his riches, and strengthened himself in his wickedness."

Fall will soon be here, and the leaves will change their color and then fall to the ground. The hillsides will be covered with beauty beyond description, and then the leaves will be gone and the cold of winter will set in. I know spring will then soon be coming, but as I thought on this, I also thought about the Christians that have lost what they once had. May we keep growing in the Lord. May the Word of God stay precious to us. May we seek ways to daily serve the Lord. May we walk with Him faithfully. May we be an encouragement to others. Psalm 52:9, "I will praise thee for ever, because thou hast done it: and I will wait on thy name; for it is good before thy saints." God wants to use you. Let God have His way in your life today.

Don't forget what God has done for you.

August 28

Ecclesiastes 9-10 Psalm 53 Proverbs 28 Luke 11

Spiritual Maintenance

Good morning! This morning is one of those mornings that as I read my Bible, I just sat and tried to feel the heart of God behind the words. Luke 11:23, "He that is not with me is against me: and he that gathereth not with me scattereth." I know the longer we live, the closer we are to the return of the Lord, but my heart is breaking as we all see the signs of the Lord's return and yet there is not the urgency to stay faithful to God, to be more fervent in reaching the lost. It even seems there is an attack like never before on the church and many of the church are scattering. There are blessings for those that stay faithful, Luke 11:28, "blessed are they that hear the word of God, and keep it." Proverbs 28:14, "Happy is the man that feareth alway: but he that hardeneth his heart shall fall into mischief."

I had to change fuel filters on one of the mowers. That job was finished and I headed out to mow. Things were going great and then I noticed one of the tires was losing air, so back to the barn, jack up that side of the mower that had the low tire, which is now almost flat, take off the tire, air it up to find where the leak is so that it can be repaired. As I found the hole, I noticed it is on the same side of the mower as another leak I had a couple of weeks ago. I told my wife there must be something in the ground, that I am not seeing, that is puncturing the tires. As I was loading the tire in the truck to go and have it repaired, I thought about Christians that constantly need to be pumped up or spiritually repaired. They just can't stay serving and they do not stay faithful. They have excuse after excuse. I read on in Psalm 53:3, "Every one of them is gone back: they are altogether become filthy; there is none that doeth good, no not one." It was late when I got home so I could not go out to try to find what had made the hole in the mower tire, but I will when the sun comes up. Is there something in your life that keeps draining your spiritual fire? Is there an area that you have trouble keeping in tune with the Lord?

Are you making excuse or trying to justify your lack of faithfulness? I read again Ecclesiastes 9:10, "Whatsoever thy hand findeth to do, do it with thy might; for there is no work, nor device, nor knowledge, nor wisdom, in the grave, whither thou goest." Let us all get busy serving and stay busy. We all live in some type of housing and we all know there is maintenance and upkeep. We must do spiritual maintenance also, or we will become backslidden. Ecclesiastes 10:18, "By much slothfulness the building decayeth; and through idleness of the hands the house droppeth through."

One mower I pull behind the tractor has twelve tires on it plus the four tractor tires. I have to find what is causing the flat tires. Can I challenge us all to find out what might be draining us spiritually and plug that hole? We must do the maintenance that is needed or this leak, or needed maintenance, will cause us to become hard spiritually. "He that trusteth in his own heart is a fool: but whoso walketh wisely, he shall be delivered." I lose mowing time when I have to make those repairs, the work builds up, and I get behind. What spiritual ground are we losing when we do not stay faithful to the Lord? Keep on, my brother and sister. Do the spiritual maintenance that is needed, or you will soon be out of service for the Lord.

What spiritual ground are we losing when
we do not stay faithful to the Lord?

August 29

Ecclesiastes 11-12 Psalm 54 Proverbs 29 Luke 12

Are You Ready?

Good morning! We hear of tornados, hurricanes, destruction of homes, businesses and much more. I ask myself, why will people not turn to the Lord? His promises are sure. Proverbs 29:25, "whoso putteth his trust in the LORD shall be safe." God is our comfort in the time of the storm. Psalm 54:7, "For he hath delivered me out of all trouble." The neighbors had lost some cows and they thought they had broken through the fence and came over on the camp property. Sure enough, I found them down in the valley, all huddled together safe from the storm. I looked at those cows and thought how man just keeps on going instead of seeking the Lord and preparing for His return.

The Lord Jesus is coming again, and it is going to be soon. Where will He find us and what will He find us doing? One of the neighbors had a rope halter and they told me that they were going to lead this one cow home. I got tears in my eyes as I thought how God is trying to draw us close to Him and lead us home, not with halter, but with His love and compassion. Yet like many of those cows that I pushed out of the timber back home, we fight everything God is trying to do in our lives. Where the cows were there was no water or hay. It was just timber and yet that is where they wanted to be. Just like us when we stay away from reading God's Word and spending time in prayer to refresh our souls as we communicate with God. Ecclesiastes 12:13, "Let us hear the conclusion of the whole matter: Fear God, and keep his commandments: for this is the whole duty of man.." There is no time to waste. We need to be focusing on being ready for the Lord's return. Luke 12:40, "Be ye therefore ready also: for the Son of man cometh at an hour when ye think not." I enjoy every bit of the time that I get to spend with my wife and family, but I cannot neglect telling others about Christ's gift of salvation to a lost and dying world. Be a witness wherever you go, pass out every tract that you can. Pray for the Lord to help you be sensitive for souls. Ecclesiastes 12:14, "For God shall bring every work into judgment, with every secret thing, whether it be good, or whether it be evil."

The cows were found and herded back home. May we be used of God to help a lost world find Christ and show them the hope of an eternal home in Heaven. It has always amazed me how when you open the gate and head the cows toward that opening, they know that is where they are supposed to go and supposed to be. Will God find us where we are supposed to be, doing what we are supposed to be doing? I know we are not steers and cows, but sometimes I think we are pretty close. Have a blessed day.

We need to be focusing on being ready for the Lord's return.

August 30

Song of Solomon 1-2 Psalm 55 Proverbs 30 Luke 13

Spiritual Pruning

Good morning! As Mrs. Smith and I are approaching the fifty-year mark of being married, I am constantly growing in the love I have for her and I believe she would say the same. This morning we begin reading in Song of Solomon, the book of showing God's love for us and our love for God. As I read in Song of Solomon 1:4, the two words, "Draw me" caught my attention. I hunger to grow in the Lord so that His Word and His will would "draw me" closer to Him. I watch so many who say they love the Lord but give excuse for not living for Him and serving Him. I read on down to 1:7, "why should I be a one that turneth aside." Let us all take a moment and ask ourselves a question. Has this time of fear that we are living in brought us closer to God, or has it caused us to turn away and hide out of fear of the unknown? Where does our love for God and our calling of reaching people for Christ fit into this time of fear and separation?

Song of Solomon 2:10, "My beloved spake, and said unto me, Rise up, my love, my fair one, and come away." Should this not be a time for God's army to rise up and fill this world with the love of Christ for them and their lost soul? In Luke 13 we read the parable of the barren fig tree. The "dresser" of the vineyard wanted to cut down a tree that had not produced but Jesus said in verse 8, "let it alone this year also, till I shall dig about it, and dung it." That is exactly what needs to happen to so many of us. We need the contentment dug up and fresh spiritual fertilizer put in our lives. Fertilizer feeds and stimulates, and that is what we need. Proverbs 30:5, "Every word of God is pure: he is a shield unto them that put their trust in him." Psalm 55:22, "Cast thy burden upon the LORD, and he shall sustain thee: he shall never suffer the righteous to be moved."

We have an old, and I mean old, pear tree at the camp. I went and cut a lot of old dead branches out of it and trimmed it back a little. As

I was trimming around it this week and mowing, I stopped and looked at it, and it is full and drooping with pears. It is like the pruning had stimulated this old tree. I think we need some spiritual pruning and some spiritual fertilizer that will help us to love our Saviour like we should. Show your love today by bringing forth the fruit of your life that you should. Let us say, "Draw me" close to you, Lord, that I can better love and serve you. Our lives are to be bearing much fruit. Maybe we need to ask God to trim us back a long way so we can get all the old dead out. Have a very blessed and fruitful day.

Show your love for the Saviour by bringing forth the fruit that you should.

August 31

Song of Solomon 3-4 Psalm 56 Proverbs 31 Luke 14

True Love

Good morning! All of us have things that we love very much, but there are differences in the types of love. We might say, I sure love that truck, or I sure loved our last vacation. One is an object and the other is time or an adventure. We could also say, I long to spend more time with my family that I love, or I love every moment that I spend with my love. One is a group time and one is time with an individual. As I read in Song of Solomon 3:1, "I sought him whom my soul loveth." I spent time looking for the one that I had deep heart love for. "Song of Solomon 3:2, "I will see him whom my soul loveth." One word is different in these two verses, and yet both mean a going after.

Do you spend time seeking the Lord because of desiring a relationship with Him and because you love Him with a deep soul-felt love? Do we give God the full focus of our heart? In Luke 14 we read the parable of a certain man that made a great supper and "bade many." Luke 14:17, "Come, for all things are now ready." The food was prepared, the table was set, the guests were invited and then we read in verse 18, "And they all with one consent began to make excuse." How could they do this when a special banquet was made just for them? It is just like us when we make excuse why we do not come to church or Sunday School, why we do not spend time in God's Word, why we do not spend time in prayer, why we do not spend time serving the Lord. Excuse is nothing more than a lack of true love. In Proverbs 31 we read the word "she" fifteen times and then an action after. Why? Because she loves her family with a deep heart and soul-felt love. Our true love for God is shown by the actions we do toward and for God. Our love for God is demonstrated by our seeking after God for a relationship with God. God is not against us. Psalm 56:9, "for God is for me." Oh, that we would have a hunger for God and teach our children to have that same, and greater, hunger. When we make excuse, what example is being set for our children, grandchildren and all those watching our lives? The Psalmist wrote in Psalm 56:11, "In God have I put my trust."

You can take a little puppy that has been taken from its mother and spend time with this pup and there will be a trust, a bond that the pup will have with you. My wife and I were visiting in a home and a large dog came toward me. I stood still, talked softly, and let the animal smell me as I reached out and touched it. In a matter of moments, that watch dog settled down and leaned into me to establish a relationship with me. God is waiting for us to stop, seek Him, search His Word, and spend time in conversation with Him in prayer. He loves us. Is it not important for us to show Him how much we love Him? "I sought him whom my soul loveth." Keep seeking Him today and walk with Him throughout the day.

Our true love for God is shown by the actions we do toward and for God.

September 1

Song of Solomon 5-6 Psalm 57 Proverbs 1 Luke 15

Don't Lose What You Love

Good morning! It can never be stressed enough to be very careful that you do not lose what you love. By that I mean so often the things that we love dearly will not be there, if you just take them for granted. Song of Solomon 5:6, "I opened to my beloved; but my beloved had withdrawn himself, and was gone: my soul failed when he spake: I sought him, but I could not find him; I called him, but he gave me no answer."

How much do you appreciate your church, your pastor, those that love you and have tried to help you? They stayed faithful, but you gave excuse and quit or just gave up and now what you loved is gone. In Luke 15 we read about the lost sheep, lost coin, and the lost son. They were all missing and they were all sought for. In Luke 15:10, "Likewise, I say unto you, there is joy in the presence of the angels of God over one sinner that repenteth." Oh, the joy to see someone walk back in church that has not been there in a long time! The joy to see someone rededicate their life to the Lord. The joy of seeing a sinner sit down and have someone take the Bible and show them how to be saved. The excitement that they are saved, they follow in baptism, they start attending and then miss one service and then the next and next. We must look at our lives and see where we are letting the devil keep us from being faithful, not to man, but to the LORD. Proverbs 1:10, "My son, if sinners entice thee, consent thou not." God has not moved. He is there and waiting. We must come to ourselves, just as we read about the prodigal son in Luke 15:17, "And when he came to himself."

There is safety in staying faithful to the Lord. Proverbs 1:33, "But whoso hearkeneth unto me shall dwell safely, and shall be quiet from fear of evil." I ask the question this morning, have we allowed the world to put fear in us to keep us from being faithful to the Lord and our service to Him? God has not left us. He is not deaf unto our cry to Him. God's mercy is everlasting. Psalm 57:1, "Be merciful unto me, O God, be merciful unto me: for my soul trusteth in thee." Let it not be said of us, "I opened to my beloved; but my beloved had withdrawn himself." Proverbs 1:25, "But ye have set at nought all my counsel, and would none of my reproof." We need revival, personally and as a nation. May we seek Him today, He is waiting just as the father was for the prodigal son.

Often the things we love will not be there if we take them for granted.

September 2

Song of Solomon 7-8 Psalm 58 Proverbs 2 Luke 16

An Unstoppable Love

Good morning! In Luke 16:15, there are four words that I read over and over this morning. Those words from verse 15 are "God knoweth your hearts." There are times that our intentions are not understood. We say the wrong words or they are taken the wrong way. We are misunderstood by the actions that we take or the lack of taking action. I read these words several times, "God knoweth your hearts." We cannot hide from God and especially we cannot hide the feelings in our hearts. How is your love for God this morning? Is your love for God growing? Are the actions of your life showing forth the words that you say? Song of Solomon 8:7, "Many waters cannot quench love, neither can the floods drown it: if a man would give all the substance of his house for love, it would utterly be contemned." The word "contemned" means despised, scorned, slighted, neglected, rejected with disdain. May I simply say, God and God alone knows our love for Him and even if we gave all we had, you cannot put out with all the water in the world a true love for God.

How is your love for God this morning? Does your love for Him show forth in your life for Him, service for Him, faithfulness to Him, faithfulness to stand for Him, faithfulness to witness for Him? Proverbs 2:10-11, "When wisdom enters into thine heart, and knowledge is pleasant unto thy soul; discretion shall preserve thee, understanding shall keep thee." Our love for God should be unstoppable in word, action, and practice. God sees the heart and He sees through every excuse that we give. Psalm 58:11, "Verily there is a reward for the righteous: verily he is a God that judgeth in the earth."

Last night as the day ended, Mrs. Smith and I went on a brief ride on my side by side four- wheeler. As I looked down through the timber, I saw one of my horses down. I ran quickly to see what was wrong and the horse had stepped in a hole between some roots of a tree and rocks. I went and got some neighbors for help. We cut the roots away, dug the rocks out, called the fire department with ropes to help pull the horse out. We worked many hours into the night to get the horse back on her feet. The vet was called and a decision was made. As I knelt by the horse and was told the horse will not be able to make it, my love for that horse overwhelmed my heart, but a decision had to be made. Let your love for God grow so deep that when tough decisions need to be made and you seem to be all alone, you can say, "God knoweth my heart." Tough decisions made with God and for God will strengthen us to stand for Him and serve Him with a greater love in our hearts.

Our love for God should be unstoppable in word, action, and practice.

September 3

Isaiah 1-2 Psalm 59 Proverbs 3 Luke 17

Fulfilling Your Purpose

Good morning! A rejected tomato caught my eye. Why did that tomato not make it to the table? It did not make it to a salad, a grilled hamburger, a slice on a plate, into a delicious sauce. Why did the tomato not make it? It just lay there beside the garden. I am sure you are thinking that Bro. Smith has now lost what mind he had left, feeling sorry for a tomato. No, I have not lost my mind. As I went to help some men pick some tomatoes, my eye caught this one that was discarded. As I read this morning in Isaiah 1:2, "Hear, O heavens, and give ear, O earth: for the LORD hath spoken, I have nourished and brought up children, and they have rebelled against me." That tomato was one day just a blossom and then a small green tomato began to develop and then the sun and rain began to cause that tomato to ripen. It could have just fallen off the vine before it was picked or it could have just laid on the ground and rotted. Whatever happened, the tomato will never be used for the purpose it was designed by God.

Are we being used by God in the way that He designed for us to be used? What a shocking statement we read in Isaiah 1:21, "How is the faithful city become an harlot!" The city of God, Jerusalem, is now a city of sin. Has America forsaken God and become a country of sin? Have we allowed our lives to quit shining for the Lord? Isaiah 2:28, "they that forsake the LORD shall be consumed." The tomato has no soul, no life, no calling of God; but it did have a purpose. Luke 17:33, "Whosoever shall seek to save his life shall lose it; and whosoever shall lose his life shall preserve it." Is there more of a fear of the pandemic, the economy, retirement, self-gain, than there is a fear of not doing the will of God? We must repent and lose our self and gain back the purpose and will of God for our lives. Proverbs 3:3, "Let not mercy and truth forsake thee: bind them about thy neck; write them upon the table of thine heart."

Oh, how Mrs. Smith and I hate to see the fruit of a garden wasted, but how much more in the eyes of our Saviour to see a life wasted instead of serving the LORD. Psalm 59:16, "But I will sing of thy power; yea, I will sing aloud of thy mercy in the morning: for thou hast been my defense and refuge in the day of my trouble." I continued to walk in the rows of the neighbor's garden and helped pick some beautiful, very delicious tomatoes that will be used for the purpose that our Lord made them for. May we purpose to please the Lord and be what He has created us to be. May we sing and exalt the KING with our lives and be in His perfect will doing what He saved us to be. Have a blessed day.

Are we being used by God in the way that He designed for us to be used?

September 4

Isaiah 3-4 Psalm 60 Proverbs 4 Luke 18

The Power of Words

Good morning! Have you ever said, "I wish I could tell them how I really feel?" Are you really sure you want to say those words to them? I have often said, "the last words you say to someone could be the last words you say." Our world is so filled with hateful words, cutting words, words that are meant to hurt. Why? Should not our words be words to encourage, uplift, be a blessing?

A city, a nation was judged because of their tongue and their actions. Isaiah 3:8, "For Jerusalem is ruined, and Judah is fallen: because their tongue and their doings are against the LORD, to provoke the eyes of his glory." I am very thankful that I was taught, "if you cannot say something nice, then do not say anything." It is not constructive criticism; it is words of destruction. Proverbs 4:24, "Put away from thee a froward mouth, and perverse lips put far from thee." Do not fight with your mouth. Words once spoken cannot be taken back. Words will cut deeper than we know. God is our defense. God sees and hears what is going on. Luke 18:7, "And shall not God avenge his own elect, which cry day and night unto him, though he bear long with them?" It is always better to say nothing, than to say something that will deeply hurt another. I have heard people say, I am just a person that speaks my mind. Yes, and you do not have much of a mind. This world is set on edge and our mouths show it. Stop, think, and get yourself under control before you allow yourself to say words that you will regret. If someone wants your opinion, they will ask for it. It is so disrespectful when people talk under their breath, or behind someone's back, or when someone else is talking. Words should not be spoken unless they can be correctly heard.

Psalm 60:12, "Through God we shall do valiantly: for he it is that shall tread down our enemies." Peace in our homes could come from the right words spoken. A marriage could be healed from saying the right words. A child could be encouraged to work harder in school by saying the right words. A comfort to a discouraged brother or sister in Christ could come from saying the right words. Take time and let us all think before we speak and remember, "the last words that you say to someone, could be the last words you say." Speak words that strengthen and encourage, even in times of correction. As mom said many times, "think before you speak."

The last words you say to someone could be the last words you say.

September 5

Isaiah 5-6 Psalm 61 Proverbs 5 Luke 19

Occupy Till Jesus Comes

Good morning! As I read in Isaiah this morning, and understanding that it is judgment on the children of Israel for their sin, I still see something that I think we should apply to our lives. The Bible contains stories of real people and real events. The children of Israel were blessed of God and yet allowed sins to destroy God's blessing. Now to us. America was allowed to be established through all the bloodshed and sacrifice of men but we can continually see the hand of God and His blessing from the very beginning. America has welcomed people from around the world, and we have sent missionaries around the world to share the Gospel of Jesus Christ and yet we are at a point of the greatest denial of God that this country has ever known. As I read Isaiah 5:1-2, "My wellbeloved hath a vineyard in a very fruitful hill. And he fenced it, and gathered out the stones thereof, and planted it with the choicest vine, and built a tower in the midst of it, and also made a wine press therein: and he looked that it should bring forth grapes, and it brought forth wild grapes."

Our country has been often called the breadbasket of the world. People of all nations have sought freedom in America. We have been a land with a Constitution that has the hand of God all over it, and yet the forces of evil have attacked and we have raised a generation that seems to seek peace at any price. A beautiful vineyard, fenced, rocks removed, tower built, winepress, choicest vines planted and yet it brought forth wild grapes, wall broken down and thorns and briers came up (Isaiah 5:4-7). We turn to look this morning and read in Luke 19:13, "And he called his ten servants, and delivered them ten pounds and said unto them, Occupy till I come." "Occupy" means work, invest, take care of, guard, protect. What happened? Proverbs 5:12-13, "How have I hated instruction, and my heart despised reproof; and have not obeyed the voice of my teachers, nor inclined mine ear to them that instructed me!" That is it! We have turned our backs on principles that brought God's blessing.

What is it today in our lives that we need to heed the Words of God about? What do we need to personally repent of? We must stand for Biblical truth. We must be faithful. We must press on and keep the "stones," the "briers" out, keep the "fences" in good repair, and keep the "tower" in good repair and keep the vigilance on guard against the enemies. Psalm 61:5, "For thou, O God, hast heard my vows: thou hast given me the heritage of those that fear thy name." We have an heritage for which each generation must pay the price of preservation. We must continually strive to walk with God. My brother and sister, "occupy" till Jesus returns.

We must be faithful, press on, and continually strive to walk with God.

September 6

Isaiah 7-8 Psalm 62 Proverbs 6 Luke 20

God's Unchanging Word

Good morning! Somebody is always wanting to change the rules. I am so very thankful that our Lord is always the same. He cautions us about change. Isaiah 8:11, "For the LORD spake thus to me with a strong hand, and instructed me that I should not walk in the way of this people." God's Word is unchanging. We are living in a generation that wants to block streets, burn buildings, get their own way. My folks had a way to handle us children when one of us wanted our own way. You know, I did the same thing to my children as my parents did. Isaiah 8:12, "Say ye not, A confederacy." Isaiah 8:13, "Sanctify the LORD of hosts himself; and let him be your fear." We need to fear not pleasing God, not reading His Word, not following His Word, not spending time with Him in prayer. Jesus' authority was questioned in Luke 20:2, "Tell us, by what authority doest thou these things? Or who is he that gave thee this authority?." He did not answer and just continued on, and then in Luke 20:38, "For he is not a God of the dead, but of the living: for all live unto him."

I am thankful there are stop signs, yield signs, speed limit signs, road direction signs, caution lights, stop lights, lane direction signs; and that is just a few of the guidelines we have for safety. Our rebellion comes from the great deceiver himself, Satan. Proverbs 6:20, "My son, keep thy father's commandment, and forsake not the law of thy mother." Verse 21 goes on to say, "Bind them continually upon thine heart, and tie them about thy neck." I love those words we read this morning in Psalm 62:8, "Trust in him at all times; ye people, pour out your heart before him: God is a refuge for us. Selah." I choose to take the advice of a couple that has been married between 60 and 70 years, has raised their children to work hard, has paid their bills and paid them on time, spent time with family, reverenced the Lord's day, and stayed true. Psalm 62:10, "Trust not in oppression, and become not vain in robbery: if riches increase, set not your heart upon them."

Give us another generation that just does right in the sight of God, has a determination that cannot be stopped, does their best to live Godly before the Lord. Stand up, my brother and sister, for Biblical truth and principles. Stand up!! I love playing board games, and I love to win. When I play with some of my grandchildren, they sometimes want to change the rules. I remember being told, "rules are not made to be broken." Let us live each day under the authority of God's rules, His unchanging Word.

Our Lord is always the same and His Word is unchanging.

September 7

Isaiah 9-10 Psalm 63 Proverbs 7 Luke 21

God's Outstretched Hand

Good morning! I was sitting on the porch of my great uncle's home. This was my Granny's brother. I could listen to story after story as Uncle Bob Carson told story after story. America today is not the same America that he used to talk about. His generation loved America and sacrificed personally for it. He talked of men volunteering for war, rationing of gas, tires, sugar, flour and the such. He talked about how everyone was ready to do their part.

As I read this morning in Isaiah 10:1, "Woe unto them that decree unrighteous decrees, and that write grievousness which they have described." Even though we are seeing so much negative, so much crime, wrongdoing, and wrong priorities I was encouraged as I read Isaiah 10:21, "The remnant shall return, even the remnant of Jacob, unto the mighty God." My Uncle Bob has been gone many years and I know he would be shocked at the America he would see today. I read Luke 21:13, "And it shall turn to you for a testimony." Luke 21:8, "Take heed that ye be not deceived." We are the generation now living and we, as saved sinners washed by the blood of the Lamb, need to evaluate every area of our life and ask ourselves, just what kind of testimony are we leaving for this and the next generation? Have we raised a generation to take care of the flesh only and not the spirit? Are we the generation that is bowing a knee and not standing in honor? We are like the bird that took the bait in the trap. Proverbs 7:23, "as a bird hasteth to the snare, and knoweth not that it is for his life." We need to be on our knees in prayer more than anything else we do. Psalm 63:1, "my soul thirsteth for thee; my flesh longeth for thee in a dry and thirsty land, where no water is." God's hand is still stretched out to us and the power of the Holy Spirit is still available to us. Even in God's judgment on Israel, His hand was still stretched out to them. Isaiah 9:12 and 10:4, "For all this his anger is not turned away, but his hand is stretched out still."

Reach out to the Lord this morning. Hunger for His presence and power. Go to Him for that water that is satisfying. We must stand for the cause of Christ. One of the things that drew me to talk with Uncle Bob was that he was a fighter and yet a gentle man. I would listen as he told about tough times and how they kept on. Let us keep on for God today.

God's hand is still stretched out to us and the power of the Holy Spirit is still available to us.

September 8

Isaiah 11-12 Psalm 64 Proverbs 8 Luke 22

Protect Your Boundaries

Good morning! I read in Isaiah 11:6, "The wolf also shall dwell with the lamb." One wild, one gentle. One very strong in defense and one very weak. One with the ability to exist alone and the other must have a protector. My dogs were laying down and very content. They had been fed and watered and I had spent a little time with them. As I was typing this devotion, the barking started and they took off in a full run. Why? The farmer behind us drove slowly down the lane. He usually has his dog with him, but I do not know if he did this morning. My dogs knew his truck and assumed his dog was there. What does it matter? I thought for a few moments and read on.

Isaiah 11:6, "The wolf also shall dwell with the lamb, and the leopard shall lie down with the kid; and the calf and the young lion and the fatling together; and a little child shall lead them." What peace will come to this earth one day! As a matter of fact, in Isaiah 12:1 and 12:4, we read "in that day." Let another dog come on the camp property and my dogs are on the attack. Why? Because they have set boundaries to be protected. In Luke 22:4 we read how Judas made a covenant to betray Jesus because "he went his way." In the garden before the betrayal of Jesus, He told Peter in Luke 22:32, "But I have prayed for thee, that thy faith fail not." There will come "that day" when there will be peace and the "wolf also shall dwell with the lamb," but that day has not come and we must remain vigilant to stand for Christ. Luke 22:40, "Pray that ye enter not into temptation." Proverbs 8:32, "Now therefore hearken unto me, O ye children: for blessed are they that keep my ways."

Have you set spiritual boundaries in your life that you are vigilant to keep? Are we allowing the wickedness of this world to penetrate our lives? Have we arrived at the point of a willingness to just get along and boundaries of Christlikeness have been broken down? Have we allowed compromise to settle in? As the Psalmist cried out in Psalm 64:1, "Hear my voice, O God, in my prayer: preserve my life from fear of the enemy." I am thankful for the dogs being alert to any intruder. May our hearts be challenged to be on alert for the slyness of the devil.

We must be vigilant to keep the spiritual boundaries in our life.

September 9

Isaiah 13-14 Psalm 65 Proverbs 9 Luke 23

God's Purpose

Good morning! Think with me this morning and ask yourself, have you ever not done something that you know you should have done? In other words, "I knew I should have." There have been times that I knew I should have done something and then I lived to regret that I did not do what I knew I should have done. Are you with me this morning? Why did we not do what we knew we should have done? We cannot go back in time so we must look to the present and then the future.

Isaiah 14:24, "The LORD of hosts hath sworn, saying, surely as I have thought, so shall it come to pass; and as I have purposed, so shall it stand." God has a purpose for each one of us and in that purpose is the will of God that will bring joy, happiness, and peace. We read this morning about Satan being the great deceiver of this world that we live in and how he has a purpose, and yet God our Redeemer has a greater purpose. I asked myself, do I listen to the purpose that the devil has for my life or do I listen and follow the purpose God has for my life? In Luke 23:4, Pilate said, "I find no fault in this man." As we read on, we read three times this same statement and yet the purpose of God is found in Luke 24:46, "Father, into thy hands I commend my spirit." God's purposed will for all of us is that we give ourselves fully in the hands of God. We have been chosen by God to fulfill God's purpose, and yet we allow ourselves to turn a deaf ear to the Holy Spirit when He speaks.

Proverbs 9:6, "Forsake the foolish, and live; and go in the way of understanding." We need to quit fooling ourselves and live God's purpose in every area of our life. Psalm 65:4, "Blessed is the man whom thou choosest, and causest to approach unto thee." God is calling us to Him. He is in full control of what is going on in this world and it is God calling us unto Him. Seek His face today. Let your heart be drawn to Him and be doing His purpose for your life. Let us say today and every day, I purpose to do the purposed will of God for my life.

We have been chosen by God to fulfill God's purpose.

September 10

Isaiah 15-16 Psalm 66 Proverbs 10 Luke 24

Jesus is Coming Again!

Good morning! Isaiah 15:6, "The hay is withered away, the grass faileth, there is no green thing." When we think something is dried up and dead it is not necessarily gone. As I read this phrase, I thought how we had just finished another cutting of hay and what is left of stubble looks so dry and dead, but it is not. The judgment of God is falling and destruction is ahead, but God is still in control. The question was asked in Luke 24:5, "Why seek ye the living among the dead?" They had looked in the tomb and Jesus was not there. It is like they had forgotten all that He had taught.

As we look at the world today, have we forgotten what the Bible has let us know? Luke 24:25, "O fools, and slow of heart to believe all that the prophets have spoken." We have said it, but have we believed it? Jesus is coming again and we are being forewarned again. Even though the grass looks dead that the hay was just cut from, it is not. Even though it will lay like it is dead this winter, it is not dead. I have been in and around several tornados. You know what all tornados do? They pass on by. Proverbs 10:25, "As the whirlwind passeth, so is the wicked no more: but the righteous is an everlasting foundation." The tomb was empty and it is taking us closer to His return. The times we are now living in are reality that Jesus is coming soon. It is time for us to be louder than the protestors, louder for Godliness, and our testimony for Christ should be louder.

Psalm 66:16, "Come and hear, all ye that fear God, and I will declare what he hath done for my soul." The rebellion, the pestilence, wars and rumors of wars, hatred, earthquakes, are all signs Jesus is coming again. Psalm 66:7, "He ruleth by his power forever; his eyes behold the nations: let not the rebellious exalt themselves. Selah." Let us cry out today. JESUS IS COMING AGAIN!!

The times we are now living in are reality that Jesus is coming soon.

September 11

Isaiah 17-18 Psalm 67 Proverbs 11 John 1

Never Forget

Good morning! My father said to me several times growing up, "do not forget where you came from." He was not talking about an address, a state, a house. He was talking about how we were raised; principles of life to live by. Today is a day to remember because of the tragedy back on September 11, 2001. Isaiah 17:10 warned the people of God about forgetting; "Because thou hast forgotten the God of thy salvation, and hast not been mindful of the rock of thy strength." We must never forget what God has done for us by giving us a free gift of salvation, eternal life, His preserved Word, the opportunity to communicate with Him in prayer and an endless list of other things. Most of the rioters we see destroying in the streets of many cities today were not even possibly born during 9-11, or they were very young. Oh, that we would be a people that will remember our Lord and not forget that He is our God.

I love what I read in John 1:34, that John the Baptist said about Jesus, "And I saw, and bare record that this is the Son of God." May we "bare record" with our lives of all that God has done and is doing in our lives. Give us a generation that remembers and another generation will be taught, but if we forget, the next generation will never know, let alone remember. It is up to us, the living, to proclaim the goodness of God. It is up to us to keep the fire of God burning. It is up to us to stand strong and keep going forward for the Lord. I am thankful for all the flags that will be flying today, the songs that will be played, the names that will be mentioned, but let us not forget what the Giver of life has done for all of us. Proverbs 11:3, "The integrity of the upright shall guide them: but the perverseness of transgressors shall destroy them."

Let us be a people of holiness and righteousness in every area of our lives. May our cry today be what we read in Psalm 67:1-2, "God be merciful unto us, and bless us; and cause his face to shine upon us; Selah. That thy way may be known upon earth, thy saving health among all nations." Let us not forget! Let us remember and stand strong on God's unchanging Word!

Let us not forget what the Giver of life has done for all of us.

September 12

Isaiah 19-21 Psalm 68:1-18 Proverbs 12 John 2

A Zeal for God

Good morning! Isaiah 19:2, "And I will set the Egyptians against the Egyptians: and they shall fight every one against his brother, and every one against his neighbour; city against city, and kingdom against kingdom." God always has a purpose in everything. Isaiah 19:22, "And the LORD shall smite Egypt: he shall smite and heal it: and they shall return even to the LORD, and he shall be intreated of them, and shall heal them." With all that God is allowing to go on in our world, there is a greater purpose than what we can see, but it must put us on our knees before our God. John 2:17, "The zeal of thine house hath eaten me up." He drove the money changers out of the house of God. We must use this time we are going through to be driven closer to our Lord.

As my wife and I drove down the road there was a spot where I slowed down because of at least five squirrels in the road. They all seemed to be working to get something. I could not see what it was, but they were consumed to get it. They know winter is coming and they are doing everything they can to be prepared. Proverbs 12:27, "The slothful man roasteth not that which he took in hunting: but the substance of a diligent man is precious." The purpose behind the hunt is for food.

God has a purpose in what is going on in this world and it is high time for us to have a "zeal" for God that we are "eaten" up with. Psalm 68:1, "Let God arise, let his enemies be scattered: let them also that hate him flee before him." The world has its agenda, but the will of our God is greater. He can bring a world to its knees in a matter of a virus, a fire, a wind, a rain, an earthquake and whatever He sees fit. As God wills, His time will come. May He find us with a "zeal" for His will to be done. John 2:17, "The zeal of thine house hath eaten me up." How is your love for the work of God in these times we are in?

It is high time for us to have a "zeal"
for God that we are "eaten" up with.

September 13

Isaiah 22-23 Psalm 68:19-35 Proverbs 13 John 3

Keep the Ditches Open

Good morning! Well, the rain is coming and the ditches are overflowing with water. When I was a young boy the country roads were mostly dirt with some gravel. What kept the roads from washing away was the grader ditches. Isaiah 22:11, "Ye made also a ditch between the two walls for the water of the old pool." As I read this word "ditch" I thought about a part of a road that helps keep the road in place. This ditch between these two walls kept the water flowing and prevented the walls from washing out and falling. A road has what is called a "crown" in it to allow the water to flow off into the ditch and the ditch carries the water away toward the creek, river, or lake.

We must not allow sin to be part of our life because it will prevent the Holy Spirit from working in our life and this sin will rob us of victory. John 3:30, "He must increase, but I must decrease." If the water from a rainstorm stands in the road in will cause potholes and ruts that could eventually wash the road away. Proverbs 13:14, "The law of the wise is a fountain of life, to depart from the snares of death." God's law is like a ditch along the side of the road. It keeps the sin flowing away and keeps us strong in the Lord. Psalm 68:28, "Thy God hath commanded thy strength: strengthen, O God, that which thou hast wrought for us." The word "wrought" means molded or shaped.

My granddad used to allow me in the summer to ride with him in the town's road grader and much of the time we spent repairing the ditches to keep the water from destroying the roads. He would often say when I was riding with him, "the ditches have to stay open, or the road will get washed away." We need spiritual ditches to keep the sin away from our lives. When the storms of life come, make sure the ditch is open so that your walk with God can be maintained. Sin must daily be confessed and forsaken. Keep the ditches open in your life and keep that sin away that will destroy. Something to think about.

*Sin will prevent the Holy Spirit from working
in our life and will rob us of victory.*

September 14

Isaiah 24-25 Psalm 69:1-15 Proverbs 14 John 4

Praise in Trials

Good morning! What draws our attention each day? Do blessings or trials, times of rejoicing or times of testing control most of our attention? A small sliver of wood underneath a nail seems to bring hurt that the whole body feels. Isaiah had a way of looking through trials and seeing a blessing. Isaiah 25:1, "O LORD, thou art my God; I will exalt thee, I will praise thy name; for thou hast done wonderful things; thy counsels of old are faithfulness and truth." Isaiah 25:4, "For thou hast been a strength to the poor, a strength to the needy in his distress, a refuge from the storm, a shadow from the heat." Isaiah 25:8 is a sister passage to Revelation 21:4, "He will swallow up death in victory; and the Lord God will wipe away tears from off all faces."

I asked myself this morning a simple question. Is the Lord closer to us in blessings or in trials? I answered my own question by saying to myself, He is always there. We are the ones that move and only draw to Him close in trials. Is it not time to give Him praise all the time? The lady at the well, even with the negativity of sin in her life being revealed, still said in John 4:29, "Come, see a man, which told me all things that ever I did: is not this the Christ?" God is always right there for us. It is us and our sin that dims His presence. Proverbs 14:6, "knowledge is easy unto him that understandeth." The writer in Psalm 69:5 put it this way, "O God, thou knowest my foolishness; and my sins are not hid from thee."

I think we need to get out of the mud and quit complaining and start praising like we should. Psalm 69:14, "Deliver me out of the mire, and let me not sink." To a little boy that does not have to wash his clothes, a mud hole is a lot of fun. To a mom that has to wash the clothes and clean the little fellow up, the mud hole causes more work. Let us just stay out of the hole of sin and enjoy praising our Lord even in the middle of trials and testings because He is right there.

God is always there for us. It is us and our sin that dims His presence.

September 15

Isaiah 26-27 Psalm 69:16-36 Proverbs 15 John 5

Are You Ready?

Good morning! I can remember laying in my bunk at scout camp. The day had been a wonderful day, and now all was quiet and everybody was in their bunks. In the distant silence you could hear the bugler sounding taps. It was a perfect ending to a great day. The sound of the bugle brought a peace in the night.

As I read today in Isaiah 26:13, "And it shall come to pass in that day, that the great trumpet shall be blown." And as we read and closed out Isaiah 27:13, "and shall worship the LORD in the holy mount at Jerusalem." There will soon be another trumpet sounding and we that are alive and waiting will meet the Lord in the air. Are you ready? John 5:39, "Search the scriptures; for in them ye think ye have eternal life: and they are they which testify of me." The promises of God are there for us to find, study and apply to our daily lives. Proverbs 15:28a, "The heart of the righteous studieth to answer." Psalm 69:32, "The humble shall see this, and be glad: and your heart shall live that seek God."

I am so thankful for the peace in my heart that only God can give, that soon the trumpet of the Lord will be sounding. That night in my bunk at scout camp brought a peace that things were okay, but nothing will be like the trump of God when it sounds, and we leave this earth. Are you ready for the trump to sound?

There will soon be a trumpet sounding and we that are waiting will meet the Lord in the air.

September 16

Isaiah 28-29 Psalm 70 Proverbs 16 John 6

Don't Leave Out the Fitches

Good morning! Have you ever tasted something that was absolutely delicious but you could not detect the exact flavor? As we read this morning of upcoming discipline for Judah and Jerusalem, a couple of words caught my attention. Isaiah 28:27, "For the fitches are not threshed with a threshing instrument, neither is a cart wheel turned about upon the cumin; but the fitches are beaten out with a staff, and cumin with a rod." These are seasonings that are to be handled delicately. These seeds were sprinkled over bread before it was baked to add an aromatic flavor. The seeds were so small but added an important flavor and aroma.

Isaiah 29:15, "Woe unto them that seek deep to hide their counsel from the LORD, and their works are in the dark, and they say, Who seeth us? And who knoweth us?" It is what we think that we hide that brings out the result of sin in our lives. In John 6:26, "Ye seek me, not because ye saw the miracles, but because ye did eat of the loaves, and were filled." The Christian's walk with God is much more than the blessings; it is the relationship. Too many look at a walk with God for what they desire to get instead of hungering for a relationship. Proverbs 16:16, "How much better is it to get wisdom than gold! And to get understanding rather to be chosen than silver!"

The "fitches" were handled so carefully because they were so vital to the outcome of the bread being baked. Psalm 70:5, "O God: thou art my help and my deliverer." What we deem as the least in our walk with God could be the most important element. We must daily spend time alone with God in His Word and on our faces in time of prayer. What "fitches" are you trying to leave out?

What we deem as the least in our walk with God could be the most important element.

September 17

Isaiah 30-31 Psalm 71:1-16 Proverbs 17 John 7

Renew and Recommit

Good morning! Isaiah 31:1, "Woe to them that go down to Egypt for help; and stay on horses, and trust in chariots, because they are many." Many years ago, I learned a lesson that has helped me many times. The Lord sees the war, I see a battle. Many a Christian has given up because they looked at what the world offered and thought, I am missing so very much. Why do we turn to the world for help instead of staying faithful to the Lord? Why do we drop separation standards that we once held? Why do some quit being faithful?

Isaiah 31:3, "Now the Egyptians are men, and not God; and their horses flesh, and not spirit." Jesus was continually challenged about His authority and yet He never let their challenge to Him distract Him. John 7:46, "Never man spake like this man." Renew your determination to stay with God. Recommit your life to stay faithful and true. Quit looking to the world and comparing. Learn from the mistakes of others. Proverbs 17:10, "A reproof entireth more into a wise man than an hundred stripes into a fool." That word "reproof," which means rebuke, spoke to me this morning.

Are we living in self-denial or are we allowing the Lord to purge us of ourselves, the world and sin? The world will soon pass, and what is done for Christ will last. Psalm 71:12, "O God, be not far from me: O my God, make haste for my help." The things in this world that we think we need could be the things that destroy us. Remember, God sees the entire war, we are only seeing the battle at present. Stay faithful to the task at hand.

Renew your determination and recommit your life to stay faithful to God.

September 18

Isaiah 32-33 Psalm 71:17-24 Proverbs 18 John 8

God's Word the Guide

Good morning! I love reading how the Lord led in the history of our country, His protection of patriots that gave everything they had, and more, that we will ever know. I love to travel across our great land and to see how God worked miracle after miracle in the settling and expansion of our country.

I read this morning in Isaiah 33:22, "For the LORD is our judge, the LORD is our lawgiver, the LORD is our king, he will save us." James Madison read this very passage in history and the Lord led him in the forming of our government. Mark it in your Bible and never forget it. Isaiah 33:22, "our judge" (judicial branch), "our lawgiver" (legislative branch), "our king" (executive branch). In John 8:31-32, we are commanded to make God's Word a daily part of our lives, "If ye continue in my word, then are ye my disciples indeed; and ye shall know the truth, and the truth shall make you free."

Each generation must continually seek the wisdom of the Lord through His Word. John 8:47, "He that is of God heareth God's words: ye therefore hear them not, because ye are not of God." Let God's Word be a guide in every decision. Proverbs 18:15, "The heart of the prudent getteth knowledge; and the ear of the wise seeketh knowledge." Oh, that we would continue as our forefathers did to seek God and His guidance through His everlasting Word.

Each generation must continually seek
the wisdom of the Lord through His Word.

September 19

Isaiah 34-35 Psalm 72 Proverbs 19 John 9

Days of Praise

Good morning! There is a chorus that says, "Therefore the redeemed of the Lord shall return and come with singing unto Zion." I wish we could sing the whole chorus together today. It came to my mind as I read Isaiah 35:10, "And the ransomed of the LORD shall return, and come to Zion with songs and everlasting joy upon their heads: they shall obtain joy and gladness, and sorrow and sighing shall flee away." We need to spend time each day singing praise to the Lord! Make a point to learn new choruses and sing them often.

In John 9, Jesus takes mud and heals the blind man and his parents were asked who did it. I love what they said in John 9:21, "ask him: he shall speak for himself." On down in verse 25 when he is pressed to give an answer for who gave him sight, he says, "one thing I know, that whereas I was blind, now I can see." This was his testimony of praise from his own lips. There is life-fulfilling satisfaction in learning to give praise to the Lord. Proverbs 19:23, "The fear of the LORD tendeth to life: and he that hath it shall abide satisfied."

Let this day be a day of praise unto the Lord. Psalm 72:17, "His name shall endure for ever." Psalm 72:19, "let the whole earth be filled with his glory; Amen and Amen." Oh, that our days would be filled with praise to our King.

There is life-fulfilling satisfaction in learning to give praise to the Lord.

September 20

Isaiah 36-37 Psalm 73:1-14 Proverbs 20 John 10

How to Have a Good Day

Good morning! The alarm goes off, you hit the snooze, pull the covers a little tighter around you and say to yourself, I can sleep just a little longer. The next time the alarm goes off, instead of hitting the snooze you just shut the alarm off. How many mornings has the alarm gone off and we say to ourselves, "it cannot be morning yet!" When we finally get up, we are running late and another day has started off bad.

The devil wants us to throw a day away. The devil wants us to get so frustrated that we do not take the time to be alone with God. In Isaiah 36, Rabshakeh belched out threats of what was going to happen to Israel by the king of Assyria. Isaiah 36:21, "But they held their peace, and answered him not a word: for the king's commandment was saying, answer him not." Don't give the devil place to claim victory. When we let the devil get us down it is like we have forgotten all that we can do to have the victory in Christ that is ours. We cannot lose what we did not pay the price for. Jesus paid the price for our salvation and the fact is, we need to quit listening to our flesh and the devil and claim the victory of John 10:29, "no man is able to pluck them out of my Father's hand." Quit trying to live the Christian life in your own strength and start living in the strength of God and His Word. Proverbs 20:9, "Who can say, I have made my heart clean, I am pure from my sin?" It is vitally important for us to live in the strength of a walk with Christ and not in the strength of our flesh. Proverbs 20:17, "Bread of deceit is sweet to a man; but afterwards his mouth shall be filled with gravel."

All of us have days that start out bad, but they do not have to stay that way. We all have times that it seems those not living for the Lord are having a better day than us. Psalm 73:14, "For all the day long have I been plagued, and chastened every morning." Look up, take time with God, dwell on His Word, speak with Him. Proverbs 20:22, "Say not thou, I will recompense evil; but wait on the LORD, and he shall save thee." One time I was late milking a cow, and she was carrying on by the barn. The sound she was making was terrible because she was in pain and needed to be milked. When I got out there and milked the old cow, her pain stopped, the noise stopped, and I did not get in trouble. Stop right now and do what you are supposed to do and watch how the day will be a great day. Some things to think about.

Don't give the devil place to claim victory.

September 21

Isaiah 38-39 Psalm 73:15-28 Proverbs 21 John 11

Sitting in the Corner

Good morning! As I read Isaiah 38:2 this morning, my mind went many years back when I had been told by the teacher to go sit in the corner and think about what I had done. Look at these words we read in Isaiah 38:2, "Then Hezekiah turned his face toward the wall, and prayed unto the LORD." Thank the Lord for teachers that meant business, parents that stood behind the teacher's authority, and I am so thankful that I had to learn a lesson of being sent to sit in the corner. What goes through the mind of the student set in a corner? What went through the mind of king Hezekiah as he faced the wall, and the tears came down? You face your wrong, should feel the shame and regret, and you are ready to confess your fault. Isaiah 38:17, "for thou hast cast all my sins behind thy back."

When was the last time you had a seat in the corner and faced the sins of your life like we all should? When was the last time you repented, begged the Lord's forgiveness and came away feeling cleansed and ready to get back to going forward in your walk with God? As we read on in John 11, we find Lazarus in the tomb, everybody thinking he is dead and Jesus approaches. Martha goes running to Jesus and we read in John 11:20, "Mary sat still in the house." What is Mary pondering? Is there bitterness in her heart or is she trying to learn the lesson that is being taught? John 11:29, Martha tells Mary, "The Master is come, and calleth for thee." John 11:29, "As soon as she heard that, she arose quickly, and came unto him." In verse 32, "Then when Mary was come where Jesus was, and saw him, she fell down at his feet." There was never a moment that Jesus did not know what He was doing, but I believe there are times we just need to go sit in the corner and ponder things that God is trying to do in our life. John 11:40, "Said I not unto thee, that, if thou wouldest believe, thou shouldest see the glory of God?"

Maybe this morning we need to sit in the corner for a while and ponder the things of God. Proverbs 21:21, "He that followeth after righteousness and mercy findeth life, righteousness, and honour." Does the Lord seem far away? Has it been a while since you have felt close to the Lord? Do you need to go sit in the corner for a while and seek the forgiveness of God? Psalm 73:17, "Until I went into the sanctuary of God; then understood I their end." Psalm 73:28, "But it is good for me to draw near to God: I have put my trust in the Lord GOD, that I may declare all thy works." I know when I was sent to the corner, I did a lot of seeing how I was wrong about some things. Let God take you to the corner today. I promise, if you will be honest with yourself, you will come away a stronger person.

There are times we need to go sit in the corner
and ponder what God is trying to do in our life.

September 22

Isaiah 40-41 Psalm 74:1-11 Proverbs 22 John 12

Our Way or God's Way?

Good morning! As I began reading this morning, I stopped and wrote on the top of my paper, is my way blocking God's way? Am I yielding my life to God, or am I trying to fit God in to my life? Is my priority of life the will of God, or is my priority of life me and what I would like to see accomplished? Does God have His place in our life, or do we just place Him in our life where it is convenient?

Isaiah 40:18, "To whom then will ye liken God? Or what likeness will ye compare unto him?" Is God and His will first place in our lives? We all want the blessings of God, but do we want them our way or God's way? We say, I love the Lord and want to serve Him, but do we do things His way or our way? Isaiah 40:22, "It is he that sitteth upon the circle of the earth,." Isaiah 40:25, "To whom then will ye liken me, or shall I be equal? saith the Holy One." It is God that rescues us, provides for us, gives us our health, and gives us life. Isaiah 40:29, "He giveth power to the faint; and to them that have no might he increaseth strength." I love listening to the birds sing, the crickets making their clicking noise, the beautiful sound as the wind blows through the trees. Can you imagine nature if there were no sounds of praise to God? Jesus did miracle after miracle and yet they rejected Him. John 12:9, "Much people of the Jews therefore knew that he was there: and they came not for Jesus's sake only, but that they might see Lazarus also, whom he had raised from the dead." My heart was so convicted this morning as I thought, the crowd was more interested in the miracle than the One that brought about the miracle. Psalm 74:9, "We see not our signs: there is no more any prophet: neither is there among us any that knoweth how long."

Oh, that today we would take the time to look at our LORD and take time to be with Him, walk with Him, learn of Him, fellowship with Him. Proverbs 22:17, "Bow down thine ear, and hear the words of the wise, and apply thine heart unto my knowledge." Proverbs 22:19, "That thy trust may be in the LORD." The trees are starting to turn to the fall colors. That is God painting the forest. The squirrels are starting to fatten up. That is God preparing them for winter. Is it not time for us, whom Jesus died for, to take time to praise our Redeemer and spend time with Him? Don't just enjoy the result of a miracle, learn to enjoy the Creator of the miracle. Have a blessed day.

We all want the blessings of God, but do we want them our way or God's way?

September 23

Isaiah 42-44 Psalm 74:12-23 Proverbs 23 John 13

Our Spiritual Compass

Good morning! As a young boy in Boy Scouts, I learned how to use a compass. The function of a compass has always amazed me. As I drove down the winding road coming to the ranch from town, I would glance at the compass in my truck and watch it change as the curves in the road caused the direction of the compass to change. It is unseen and yet very real in our lives; the magnetic draw of the North Pole. Isaiah 42:16, "And I will bring the blind by a way that they knew not; I will lead them in paths that they have not known: I will make darkness light before them, and crooked things straight. These things will I do unto them, and not forsake them."

We take so very much for granted in life. God and His power is all around us and yet we deny Him in so many ways. In John 13, we see Jesus on His knees washing the feet of the disciples, and I am afraid the focus is on the feet and not the picture of salvation in us humbly accepting Him and serving Him. John 13:8, "If I wash thee not, thou hast no part with me." Notice the words, "if I wash thee not." His precious blood was shed to wash our sins away and provide salvation for us who by faith trust Him. So many pictures of God, His direction, His provision, His love and yet we have trouble in being faithful and true to Him. What has our attention today? Proverbs 23:5, "Wilt thou set thine eyes upon that which is not?"

No matter which direction I turn, the needle of the compass will always point in the direction of north. The compass in my truck shows the direction I am going because the true direction is focusing on north, and it is always the same. Psalm 74:16, "The day is thine, the night also is thine: thou hast prepared the light and the sun." The sun was placed by God for the day and the moon for night. Psalm 74:17, "Thou hast set all the borders of the earth: thou hast made summer and winter." No matter where we go on this earth, God set the boundaries of north, south, east and west. No matter where we go on earth, God has set all the seasons. Why not face our lives in the direction that He is wanting to lead us? In our first verse, Isaiah 42:16, "And I will bring the blind by a way that they knew not." I think we need to take a good look today at our spiritual compass and see if we are blinded or going in the right path. I can hear the man teaching me how to use the compass. Always trust the compass, it will not lie to you and when you feel lost, trust your compass. Trust the Bible, trust the Holy Spirit, and walk the path that is so clear when following the LORD.

Why not face our lives in the direction that He is wanting to lead us?

September 24

Isaiah 45-46 Psalm 75 Proverbs 24 John 14-15

What is Your Name?

Good morning! Does a horse, dog, cat, or any pet really know their name when you and I call them? As we read this morning in Isaiah 45:4, "I have even called thee by thy name: I have surnamed thee, though thou hast not known me." Let us take a moment and look at the word "surnamed." Our parents gave us a name and as I looked up and read about "surnamed," it means "a name added" or can I say, a name God knows us by, or a special name given to us. Let us read on in Isaiah 45:5,

"I am the LORD, and there is none else, there is no God beside me: I girded thee, though thou hast not known me."

If our Lord could tell us today, what would your "surname" be? Does God see us faithful, consistent, serving, or does he see us unfaithful, very inconsistent, very selfish, our life is ours to live the way that we want? Also this morning, we kept seeing the phrase, "I am the LORD, and there is none else." My heart was convicted to ask myself, what do I put before God? What is more important to me than putting God first in everything? Just think, God has a special name for each of us. As we read on in John 14:1, "Let not your heart be troubled: ye believe in God, believe also in me." Jesus was teaching the truth that He and the Father are one. Oh, that we would be on the same page with God. Most of us will have a special name that somebody who loves us calls us. There is something special about us to them and that is why we have that special name. What is the name that God has given you? We see the importance of consistency and stability in our walk with God as we read Proverbs 24:21, "My son, fear thou the LORD and the king: and meddle not with them that are given to change."

Our parents gave us a name at birth and our lives will be known by our name. Thank the Lord that God loves each of us in a very special and personal way. What is your name given to you by God? Psalms 75:7, "But God is the judge: he putteth down one, and setteth up another." I hunger for God to be pleased with my life, and yet I know that I often fail. I think more than anything today, my God does not see me as I see me. He loves me, gave His Son for me, has a will for my life, and has given me a very special name. May we live up to the name that our God knows us by.

Thank the Lord that God loves each of us
in a very special and personal way.

September 25

Isaiah 47-48 Psalm 76 Proverbs 25 John 16

Harvest or Stubble

Good morning! I walked through a field of corn that is just about ready for harvest and I looked at a field of soybeans that are starting to dry. Just a short time ago both crops were just coming up through the ground and now they are both close to harvest. As I read Isaiah 47:10, "For thou hast trusted in thy wickedness: thou hast said, None seeth me, Thy wisdom and thy knowledge, it hath perverted thee; and thou hast said in thine heart, I am, and none else beside me." I sat this morning and thought about fields of corn and soybeans that did not make it to harvest this year, and I thought about my brothers and sisters in Christ that have fallen away from their walk with God. The winds come and can destroy a fine crop, too much water, not enough water, too many weeds, not being cultivated; all of these things and more can destroy a crop. Staying in fellowship with the Lord is a daily task. The crops can make it with labor from the farmer, and God's blessing of just the right amount of rain and sun.

I read in Isaiah 47:14, "Behold, they shall be as stubble." Let us consider for a moment the word "stubble." Stubble can be what is left after harvest or stubble can be an undeveloped crop in the field. The same is with a Christian that lives for God and leaves an inheritance of a Godly testimony or it can be a Christian that quit growing and being faithful to the LORD. John 16:17, "A little while and ye shall not see me: and again, a little while, and ye shall see me: and Because I go to the Father." Jesus walked this earth and left so the Holy Spirit could come and have a walk with us. The phrase, "a little while" is mentioned seven times in this chapter of John. I thought how short of a season it is from planting to harvest and how fruitful a good harvest can be or how destructive a bad harvest can be to the famer, with nothing left but "stubble." Proverbs 25:13, "As the cold of snow in the time of harvest, so is a faithful messenger to them that send him: for he refresheth the soul of his masters."

What a blessing to see laborers for the Lord faithful in the days of harvest because they have stayed faithful to the Lord in their walk and labor for Him. I think it is time for us this morning to dwell on the words found in Psalm 76:11, "Vow, and pay unto the LORD your God." Maybe we need to be on our knees and get right with God before we turn into "stubble." There are those that need to keep on and keep their "vow" to the master and reap a great harvest for the Lord. Some things to think about this morning.

Staying in fellowship with the Lord is a daily task.

September 26

Isaiah 49-50 Psalm 77 Proverbs 26 John 17

A Very Special Purpose

Good morning! Can I invite you go to out to the pumpkin patch with me? The air is brisk this morning, but it is that time of the year. The plants that grew from a seed and brought forth a beautiful blossom, soon had a beautiful pumpkin growing on it. It was once a dark green and is now a beautiful orange. The vines are all dried up and the pumpkins lay on the ground ready to be picked up and become a decoration or a delicious pie. Wait a minute, the seeds were all the same size when we planted them, but the pumpkins that we see are different sizes. How come? I gazed at the different sizes and I thought, is size all that matters, is shape all that matters, or the pumpkin meat inside, is that what really matters?

Isaiah 49:2, "And he hath made my mouth like a sharp sword; in the shadow of his hand hath he hid me, and made me a polished shaft; in his quiver hath he hid me." Not just a sword, but a "sharp sword," not just any arrow but one with a "polished shaft." That "polished shaft" is hidden for a special purpose. To each of us the different sizes of the pumpkin make each one special in its own way. Isaiah 49:16, "Behold, I have graven thee upon the palms of my hands." We each are created in the image of God, but each of us has a very special purpose in the hand of God. John 17:10, "And all mine are thine, and thine are mine; and I am glorified in them." Oh, how all of us that know the Lord can be used of God for a special purpose just for Him.

I thought of my dad this morning that is in Heaven as I read Proverbs 26:7, "The legs of the lame are not equal." You see, my dad was born with polio and one of his legs was shorter than the other. I told my dad many times that God must have had a special purpose for him. Psalms 77:19, "Thy way is in the sea, and thy path in the great waters." God has a will and way that to us might be a mystery, but to God it is very special and just for us. I will never know why the same pumpkin seeds produce different sizes of pumpkins, but God does. We are created in His image for a purpose that we should be no matter what we think, because God made us all very special in His eyes. He wants us to be that "polished shaft" for Him.

Each of us has a very special purpose in the hand of God.

September 27

Isaiah 51-52 Psalm 78:1-20 Proverbs 27 John 18

Remember His Works

Good morning! As a grandpa I often wish I had another life to live. Daily I take each one of my grandchildren and children before the Lord in prayer and I often call just to hear their voice. I hunger to be part of their lives. I looked in the fishing tackle box of one of my grandsons last night and saw all the fishing tackle that he has accumulated. I remember the days he and the other grandsons began to take an interest in fishing. They have come so far in growing older. Isaiah 51:1, "look unto the rock whence ye are hewn, and to the hole of the pit whence ye are digged."

I try to be a goal-oriented person, and yet I find myself frustrated so often in what I have not completed instead of seeing what has been completed. Let us this morning step back, look at where God has brought us from and what He has done and is doing in our lives, and give Him some extra praise for all that He has done. I remember when the grandsons got a fishing pole, some sinkers, bobbers, and a few hooks. They were happy and now the tackle boxes are full of lures, fishing flies and a whole lot more of different kinds of fishing tackle. Isaiah 51:22, "Thus saith the Lord the LORD, and thy God that pleadeth the cause of his people, Behold, I have taken out of thine hand the cup of trembling, even the dregs of the cup of fury; thou shalt no more drink it again." Have we forgotten all that God has done and where He has brought us from? Have we lost the joy of the early days of being born again? I love the words of Jesus in John 18:9, "Of them which thou gavest me have I lost none." I will not be lost or cast off by Jesus, but have I forgotten all that Jesus has done for me? Proverbs 27:20, "Hell and destruction are never full; so the eyes of man are never satisfied." I am not against growth. I beg the Lord constantly to grow in Him and I hunger so for Him, but I asked myself this morning if I have forgotten all that He has done for me. Psalm 78:10, "They kept not the covenant of God, and refused to walk in his law;" Psalm 78:11, "And forgat his works, and his wonders that he had shewed them."

I am a proud grandpa and thankful for our children and grandchildren. I love and am so very thankful how they each are growing and maturing, but I have more of a hunger to see them grow in the Lord and never forget all that God has done for them and through them. May I ask this question this morning? Have we come so far that we have forgotten all that God is and has done? Have we lost the child-like faith that we once had? Have we lost the burning desire to see God and to grow in faith for God? Psalm 78:19, "Can God furnish a table in the wilderness?" He sure can. Do not forget the joy of catching a fish on a simple hook and worm. Quit focusing on finding a better way to catch a bigger fish and just learn to enjoy fishing. I remember the days of a cane pole, can of worms and a creek bank. Never forget all that God has done and is doing.

Have we forgotten all that God has done
and where He has brought us from?

September 28

Isaiah 53-54 Psalm 78:21-33 Proverbs 28 John 19

Stay in the Plow

Good morning! Do you ever feel like you have given everything and you have no more to give? I am speaking of life. You are tired emotionally, physically, and most of all spiritually. Please do not think that I am down because I am not. As we began our reading this morning, my heart did become heavy as I read how our Saviour gave all, and to this world it seems that it was not enough. I love watching horses plow, pull and do work around a farm. I remember an old farmer that has been gone many years said to me one day, I do not use those two horses over there, because they have given everything they had. What did he mean? Those two horses would pull themselves to death if he let them. They were raised, trained and hooked to the plow, disc, planter, and wagons to work. The old farmer loved those animals and he knew they would pull until they died. He had grown to love them so much he wanted them to have a time of rest.

Isaiah 53:12, "he hath poured out his soul unto death: and he was numbered with the transgressors: and he bare the sin of many, and made intercession for the transgressors." Jesus paid it all, my friend, and we owe Him our all. Isaiah 54:17, "No weapon that is formed against thee shall prosper; and every tongue that shall rise against thee in judgment thou shalt condemn. This is the heritage of the servants of the LORD, and their righteousness is of me, saith the LORD." The best I can say is, we have an "heritage," and our God is in full control. There is such a fear and laziness in the average Christian today. Pilate looked at Jesus and said in John 19:10, "knowest thou not that I have power to crucify thee, and have power to release thee?" I wish I could have been there and seen the face of Pilate and all that heard these next words of Jesus in John 19:11, "Thou couldest have no power at all against me except it were given thee from above: therefore he that delivered me unto thee hath the greater sin." Amen!! Proverbs 28:5, "Evil men understand not judgment: but they that seek the LORD understand all things."

The old horses were made to work and they knew their purpose. When the old farmer hooked the younger horses up to the plow, the old horses would run back and forth, and it was like they were saying, I am not dead yet! Let me pull that equipment! Have you quit? Do you feel like it is time for you to be turned out to pasture? If you have life, God has a plan and purpose. Believe God that He has a plan and purpose for you. Psalm 78:32, "For all this they sinned still, and believed not for his wondrous works." My brother and sister, it is not time to head to the pasture, it is time for harvest and we need to stay hooked to the Gospel plow. Rest is needed and rest is good, but as has been said a multitude of times, there is no discharge from this war. You might not plow as fast as you used to, but stay hooked to the Gospel and spread it, for the field is ready to be planted with the seed of salvation for all mankind.

If you have life, God has a plan and purpose.

September 29

Isaiah 55-56 Psalm 78:34-55 Proverbs 29 John 20-21

Come When He Calls

Good morning! I have called many times for my dogs to come and be fed and watered. I have stood at the fence and called the horses, so that I can give them grain. I have watched the cows run to the feed troughs as I have dumped the grain for them to eat. As I began reading in Isaiah 55:3, these words caught my eye, "Incline your ear, and come unto me: hear, and your soul shall live; and I will make an everlasting covenant with you." This is a personal invitation from God and it is much more than being fed some dog food or grain to just fatten you up. It is an "everlasting covenant." I had to dump some grain the other day and not give it to the horses, because I noticed a little mold from moisture, and I did not want to make them sick. God and His Word is always fresh.

Oh, that we would "come unto" the Lord. Isaiah 55:6, "Seek ye the LORD while he may be found, call ye upon him while he is near." Our Lord is never far away. The problem is when He calls, do we respond? John 20:31, "But these are written, that ye might believe that Jesus is the Christ, the Son of God; and that believing ye might have life through his name." As I read John 20 and 21, I noticed the words, "cometh, came, come" mentioned thirteen different times and then I noticed these words also mentioned several times, "follow, following." When an animal is obedient to come, they are fed and watered. When we are obedient to come to the Saviour, we receive life everlasting, with a multitude of blessings. Proverbs 29:25, "The fear of man bringeth a snare: but whoso putteth his trust in the LORD shall be safe." The animals have no soul, and when they die, life is over. For you and me, there is life everlasting and even though we sin and sometimes turn our back on God, we can still come back and He will forgive. Psalm 78:38, "But he, being full of compassion, forgave their iniquity, and destroyed them not: yea, many a time turned he his anger away, and did not stir up all his wrath." Psalm 78:39, "For he remembered that they were but flesh."

I can stand and call a dog, horse, or a cow and most all the time they will come right away. You know something very amazing? When I feed them and spend time with them, they want to follow me and be wherever I am. Why is that not the same with us as humans? Thirteen times we read in two chapters the words, "cometh, came, come" and we saw the response of "follow, following." What do you do when the Lord is calling? Have you heard His voice and not responded? He is still calling. Come to Him, He will forgive. Come to Him and live that joyous life that can be yours. Listen to those words in Isaiah 55:3, "come unto me." He is calling today, why not "follow?"

When we come to the Saviour, we receive life everlasting and a multitude of blessings.

September 30

Isaiah 57-58 Psalm 78:56-72 Proverbs 30-31 Acts 1

Revival of the Contrite

Good morning! Throughout the years I have listened to a lot of leaders teach and preach on leadership. I have a lot of books on leadership in my office. Through all that I have listened to and all that I have read, I have come to the simple conclusion that leadership must be earned. It cannot be demanded, it cannot be bought, it cannot be positional, it must be earned. We are living in a time of demand, and "I want my way," instead of understanding respect, honor, humility, and patience. A young preacher boy just recently walked up to me and asked me how to attain the power of God and I said four simple words to him, "learn how to die." I waited for his response. He looked at me with a surprised look because he is part of a generation, or should I say a time in his life, that he wants something, but not sure that he wants to pay the price. He is a good young man, and we talked quite a long time.

Isaiah 57:15, "For thus saith the high and lofty One that inhabiteth eternity, whose name is Holy; I dwell in the high and holy place, with him also that is of a contrite and humble spirit, to revive the spirit of the humble, and to revive the heart of the contrite ones." Two times the word "contrite" is used in this verse. As I looked up the definition of "contrite," I read this, "feeling or expressing remorse or penitence; affected by guilt." How is your spirit toward known sin in your life? How is your spirit toward your true walk with God? Isaiah 58:1, "Cry aloud, spare not, lift up thy voice like a trumpet, and shew my people their transgression, and the house of Jacob their sins." Did you stop this morning and ask God to show you unconfessed sin so that you can ask Him for forgiveness? Are there things in your life that you know are not right? Acts 1:24, "Thou, Lord, which knowest the hearts of all men." Oh, that we would focus on getting right with God, staying right with God, and walking right with God. Psalm 78:56-57, "Yet they tempted and provoked the most high God, and kept not his testimonies. But turned back, and dealt unfaithfully like their fathers."

These last few months I have had part in several funerals. To face a family that has lost a loved one and will never again speak to each other on this earth, is a very sobering thought. For those that are saved the Scriptures comfort us that we will see them again. Why would we want to live the Christian life and walk separately from God? Take time right now and ask the Lord to look deep into your heart and let Him bring to your mind sin that needs to be confessed and forsaken. He wants to walk with you and me. Let Him be the Saviour that He wants to be. Let us think on that word "contrite" today.

We need to focus on getting right with God,
taying right, and walking right with God.

October 1

Isaiah 59-60 Psalm 79 Proverbs 1 Acts 2

Selective Hearing

Good morning! For every child there seems to be that time of selective hearing. My mother had to say to me, "David Lynn, you heard me, now get to the house." Selective hearing has led more people down a wrong path than we will ever know. I would like for us to spend a little time thinking about hearing this morning. Isaiah 59:2, "But your iniquities have separated between you and your God, and your sins have hid his face from you, that he will not hear." The longer that we disobey God, the farther we go from Him. We have a promise in Isaiah 60:20, "the LORD shall be thine everlasting light, and the days of thy mourning shall be ended." More pastors have arrived at a point of major discouragement just because people that they love and hunger to be a shepherd to have decided not to listen or to ignore that which they have heard.

As we read in Acts 2:6, "Now when this was noised abroad, the multitude came together, and were confounded, because that every man heard them speak in his own language. What a day for the church of God to get the message of salvation out to lost man. Listen to the testimony of many in Acts 2:11, "we do hear them speak in our tongues the wonderful works of God." They testified, "the wonderful works of God." Are you a Christian that heeds to what you hear? Acts 2:37, "Now when they heard this, they were pricked in their heart." That is why we need to hear preaching as often as possible and listen to the voice of God speak through the man of God. As we read the words of God, we need to allow the Holy Spirit of God to speak to our hearts. The result of listening and heeding to what we hear, we read about in Acts 2:42, "And they continued steadfastly in the apostles doctrine and fellowship." There was unity because many that heard responded to what they had heard. Proverbs 1:5, "A wise man will hear." Proverbs 1:8, "My son, hear the instruction of thy father." Let us face the fact we do not listen because we know the truth and we do not want to face the truth. Psalm 79:9, "Help us, O God of our salvation, for the glory of thy name: and deliver us, and purge away our sins, for thy name's sake."

I can hear it today, just like it was said many times, "David Lynn, you heard me, now get to the house." You know, when I obeyed those words there was peace; and when I did not obey, I heard these words, "when your dad gets home, he will hear about this." I did not want dad to hear that I had disobeyed, so I ran to the house. Let us run to God today. It sure will bring a peace that is wonderful.

Are you a Christian that heeds to what you hear?

October 2

Isaiah 61-62 Psalm 80 Proverbs 2 Acts 3

True Teamwork

Good morning! We hear so much in life about teamwork and yet it seems there is not team unity. Our country is a melting pot of every walk of life. At one time we were the land of the free and the home of the brave. It seems that now we are the home of the fearful and the land of the accusers.

It has been said often that God wants to use all of us in a special way. Isaiah 61:1-2, "The Spirit of the Lord God is upon me; because the LORD hath anointed me to preach good tidings unto the meek, he hath sent me to bind up the broken-hearted, to proclaim liberty to the captives, and the opening of the prison to them that are bound. To proclaim the acceptable year of the LORD, and the day of vengeance of our God; to comfort all that mourn." Jesus read this exact passage in Luke 4:18-19. God has His timing, God has a call for each of us, and God has a place for us. Are you serving in the place that God has you or are you looking at another place instead of being everything God wants you to be in your place? God wants to use you in the place where you are. Have you been willing to be used how He wants in that place? A lame man was healed and the people wanted to bring the glory to Peter and John, but listen to Peter's response in Acts 3:12, "And when Peter saw it, he answered unto the people, ye men of Israel, why marvel ye are this? Or why look ye so earnestly on us, as though by our own power or holiness we had made this man to walk? Acts 3:16, "the faith which is by him hath given him this perfect soundness in the presence of you all." God wants to powerfully use us all. Are you allowing Him? Are you part of the team that is God's team? Where is your focus? Are you seeking the power of God where you are? Are you asking God to use you in the place that you are? Have you yielded to God so that God can use you?

Proverbs 2:11, "Discretion shall preserve thee, understanding shall keep thee." Proverbs 2:20, "That thou mayest walk in the way of good men, and keep the paths of the righteous." God is waiting on us. God is ready to use us. The problem is we are not fully yielded to Him and I fear there is so much unconfessed sin. Psalm 80:17, "Let thy hand be upon the man of thy right hand, upon the son of man whom thou madest strong for thyself." God's strength and power is available to all who yield to Him with a clean and confessed heart and a fully yielded life. May our Lord use us in the way that pleases Him. True teamwork starts with God and us. Are you letting God be on your team?

Have you yielded to God so that He can use you?

October 3

Isaiah 63-64 Psalm 81 Proverbs 3 Acts 4

Do All You Can

Good morning! When we were early in our marriages and the Lord gave us children, we did everything we could to take care of them, provide for them, and meet their every need. I thought this morning as

Mrs. Smith and I are crossing some very big lines in our ages, how our children are so concerned that we are taken care of. Dad and mom, are you okay? What do you need? What can we do? How can we pray? God has done so much for all of us. I asked myself this morning, am I doing everything I can for my Lord that saved me and gave me life eternal?

Isaiah 63:9, "In all their affliction he was afflicted, and the angel of his presence saved them: in his love and in his pity he redeemed them; and he bare them, and carried them all the days of old." God has done so much. What are we doing for God? How sad as we read on down to Isaiah 63:10, "But they rebelled, and vexed his Holy Spirit." Isaiah 63:15, "where is thy zeal and thy strength, the sounding of thy bowels and of thy mercies toward me? Are they restrained?" How sad it is when a parent does everything they can to raise that child, and then that child turns bitter against their parent, or rejects all that they were taught. It is even more sad to see a saint of God reject a walk with God. The religious crowd said about Peter and John; "we cannot deny it," in Acts 4:16. Acts 4:13, "Now when they saw the boldness of Peter and John, and perceived that they were unlearned and ignorant men, they marveled; and they took knowledge of them, that they had been with Jesus." Oh, that our lives would show that we have "been with Jesus!"

Picture with me a mother and father loving that newborn baby, and now picture with me that mother and father at the end of their lives and their children now making sure their parents are taken care of. How did that happen? A life of building a relationship of love, compassion and concern. Proverbs 3:1, "My son, forget not my law; but let thine heart keep my commandments." We have called out to God so many times and He has been there. May we take a good look at what kind of relationship we are building with God today. Psalm 81:7, "Thou calledst in trouble, and I delivered thee; I answered thee in the secret place of thunder." Are you in that walk with God that you should be? Are you daily seeking His face and will? He was always there for us. We as humans love our families; should we not even have a much greater love for our Heavenly Father? Some things to think about this morning.

We have called out to God so many times and He has been there.

October 4

Isaiah 65-66 Psalm 82 Proverbs 4 Acts 5

Just Step Aside

Good morning! Oh, what a Saviour! He takes care of me, even when I have no idea what He is doing. He knows my every need, He knows my every want, He is constantly watching out for me. Isaiah 65:24, "And it shall come to pass, that before they call, I will answer; and while they are yet speaking, I will hear." The apostles have been thrown in prison and we read in Acts 5:19, "But the angel of the Lord by night opened the prison doors, and brought them forth." I often wonder if we would step aside and let God do the work, if so much more could be done. The prison guards looked and the apostles were gone. Where did the prisoners go? They are down teaching in the temple. Word gets to the chief priest, and he personally sees that the men are gone and the jail doors are locked. Boy, there is going to be trouble now and we read how a very educated man named Gamaliel tells these Jews to be careful. Acts 5:38, "if this counsel or this work be of men, it will come to nought." Acts 5:39, "But if it be of God, ye cannot overthrow it; lest haply ye be found even to fight against God."

Oh, that we would allow the Lord to do His will in our lives and just step out of the road. Mrs. Smith and I were talking last night as we were traveling, how the Lord is always right ahead of us making the path clear. Proverbs 4:18, "But the path of the just is as the shining light, that shineth more and more unto the perfect day." Do not fight what God is trying to do in your life. Do not mess up what God is trying to do. Keep walking in the light, which is Christ. Proverbs 4:26, "Ponder the path of thy feet, and let all thy ways be established." That word "ponder" means to consider, think upon, take time and look. Oh, that we would walk in the will of God, be in God's timing and be faithful in the place where God wants us to be.

This world is on a crash course and they do not even know it. Psalm 82:5, "They know not, neither will they understand; they walk on in darkness: all the foundations of the earth are out of course." Keep listening to the Holy Spirit, keep reading the Word of God, and keep walking with Him because He is there all the time for us. Those prison doors opened without a key. What is God ready to open for us if we would just let Him?

If we would step aside and let God do the work,
how much more could be done?

October 5

Jeremiah 1-2 Psalm 83 Proverbs 5 Acts 6

Sanctified and Surrendered

Good morning! Mrs. Smith and I just recently spent a few days with our children and our grandchildren. It was a wonderful time. We all wish that we would have had more time. The time brought back memories of when each one was born, and the time of life watching them grow. I sat along a lake bank watching each of them fish and spent time with our daughter-in-law, daughter and granddaughter. Each of them holds a special place in our hearts. As we have watched them grow in life and grow in the Lord, and as we daily watch them mature, I cannot even come close to imagining what God must feel as He watches each one of us. He gave each of us a free will to accept Him or reject Him as our Saviour, but what then?

As I read God's Word to Jeremiah in Jeremiah 1:5, "Before I formed thee in the belly I knew thee; and before thou camest forth out of the womb I sanctified thee, and I ordained thee a prophet unto the nations." As has often been said, the word "sanctified" means set apart. Mrs. Smith and I thought about the plan of God for each member of our family. May I ask you, as I often ask myself and my Lord in prayer, am I doing the will of God for my life? He knew us before we were born. How God's heart must break when we reject Him or live our own lives to please ourselves instead of living the will of God. I do not know what all of our grandchildren will be in twenty years if the Lord tarries, but I do know that I want to set the example of a surrendered life before them and that when my path on this earth is done, they will be able to see a life lived for the Lord. Jeremiah 2:32, "Can a maid forget her ornaments, or a bride her attire? Yet my people have forgotten me days without number." "Days without number." Oh, that we would not live one day without seeking the face of the Lord and doing His will. Acts 6:3, "Wherefore, brethren, look ye out among you seven men of honest report, full of the Holy Ghost and wisdom, whom we may appoint over this business." God is still looking for men and women ready to serve, walking with God, seeking His daily power.

Do you hunger for God? Do you hunger to be in His will? Proverbs 5:12-13, "How have I hated instruction, and my heart despised reproof; and have not obeyed the voice of my teachers, nor inclined mine ear to them that instructed me!" Psalm 83:16, "Fill their faces with shame; that they may seek thy name, O LORD." We must seek God and not turn from Him. May our life be filled with a desire to be "set apart" for our Lord's purpose. Psalm 83:18, "That man may know that thou, whose name alone is JEHOVAH, art the most high over all the earth." Are you seeking the Saviour today and listening, learning, and leaning on Him? I beg the Lord daily for my son and son-in-law, that they may lead their families in the will of God. This morning my heart has been greatly stirred to keep pressing on in daily walking with God and living in His perfect will.

May we not live one day without seeking
the face of the Lord and doing His will.

October 6

Jeremiah 3-5 Psalm 84 Proverbs 6 Acts 7

Love Your Undershepherd

Good morning! Several shepherds stood talking as their different herds of sheep waited patiently, all mixed together. As one by one the shepherds said a few words and walked away, the large group of sheep began to separate as they heard the voice of their shepherd and they began to follow. I have read many stories like this and I have personally observed this amazing picture myself. How did the sheep know to follow their shepherd? Their shepherd was their protector from harm. Their shepherd made sure they had a green pasture to graze in and cool water to drink. Their shepherd was strong and kept them in a herd, and when one got away, it was their shepherd that went after them and was hard, firm and loving toward them all at the same time.

Thank the Lord daily that you have an undershepherd that has been called of God and placed in your life. Isaiah 3:15, "And I will give you pastors according to mine heart, which shall feed you with knowledge and understanding." Each shepherd heard a call from God as they yielded to this special office. Isaiah 5:5, "I will get me unto the great men, and will speak unto them; for they have known the way of the LORD." Moses heard God say, as it is recorded in our reading in Acts 7:43, "I have seen, I have seen." Each of us needs our God-given, God-called shepherd to be what God has called him to be. Acts 7:35, "Who made thee a ruler and a judge? The same did God send to be a ruler and a deliverer by the hand of the angel which appeared to him in the bush." We live in a day that lack of respect and honor for leadership is out of control and God warns us about sowing "discord." Proverbs 6:19, "A false witness that speaketh lies, and he that soweth discord among brethren."

Be careful, my brother and sister. Pastors are not perfect but they did surrender to the call of God, and I believe in my heart that they mean to do right. God's call is a call to humility and followship of HIM. What great responsibility each pastor has. Pray for your pastor. Be loyal to your pastor. Be an encourager to you pastor. Psalm 84:10, "I had rather be a doorkeeper in the house of my God, than to dwell in the tents of wickedness." If each of us sheep would just listen to the voice of the shepherd that God has given us from God's Word, it would have God's greatest blessing on each of our lives. Why not send a note of thankfulness and appreciation to your pastor today? Smile when you see him. Love his family. Be loyal and enjoy the blessings of God.

Pray for your pastor, be loyal to him and encourage him.

October 7

Jeremiah 6-7 Psalm 85 Proverbs 7 Acts 8

A Tower for Christ

Good morning! As I was driving back from Lexington yesterday headed to the ranch, I noticed something that I see almost every day. It was the water tower of Lancaster, Kentucky. I remember when I was younger, how excited I was as a young boy to see the construction of our water tower in the little town in Missouri where I lived. When they were done putting up that tower, you could see it for miles outside of town. As I drove home yesterday, I could see the water tower miles before I drove to town.

My heart was convicted this morning that people should see Christ in us before we ever say a word or introduce ourselves. People should see Christ in us as we speak on the phone, as we pass them at the store, in our driving habits, and in every area of our life. Jeremiah 6:27, "I have set thee for a tower, and a fortress among my people." We are set as a tower for Christ in the middle of a darkened, blinded world. Jeremiah wrote on to say, "Stand in the gate of the LORD's house, and proclaim there this word, and say, Hear the word of the LORD." I hunger to win souls. I hunger to be a better soul winner. I hunger to spread the Word of God. As I write the three previous statements, I ask myself and I ask you, are we standing as a tower for Christ proclaiming the truth of God through our lives? The people of God in Acts were scattered abroad and many had been jailed, tortured and some had met death, and yet we read in Acts 8:4, "Therefore they that were scattered abroad went every where preaching the word." Are you standing as a tower for Christ? Acts 8:6, "And the people with one accord gave heed unto those things which Philip spake, hearing and seeing."

As the water tower caught my eye in a different way, may the words of God cause us this morning to think about how we are to have a testimony for Christ that is true, tall, and a testimony to bring honor to His name. Proverbs 7:24, "Hearken unto me now therefore, O ye children, and attend to the words of my mouth." The return of the Lord draws closer every day and the gift of God's salvation must be proclaimed in a way that all can see, hear and understand. Psalm 85:9, "Surely his salvation is nigh them that fear him; that glory may dwell in our land." Psalm 85:11, "Truth shall spring out of the earth; and righteousness shall look down from heaven." May our lives be a greater living testimony for Christ than any tower that will ever be built. Stand today, my brother and sister, stand tall for Christ.

People should see Christ in us before we ever say a word.

October 8

Jeremiah 8-9 Psalm 86 Proverbs 8 Acts 9

A Path to the Master

Good morning! As I was walking to the barn yesterday morning, I looked at the path the dogs have made in the grass from the barn to the house. Sometimes the dogs spend the night in the barn, sometimes they will sleep under one of our bedroom windows, and sometimes depending if we have campers at the ranch or not, they will find a place in the cowboy town to stay close to the campers. How come our two dogs have chosen the path? The path is not a straight path, but it is a path that they have walked so much it is well worn, and when I cut the grass, this path is so worn that it has worn some of the grass away and you can clearly see the dirt. Two dogs have chosen a direct path to where their master lives, where they drink fresh water, eat the food provided, receive special treats like bones left over from pork chops or some fresh bacon grease poured over their dog food. These two dogs chose the path to their master.

What path have we chosen to our master? Is it the shortest path or do we go another way? Jeremiah 9:23-24, "Thus saith the LORD, let not the wise man glory in wisdom, neither let the mighty man glory in his might, let not the rich man glory in his riches: But let him that glorify glory in this, that he understandeth and knoweth me that I am the LORD which exercise loving kindness, judgment, and righteousness, in the earth: for in these things I delight, saith the LORD." It is dark and early in the morning right now while I am writing. Do you know if I walk out into the dark, I will not have to call the dogs, they will just show up because they are listening for their master to come to the door and they want to see him. I stood and looked at the worn path and I thought, do two dogs have more of a love for their master that they have worn a path to be with him, than we do for a Master that forgave our sins and has given us eternal life? Is there a worn path where you kneel and pray? Is there a worn Bible because you have spent time reading it? Is there a worn prayer list because of the prayers that you bring to our LORD? Acts 9:6, "Lord, what will thou have me to do?" That was the words Saul said when he heard the Lord say, "Saul, Saul, why persecutest thou me?" Do not use the excuse of not living for God and serving Him because of difficulties in your life. Saul was blind three days. Acts 9:9, "And he was three days without sight, and neither did eat nor drink." There was a humility and desire to do what he did not even yet know. Proverbs 8:20, "I lead in the way of righteousness, in the midst of the paths of judgment." Oh, that we would stay faithful to God, His Word, and His ways. Make a straight path to Him today. Seek His face today. Wait upon Him today. Praise Him today. Psalm 86:12, "I will praise thee, O Lord my God, with all my heart: and I will glorify thy name for evermore."

Those dogs will walk that same path in just a few minutes, not because I taught them or told them to. Those two dogs desire to be with and walk with the master that loves them and cares for them. Do you hunger to be with the Master today? He is always ready to spend time with us and be there for every need and burden we have. The Master is waiting to be with you.

Have you worn a path to the Master?

October 9

Jeremiah 10-11 Psalm 87 Proverbs 9 Acts 10

Creatures of Habit

Good morning! All of us are creatures of habit. Some habits are very good and some are very bad. It seems as though the bad habits that we have we know we need to break, but we do not have the strength, willpower or discipline to conquer them. Such is like a dog chasing things like a car, cat, rabbit, squirrel, or even the neighbor's chickens. I asked myself this morning, what habits of the world do I have? Jeremiah 10:2, "Thus saith the LORD, Learn not the way of the heathen, and be not dismayed at the signs of heaven; for the heathen are dismayed at them." The world continues on and ignores the way of the Lord. The world rejects Christ and feels just like they will be fine. A Christian knows what is right to do and yet goes the ways of the world and thinks they do not need to honor Christ in their lives. Jeremiah 10:24, "O LORD, correct me, but with judgment; not in thine anger, lest thou bring me to nothing."

A neighbor's dog used to come over and play with one of my dogs and that neighbor's dog loved to chase cars. One day while chasing a car, the neighbor's dog was hit just down around the corner from our house. I did not know this had happened and we called and called for our dog and she did not come. Later that day I had to go to town and as I came around that corner, there was my dog laying by the neighbor's dog that had been killed from being hit by the car. How often has it been that the habits of another person have pulled a faithful Christian away from being what God wanted them to be? Our fear of this world is pulling many away from serving and being faithful to the Lord. Jeremiah 10:19, "But I was like a lamb or an ox that is brought to the slaughter; and I knew not that they had devised devices against me." We try to justify the bad habits and before long those habits can pull us away from the relationship we once had with God. Acts 10:34, "Then Peter opened his mouth, and said, of a truth I perceive that God is no respecter of persons." Proverbs 9:6, "Forsake the foolish and live; and go in the way of understanding."

It took me awhile, but I am very thankful that we broke our dog of chasing cars. What excuse of a habit will you give God when you stand face to face with Him? What excuse will you give for not being what you know God wanted you to be? Psalm 87:6, "The LORD shall count, when he writeth up the people." We need to check out our habits that keep us from being the Christian that God wants us to be. Something to think about. How about asking the Lord for strength to conquer that bad habit and get on track with God?

What excuse will you give for not being what God wanted you to be?

October 10

Jeremiah 12-13 Psalm 85 Proverbs 10 Acts 11

Handling Pride Properly

Good morning! As I read Jeremiah 13:15, "Hear ye, and give ear; be not proud: for the LORD hath spoken." Pride blocks our hearing, pride blocks the Lord doing His work in our lives, pride is a destroyer and a divider. Pride out of control can ruin everything it touches. Good pride is doing a job right. Good pride takes care of things that the Lord has given us. Good pride will bring obedience. May I ask this morning, has your pride been handled the right way? God said through the prophet Jeremiah in Jeremiah 13:16, "Give glory to the LORD your God, before he cause darkness, and before your feet stumble." Have you forgotten to give God the glory for answered prayer?

As I was praying this morning, I noticed several answered prayers and I had to stop and ask God to forgive me because I had not given Him the praise He deserved. The great commission that we have been given to reach the world for Christ can turn into a pride problem if we are not careful. We work hard and yet we do not see the results, and our pride gets hit. Acts 11:2, "And when Peter was come up to Jerusalem, they that were of the circumcision contended with him." There was contention because of pride. Conviction of sin will affect our pride instead of having a humbled heart. Pride can create a negative spirit toward a brother or sister in Christ. Proverbs 10:12, "Hatred stirreth up strifes: but love covereth all sins." May we learn to rejoice in what God is doing in our life, and also rejoice when God is doing a great work in the lives of others. Maybe we do not see the fires of revival stirring because of our pride. Maybe we do not head to the altar at church because of our pride when the Spirit of God mentions our sins through the preacher.

As I was on my knees this morning and stopped asking and began rejoicing in what God has done and is doing, I began to see how Jeremiah was so broken over the pride of the people of Israel. Oh, that God would help us see our pride that blinds us from seeing as God sees. Psalm 85:6, "Wilt thou not revive us again: that thy people may rejoice in thee?" Oh Lord, help me to have the right pride and keep the wrong pride confessed and forsaken.

Pride out of control can ruin everything it touches.

October 11

Jeremiah 14-15 Psalm 89:1-18 Proverbs 11 Acts 12

The Perfect Passage

Good morning! I love the mountains. I love to look at the majestic Rocky Mountains, I love to drive through the beautiful Smokey Mountains. I love those curving roads through the Appalachian and Blue Ridge Mountains. As my wife and I drive toward the mountains I often say, how did they get through them when there was no road, no known passageway? To the pioneers there was a way. To the explorer there was a way. To those that had the character to push on there was a way, and when they found the way, it became a way for others.

Those of us that know Christ as our personal Saviour have found the way of eternal life. We have found the way for our sins to be forgiven. We have found the way to joy, peace, and a usefulness for life, and that is to live for Christ. Our reading in Jeremiah 14 and 15 this morning takes us to the place where Israel has refused God's way so long, that it is like God has left them. Jeremiah 14:19, "why hast thou smitten us, and there is no healing for us? We looked for peace, and there is no good." When we come to that point in life that there is a standstill and we do not know what to do, we have arrived at a good place. We do so much without God, or ignore what we know God would want, that it is like we have arrived at the mountains and we cannot find the right path to take. Jeremiah 15:16, "Thy words were found, and I did eat them; and thy word was unto me the joy and rejoicing of mine heart: for I am called by thy name, O LORD of hosts." The way of the world is the way of destruction. The way of the Lord is the path of life and blessings. In Acts 12, Herod had killed James, and Peter was locked in chains in jail and yet as the people came together in prayer, the chains fell off and we read in Acts 12:10, "they came unto the iron gate that leadeth unto the city; which opened to them of his own accord." Peter came to a place where he and others thought his life would end, and yet this mountain passage was found and he walked out without one problem.

Is a mountain in front of you today and you have no idea how to get around it, over it, or through it? Look to the Lord, confess sin, forsake the sin, turn to Him and watch Him guide you through. God is waiting on us to do right in His eyes, not ours. The words *righteous* and *righteousness* both mean right in the eyes of God. Proverbs 11:3, "The integrity of the upright shall guide them." It is when we do what we know is right. Proverbs 11:5, "The righteousness of the perfect shall direct his way." The word "perfect" means those who are redeemed and do what they know is right in God's eyes. Proverbs 11:6, "The righteousness of the upright shall deliver them." Proverbs 11:8, "The righteous is delivered out of trouble." Is there a mountain range in front of you? Look to the ONE who can show the perfect passage through that trial, discouragement, battle, frustration. Psalm 89:15, "Blessed is the people that know the joyful sound: they shall walk, O LORD, in the light of thy countenance." Our Lord will not only show us the path to go, but He also lights the way. You can make it through that mountain in front of you if you will go God's way.

The way of the Lord is the path of life and blessings.

October 12

Jeremiah 16-17 Psalm 89:19-37 Proverbs 12 Acts 13

What's on Your Plaque?

Good morning! Have you ever gone to a craft store and taken the time to just read the quotes or phrases on the plaques? During my reading I wrote down a couple of phrases that came to my mind. "Friendships are Forever." "Enjoy it while you have it, it will not be there forever." God loves His people with a love that is beyond our understanding. His longsuffering is beyond what any human could have. God does have a limit of His patience with us. I thought Jeremiah 16:5 might be a good verse to put on a plaque and hang it in our homes so that we can often see it and think about it. "I have taken away my peace from this people, saith the LORD, even loving kindness and mercies." How about this to hang above the door, and we could see it every time we leave the house? Jeremiah 16:12, "ye walk every one after the imagination of his evil heart." Those two statements give a person something to think about, and yet we still reject what God has for us. Can you picture with me a beautiful rustic plaque hanging in our home's dining room where we as a family eat our meals? Jeremiah 17:5, "Cursed be the man that trusteth in man, and maketh flesh his arm, and whose heart departed from the LORD." No, we would not hang these types of plaques in our home, but they are in the Word of God and they should pierce our hearts deeply. How about these plaques hanging in our living room where we sit and talk, read books, or maybe mom and dad tell stories of their childhoods? Jeremiah 17:7, "Blessed is the man that trusteth in the LORD, and whose hope the LORD is." Jeremiah 17:22, 24, 27, "hallow the sabbath day."

I have plaques that hang in my office for me to see every day. One just says, "FAITH." Another one reads, "When the going gets tough, the tough get going!" You and I have life to be a light in this world, and that light is to be a bright light. Our lives should be under great conviction when we read verses such as Acts 13:10, "wilt thou not cease to pervert the right ways of the Lord'? We need to take a look at what plaques our lives display for everyone around us. Take a look at what is daily a testimony of your life. Let us this morning decide we are going to be a plaque that shows forth glory to the King of Kings. Proverbs 12:3, "the root of the righteous shall not be moved." Proverbs 12:7, "the house of the righteous shall stand."

As we walk out to take the children to school, go to work ourselves, or set out to do the things on our "to do" list, may we read this plaque as we head out into the world before us. Psalm 89:28, "My mercy will I keep for him for ever more, and my covenant shall stand fast with him." God has not changed. Maybe we need to change some plaques that hang about our lives.

We need to take a look at what plaques our lives display for everyone around us.

October 13

Jeremiah 18-19 Psalm 89:38-52 Proverbs 13 Acts 14

Get Up!

Good morning! I can remember hearing the wrestling coach say so many times to the wrestlers, "GET UP." I can remember boxing coaches telling a boxer to "GET UP." I can remember one of my all-time favorite messages I heard preached by Dr. Jack Hyles, and I bought the tape (cassette tape) and wore several out, "Knocked Down, but Not Knocked Out." So many times, we get knocked down or just fall. Can I give you a simple thought? GET UP! A farmer does not quit farming because he had a bad crop. A rancher does not quit raising beef cows because he lost some newborn calves. A ball player does not quit playing ball because he struck out. Why do we as God's people quit because we fell or we feel the Christian life is so hard? Just GET UP!

We read of the potter in Jeremiah 18:4, "so he made it again." He did not like what he saw so he "made it again." God's Word records for us to read, apply and live in Jeremiah 18:6, "cannot I do with you as this potter? saith the LORD. Behold, as the clay is in the potter's hand, so are ye in mine hand." If you have sinned and departed from walking with God, listen to the words in Jeremiah 18:11, "return ye now every one from his evil way, and make your ways and your doings good." GET UP! We read of the impotent man in Acts 14:8, "being a cripple from his mother's womb, who never had walked." Acts 14:9, "The same heard Paul speak: who steadfastly beholding him, and perceiving that he had faith to be healed." Acts 14:10, "Said with a loud voice, Stand upright on thy feet. And he leaped and walked." He GOT UP!

Sin is a destroyer. Sin will take you deeper than you want to go. Sin will cause you to feel it is all over. Sin will give you the attitude, I can't. Sin will destroy relationships with those you love and those that have been there for you. Proverbs 13:18, "Poverty and shame shall be to him that refuseth instruction: but he that regardeth reproof shall be honoured." The end of life will come soon enough, but while we have life, we need to be standing and serving. Psalm 89:48, "What man is he that liveth, and shall not see death? shall he deliver his soul from the hand of the grave? Selah." Some things to think about. While you are thinking, just GET UP!

While we have life, we need to be standing and serving.

October 14

Jeremiah 20-21 Psalm 90 Proverbs 14 Acts 15

What Are You Chained To?

Good morning! Have you ever watched how a dog acts that is kept on some type of chain or cable? Maybe the dog is tied up because it runs off and the owner does not want to keep chasing it. Maybe the dog is tied up or chained up because of it attacking people. Have you ever watched what happens when the owner of the dog lets the dog loose? The dog will never just sit there, it runs and runs and runs. That dog now has its freedom. When the dog gets tied up or chained up or even put on a cable so that it has a little more running room, it is still not free.

As I read in Jeremiah 20:4, "I will make thee a terror to thyself, and to all thy friends." Sin will chain us. Sin will rob us. Sin binds us and controls us. Jeremiah 21:8, "I set before you the way of life, and the way of death." Before each of us is an opportunity to walk with God or to be bound in sin. It takes work to live the Christian life, but it is worth the joy and peace and the relationship with the Lord. I watched a neighbor's dog that is on a cable so it can run. When they first got the dog, it came over to our house and I sat and talked with it, spent a little time letting the dog smell me and be comfortable around me. As a matter of fact, my wife and I really liked the dog. The neighbor spends no time with his dogs and has several tied up. That same dog that I have petted, talked with, gave a little treat to, attacked me one day when someone else other than the owner let it loose. That dog's personality totally changed because of being chained. We read in Acts 15 about men of God who were called of God but had a contention, and we read in Acts 15:39, "And the contention was so sharp between them, that they departed asunder one from the other." I do not believe for a moment that the apostles were involved in any kind of sin, but self and pride and a wrong spirit did get in the road of having a right spirit.

We need to be very careful about what could bind us or control us, and whatever it is that could create a bad spirit in us and cause us to even attack those that we love. I heard this quote many years ago that went like this; "Be careful what you say or do, you will live with it the rest of your life." Proverbs 14:10, "The heart knoweth his own bitterness." Proverbs 14:14, "The backslider in heart shall be filled with his own ways." It is time for us this day to do a self-evaluation. Do we have some things that we are chained to that have created a wrong spirit in us? Are we living for the Lord because we want to please Him and have a love in our heart? Proverbs 14:33, "Wisdom resteth in the heart of him that hath understanding: but that which is in the midst of fools is made known." Walk with the Lord in peace, because you have nothing between you and the Lord. Psalm 90:14, "O satisfy us early with thy mercy; that we may rejoice and be glad all our days." I stopped and looked at the dog that had been chained. I talked softly and gently. The dog settled down, and we began to rebuild a relationship. What has you chained that has caused you to lose your joy? Find out what it is because you might just be attacking the one that cares for you. Some things to consider this morning.

Do we have things we are chained to that have created a wrong spirit in us?

October 15

Jeremiah 22-23 Psalm 91 Proverbs 15 Acts 16

A Secret Place

Good morning! Do you remember playing hide and go seek? One person began to count to 100 and that gave the rest of us time to go and hide. We were hiding so that we could not be found and we could be the winner. If we were not found, we did not want to tell anybody where that special place of hiding was. Life is not a game. We will not win in trying to hide from God. Sin will always be revealed. Jeremiah 23:24, "Can any hide himself in secret places that I shall not see him?" Our lives should be lived to have victory over sin. Jeremiah 23:28, "What is the chaff to the wheat?" Chaff is the part of the grain that is thrown away. The chaff is of no value and is totally worthless. The chaff is the inedible part of the grain. The chaff is a picture of sin in our lives and it must be separated because sin has no value.

As we find Paul and Silas in prison, they were praying and singing praises unto God in Acts 16:25. The prison was shaken, the chains unlocked and the prison doors opened. We read how the jailer "brought them out." Acts 16:30, "And brought them out, and said, Sirs, what must I do to be saved?" They were separated from bondage and set free by God. Quit trying to hide from God and quit justifying sin. God will always find our hiding place. There is another hiding place that we should be seeking. Proverbs 15:29, "The LORD is far from the wicked: but he heareth the prayer of the righteous."

It is time for us to have a special place, a private place, a "secret place" to meet in prayer with God, to plead for His cleansing, to hunger to fellowship with Him, to find His leadership in our lives. Psalm 91:1, "He that dwelleth in the secret place of the most High shall abide under the shadow of the Almighty." There is a "secret place" to hide from God, and there is a "secret place" to be with God. I choose to be in the "secret place" of prayer, fellowship, and communing with God. Are you in the right "secret place" today?

There is a secret place to hide from God and a secret place to be with God.

October 16

Jeremiah 24-25 Psalm 92 Proverbs 16 Acts 17

Fresh Oil

Good morning! Sometimes I find myself looking back too much instead of looking ahead. There are things in our past that cannot change, but there are many ways in the future that we can change what we need to change. Remember the use of an eraser in school. When you made a mistake, you could just erase it, correct it, and go on. When we were younger, our schoolwork was done with a pencil, and then when we were older, we were allowed to use an ink pen. We were more confident in not making mistakes, so we did not worry about having to erase something. I often get notes from campers, and the younger campers almost always write with a pencil and the teen campers write with a pen. I wrote today at the top of my notes as I was reading the daily Scriptures, this simple statement, "Things I wished I had changed and cannot; and things I can by God's grace will change.

Jeremiah 25:4, "And the LORD hath sent unto you all his servants the prophets, rising early and sending them; but ye have not hearkened, nor inclined your ear to hear." I want to learn and by desiring to learn, I might have to make some changes. As we all grow in the Lord and begin to have a closer walk with the Lord, we make some changes in our lives. We all have and probably will make mistakes. Mistakes that we have made and can correct we should. Jeremiah 25:5, "They said, turn ye again now every one from his evil way, and from the evil of your doings." There are a couple of things I want to bring out in this verse. "Turn ye again"; they had turned to sin before, and God is saying ye must "turn away again" from that which is keeping you from being obedient. Look also at the two words, "every one." All of us fight sin. Did you ever think we sin not because of any other reason than we are sinners? That is the main reason we must focus on walking with God, because we are sinners. Sinners sin and we need to learn how to walk with God and, as sinners, have victory over sin. That is why we need to go to Sunday School, hear preaching and teaching, read our Bibles, go to revival meetings, have daily devotions, etc. We are sinners and when we get saved, we have invited the Spirit of God to forgive us and come into our heart, but we are still sinners and we need the Spirit of God to keep convicting us of our sin. Thank God we can be forgiven and grow in our relationship with God. Acts 17:27, "That they should seek the Lord, if haply they might feel after him, and find him, though he be not far from every one of us."

When we sin, our flesh wants us to run from God instead of allowing the conviction of sin to draw us to God and obtain the victory over the sin. Acts 17:30, "And the times of this ignorance God winked at; but now commandeth all men every where to repent." God knows we are sinners, but we must face the sin and ask forgiveness of sin. Sin is not the right way. Sin will take us farther away from God. That is why we skip church, skip our Bible reading, skip our prayer time, and we feel we can make it without God. Then we are so far away we feel that we cannot come back to God. THAT IS A LIE OF THE DEVIL! Proverbs 16:25, "There is a way that seemeth right unto a man, but the end thereof are the ways of death." As I read in Psalm 92 this morning, my heart rejoiced that we can correct and forsake sin in our lives by asking God for "fresh oil" of the Holy Spirit's conviction and forgiveness. Psalm 92:10, "But my horn shalt thou exalt like the horn of an unicorn: I shall be anointed with fresh oil." AMEN! There is fresh forgiveness and a fresh start by the power of the Holy Spirit of God. We do not need an eraser, we do not need a bottle of white out, we do not need to backspace, we do not need to hit the delete button. We just need the conviction and forgiveness of

God. Yes, we can have the "fresh oil" of God. Yes, we can change and forsake sin. Do it today, right now. God is there waiting.

God gives fresh forgiveness and a fresh start by the power of the Holy Spirit.

October 17

Jeremiah 26-27 Psalm 93 Proverbs 17 Acts 18

Spiritual GPS

Good morning! I received an email yesterday from a pastor asking for a GPS address so that he can come to a camp activity. This pastor has only come to the camp one time and he is pastoring a different church now, so he wanted to find directions and figure when they should leave the church to make it to the camp on time. Simple request, and things should be okay, but not necessarily. What do I mean? All GPS's are not the same and several GPS's have led people driving to the camp the wrong direction. You say, that could never happen. Well, it does, depending on the direction you are coming, the update of the GPS, and possible road changes. I will never forget one church that called the camp with a bus load of kids, that found themselves on a dead-end road facing a creek that could not be crossed.

Thank the Lord there is only one way of salvation. Jeremiah 26:13, "Therefore now amend your ways and your doings, and obey the voice of the LORD your God." Do you know money has a voice, a vehicle has a voice, things have voices? You say a vehicle does not speak. You have never heard the voice tell you that you need that truck or you need that car? We hear all kinds of voices. Have you ever heard the voice that says, you do not need to go to church today, or you do not need to read your Bible or pray? Yes, in our wicked sinful life we do hear other voices. Let us look at the word "amend." It means to correct, to make better, to change. God is saying to change your ways and obey HIS voice. Our GPS's are wonderful devices, but they can still direct us in a wrong way. What voice are you listening to this morning? What voices do you listen to throughout the day? We read in Acts 18:5, "Paul was pressed in the spirit," and in Acts 18:9, "Then spake the Lord to Paul in the night by vision." Paul was tuned in to the voice of God. Too often we listen to the wrong voice and go in the wrong direction.

You might say, how do we know the voice of God above all other voices? The voice of God never contradicts Biblical principles. The voice of God never leads us away from God. The voice of God never leads us to sin. Yes, we go through trials that do not seem to be of God, but He could be preparing us for our next step. He could be making us stronger for His service. He could be drawing us closer to Him for greater strength. Proverbs 17:3, "The fining pot is for silver, and the furnace for gold: but the LORD trieth the hearts." God's voice is clear and strong. God's voice may be heard if we hunger to listen. Psalm 93:4, "The LORD on high is mightier than the noise of many waters, yea, than the mighty waves of the sea." We need to be very careful that we are not listening to something that will take us away from the will of God and lead us down a wrong path. Do you need to update your spiritual GPS? It is never wrong when our focus point is God.

The voice of God never contradicts Biblical principles.

October 18

Jeremiah 28-29 Psalm 94 Proverbs 18 Acts 19

A True Foundation

Good morning! As I opened the car door for Mrs. Smith I said, well, look there on the ground. Again, when I started up to the steps to the back door of the house, I said to Mrs. Smith, well look, there is another one. What I was telling her to look at was wooly worms. She asked me, what do the different width of stripes mean? I think I have driven my wife nuts with old folklore sayings through the years of our marriage. I was taught and am still learning many things about what we can learn through signs in nature and animals. First of all, a definition for the word "folklore." Let us break the word down. "Folk," meaning people in general or certain people, such as older people or younger people. "Lore" means to learn. When we put the two words together, we have "folklore," meaning a certain group of people passing lessons of life to other people. Such as my parents or adults in my life passing things they had learned on to me. It is an interesting thought about the stripes and colors about a wooly worm.

This is the point that I want to make this morning; it is an interesting thought. Jeremiah 28:15, "Then said the prophet Jeremiah unto Hananiah the prophet, Hear now, Hananiah; The LORD hath not sent thee; but thou makest this people to trust in a lie." Hananiah was going to die because as a prophet, he told the people a lie. In Acts 19 Paul was judged by the Jews because he told the truth about their false gods, especially about those that were making money for making "silver shrines for Diana" (Acts 19:24). Acts 19:26, "Moreover ye see and hear, that not alone at Ephesus, but almost throughout all Asia, this Paul hath persuaded and turned away much people, saying that they be no gods which are made with hands." Our foundation is the Word of God that has been preserved for us. This world is full of believing lies. The truth must be told. Proverbs 18:7, "A fool's mouth is his destruction, and his lips are the snare of his soul." Many a church do not preach and teach the truths of the Bible. Thank the Lord when a false prophet is called out. Psalm 94:12, "Blessed is the man whom thou chastenest, O LORD, and teachest him out of thy law." Psalm 94:13, "That thou mayest give him rest from the days of adversity, until the pit be digged for the wicked." The truth will be told. "Jesus is the way, the truth and the life" (John 14:6).

I pray you get the truth from my thoughts today. Let me end with what I was taught, though I do not know if it is the truth or not. When you see brown wooly worms it means a harsh winter. When you see wide brown bands on a wooly worm it means a mild winter. When you see black wooly worms it means a severe winter. When you see light brown or white worms it means a snowy winter. Every year of my life I have seen all the different colors in the fall months. You know what I decided? We are going to have winter. Have a blessed day and always believe the truth of the Words of God.

Our foundation is the Word of God that has been preserved for us.

October 19

Jeremiah 30-31 Psalm 95 Proverbs 19 Acts 20

The Family of God

Good morning! It was the day after Christmas, 1963. We had our Christmas and packed everything up in a grain truck and headed to a new home. Mom and dad had been raised around the town where I was born and spent the first twelve years of my life. As a young man, I did not want to leave the place that I had called home, and yet dad and mom believed it was the right thing to do. It was hard leaving my cousins, aunts, and uncles, and especially my grandparents. Before Christmas break dad had picked me up at school; he wanted to talk with me. For six months dad had worked a new job in Iowa and came home once a week. I will never forget that day. Dad told me we were going to move to Iowa and leave Missouri. I thought, leave family and friends? By that move, God had a work to do in my life far greater than I would ever know. I was about to start a journey that would lead me down a path to give my life in full surrender to the Lord. Oh, there have been those times that I have fought being surrendered to the Lord.

I read this morning the words Jeremiah wrote in Jeremiah 30:22, "And ye shall be my people, and I will be your God." My parents and grandparents went to Heaven many years ago. Many of my friends I had growing up have died long ago. My brother and sister live many miles away. Our children and grandchildren live many miles away. Please do not think that I am not happy because I have family and friends all over this world. We are the family of God. Throughout the years I have met missionaries that have served and are serving around this world. I sat last evening and looked at photo albums of staff that have served with us summers gone by and many are serving the Lord today. My brother and sister, we are part of the greatest family in the world, the family of

God, and God loves us more than we will ever know. Jeremiah 31:1, "At the same time, saith the LORD, will I be the God of all the families of Israel, and they shall be my people." Jeremiah 31:14, "my people shall be satisfied with my goodness." Jeremiah 31:33, "will be their God, and they shall be my people."

That move from Missouri to Iowa started a chain of events that have given me part of being in a family that is larger and greater than any family that will walk this earth, the family of God. Listen to the words of Paul as he was continuing his missionary journeys and telling some believers good-bye in Acts 20:32, "And now, brethren, I commend you to God, and to the word of his grace, which is able to build you up, and to give you an inheritance among all them which are sanctified." Did you see the words "all them?" We are so blessed to be part of the family of God. Spend time at church speaking to those that are part of your local church family. Get an understanding that your local church family is a family that will be there for you. Proverbs 19:8, "He that getteth wisdom loveth his own soul: he that keepeth understanding shall find good." Yes, our earthly blood families might be gone or far away, but we have the family of God there by us to pray with and for us, to fellowship with and to be a blessing to and for. Church is meeting with God and being with family. Psalm 95:6, "O come, let us worship and bow down: let us kneel before the LORD our maker." Learn to love and care for the family God has given you in your local church. Folks in your church care more for you than you know. Have a blessed day with family today.

We are part of the greatest family in the world, the family of God.

October 20

Jeremiah 32-33 Psalm 96 Proverbs 20 Acts 21

Be Strong

Good morning! I ask you, is there anything too hard for God?? The easy answer is no, there is not. How is your faith in God this morning? How is your walk with God this morning? Have you taken the time to praise Him this morning? We have an inheritance, and that inheritance is eternal. Jeremiah 32:8, "the right of inheritance is thine, and the redemption is thine." Jeremiah 32:17, "Ah Lord God! behold, thou hast made the heaven and the earth by thy great power and stretched out arm, and there is nothing too hard for thee." What is your fear this morning? Give it to God. Why have weak faith? Be strong in the Lord.

Jeremiah 32:19, "Great in counsel, and mighty in work: for thine eyes are upon all the ways of the sons of men: to give every one according to his ways, and according to the fruit of his doings." Do not forget, Jeremiah is in prison and the prison that he is in is not a place of comfort. Jeremiah 32:27, "Behold, I am the LORD, the God of all flesh: is there any thing too hard for me?" In Acts 21, the people were pleading with Paul to be careful and to leave town, and this is the spirit and attitude of Paul and the people in verse 5, "we kneeled down on the shore, and prayed." Acts. 21:14, "And when he would not be persuaded, we ceased, saying, The will of the Lord be done." Our faith in God is our hope and our light. Our spirit will be strengthened in God when we keep going forward by faith. Proverbs 20:27, "The spirit of man is the candle of the LORD, searching all the inward parts of the belly."

Look at the morning sun, look at the evening sun. Nothing will stop them because God is in control. Try to stop the wind, the snow, the rain. God controls more than we can ever imagine. Be strong in the Lord! Psalm 96:2, "Sing unto the LORD, bless his name; shew forth his salvation from day to day." Psalm 96:10, "Say among the heathen that the LORD reigneth." I think we need to move forward by faith in God and not stand still in fear. Press on, my brother and sister.

Our spirit will be strengthened in God when
we keep going forward by faith.

October 21

Jeremiah 34-35 Psalm 97 Proverbs 21 Acts 22

An Encourager

Good morning! When was the last time you went out of your way to do something for someone else without being asked? Our Lord Jesus set the example of serving others and putting others first before ourselves. It is easy to want to do something for a friend or to do things with friends that have the same interests that we do. When was the last time that you took time to go out of your way to be a blessing, or reach out and spend time with somebody that might not be just like you or have the same interests as you?

Jeremiah 34:9, "that none should serve himself." I am afraid too often a father does not do things with his children because he says he is tired from a week's work. A mother does not take the time to work with her daughters, teaching them how to develop in being a housewife. So often it gets said, I can do it myself faster and better. How about someone in church that you never or very seldom say hello to or even pass by and smile at and say, it is sure good to see you today. How about encouraging someone to go to a church activity with you, and spend some time with someone other than just your friends? I read that phrase again in Jeremiah 34:10, "that none should serve themselves." Our world is not hearing the story of God's love and forgiveness because we are so focused on what we are doing or want to be doing. Acts 22:15 in our reading today about Paul, "For thou shalt be his witness unto all men of what thou hast seen and heard." There is a hurting world and there are not enough servants of the Lord to answer that hurt with the healing of the Lord Jesus. My mother never taught a Sunday School class and never was asked to sing in the choir, but boy, was my mom a servant! She sought out the hurting. I can remember many a meal that mom served to those in need. She did not drive but she would have my dad take her to those shut in or going through a tough time. At a church VBS you would find my mom in the kitchen serving.

Have we shut our ears to those in need, to those that might not be the most talented? Proverbs 21:3, "Whoso stoppeth his ears at the cry of the poor, he also shall cry himself, but shall not be heard." Some of the happiest people I know are those that are always asking, what can I do? I have no doubt that some of the people that are the strongest in a walk with God are those that see the needs of others and look for what they can do for others. Psalm 97:11, "Light is sown for the righteous, and gladness for the upright in heart." If we just open our eyes, there is a world of hurting, lonely, empty people that do not think anybody cares. Let God use you today to be that servant of the Lord that is the encourager to the discouraged.

Some of the happiest people are those that are always asking what they can do for others.

October 22

Jeremiah 36-37 Psalm 98 Proverbs 22 Acts 23

The Words of God

Good morning! There has been an ongoing battle for the truth of the teachings and preservation of the Scriptures. This battle will continue, but from the beginning of time the Words of God have been sealed in Heaven. Jeremiah was told by God to record God's Words. Let us look together at Jeremiah 36:2, "Take thee a roll of a book, and write therein all the words that I have spoken unto thee against Israel, and against Judah, and against all nations, from the days of Josiah, even unto this day." The Words of God have been written and preserved by God to be used to guide us, warn us, protect us, convict us, draw us to God, teach us how to love God and be loved of God. The importance of God's Word will never end in explanation. That is why it is so important to read God's Word, learn and memorize God's Word, and apply it to every area of our lives.

The words that God gave to Jeremiah were recorded and read to the king and we read the king's reaction. Jeremiah 36:16, "when they had heard all the words, they were afraid both one and other." Jeremiah 36:23, "He cut it with the penknife, and cast it into the fire." Know that God's Word will be preserved, so God told Jeremiah what to do in Jeremiah 36:28; "Take thee again another roll, and write in it all the former words that were in the first roll." Thank the Lord! In Acts 23, we read how Paul spread the Words of God and they tried to kill him several times and this is what God said to Paul in Acts 23:11, "Be of good cheer, Paul: for as thou hast testified of me in Jerusalem, so must thou bear witness also at Rome." We must hear the Words of God and we must live the words that we hear. Proverbs 22:17, "Bow down thine ear, and hear the words of the wise, and apply thine heart unto my knowledge."

We cannot forget the commission that we have been given to spread the Word of God to every language and nation. Psalm 98:3, "He hath remembered his mercy and his truth toward the house of Israel: all the ends of the earth have seen the salvation of our God." You might be thinking we are losing some battles but keep reading the Word of God and you will soon see we are going to win the war. Read the Word of God and let us spread its truth everywhere.

We must hear the Words of God and we must live the words that we hear.

October 23

Jeremiah 38-39 Psalm 99 Proverbs 23 Acts 24-25

Step Forward

Good morning! What determines the lead goose in the flock as we look into the sky and see that V-shape of geese flying through the sky? Please stop and think with me this morning. Who really is the leader? We are challenged in many places in the Word of God to watch nature. Who is the real leader in the flock of geese? Jeremiah has been cast into prison, and then there steps forth a man named Ebed-melech, an Ethiopian eunuch. Jeremiah 38:8, "Ebed-melech went forth out of the king's house, and spake to the king, saying." He was not picked, he "went forth." It was not his position, it was not his authority, but he decided and "went forth." Ebed-melech decided on his own accord to go to the king and ask the king to listen to Jeremiah. Jeremiah 38:15, "Then Jeremiah said unto Zedekiah, If I declare it unto thee, wilt thou not surely put me to death? and if I give thee counsel, wilt thou not hearken unto me?" Jeremiah 38:17, "Then said Jeremiah unto Zedekiah, Thus saith the LORD, the God of hosts, the God of Israel; If thou wilt assuredly go forth unto the king of Babylon's princes, then thy soul shall live, and this city shall not be burned with fire; and thou shalt live, and thine house." Zedekiah did not listen to Jeremiah because of his fear.

Many a Christian are fearing the news reports and a virus more than doing what God has for them to be doing. Fear will keep us from being obedient to the Lord and while our fear is controlling us, a world is going to Hell. My brother and sister, a man stepped forward and a people could have been spared if there had been obedience to the Word of God. I am afraid we are expecting just a few to carry the load while others are stepping back in fear of the unknown, calling it wisdom. We are seeing many a Christian backslide, not be faithful, lose their burden, and say they are waiting. Waiting for what???? Jeremiah 39:18, "because thou hast put thy trust in me, saith the LORD." Ebed-melech was spared while the king had his eyes put out and he was bound in chains. Paul said in Acts 24:16, "And herein do I exercise myself, to have always a conscience void of offence toward God, and toward men." Paul spoke the Word of God and did the will of God no matter the consequence. Proverbs 23:17, "Let not thine heart envy sinners: but be thou in the fear of the LORD all the day long." During this time of confusion, trouble, trials, turmoil, unrest, we need a people to step forward like Ebed-melech and be what God wants them to be. Psalm 99:9, "Exalt the LORD our God, and worship at his holy hill; for the LORD our God is holy."

Who is the leader of the flock of geese? All of them. That is right, all of them. Every few minutes or less the lead goose moves, and another comes to lead. They work as a team. Each goose takes turns at the lead and they all do their part. The lead goose at the point starts the breaking of the wind and each goose following just flies slightly higher to get the updraft of the wind, so the lead is constantly being changed so the entire flock can fly for three to eight hours to get to their destination. If all of God's people would do a little and step up to do their part, we could reach this lost world for Christ. May God give us more Ebed-melech's.

While our fear is controlling us, a world is going to Hell.

October 24

Jeremiah 40-41 Psalm 100 Proverbs 24 Acts 26

No Outlet

Good morning! As Mrs. Smith and I were driving home from church Sunday afternoon, she said to me, look at those beautiful colors of the trees. As I looked, I said to her, why don't we take a long road home? Before we left Lexington we drove through several neighborhoods where the trees were so beautiful. As I was watching for traffic and admiring the trees, I turned down several streets that were not through streets and we had to turn around at the end of the street. I missed the signs that said, "no outlet" or "dead end."

I have thought about those signs for a couple of days and as I read this morning in Jeremiah 40:3, "because ye have sinned against the LORD, and have not obeyed his voice, therefore this thing is come upon you." Let us look at the words, "this thing is come upon you." If we are not careful, we are going to also reap what we are sowing and God just might say, "this thing is come upon you." We give excuse why we cannot come to Sunday School, why we cannot be at church on time, why we cannot help in a class, why we cannot drive a bus route, why we cannot go soul winning and the "why we cannot's" will never end until the Lord says, "because ye have sinned." Our God is so patient but there will come that day when we will see, "this thing is come upon you." Paul stood before king Agrippa and said in Acts 26:22, "Having therefore obtained help of God, I continue unto this day, witnessing both to small and great, saying none other things than those which the prophets and Moses did say should come." Did you catch the words, "should come?" You see, we will reap what we have sown. The signs were there, "dead end" and "no outlet," but I was more interested in looking at the trees. Proverbs 24:12, "If thou sayest, Behold, we knew it not; doth not he that pondereth the heart consider it? And he that keepeth thy soul, doth not he know it? And shall not he render to every man according to his works?" My friend, our justification for why we cannot will come to an end and it will be said to us, "doth not he know it" or as Moses said, "should come," or we will face the fact, "this thing is come upon you."

God is looking for our faithfulness and full surrender without excuse. Psalm 100:3, "Know ye that the LORD he is God: it is he that hath made us, and not we ourselves; we are his people and the sheep of his pasture." That road will soon come to a "dead end," and we will have to face our Lord. The path that we often take has "no outlet," and we will have to look at our Lord and ask forgiveness to get back on the right path. My friend, my brother and sister in Christ, quit making excuse why you can't, because we might sooner than later have to face a situation that "this thing is come upon you." Walk with God today, be faithful and you will not come down to a "dead end" road.

God is looking for our faithfulness and full surrender without excuse.

October 25

Jeremiah 42-43 Psalm 101 Proverbs 25 Acts 27

Obedience

Good morning! There is a word that we all have heard many times during our life, no matter our age, and that word is "obedient." As I looked in my 1828 dictionary this morning, the definition reads like this: submissive to authority; yielding compliance with commands, orders or injunctions; performing what is required, or abstaining from what is forbidden. That is very simple to understand. The children of Israel cried out to Jeremiah to go to the Lord and find the way they should go. Jeremiah 42:3, "That the LORD thy God may shew us the way wherein we may walk, and the thing that we may do." Jeremiah 42:6, "Whether it be good, or whether it be evil, we will obey the voice of the LORD our God, to whom we send thee; that it may be well with us, when we obey the voice of the LORD our God." I have heard many a person say, I want to do what is right and what God wants me to do. I have prayed with many that have rededicated their lives to the Lord. I have seen many tears by those that want things to be right with them and God.

It seemed that the children of Israel wanted to do right and then we read in Jeremiah 43:2, "all the proud men, saying unto Jeremiah, thou speakest falsely." Jeremiah 43:4, "and all the people obeyed not the voice of the LORD." Jeremiah 43:7, "they obeyed not the voice of the LORD." What happens? Lack of obedience. It is just as simple as that. Why a lack of obedience? Lack of character to stay in fellowship with God. We all must realize our flesh is weak. Discipline to do right in a walk with God is of the most importance. Telling our flesh, I am not going to stay in bed. I am going to be on time for Sunday School and church. Nothing is going to keep me from serving the Lord. It is our flesh controlling us, and us weakening to our flesh. Paul heard from the Lord what to do and he shared this with the ship's owner and master in Acts 27:10, "Sirs, I perceive that this voyage will be with hurt and much damage." The owners thought they knew more than the man walking with God, and their pride caused them to lose the ship. Acts 27:11, "Nevertheless the centurion believed the master and owner of the ship, more than those things which were spoken by Paul." Acts 27:21, "Paul stood forth in the midst of them, and said, Sirs, ye should have hearkened unto me." Paul was just telling what God told him. Acts 27:25, "I believe God, that it shall be even as it was told me."

You cannot have God's blessing without putting God first place. God will never bless less than full obedience. We must keep our flesh under control and walk in the spirit. Proverbs 25:28, "He that hath no rule over his own spirit is like a city that is broken down, and without walls." How is your obedience to the Lord today? How are you doing at keeping your commitment to the Lord? How is your faithfulness in comparison to your fear of the unknown? Psalm 101:3, "I will set no wicked thing before mine eyes: I hate the work of them that turn aside;

it shall not cleave to me." Our word for today is "obedient"; immediate surrender, constant surrender, full surrender. We all need to check every area of our lives and see if we are "obedient" to the Lord.

You cannot have God's blessing without putting God first place.

October 26

Jeremiah 44-46 Psalm 102:1-10 Proverbs 26 Acts 28

Stubborn Spirit

Good morning! One of the things that so bothered me as I was growing up was all the whippings that I got. I asked my mom one day why I got so many, and she said the problem was me. My parents, and my precious wife have told me on many occasions that I have a very stubborn spirit. That stubborn spirit has hurt me and those I love too many times. There is a place for stubbornness, but not when it comes to walking with God. Jeremiah 44:2, "Thus saith the LORD of hosts, the God of Israel; ye have seen all the evil that I have brought upon Jerusalem, and upon all the cities of Judah; and, behold, this day they are a desolation, and no man dwelleth therein." God is saying through the writings of Jeremiah, can you not see how the stubbornness of the people have brought total ruin? Jeremiah 44:4, "Howbeit I sent unto you all my servants the prophets, rising early and sending them saying, Oh, do not this abominable thing that I hate." God said, I sent men of God to you to warn you, to advise you, to let you know what I would do, and yet we see their response in Jeremiah 44:5, "But they hearkened not, nor inclined their ear to turn from their wickedness, to burn no incense unto other gods." You might think this morning, I do not burn incense. Let me explain what is being said. Anything that we have in our lives that we put ahead of God is like worshipping another god. God then lets us know that what He says, He means. Jeremiah 44:9, "Have ye forgotten." Jeremiah 44:28, "shall know whose words shall stand, mine or theirs." Jeremiah 44:29, "that ye may know that my words shall surely stand."

Many years back we had a beautiful longhorn bull we called "Shadow." He had a solid body structure, beautiful full set of horns and walked with great pride. My son and I worked hours, days, and weeks with him to get him to settle down. He had an unpredictable spirit in him. A friend of ours that raises longhorns and different stock for rodeos came to see this bull. He made several suggestions and we tried them. We made a very hard decision to sell him and the owner of an exotic animal farm heard that we had this beautiful longhorn bull and he wanted him for his farm. We sold that bull, but the owner of the exotic animal farm did not keep him very long because he was charged by "Shadow" and got penned up next to a corner gate and almost killed. I have no idea what happened to "Shadow" after that, but he had a spirit that could not be controlled.

In Acts 28 this morning we read about Paul's teaching and preaching, and we read this in verse 27, "For the heart of this people is waxed gross, and their ears are dull of hearing, and their eyes have they closed." How sad to hear and still reject God's teaching. Don't turn back on God. Please do not reject what God is trying to do in your life. Sometimes we go through difficult times in our walk and growth in the Lord, but don't quit on God. Proverbs 26:11, "As a dog returneth to his vomit, so a fool returneth to his folly." How sick to see a dog eat its food, and then vomit and eat that vomit. Do not return to the sin God saved you from. If you have fallen prey to the flesh, get up and renew your walk with God. Psalm 102:2, "Hide not thy face from me in the day when I am in trouble; incline thine ear unto me: in the day when I call answer me speedily." There are none of us exempt from the possibility of falling away from God. Even the Psalmist cried out to God, for God to hear his cry. I had to sell that beautiful bull because his spirit could not be conquered. I took too many a paddling because of my stubborn spirit. Let God lift you back up this morning. Stay close to Him and do not reject the teachings of His Word. He loves you and me and has a very special plan for us. Have a blessed day.

There is a place for stubbornness,
but not when it comes to walking with God.

October 27

Jeremiah 47-48 Psalm 102:11-17 Proverbs 27 Romans 1-2

A Daily Walk with God

Good morning! I looked at a picture of an older lady that is probably days from going to Heaven. For many years she read her Bible daily and read it entirely through each year. It was testified about her that there were times her children and grandchildren heard her praying and even saw her on her knees. Now she sits, blind, cannot get on her knees and is just waiting on the Lord to take her Home. As I looked at the picture, I asked the Lord to help me to be faithful to the very end in daily reading His Word and not just spending a little time in prayer, but walking throughout the day in constant prayer with the Lord.

Our reading today is full and overflowing. We live in a world where people boast of living a life without God. A world that is doing what is right in their own eyes and rejecting God's holiness. Not worshiping God but mocking God. Jeremiah 48:14, "How say ye, we are mighty and strong men for war?" Jeremiah 48:39, "They shall howl, saying, How is it broken down!" Jeremiah 48:42, "And Moab shall be destroyed from being a people, because he hath magnified himself against the LORD." We read this morning of the power of God to destroy a people because of their rejection of God. As we turned to Romans 1 and 2, the Scriptures continue in teaching us not to be ashamed of being a Christian, and how important it is to separate ourselves unto God. Romans 1:16, "For I am not ashamed of the gospel of Christ: for it is the power of God unto salvation to every one that believeth; to the Jew first, and also to the Greek." God will have His day to bring judgment against sin in this world. Romans 1:18, "For the wrath of God is revealed from heaven against all ungodliness and unrighteousness of men, who hold the truth in unrighteousness." We read in Romans 2:24, "For the name of God is blasphemed." The word "blasphemy" means one whose speech or actions are against God. As I read that definition I thought, may my words never be against God, but how about my daily actions? We should respond to the love of God. Romans 2:4, "the goodness of God leadeth thee to repentance." Proverbs 27:12, "A prudent man forseeth the evil, and hideth himself; but the simple pass on, and are punished." The word "prudent" means practically wise. Are we thinking about how God sees us?

This precious elderly lady now cannot read, cannot get on her knees and pray like she used to, but I believe while she waits on her Saviour to take her Home, she is dwelling on His Word and having a wonderful talk with Him in her heart. I asked myself this morning, how would I be if I could not read God's Word daily and get on my knees to talk with my Lord? My friend, God loves you. May we love Him by spending time with Him and letting His Word grow in us. May we be found living God's Word in every area of our lives. Enjoy your time with the Lord because you will be spending eternity with Him soon. If you do not know Him, may you trust Him today. Ask Him to forgive you of your sins, because you are sorry for your sins, and by faith ask Him to come into your heart and save your soul and give you life eternal. Live today like you are thankful He has given you eternal life.

Enjoy your time with the Lord because you will be spending eternity with Him soon.

October 28

Jeremiah 49-50 Psalm 102:18-28 Proverbs 28 Romans 3-4

Stay on the Main Road

Good morning! It used to be when we traveled, we used a road map and now we use our phone as a guide, or even our car has some type of navigation system. Let us return this morning to the road map. I have to chuckle at talking about a road map, because I know there might be some that say, "a road map," what is that? Can you remember how the different types of roads were printed a different color? Interstates were yellow, two lane main highways were red and other highways or county roads were black. My wife and I sometimes enjoy taking a map and hitting the back roads just to discover new areas that we have never seen before. Often when we travel the back roads, we look for intersections of main roads to keep ourselves from getting lost or losing the directions of just where we are.

Sometimes in life we get off on a side road and find ourselves away from the Lord and we need to get to an intersection to get back on the right road with Christ. Jeremiah 50:5, "Come, and let us join ourselves to the LORD in a perpetual covenant that shall not be forgotten." I want to look at the word "perpetual," which means never ceasing, continuing forever in the future time. Wow, our Lord wants us to stay on the main road of life with Him and this road will lead us to a future of never-ending time with him! Romans 4:8, "Blessed is the man to whom the Lord will not impute sin." Now let us look at the word "impute." When we get off into sin, we can get right back in relationship with God by confessing and forsaking that sin and we can be back on the main road that is a blessed relationship with God. "Impute" means to charge, to make charge to the account, but Romans 4:8 reads, "the Lord will not impute sin." He will forgive and help us get back on the main road.

Oh, how I love to see the new sights on a back road. We think that sometimes sin is fun or satisfying, but the back roads will never take us home or back to where God wants us to be. Romans 4:20, "He (Abraham) staggered not at the promise of God through unbelief; but was strong in faith, giving glory to God." Romans 4:21, "And being fully persuaded that, what he had promised, he was able also to perform." Abraham got on a side road and sinned but praise the Lord, he got back on the main road with the Lord and received the blessings of God. Proverbs 28:20, "A faithful man shall abound with blessings." Proverbs 28:25, "he that putteth his trust in the LORD shall be made fat." There are main roads in our country that seem like they never end, and you can travel border to border or coast to coast, but there is nothing like a blessed walk with God that is a "perpetual" walk that never ceases. Psalm 102:27, "But thou art the same, and thy years have no end." Stay on God's main road.

The back roads of life will never take us home
or to where God wants us to be.

October 29

Jeremiah 51-52 Psalm 103 Proverbs 29 Romans 5-6

God's Never-Ending Love

Good morning! Come with me down by the pond. The air is so calm that the water is not even moving. The water is reflecting an image of the trees and sky all around. Reach down and pick up a stone. The stone can be of any size. Now toss the stone into the pond, anywhere will be just fine. Watch the ripples that never end until they reach the shoreline. It does not matter where you throw the stone in the water because some of the ripples will not stop until they reach the shore. As I was reading my Bible this morning, I thought how God's love to us will never end and it will always be there until we reach the Heavenly shore and then we will be with the Lord forever. AMEN!!!!

Jeremiah 51:5, "For Israel hath not been forsaken, nor Judah of his God, of the LORD of hosts; though their land was filled with sin against the Holy One of Israel." Sin has bought a price on Israel and it will bring a price to pay upon us, but that does not mean God has forsaken us. Jeremiah 51:10, "The LORD hath brought forth our righteousness: come, and let us declare in Zion the work of the LORD our God." God does not quit on us, so let us not quit on God. Yes, we sin and that is because we are sinners, but God is there and ready to forgive us our sins. We must face the sin, request forgiveness of sin and forsake the sin. God wants to use us. Israel has sinned, and God's judgment has fallen but we read four words, ten times, in Jeremiah 51:20-24; "with thee will I." "With thee will I," God wants to use us sinners for His work. What needs to be done in our lives was a phrase found in Jeremiah 51:12 and 27. We need to "Set ye up a standard," and that "standard" is the Lord Jesus Christ and His never-failing Word, the Bible. Romans 5:15, "For if through the offense of one many be dead, much more the grace of God, and the gift by grace, which is by one man, Jesus Christ, hath abounded unto many." The "gift of grace" is salvation to all men. Our sin came through one man, Adam, and God's grace came through Jesus Christ.

We need to constantly, daily, every moment of the day live Romans 6:11, "Likewise reckon ye also yourselves to be dead indeed unto sin, but alive unto God through Jesus Christ our Lord." Quit saying you can't live the life of a Christian. Proverbs 29:25, "The fear of man bringeth a snare: but whoso putteth his trust in the LORD shall be safe."

Throw another stone into the pond and watch that ripple continue until it reaches the shore. The mercies of the Lord are everlasting. Psalm 103:17, "But the mercy of the LORD is from everlasting to everlasting upon them that fear him, and his righteousness unto children's children." I think we need to take our children and grandchildren down to the pond and let them throw a stone in and watch the ripples to teach an everlasting lesson.

God's love will always be there until we reach the Heavenly shore.

October 30

Lamentations 1-2 Psalm 104:1-17 Proverbs 30 Romans 7-8

Where Did the Time Go?

Good morning! Have you ever said, where did this day go? Or have you ever gone on a vacation and asked yourself, how did this vacation go so fast? I remember the day that our children got married and it seemed like it was the day before that we had brought them home from the hospital. Where has life gone? How did it go by so fast? Just yesterday they were learning how to tie their shoes and now they are the ones teaching their children how to tie their shoes. The words I said to the young lady that I wanted to spend my life with were just said yesterday and now almost fifty years later, life has just flown by. As we grow older, we face something that I do not know how to prepare for, and that is the passing of a loved one. Life goes so fast and especially time with the ones we love so much.

The question is asked in Lamentations 1:1, "How doth the city sit solitary, that was full of people! How is she become as a widow! She that was great among the provinces, how is she become tributary!" What once was, is now not anymore. Gone! What happened? Why? Lamentations 1:8, "Jerusalem hath grievously sinned; therefore she is removed." The world wants the flesh to be satisfied. The world hungers for peace at any price. Do not point out my sin! Do not put boundaries on what I want to do! It is my life and I will live it the way I want! God's heart is broken, and yet what He had to do was because He loved beyond what flesh could understand. Jeremiah's heart is broken, and he writes in Lamentations 1:12, "Is it nothing to you, all ye that pass by? Behold, and see if there be any sorrow like unto my sorrow, which is done unto me, wherewith the LORD hath afflicted me in the day of his fierce anger." All of us want our children to "turn out," as we would say. But turn out how? Are we teaching them to live for the Lord and to walk daily with Him? Are we living a life before our children and grandchildren consistent with the Word of God? Romans 8:1-2, "There is therefore now no condemnation to them which are in Christ Jesus, who walk not after the flesh, but after the Spirit. For the law of the Spirit of life in Christ Jesus hath made me free from the law of sin and death." Oh, that we would put Christ and a walk in the Spirit first place in every area of our life. The great nation of Israel in our reading in Lamentations is now in captivity because of sin and rejection of God and God's way. Proverbs 30:12, "There is a generation that are pure in their own eyes, and yet is not washed from their filthiness."

Life is so short. We must not lose one moment in teaching generations to come about the love of Christ to save their soul, and the blessings of God to live for Christ. As I read this phrase in Psalm 104:16, "The trees of the LORD are full of sap." The trees have the sap flowing because they are alive. Our life in Christ must be flowing with the presence of the Holy Spirit leading us, convicting us, drawing us closer to a life that can be blessed in Christ. Today will be gone soon, so live today for Christ because tomorrow may never come. If tomorrow comes, live and enjoy the blessed life walking with Christ. Some things to think about this morning.

Live today for Christ because tomorrow may never come.

October 31

Lamentations 3-5 Psalm 104:18-35 Proverbs 31 Romans 9-10

Be Patient

Good morning! In just a couple of hours there will be four-legged friends showing up at a set of glass doors. I will be sitting in a chair close to my wife with my Bible in my lap, getting ready to have devotions together. These four-legged friends will sit and look at the glass to see if they can see me. If they can see through the glass and take a look at me, their tail will begin to wag, they will begin to whine and make a couple of circles and go back and forth to get my attention. The impatience of these little friends will get stronger and stronger and there might even be a couple of times that there will be a little bark, and that is saying we are ready for you to pet us, feed us and pay a little attention to us. I have learned that those dogs waiting on me and wagging their tails and giving the little bark to draw my attention, works on me. I love it that the dogs are waiting to see me. You know even when I feed them, they want to be petted, played with, and they want to go wherever I go. When I get in my truck, they will run right alongside of the truck until I get to the end of the drive. Those dogs will be waiting for me when I return tonight. I said a lot about the dogs to use a simple picture to get our attention on some thoughts from God's Word about waiting and seeking the Lord.

Lamentations 3:25, "The LORD is good unto them that wait for him, to the soul that seeketh him." Lamentations 3:26, "It is good that a man should both hope and quietly wait for the salvation of the LORD." We so often miss the will of God because of impatience. We miss the joy of seeing His hand work things out for His purpose. As I read Romans 10:1, "Brethren my heart's desire and prayer to God for Israel is, that they might be saved." Be patient and let God work in the hearts of those that you love that are not saved. Be patient and let the Word of God work that has been sown in a lost co-worker's heart. Be patient as your children go through battles that will help them develop a walk with God. Be patient with each other, in every relationship.

There is a joy beyond words when we wait on the perfect will of God and see it develop before our very eyes. God gives us a picture in Proverbs 31:20 as we read, "She stretcheth out her hand to the poor; yea, she reacheth forth her hands to the needy." Here we see love and patience with those hands that reach out. Psalm 104:27, "These wait all upon thee; that thou mayest give them their meat in due season." God's will is going to be done in God's timing. Have patience, "it is good."

There is a joy beyond words when we wait on the perfect will of God.

November 1

Ezekiel 1-3 Psalm 105:1-15 Proverbs 1 Romans 11-12

A Hunger for God

Good morning! It seems the colder the weather gets the more we stay inside, and the more we stay inside, the more we eat. Can anybody relate? I remember as a teenage boy, my mother saying to me, "David, you did not even taste what you just ate." I was a growing boy and seemed to never be full even though I ate all the time, or that is what my parents said. Growing as a teen was going forward toward manhood. I was growing in stature, in mind, setting goals and having direction for my life. I asked myself this morning, am I still hungering to keep going forward? Am I hungering for the truths of the Word of God and hungering for the power and leadership of the Lord?

Ezekiel 1:12, "And they went every one straight forward: whither the spirit was to go, they went: and they turned not when they went." Are you hungering for the leading of the Lord? Are you hungering for Him to feed you from His Word? Ezekiel 2:1, "And he said unto me, Son of man, stand upon thy feet, and I will speak unto thee." We need to have our spirits set on fire for the Lord. We, as a world of Christians, are backslidden. My brother and sister, we need revival! Have we forgotten those words recorded in Ezekiel 3:18, "his blood will I require at thine hand?" Ezekiel 3:19, "Yet if thou warn the wicked, and he turn not from his wickedness, nor from his wicked way, he shall die in his iniquity; but thou hast delivered thy soul." My friend, we need more than a hunger for food; we need a hunger for God. We are the generation now living and we have a world before us that needs Christ. We need to not forget why we have life. Romans 11:29, "For the gifts and calling of God are without repentance."

When is the last time you begged God for a vision for your neighborhood, your town, your state, your country, your world, and had a hunger for God's power to move through you? Proverbs 1:23, "Turn you at my reproof: behold, I will pour out my spirit unto you, I will make known my words unto you." We need to beg God for a spiritual hunger for Him many times, more than a teen boy hungers for food that will truly never satisfy. Psalm 105:4, "Seek the LORD, and his strength: seek his face evermore." It is time for us to sit at the spiritual table and eat a meal of spiritual food, to cause us to stand and move forward for Christ. Some things to consider.

When is the last time you had a hunger for
God's power to move through you?

November 2

Ezekiel 4-5 Psalm 105:16-45 Proverbs 2 Romans 13-14

The Season of Joy

Good morning! As I was reading the Word of God this morning, a phrase kept running through my mind. "Reading the times of the seasons." Is it fall, is it winter, is it Thanksgiving, is it Christmas? What season is it now in this time of confusion? Is the Lord Jesus and His will for our life in the forefront of our mind? Are we waiting for something to pass? Is there a fear that we have never had before? Have we lost our love for being in church and being with the family of God? What season of life is it? What season of time are we living in? Are we hiding in sin, or are we pressing forward for the season in time of our Lord's return?

Ezekiel 4:14, "Then said I, Ah Lord God! Behold, my soul hath not been polluted." Has the news media and fear of the unknown caused us to be in a season of time when there is more fear of something that cannot be described than a fear of pleasing God? Ezekiel 5:6, "For they have refused my judgments and my statutes, they have not walked in them." Do we pay more attention to the media than the Word of God? Romans 13:11, "And that, knowing the time, that now it is high time to awake out of sleep: for now is our salvation nearer than when we believed." Romans 13:12, "The night is far spent, the day is at hand: let us therefore cast off the works of darkness, and let us put on the armour of light." It is the season for all of God's people to shine the light of salvation into a darkened world of sin. We have not been forsaken. God has not turned His back. God is still ready to hear our prayers and to guide us in every step. Proverbs 2:7, "he is a buckler to them that walk uprightly."

Oh, it is the season of joy! It is the season for God's people to have faith in our living Saviour. Psalm 105:43, "And he brought forth his people with joy, and his chosen with gladness." Put a smile on your face. Step out today with a joy in your heart because of the promises of God, so that a world doomed because of sin can see the light of salvation in Jesus Christ. Yes, this is the season of spreading the Gospel. Have a very blessed day.

It is the season for God's people to shine the light of salvation into a darkened world of sin.

November 3

Ezekiel 6-7 Psalm 106:1-16 Proverbs 3 Romans 15

Press Forward

Good morning! I often have stood at the camp and just looked over the hills and valleys and wondered what they would say if they could speak. The quietness, the peace, the beauty. The sound of the wind blowing through the trees, the comforting relaxing sound as the water slowly makes its way through the creeks. This morning, as I do almost every morning, I stepped outside into the quietness of the night. As I look up into the sky it seems as though the stars would like to say something. Does all of creation know the burden of God? Does creation sense the urgency of God?

Ezekiel 6:3, "Ye mountains of Israel, hear the word of the Lord God; Thus saith the Lord God to the mountains, and to the hills, to the rivers, and to the valleys." Ezekiel 7:2, "Also, thou son of man, thus saith the Lord God unto the land of Israel; An end, the end is come upon the four corners of the land." Judgment was falling on the sins of Israel. Is it close for the judgment of God to fall upon us? Have we turned our backs on God? Have we had the urgency to spread the gospel to our neighbors, communities and around the world like we should? Has the push by Satan and his workers been stronger than the spreading of the gospel by us, the redeemed of God? My heart is so convicted as I see the world running in fear to hide and yet forgetting the reason we have life. Listen to the words of the apostle Paul in Romans 15:20, "Yea, so have I strived to preach the gospel, not where Christ was named, lest I should build upon another man›s foundation." Romans 15:21, "But as it is written, To whom he was not spoken of, they shall see: and they that have not heard shall understand." Did God speak to His creation because man would not listen?

Oh, that we would have the fervency that we should have to spread the gospel! Proverbs 3:27, "Withhold not good from them to whom it is due, when it is in the power of thine hand to do it." Spread the Word of God! We must reach a lost and doomed world with the Gospel message, throughout the land. Psalm 106:7, "Our fathers understood not thy wonders in Egypt; they remembered not the multitude of thy mercies; but provoked him at the sea, even at the Red Sea." Psalm 106:8, "Nevertheless he saved them for his name's sake, that he might make his mighty power to be known." Through His voice the waters came, the earth opened, the seas have turned back, the waves have quieted, the sun has turned back. Yet we as man have refused to hear. While we have time, may we press forward to win a lost world to Christ and be a living testimony of His grace, and may our faith be increased daily to do a greater work for Him. The hills, valleys and rivers have kept on. May it be said of us that we have pressed on for the cause of the Gospel.

While we have time, may we press forward to win a lost world to Christ.

November 4

Ezekiel 8-9 Psalm 106:17-33 Proverbs 4 Romans 16

God's Jealousy

Good morning! Have you ever been jealous? I thought of times that I have been jealous and in some cases I was very immature, and yet there have been times that it was very important. Let us look at the definition. Jealousy: "That passion or peculiar uneasiness which arises from the fear that a rival may rob us of the affection of one whom we love, or the suspicions that he has already done it; or it is the uneasiness which arises from the fear that another does or will enjoy some advantage which we desire for ourselves." The definition is quite long but very important to understand when it comes to God's relationship with us.

Ezekiel was caught up in a vision from God and we read in Ezekiel 8:5, "So I lifted up mine eyes the way toward the north, and behold northward at the gate of the altar this image of jealousy in the entry." God is jealous of His people and how the devil and his demons work to take, steal, and detract our love for our Saviour! Ezekiel continued in Ezekiel 8:12, "hast thou seen what the ancients of the house of Israel do in the dark, every man in the chambers of his imagery? For they say, the LORD seeth us not." When we sin and try to hide it, God's jealousy is stirred, and we should be very thankful that God hungers for our love and loyalty. Paul wrote in Romans 16:19, "but yet I would have you wise unto that which is good, and simple concerning evil." Why do we hide from God? Why do we let the flesh, yes, our own flesh, deceive us? Proverbs 4:14-15 warns us, "Enter not into the path of the wicked, and go not in the way of evil men. Avoid it, pass not by it, turn from it, and pass away."

We need to take a long look at what is trying to draw us away from God. What is keeping us from our walk with God? What is keeping us from the house of God and our service for God? Proverbs 4:19, "The way of the wicked is as darkness: they know not at what they stumble." Judgment of God was brought upon Israel because of God's jealousy, and I fear the jealousy of God being turned loose on this generation. Psalm 106:21, "They forgat God their Saviour, which had done great things in Egypt." Do not forget God's love for us, His sacrifice for us, His preparation of an eternal Home for us, the cleansing blood of His Son for our sins. Oh, that we would be honest with ourselves and fight back with our jealousy for God! Some things to consider.

We should be very thankful that God hungers for our love and loyalty.

November 5

Ezekiel 10-11 Psalm 106:34-48 Proverbs 5 1 Corinthians 1-2

What Are Your Markings?

Good morning! As I came in from feeding the animals, Mrs. Smith asked me to come to the window and tell her what kind of bird it was that she was looking at. I told her what I thought it was and she said, "its markings are so different than the others." As I was reading this morning my mind came back to her statement, "its markings are so different."

As Ezekiel wrote in Ezekiel 10:19, "And the cherubims lifted up their wings, and mounted up from the earth in my sight." Ezekiel 10:22, "And the likeness of their faces was the same faces which I saw by the river of Chebar, their appearances and themselves: they went every one straight forward." "Their appearances"; what is the appearance of us in this world that we live in? What is our distinction in this world filled with sin? Can our appearance identify us with Christ and a godly appearance, godly attitude, godly spirit? What joy it is to know that our Lord has prepared special blessings for those who are willing to be set apart unto our Lord! I Corinthians 2:9, "But as it is written, Eye hath not seen, nor ear heard, neither have entered into the heart of man, the things which God hath prepared for them that love him." I Corinthians 2:12, "Now we have received, not the spirit of the world, but the spirit which is of God; that we might know the things that are freely given to us of God."

If little birds have special markings of identification and if the cherubims had special markings, what about us being godly in every area of our life? God sees and God knows. Proverbs 5:21, "For the ways of man are before the eyes of the LORD, and he pondereth all his goings. "Pondereth" means weighs out, considers, examines.

As we observed the markings of a little bird to identify it, I ask the question, is God evaluating our markings of this world and our feeble attempts of faithfulness? There should be a heartfelt drive of action toward being godly, or should I say "marked" in a way that God sees. Psalm 106:47, "Save us, O LORD our God, and gather us from among the heathen, to give thanks unto thy holy name, and to triumph in thy praise." Mrs. Smith said, "Honey what kind of bird is this?." I could only give an answer by the markings. What kind of Christian are we by our markings?

The Lord has prepared special blessings for those who are willing to be set apart unto Him.

November 6

Ezekiel 12-13 Psalm 107:1-22 Proverbs 6 1 Corinthians 3-4

Too Much Stuff

Good morning! If I say the word "stuff," what comes to your mind? Mrs. Smith and I have decided that it is time for us to go through our "stuff" and give away, throw away a lot of "stuff" that has been boxed up, pile up, stored up. Can anybody relate and admit that you have a lot of "stuff?" Why do we save so many things? I have had the grandchildren ask me, "Papa, why are you saving this "stuff?" Boy, oh boy, can stuff cause a lot of problems, become a distraction, become extra labor!

Ezekiel 12:3, "prepare the stuff for removing." The word "stuff" is mentioned five times in verses 3, 4, and 7. The "stuff" was a distraction from hearing what God wanted them to hear. Ezekiel 13:3, "Woe unto the foolish prophets, that follow their own spirit, and have seen nothing!"

"Stuff" is an excuse, "stuff" can be a distraction, "stuff" can be a time waster, "stuff" can be a deceiver, "stuff" can keep us from doing the will of God. I Corinthians 3:3, "For ye are yet carnal: for whereas there is among you envying, and strife, and divisions, are ye not carnal, and walk as men?" "Stuff" in our lives can keep us from growing in the Lord. I Corinthians 3:18, "Let no man deceive himself." We save "stuff" because we think it is important and yet we end up getting rid of most of our "stuff." Proverbs 6:9, "How long wilt thou sleep, O sluggard? When wilt thou arise out of thy sleep?" Proverbs 6:11, "So shall thy poverty come as one that travelleth, and thy want as an armed man." Let us look closely at the word "travelleth." It means to wander here and there, having no direction; time waster. Sounds like the writer of Proverbs is warning us about our "stuff." Psalm 107:4, "They wandered in the wilderness in a solitary way; they found no city to dwell in." Psalm 107:5, "Hungry and thirsty, their soul fainted in them."

Oh, how many Christians today are living in "stuff" and just wandering around, not living in the will of God, doing the work of God and enjoying the blessing of God? What "stuff" is keeping you from enjoying the fulfilled walk with God? Psalm 107:6-7, "Then they cried unto the LORD in their trouble, and he delivered them out of their distresses. And he led them forth by the right way, that they might go to a city of habitation." YES, they got out of the "stuff" and away from the "stuff" and walked in the promises of God. My brother and sister in Christ, do you have some "stuff" in your life that needs to be confessed and forsaken? Let me encourage you today, right now, get rid of the "stuff" and enjoy a walk with the Lord.

What "stuff" is keeping you from enjoying the fulfilled walk with God?

November 7

Ezekiel 14-15 Psalm 107:23-43 Proverbs 7 1 Corinthians 5-6

A Constant Source

Good morning! I stood beside a flowing creek, and I went and stood beside a creek bed where water once flowed and now it is dry. One is flowing because it has a mouth where it is being fed and the other is dry because its source is runoff water. As I stood in the woods and observed both creeks, I thought how that is like the life of many Christians. Some are constantly filled because of their personal walk with God and some only get what others preach, teach, or talk about what they received from the Lord in their personal walk. What kind of creek are you today, Christian?

Ezekiel 14:14 stirred my heart today; "Though these three men, Noah, Daniel, and Job, were in it, they should deliver but their own souls by their righteousness, saith the Lord God." As I read on, verses 18 and 20 are almost exactly the same wording. These three men are perfect examples of getting their strength from their personal relationship and walk with God, and their walk with God is what brought them through the battle. In I Corinthians 5:7, we are challenged to "purge out" what is drying us up in our walk with God. "Purge out therefore the old leaven, that ye may be a new lump, as ye are unleavened. For even Christ our Passover is sacrificed for us." We can have a constant source when we walk in Christ and keep the sin confessed so the sin does not dry up the flow of fresh teachings from a faithful, consistent walk with God. In Proverbs 7:25, the young man is challenged to "decline" sinful ways, "Let not thine heart decline to her ways, go not astray in her paths." Branches will fall and rocks can dam a small creek, but when the source keeps supplying the water, the power of the water will keep flowing. When we are tempted to sin, the fresh source of learning from a walk with God will allow the Holy Spirit to convict us and we can flee from sin. Oh, that we would stay connected to the living source of the Word of God, and a strengthening source from a daily walk with God! Psalm 107:35,

"He turneth the wilderness into a standing water, and dry ground into watersprings."

As I looked at the flowing water of a creek that has a source, and then moved just a short distance to a creek bed that is dry because it is only fed by runoff, I said, "Father please help me to live by the fresh spiritual water that constantly flows from You." Have a blessed day, and drink from the stream that never runs dry.

Oh, that we would stay connected to the living source of the Word of God!

November 8

Ezekiel 16-17 Psalm 108 Proverbs 8 1 Corinthians 7

Praise the Lord!

Good morning! I stopped as I was walking and just looked at the pine needles all over the ground, and it was like the Lord said, that is like the love that I have for you, it is never ending. All over the ground are leaves and pine needles that could never be counted. In Ezekiel 16:6-14, we see the word "I" used to identify what God has done. An example is Ezekiel 16:9, "Then washed I thee with water; yea, I throughly washed away thy blood from thee, and I anointed thee with oil." At least sixteen times we read the word "I."

Oh, that we would praise the Lord for His endless blessings! Thank Him for His unending forgiveness. Praise Him from the mountaintops for His salvation. I Corinthians 7:23-24, "Ye are bought with a price; be not ye the servants of men. Brethren, let every man, wherein he is called, therein abide with God." God wants to use each of us and He has so abundantly blessed us. How can we not serve Him in every way that we can? Proverbs 8:17, "I love them that love me; and those that seek me early shall find me." Proverbs 8:20, "I lead in the way of righteousness, in the midst of the paths of judgement." Proverbs 8:21, "That I may cause those that love me to inherit substance; and I will fill their treasures." Proverbs 8:32, "blessed are they that keep my ways."

I do not know about you, but my heart is humbled at the goodness of God toward this sinner. Just stop this morning and look all around, think about the avenue we have to Heaven, the preserved Words of God. We have so much for which to give Him praise. Psalm 108:3, "I will praise thee, O LORD, among the people: and I will sing praises unto thee among the nations." Wherever we are in this world, let us stop and give praise to our LORD!! Have a very blessed day.

Praise the Lord for His endless blessings,
His unending forgiveness, and His salvation!

November 9

Ezekiel 18-19 Psalm 109:1-13 Proverbs 9 1 Corinthians 8-9

Unseen Enemy

Good morning! I walked along a trout stream with Mrs. Smith yesterday and observed the ducks, birds, plant life, and flow of the water, and thought about the balance of nature. Earlier in the day a tree fell with a loud thundering bang and as we walked, we noticed where this large tree had fallen. What caused this once tall, strong, and large tree to fall? I do not know, but I could assume several different things. What causes a Christian to fall? What causes a Christian to backslide? What causes a Christian to have a fire in their soul and want to serve God, and now the faithfulness of church attendance is gone?

An example is our reading this morning. Ezekiel 18:24, "But when the righteous turneth away from his righteousness, and committeth iniquity, and doeth according to all the abominations that the wicked man doeth, shall he live? All his righteousness that he hath done shall not be mentioned: in his trespass that he hath trespassed, and in his sin that he hath sinned, in them shall he die." The Christian life is not a balance of right and wrong. The Christian life is to be a growth in Christ. That tree that fell was once a sapling and it grew through all kinds of weather from cold to heat, rain to snow, winds, and mighty storms, and still it stood.

What killed that mighty tree? A small bore, a fungus, etc. Whatever it was, that mighty tree now lays on the ground. Our life in Christ should be a facing and forsaking of sin and temptation. Ezekiel 18:30, "Repent, and turn yourselves from all your transgressions; so iniquity shall not be your ruin." Many a tree has been destroyed by a small little bore or an unseen enemy. Our problem is that we do not put Christ first in everything we do. I Corinthians 9:14, "Even so hath the Lord ordained that they which preach the gospel should live of the gospel." Paul worked on disciplining his flesh, not allowing himself to be the cause of stopping what Christ wanted to do in his life. I Corinthians 9:27, "But I keep under my body, and bring it into subjection: lest that by any means, when I have preached to others, I myself should be a castaway."

I am thankful for foresters that work to protect our forests from different enemies that are often unseen but can destroy great numbers of trees. Are trees more important than our testimony for Christ? We need to get to the cause of what is or could destroy us and forsake it, confess it and work in the strength of Christ to overcome it. Do not say you are strong enough to overcome. That mighty tree that had stood for years fell with a loud thud to the ground, and so can you and I fall from a sweet relationship in Christ. Proverbs 9:6, "Forsake the foolish, and live; and go in the way of understanding." The flesh and the world are liars. Do what is right in the eyes of God. Do not let the flesh keep you from doing what God will protect you from and bless you for when you do right. Psalm 109:2, "For the mouth of the wicked and the mouth of the deceitful are opened against me: they have spoken against me with a lying tongue." We must stay alert to the lies of the devil and the lies and weaknesses of our flesh. Be alert. As the mighty tree has fallen, so can the strongest Christian fall from the weakness of their flesh. Grow strong in the Lord and stand the test of time for His glory. Stay faithful.

We must stay alert to the lies of the devil
and the lies and weaknesses of our flesh.

November 10

Ezekiel 20-21 Psalm 109:14-31 Proverbs 10 1 Corinthians 10

Keep the Fire Burning

Good morning! I have heard many messages on having your heart set on fire by God. My heart has been stirred as I listened to each man of God preach with a burden to see people serving the Lord with everything they have. As I read in Ezekiel 20:47, I began to think about the messages that I had heard preached and then I noticed in this verse about the "green tree" and "dry tree." Let us read the verse together. "Hear the word of the LORD; Thus saith the Lord God; Behold, I will kindle a fire in thee, and it shall devour every green tree in thee, and every dry tree: the flaming flame shall not be quenched." Let us also read Ezekiel 20:48, "And all flesh shall see that I the LORD have kindled it: it shall not be quenched."

I have burned a lot of wood in my 69 years of life. I have cooked many a meal over an open fire, slept on the ground by a fire, and have eaten a lot of popcorn while sitting and talking while watching a fire. Burning green wood and burning dry wood is much different. Dry wood will build a hot fire fast, while green wood will make a good bed of coals to cook on. Dry wood is easier to start while green wood is much harder to start. I burn dry seasoned wood in our wood stove to heat with, while green wood will build soot up in the flue and can cause a flue fire. Both types of wood burning in a fire are important. Just like life, when our hearts are on fire for God, we must feed the right spiritual food in our hearts to keep the fire going. I Corinthians 10:23, "All things are lawful for me, but all things are not expedient: all things are lawful for me, but all things edify not." I hunger for a spiritual fire to burn at all times in my heart. There are things that we might do that will put that spiritual fire out. I Corinthians 10:31, "Whether therefore ye eat, or drink, or whatsoever ye do, do all to the glory of God." I start a fire with dry wood and if I am going to cook a meal on the fire, I will add some green wood to build a bed of coals in the fire. Proverbs 10:32, "The lips of the righteous know what is acceptable: but the mouth of the wicked speaketh forwardness."

We need to make sure we are building the right kind of fire in our heart so that we can be what God wants us to be, for what use He has for us. Most of all, we need to focus on how to get the spiritual wood burning. Psalm 109:30, "I will greatly praise the LORD with my mouth; yea, I will praise him among the multitude." God needs us to be a burning fire for Him, wherever we are and whatever we are doing. Let your spiritual wood burn for Him and learn how to feed the right spiritual wood into the fire. Keep the fire burning.

When our hearts are on fire for God, we must keep the fire going with spiritual food in our heart.

November 11

Ezekiel 22-23 Psalm 110 Proverbs 11 1 Corinthians 11

Examine Yourself

Good morning! Have you ever been told, "Don't let yourself be distracted?" Have you ever missed one ingredient in a recipe or had a part left over when putting something together? We get distracted so easily. We must not be distracted when having a personal time with the Lord. Our focus on Him must be the most important time of every day. The judgment of God had to fall on the children of Israel, and it will fall on us if we do not keep our focus on Him. The things of this world often distract us from that daily walk with God. Do not let others, the ways of the world, personal gain, family, a job position, etc. draw you away from doing and being what the Lord wants in your life.

Ezekiel 22:30, "And I sought for a man among them, that should make up the hedge, and stand in the gap before me for the land, that I should not destroy it: but I found none." Look at the words, "I sought." God is looking for us to make time for Him. God is wanting time with us. I love being with my wife, our children, and grandchildren. It is important that I make time for each of them. Time together is time to grow together, time to learn, time to listen, time in building a relationship that will last a lifetime. In I Corinthians 11:24-25, we see the phrase, "this do in remembrance of me." As we read on in I Corinthians 11:28, "But let a man examine himself." "Examine himself." Yes, we need to stop and look at what we are not putting in its place for future life. I am not speaking of retirement. I am speaking of relationships and mostly a relationship with Christ that will grow and be fruitful, blessed and reproducing in others.

Mrs. Smith and I recently went camping and had a tremendous time of sitting by a fire, hiking, being in the great outdoors, and spending time alone with each other. The weather was tremendous, the campsite was perfect; everything was great. The day we were getting ready to leave, Mrs. Smith was taking care of everything inside and I was preparing everything outside to hook the trailer up to the truck. As I was getting the stabilizer jacks in place, the water, and electrical lines and all the details, I got distracted. We got in the truck, had a word of prayer thanking the Lord for the time together and asking for a safe trip home. We pulled out of the campsite and had not gone 100 yards and the trailer came unhooked and dragged on the road. The safety chains kept it connected to the truck. I stopped, jumped out and immediately saw what was wrong. One small pin was not properly in its place. One small little thing that is almost the size of a finger. We could have had an accident or caused an accident. Praise the Lord we were safe, and no equipment was damaged. As I worked to get us up and going again, we then pulled over and I "examined myself." How did I miss putting that pin in place? How can I avoid this happening again? I have pulled many trailers and never had this happen before. We have pulled trailers all over the U.S. and never had this happen. We sat there along the side of the road and "examined" ourselves and what we had not done.

Let us take a close look and "examine" ourselves in the eyes of God this morning. Proverbs 11:3, "The integrity of the upright shall guide them: but the perverseness of transgressors shall destroy them." My brother and sister, we need to "examine" ourselves in view of the eyes of the Lord. Psalm 110:3, "Thy people shall be willing in the day of thy power." One pin, one small detail, one piece of safety and yet it was not in its place. God "sought for a man." He is looking for us to be in our place, doing what He has called us to do, growing in our relationship with Him and reaching a lost world for Him, while holding high the standard of the Word of God. Be the one serving in the one place that is made for you.

God is looking for us to be in our place, doing what He has called us to do.

November 12

Ezekiel 24-25 Psalm 111 Proverbs 12 1 Corinthians 12-13

A Boiling Pot

Good morning! Picture with me this morning a boiling pot on the stove. In that pot is boiling water with bones in the water. We will let it boil and boil to get everything we can from those bones. As I read Ezekiel 24:3, "And utter a parable unto the rebellious house, and say unto them, Thus saith the Lord God, Set on a pot, set in on, and pour water into it." Ezekiel 24:4, "Gather the pieces thereof into it." Ezekiel 24:5, "make it boil well; and let them seethe the bones of it therein." It is a picture for us of a sinful nation, and God has come to His end with them, and God is going to have the sin purged and allow them to go through a cleansing from sin. I asked myself this morning as I looked at some commentaries on this passage, Lord, is there a deep cleansing that I need in my life? Are there things that are hidden deeply, that I need to have boiled out of me?

We who are saved and have trusted Christ as our Saviour are part of the family of God. As a family, we are like a body that was talked about in our reading in I Corinthians 12. Each part of our body has a purpose and if one part is hurting, the pain is felt throughout the body. Can you imagine if the left foot wanted to go left, and the right foot wanted to go right at the same time? We should be thankful our bodies were made to function in a way that all parts work together. What if some member of the body of Christ lives in sin and others see and feel this sin? This brings a pain throughout the body of Christ. I Corinthians 12:24, "but God hath tempered the body together." I Corinthians 12:26, "And whether one member suffer, all the members suffer with it; or one member be honored, all the members rejoice with it." Each member does not live unto itself. Everything in the boiling pot was being cleansed, and if I had space, we would see that the water and all that was in it was consumed. May our sin be boiled out and may there be a unity in the body of Christ so that we all work together as a team. One part is not more important than the other, but all parts need to function together. Oh, that we would look at the life of a fool and then look at the actions of our life. Proverbs 12:15, "The way of a fool is right in his own eyes: but he that hearkeneth unto counsel is wise."

God needed to have the boiling pot to consume the sin. May we look to the Lord for His guidance instead of having to be in a boiling pot. Psalm 111:7-8, "all his commandments are sure. They stand fast for ever and ever, and are done in truth and uprightness." Psalm 111:10, "The fear of the LORD is the beginning of wisdom: a good understanding have all they that do his commandments." As a young boy, I can remember it being said, "your mom is boiling mad." I had done wrong, I had done something that made my folks very unhappy. May we take a deep look at our life this morning and get the laziness out in our walk of faithfulness to God. May we get our lack of consistency out in our relationship with God. God loves us, saved us, and hungers to walk in fellowship with us. Let us stay out of the boiling pot of God having to deal with us.

May we look to the Lord for His guidance
instead of having to be in a boiling pot.

November 13

Ezekiel 26-27 Psalm 112 Proverbs 13 1 Corinthians 14

Godly Music

Good morning! Do you listen to music that lifts your soul in worship to the Lord? There is all kinds of music, and then there is what is called music, but it is the farthest thing from what music is supposed to be. Music has been part of every generation that has walked this earth, and we do not have to read very far to find out how music is a major part of what is going on right now in Heaven. How sad to think about not having music! Ezekiel 26:13, "And I will cause the noise of thy songs to cease; and the sound of thy harps shall be no more heard." How very sad. Why? What happened? Sin, and God's judgment. Music is played in time of victory and music is played in time of defeat. Music was played for an army to charge in battle and music was played in time of retreat. We were created by God to have music. The birds sing, the trees play a song as the wind blows through their branches. What kind of music do you listen to? Does it build your spirit in your walk with God? Does it only stir your flesh?

Yesterday I took my wife grocery shopping in the afternoon. My wife and I talked about the different music being played in the stores. Many studies have been done concerning how different types of music even causes our eating habits to be affected. I Corinthians 14:7 "And even things without life giving sound, whether pipe or harp, except they give a distinction in the sounds, how shall it be known what is piped or harped?" Godly, Christ honoring music is to be part of our lives. Be careful of what type of music you listen to and what you feed your spirit and flesh. I Corinthians 14:8, "For if the trumpet give an uncertain sound, who shall prepare himself to the battle?" Godly music will rest our soul in the time of spiritual battles. Godly music will give us peace in time of sorrow. Proverbs 13:19, "The desire accomplished is sweet to the soul: but it is abomination to fools to depart from evil." Sing the Psalms and hymns. What a joy when we gather together in church and sing together as we worship our Lord together. Psalm 112:9, "He hath dispersed, he hath given to the poor; his righteousness endureth for ever; his horn shall be exalted with honour."

May we sing for His glory, may we sing to exalt Him, may we sing from our hearts and souls in praise to Him. Take time and evaluate the type of music that you are listening to. Oh, how we need music to draw us closer to our King in every walk of life. Do not let it be said like it was said to the children of Israel in their sin; "I will cause the noise of thy songs to cease."

Godly, Christ honoring music is to be part of our lives.

November 14

Ezekiel 28-30 Psalm 113 Proverbs 14 1 Corinthians 15

Stay in Your Place

Good morning! I went to a local hospital yesterday. As I entered the hospital it was very different as to the many other times I had walked in the same doors. I had to stop, state my business, let them know who I wanted to see, have my temperature taken, and wait. Calls were made and I received an okay and a name tag to go see the patient. I walked down a long hallway and entered the elevator and selected the floor where I needed to go. As the elevator doors opened to the floor where I had selected, I looked down a long hallway. As I walked alone, I prayed as I often have prayed, Lord, please fill me with your Spirit to have the right words to say. I turned from corner to corner and then I arrived at an Intensive Care Unit. I was allowed to walk in and talked with a nurse to go to the proper room. As I stepped into the room where the patient was that I came to see, I just stood at the end of the bed, and stood in the quietness of the room where only the machines could be heard that were attached to this patient. My heart swelled within me as tears began to form. I spoke and the nurse very kindly said, he cannot respond to you, but it is okay to talk. Hoses, cords, and all kinds of devices were attached to keep his life sustained.

As I read in Ezekiel 28, several phrases spoke to me. "Thou hast been, Thou wast, Thine heart was." You see, this patient was once very faithful, and they started to let others and other things influence them. I read on this morning to Ezekiel 30:3, "For the day is near, even the day of the LORD is near." I was introduced to the head nurse and she looked at me, and then looked down and said, we are doing everything that we can. I thanked her, went back to the room, and stood there for a few moments, and prayed. As I walked back down the hall, my heart was so grieved as I thought, things do not have to be this way with so many who once were, but now are not, in their place where God wanted them to be. As I read on this morning in I Corinthians 15:57-58, "But thanks be to God, which giveth us the victory through our Lord Jesus Christ. Therefore, my beloved brethren, be ye steadfast, unmovable, always abounding in the work of the Lord, forasmuch as ye know that your labour is not in vain in the Lord." I walked out of the hospital doors and the tears came, I looked to Heaven and said, Oh Father, give me strength to stay faithful, in my place doing your work until it is time for me to come Home.

My brother and sister, stay in your place, stay faithful, do not fear, do not quit, do not give an excuse. Proverbs 14:12, "There is a way which seemeth right unto a man, but the end thereof are the ways of death." Proverbs 14:14, "The backslider in heart shall be filled with his own ways." God is there for us to help us, guide us, and strengthen us in every time of need. Stay faithful, stay in your place, stay serving the Lord. Psalm 113:7, "He raiseth up the poor out of the dust, and lifteth the needy out of the dunghill." God is faithful! I drove on to my next visit and as I drove on, I saw a busy world being busy about what they want to do, going where they want to go. As I drove, I thought, where will you be when the doors of the Lord's house are open? Where will you be and what will you be doing when God says to all of us, your time on this earth is ended? May we be busy about winning and discipling a world for Christ.

God is there to help us, guide us, and strengthen us in every time of need.

November 15

Ezekiel 31-32 Psalm 114 Proverbs 15 1 Cor. 16 & 2 Cor. 1

Are You Distracted?

Good morning! Have you ever misplaced your car keys? Have you ever laid down your cell phone and forgotten where you laid it? Have you ever looked at someone that you have known for a long time, and you forgot their name? Please tell me yes. The true answer is we have all forgotten. Mrs. Smith said to me the other day, "Honey, I am worried about you." I looked at her and said, "Why do you say that?" She said, I am watching you not finish doing something and you forget to go back and finish what you started. I took her words to heart and admitted to myself that she was right. Let me explain where I am going. We are a busy people with very busy lives, and business will sometimes cause us to only do things halfway or get distracted on what is the most important thing that we really need to be doing.

Ezekiel 32:15, "When I shall make the land of Egypt desolate, and the country shall be destitute of that whereof it was full, when I shall smite all them that dwell therein, then shall they know that I am the LORD." Look again at the words, "of that whereof it was full." Do we get so busy in our lives that we forget what is really the most important? Do we get so busy that we begin to be overcome with that which we think needs to be done and we lose what was really the most important for us to do? What I am speaking of is our faithfulness to God to be in His house, in His Word, in His service of winning souls. We are so tired at the end of the week that we make excuse as to why we cannot go to church. We have been so busy that the midweek prayer service gets skipped because we just need to stop, and we miss the spiritual strengthening that we could get if we had made it a priority to be in God's house. A couple of days ago I got home from church, got a phone call, put my ear pods in and laid my phone down and kept on moving. Then when I finished the call, I had forgotten where I laid my phone. Mrs. Smith looked at me and said, that is what I am talking about. We need to regroup and realize what is the most important for us in this life.

Are we weakening because of what we think we need to do instead of living in the promises of God? II Corinthians 1:20, "For all the promises of God in him are yea, and in him Amen, unto the glory of God by us." Yes, I am getting to that age and I find myself a little forgetful, but I must never live outside of the promises of God and living and walking in His Word and being in my place for Him. It is embarrassing but it is true of all of us. We get so busy that usually God is left out first. Proverbs 15:5, "A fool despiseth his father's instruction: but he that regardeth reproof is prudent." Proverbs 15:31, "The ear that heareth the reproof of life abideth among the wise." Proverbs 15:32, "He that refuseth instruction despiseth his own soul: but he that heareth reproof getteth understanding." Do not get so busy that you end up losing what you needed the most. Do not use something as an excuse that has kept you going the most. Psalm 114:8, "Which turned the rock into a standing water, the flint into a fountain of waters." Our God who did what this verse just said, can help us if we always put Him first and foremost in every area of our life. Do not lose what you have always needed the most.

We need to regroup and realize what is the most important for us in this life.

November 16

Ezekiel 33-34 Psalm 115 Proverbs 16 2 Corinthians 2-3

No One Left Behind

Good morning! I am asked from time to time, "Where is so and so?," meaning I have not seen them in church for such a long time. I wonder how many people that once attended church would have loved to have someone care about them enough to have a note sent to them, a text message or even a personal visit. We live in a world of such great immaturity that people are so easily offended. It is as if folks walk around with a chip on their shoulders, waiting for someone to knock it off. I want to encourage all of us to check on each other to the extent of letting others know you miss them when they are not in Sunday School or church. You never know when someone is going through a very tough time and just needs somebody to care.

As we read in Ezekiel 33 and 34 this morning, we see many verses about a shepherd and his flock. Ezekiel 34:12, "As a shepherd seeketh out his flock in the day that he is among his sheep that are scattered; so will I seek out my sheep, and will deliver them out of all places where they have been scattered in the cloudy and dark day." For sure, our days are often cloudy and dark. I believe all of us can be used of the Lord to check on those of the flock who are missing or going through a tough time in life. Ezekiel 34:16, "I will seek that which was lost, and bring again that which was driven away, and will bind up that which was broken, and will strengthen that which was sick." A phrase came to my mind that has often been used for military purposes; "No one left behind." The history of this phrase is that it is the Latin term "Nemo resideo," used first by Roman soldiers. When the Roman soldiers held their shields in a battle formation, they were so locked together that if one soldier was wounded the other soldiers kept carrying him. So, when these soldiers went into battle together, they also all left the battlefield together. II Corinthians 2:10, "To whom ye forgive any thing, I forgive also: for if I forgave any thing, to whom I forgave it, for your sakes forgave I it in the person of Christ."

Oh, how we as God's flock need to encourage, lift up, and care for one another. II Corinthians 2:10, "Lest Satan should get an advantage of us: for we are not ignorant of his devices." Picture the soldiers being locked together and moving onto the battlefield, standing strong, staying strong, and winning the victory. Proverbs 16:7, "When a man's ways please the LORD, he maketh even his enemies to be at peace with him." Proverbs 16:23, "The heart of the wise teacheth his mouth, and addeth learning to his lips." Many a soldier has risked his own life to bring home a wounded comrade. May this little phrase ring out through our lives, "No one left behind." Psalm 115:11, "Ye that fear the LORD, trust in the LORD: he is their help and their shield." Also, may we let this phrase,

"No one left behind," drive us to spread the Gospel of Jesus Christ, and win a lost world to Christ. If Christ would come today, who do you know that would be left behind? The battle is raging, let us live so that there is "No one left behind."

We as God's flock need to encourage, lift up, and care for one another.

November 17

Ezekiel 35-36 Psalm 116 Proverbs 17 2 Corinthians 4-5

The Joy of Surrender

Good morning! As I am writing this morning, Mrs. Smith and I are in another state and going to be attending a wedding of a couple that came to camp most all their lives. The bride worked on staff four years and would have worked during 2020 if we would have been able to have camp. The reason I am starting out this way is because our lives should be filled with not only living for the Lord, but also living to set the path for another generation. This young couple have yielded their lives and surrendered their wills to honor God with their lives. Both have attended Bible college in preparation for them to serve the Lord as a team.

Ezekiel 36:27, "And I will put my spirit within you, and cause you to walk in my statutes, and ye shall keep my judgments, and do them." In just a few hours this young couple will give themselves to each other and give themselves to the Lord's service. May all of us set an example of a surrendered life to the LORD. Ezekiel 36:38, "they shall know that I am the LORD." May there be an excitement in our life like a beaming light that shines in the darkest places to give the light of salvation to a lost world, and to be a light of righteousness for the next generation to be faithful to the Lord. II Corinthians 4:6, "For God, who commanded the light to shine out of darkness, hath shined in our hearts, to give the light of the knowledge of the glory of God in the face of Jesus Christ." II Corinthians 5:15, "And that he died for all, that they which live should not henceforth live unto themselves, but unto him which died for them, and rose again."

What a joy it is to see this young couple and many others going on to serve the Lord. Proverbs 17:6, "Children's children are the crown of old men; and the glory of children are their fathers." What joy to live and serve the Lord, and when we are getting older and drawing closer to the end of the trail for our lives, to be able to see another generation serving with a love in their heart for the Lord. May we all say as was written in Psalm 116:16, O LORD, truly I am thy servant; I am thy servant."

May all of us set an example of a surrendered life to the Lord.

November 18

Ezekiel 37-38 Psalm 117 Proverbs 18 2 Corinthians 6-7

There is Hope

Good morning! I wrote on the top of my paper this morning in big red letters, "NOTHING IS WASTE, ESPECIALLY A LIFE." Our world is full of people that feel they have nobody, or that nobody cares. Just last night Mrs. Smith and I were driving home,and my phone rang. As I answered I could tell in just a few words that the man talking was in a stress mode. A few years back I stood with this man in the middle of the night outside his daughter's home as the investigators were inside the home examining the crime scene from his daughter's death. Now a couple of years later I receive a call that one of his granddaughters has been making plans to take her own life. The attitude of so many is like the phrase we read in Ezekiel 37:1, "our hope is lost." No, it is not! Ezekiel 37:14, "And shall put my spirit in you, and ye shall live." What we need to do is get our eyes off our circumstances, off others' opinions, off what the world says is right, and get our eyes on the Lord. God is ready and waiting for lost people to come to Him, backslidden Christians to come to Him, and all the rest of us to put Christ first in everything.

This daughter who had taken her life did make a decision for Christ as Mrs. Smith and I stood in her hospital room, and I opened the Bible and told her of God's love and forgiveness. I so remember that night as she bowed her head and trusted Christ as her Saviour, but instead of walking in newness of life she kept heading in the way of destruction. She lost custody of her children, and then took her own life. Ezekiel 37:23, "Neither shall they defile themselves any more with their idols, nor with their detestable things, nor with any of their transgressions: but I will save them out of all their dwelling places, wherein they have sinned, and will cleanse them: so shall they be my people, and I will be their God." God will not reject anyone that comes to Him. II Corinthians 6:16-17, "as God hath said, I will dwell in them, and walk in them; and I will be their God, and they shall be my people. Wherefore come out from among them, and be ye separate, saith the Lord, and touch not the unclean thing; and I will receive you." God is ready and waiting for those saved and forgiven to return to Him, and He is ready and waiting to save the lost. Believe in miracles performed by God in all lives. God rejects no one, it is we that do not think anybody cares and that is us only seeing ourselves.

I love the words of Paul in II Corinthians 7:16, "I rejoice therefore that I have confidence in you in all things." Believe God can in anyone's life. Get up, discouraged brother or sister. Proverbs 18:14, "The spirit of a man will sustain his infirmity; but a wounded spirit who can bear?" God loves us, and people do not always realize how hurtful their words can be. At those times, remember God cares. Psalm 117:2, "For his merciful kindness is great toward us." Be encouraged today; it is a choice. While you are letting God encourage you through His Word and through your time of prayer, decide to be used of Him to encourage someone else. Put a smile on your face and realize the world is hurting and looking for hope which we have in Christ.

We need to get our eyes off our circumstances and get our eyes on the Lord.

November 19

Ezekiel 39-40 Psalm 118:1-14 Proverbs 19 2 Corinthians 8-9

How is Your Vision?

Good morning! Yesterday I went to my office and pulled a book off one of the shelves that holds books of different subjects and resources. The book that I took down is a biography of a soldier. I just let it lay on my desk yesterday and looked at the cover which has a picture of a man who was very courageous for our country in several major engagements around the world. I read this morning in Ezekiel 39:21, "And I will set my glory among the heathen, and all the heathen shall see my judgment that I have executed, and my hand that I have laid upon them." Oh, that we would be men and women of God to stand unashamedly for our Lord. Oh, that we would be faithful no matter the cost. Oh, that we would carry a vision to reach the world for Christ. In Ezekiel 40, we begin to read of the vision of the temple that would be built. The Bible says, "where there is no vision, the people perish." Oh, that we would have a vision as some soldiers did who fought an earthly battle.

We are fighting for a Heavenly cause, and I ask this morning two things. Do we have a vision for the cause of Christ? Have we lost our vision for the cause of Christ? II Corinthians 8:3, speaking of the churches of Macedonia, "For to their power, I bear record, yea, and beyond their power, they were willing of themselves." As I read on to II Corinthians 9:2, "your zeal hath provoked many." Is our zeal for the Lord encouraging and challenging others for the cause of Christ? In the biography that I have laying on my desk, the soldier made this statement, "I believe the best fighter was a man with a flag in his pack and the desire to put it on an enemy strong point." We should be the mighty army for God, ready to take a world for Christ. Proverbs 19:23, "The fear of the LORD tendeth to life: and he that hath it shall abide satisfied; he shall not be visited with evil." Our walk with God, along with our prayer life, creates the vision and fight within us. Yes, the devil will attack us, but listen and read the words of Psalm 118:13-14, "Thou hast thrust sore at me that

I might fall: but the LORD helped me; The LORD is my strength and song, and is become my salvation."

Men about whom books are written are men, but God is looking for men and women that seek Him for strength, vision, and guidance. May we daily seek the will of God that we may advance the cause of Christ to win a lost and dying world. My friend, may we pray, work, and press toward not planting a flag, but the Word of God in our own communities and around the world for the glory and honor of Christ. I am thankful for those who stand true for the freedom that we enjoy, but our calling is a Heavenly freedom for a sin bound world. Picture with me, not a flag in a soldier's pack, but the Word of God in the hands of every lost person around the world. May we press forward for Christ.

Is our zeal for the Lord encouraging and challenging others for the cause of Christ?

November 20

Ezekiel 41-42 Psalm 118:15-29 Proverbs 20 2 Corinthians 10

A Separate Place

Good morning! Can you picture with me this morning driving into a neighborhood where all the houses are built exactly alike and even painted the same? Recently Mrs. Smith and I were driving, and I asked her, did you see all those homes, how they are exactly the same and painted the same? I am not being critical; I am wanting to point out two words in our reading this morning, which are "separate place." In Ezekiel 41 and 42, we see the two words, "separate place," six different times. Ezekiel 41:14, "Also the breadth of the face of the house, and of the separate place toward the east, an hundred cubits." Notice also the words in this verse, "toward the east, an hundred cubits." As I began to look some things up, I found that this is a separate building, and it is also facing the east. When our Lord returns to catch us away, He will come from the east. This building is a holy place, such as this time we have not arrived in Heaven. This building was to picture a place we are to be preparing for, seeking to be some day, to spend eternity with God our Father.

I thought as I read on about the description of the temple for worship, our eyes must go beyond and be looking for the "separate place," that is the perfect place. We spend too much time looking at things around us and allowing them to consume us, instead of focusing on that eternal place called Heaven. II Corinthians 10:12, "For we dare not make ourselves of the number, or compare ourselves with some that commend themselves: but they measuring themselves by themselves, and comparing themselves among themselves, are not wise." We spend our time focusing on others instead of preparing for the "separate place." We should be setting our standards high for the "separate place." The world will soon perish. and we will go to the "separate place" that has nothing to do with this world. The world brings no permanent satisfaction. There will always be a better car, we think, a bigger house, or a faster new gadget. There is no satisfaction in this world, but there is a "separate place." Proverbs 20:4, "The sluggard will not plow by reason of the cold; therefore shall he beg in harvest, and have nothing." Proverbs 20:13, "Love not sleep, lest thou come to poverty; open thine eyes, and thou shalt be satisfied with bread." These two verses in Proverbs teach us a good lesson about laziness. May I also apply them to the case for spiritual laziness? We work to eat, and yet allow the things of God to slip on by. It takes work to get out of bed and spend time reading the Word of God and spend time in prayer.

I ask, is it more important for eternity's sake, family sake, personal sake to physically work and not spiritually prepare? Physical work is important, necessary, and very satisfying, but it does not prepare us for the "separate place," Heaven. Psalm 118:15-16, "The voice of rejoicing and salvation is in the tabernacles of the righteous: the right hand of the LORD doeth valiantly. The right hand of the LORD is exalted: the right hand of the LORD doeth valiantly." Who is at the right hand of God? Jesus is, and He is talking to the Father for us and about us. God is for us. Why are we not preparing and focusing on that special place called Heaven? It is that "separate place" which is being prepared for us to spend eternity with God. My heart is challenged today to check where my focus is while I am living on this old earth. Are you focusing and preparing for the "separate place?"

We must be preparing and focusing on that special place called Heaven.

November 21

Ezekiel 43-44 Psalm 119:1-16 Proverbs 21 2 Corinthians 11

Safety Gates

Good morning! When I was quite a bit younger, I heard my dad and others say a phrase that I have used all my life when someone looks shocked because of a statement or something happens in their life. The phrase is, "you look like a calf looking at a new gate." If you have ever been around raising animals that have to be kept in a pen or pasture, they often seem to get out. If you and I would get a new calf and put it in a fenced pasture, that new calf would follow the fence line to see if there is any way to get out. If that calf would get out, we would put it back in through the gate and then go repair the open spot in the fence so that it would not get out again. The gate has a purpose for getting in and letting out. The gate is a place to secure the pasture so the animals cannot, or should I say not supposed to, get out.

As we read today in Ezekiel 43:1, "Afterward he brought me to the gate, even the gate that looketh toward the east." Ezekiel 43:4, "And the glory of the LORD came into the house by the way of the gate." Ezekiel 44:1, "Then he brought me back the way of the gate." We have been reading about the construction of the temple and today we read the word "gate" being used ten different times in these two chapters. If we would go to a county fair, we would enter through the gate. If we would go to an athletic event, we would enter through the gate. If we would go to an amusement park, we would enter through the gate. The gate is a place to check all who enter and exit. It is a place of security; it is a place where authorities can control. Heaven has a gate that all must enter through. Heaven does not have multiple gates, it only has one and only those who know Christ as their Saviour may enter. It is so important for us to understand that we need gates in our lives. This world is running every direction with no gates of authority, no gates to control, no gates for emergencies, etc. II Corinthians 11:2, "For I am jealous over you with godly jealousy: for I have espoused you to one husband, that I may present you as a chaste virgin to Christ." The world wants us to believe that there are many ways to God. Paul, in his writing to the church at Corinth, saw the people being led away by false teachings. He was hated as he taught the truths of God and we read of one time in II Corinthians 11:33, "And through a window in a basket was I let down by the wall, and escaped his hands." The governor tried to have Paul killed as we read in II Corinthians 11:32, but he had the window as a gate to escape to safety. Proverbs 21:2, "Every way of a man is right in his own eyes." Proverbs 21:8, "The way of man is froward (wicked) and strange."

The fence around animals is a must and standards of life are a must in a Christian's life. There is a way that is right, and it is by the "gate" of and through the Word of God, the Bible. Psalm 119:5, "O that my ways were directed to keep thy statutes!" Psalm 119:15, "I will meditate in thy precepts, and have respect unto thy ways." It is sometimes shocking for a calf to find a new gate, but that gate is a way of access for the farmer to take care of his animals.

May we realize the gates that we are to walk through in our walk with God are the avenues to growth, safety, leadership, and direction in the Christian's life. I am thankful that Jesus is the way and the only way to Heaven. Let us decide today to go through the gates the Lord has for us and not bust a hole in the fence to have our own way. Most always that way is the way to destruction, but the ways of God are to life. Some things to think about.

It is so important for us to understand that we need gates in our lives.

November 22

Ezekiel 45-46 Psalm 119:17-32 Proverbs 22 2 Corinthians 12-13

Set Aside a Portion

Good morning! As I went to the window early this morning to look out and see if I could see the moon and stars, sure enough, there was the moon but only the lower portion of the moon was bright. I can remember being taught, when you only see the lower portion of the moon and it is like a bowl, that means it is holding water and it will soon rain. Now we know the moon does not hold water, but we do have rain coming tomorrow. The word that I would like us to think about and learn from today is the word "portion." Ezekiel 45:1, "Moreover, when ye shall divide by lot the land for inheritance, ye shall offer an oblation unto the LORD, an holy portion of the land." First of all, notice the word "oblation," meaning offered in worship or devotion. When the land is divided as an inheritance, a portion is to be given unto the LORD. The word "portion" is used seven times in the next few verses and it means an individual's part or share. Each of us have twenty-four hours in a day, so my question this morning is, how do we use the "portion" of time that we are given?

Is money more important than anything in life? Is personal time with God important enough to set aside a specific "portion" of the day? Do we give a "portion" of each day to our marriage partner? If we have children, do we give a "portion" of time to those children? Where I am heading this morning is our daily schedule. Do we run our schedule or does our schedule run us? Do we have a "portion" for God first of all, or do we just try to fit Him in? II Corinthians 12:14, "Behold, the third time I am ready to come to you; and I will not be burdensome to you: for I seek not yours, but you: for the children ought not to lay up for the parents, but the parents for the children." As I studied this verse for a while this morning, I first thought it was speaking about providing finances and leaving an inheritance. Then I thought about how Paul's heart was broken from how the church at Corinth had rejected the time he tried to spend with them, teaching them. He said,

"I seek not yours, but you." Paul had spent time and that is what we must do every day, spend a "portion" or a specific set- aside time with God every day. Proverbs 22:29, "Seest thou a man diligent in his business? He shall stand before kings; he shall not stand before mean men." "Diligent" means steady, earnest and energetic effort. We must spend time with God, with our mate and with our children, investing in each other and growing together in the Lord and in principles of life from the Scriptures. Psalm 119:27, "Make me to understand the way of thy precepts." Psalm 119:30, "I have chosen the way of truth: thy judgments have I laid before me."

I sat in the hospital again yesterday and watched as a life slipped away before it really should have. Spend the time, set the time aside to spend with God and with each other before it is too late and before that day comes and our children are leaving home and starting their own lives. No greater joy can we have than to spend time with God each day and to spend time with each other. Look at the "portion" you have in life and make sure you set a "portion" aside daily for the important things in your walk with God and each other.

How do we use the portion of time we are given?

November 23

Ezekiel 47-48 Psalm 119:33-48 Proverbs 23 Galatians 1-2

Completely Yielded

Good morning! Has there been a time in your life that you bowed before the Lord on your knees and said, "Lord, you can have me and everything I have, I completely yield myself to you?" As our Bible reading began this morning in Ezekiel, I stopped at 48:9-10, "The oblation that ye shall offer unto the LORD shall be of five and twenty thousand in length, and of ten thousand in breadth and for them, even for the priests, shall be this holy oblation." The word "oblation" mentioned eight times in our reading, meaning offered in worship or devotion, was referring to the boundaries of land and a portion given to the Lord, but let us go farther than land this morning. How about our lives, our time, our income, our talents, our goals? What have we given to the Lord and what have we held back?

As we read in Galatians 2:20, Paul said, "I am crucified with Christ: nevertheless I live; yet not I, but Christ liveth in me: and the life which I now live in the flesh I live by the faith of the Son of God, who loved me, and gave himself for me." Paul is saying, I have given my life wholly to Christ and for His use. What are you holding back from God? Are you fighting giving your life to Him, thinking He might ask more than you can give? Proverbs 23:5, "Wilt thou set thine eyes upon that which is not? For riches certainly make themselves wings; they fly away as an eagle toward heaven." The day that we give our all to God is the day of being free in Christ. By the word free, I mean we have given God our all and we are holding nothing back. Proverbs 23:23, "Buy the truth, and sell it not; also wisdom, and instruction, and understanding." Our life as a Christian will never have complete peace until we give Christ everything and hold nothing back. Psalm 119:38, "Stablish thy word unto thy servant, who is devoted to thy fear."

What a peace that day when I said to God, you can have everything. Oh yes, there have been times I have put me first and God second. The empty feeling of separation from God set in and I had to ask forgiveness and go forward by giving all back to the Lord. The book of Ezekiel ends with these words, "and the name of the city from that day shall be, The LORD is there." May that be said about our lives. The LORD has been given every part of me. The LORD has free control of all of me. Bow before Him and freshly give everything to HIM.

Our life will never have complete peace until
we give Christ everything and hold nothing back.

November 24

Daniel 1-2 Psalm 119:49-64 Proverbs 24 Galatians 3-4

God Has a Plan

Good morning! I was never abused by my parents, but I think I have a world record for being spanked. I guess I was a slow learner. I can remember saying to my parents, it seems like the harder I try, the more I get in trouble. Have you ever thought about the harder you try to do right, the more trouble comes? You say to yourself, I am going to get a plan and get organized, and then something comes along, something unexpected, and your plan has to be put aside. Have you ever noticed you only have a flat tire when you are running late for an appointment? God allows things in our lives for His purpose. He allows things that we do not and will probably never understand, to draw us closer to Him for His purpose in our lives.

I bring your attention to some phrases in some verses in Daniel this morning. Daniel 1:2, "And the Lord gave Jehoiakim king of Judah into his hand." The Lord allowed it. Daniel 1:9, "Now God had brought Daniel into favour and tender love with the prince of the eunuchs." God had a plan. Daniel 1:17, "As for these four children, God gave them knowledge and skill in all learning and wisdom: and Daniel had understanding in all visions and dreams." God had a purpose beyond what man could see. God has a purpose, plan, and program for each of us. Our purpose of life is to allow God to work through each of us as He sees fit, to draw us closer to Him and live in His will for our lives. Galatians 3:6, "Even as Abraham believed God, and it was accounted to him for righteousness." God has not asked us to do what He asked Abraham to do, but God does expect us to trust Him by faith. Galatians 3:11, "The just shall live by faith." The purpose of God in our lives will not always be understood but be assured God does expect us to trust Him and walk consistently with Him. Proverbs24:21, "My son, fear thou the LORD and the king: and meddle not with them that are given to change." As the Hebrew brothers in Daniel chapters 1 and 2 were in captivity and seemingly bad territory,

God had a plan. God has a perfect plan for each of us. May we allow God to work His plan. Psalm 119:54: "Thy statutes have been my songs in the house of my pilgrimage." Psalm 119:57, "Thou art my portion, O LORD: I have said that I would keep thy words."

In every situation of life, God has a purpose and a plan. Walk with Him and let Him do His work in and through you. The flat tire could have come because God protected you from a possible situation. Quit complaining and be obedient. Enjoy the life and walk that God's perfect plan brings. Sometimes things come because of our disobedience. Let God work His purpose in your life.

God has a purpose, plan, and program for each of us.

November 25

Daniel 3-4 Psalm 119:65-80 Proverbs 25 Galatians 5-6

God First

Good morning! A happy life is a life of proper priorities. Some of the most miserable people that I have ever been around are self-centered people. People that only see themselves are people that never see the needs of others. As we walk with Christ, the example that He set for us is to focus on the Father and we will develop a loyalty love to please Him in everything we do.

A decree was made by king Nebuchadnezzar to fall down before his image when the music was played. Why was the image built? Pride in the king. Why was the demand to fall down before the image? Pride in the king. Why was there a ruling for death if not obedient to fall before the image? Pride in the king. Pride causes us to only see us and us alone. Pride is never satisfied. Pride is justification of what self wants. Pride will not submit to any authority other than self. Daniel 3:6, "And whoso falleth not down and worshippeth shall the same hour be cast into the midst of a burning fiery furnace." Unreasonable, why? Pride of the king. What do we bow to in our lives? What is the greatest priority in our lives? What has our greatest devotion in our lives? This is the response of the three Hebrew brothers in Daniel 3:6, "But if not, be it known unto thee, O king, that we will not serve thy gods, nor worship the golden image which thou hast set up." The brothers took a stand and went to the furnace. By miracle of God and for their faith in God, obedience, and priority of God first, they were delivered. Daniel 3:29, "there is no other God that can deliver after this sort." Daniel 4:37, "those that walk in pride he is able to abase." There is a daily battle that goes on in each of us and that is "me first" or selfishness. Galatians 5:17, "For the flesh lusteth against the Spirit, and the Spirit against the flesh: and these are contrary the one to the other: so that ye cannot do the things that ye would." Galatians 5:24, "And they that are Christ's have crucified the flesh with the affections and lusts."

We need to take a long look at the priorities of our lives. What is it that we put first? What things do we have before worshipping of God and serving Him? Be careful what you put first or, may I say, fall down before. Proverbs 25:26, "A righteous man falling down before the wicked is as a troubled fountain, and a corrupt spring." A "corrupt spring" is a poisoned spring that will bring sickness and possible death. Many have fallen away from Christ because they took Him out of first place and out of being a priority of life. Psalm 119:78, "Let the proud be ashamed; for they dealt perversely with me without a cause: but I will meditate in thy precepts." The Hebrew brothers put God first and He delivered them. God always responds to our faith in HIM. God was watching the entire time to see if those Hebrew brothers would stand, and He is watching you and me, every moment of every day. Be careful what you put before God.

Many have fallen away from Christ because
they took Him out of first place.

November 26

Daniel 5-6 Psalm 119:81-96 Proverbs 26 Ephesians 1-2

Living Our Faith

Good morning! Every day in our life we have faith about different things, but how is our faith in God and what He can do? You will sit in a chair and not have fear that it will not hold you. You might go out, get in your vehicle, put the key in the ignition and there is no fear of it not starting. Earlier this morning you believed the light would turn on when you flipped the light switch. Did you talk with the men and women from the power company? Did you go and check if there was power coming through the lines? Did you go and see if you had paid the electric bill, or did you just flip the switch? When you turned the key on the vehicle for it to start, you did not see the interior of the engine. How is our faith in God today?

What was seen and known of Daniel was his faith in his God. Daniel's faith strengthened even those who did not believe, but they believed in the faith that Daniel had. May it be said of us, as it was said of Daniel, that we are people of "dissolving of doubts." Daniel 5:12, "Forasmuch as an excellent spirit, and knowledge, and understanding, interpreting of dreams, and shewing of hard sentences, and dissolving of doubts, were found in the same Daniel." Daniel 5:16, "And I have heard of thee, that thou canst make interpretations, and dissolve doubts." There was jealousy of Daniel, so a scheme to catch him was set up and, sure enough, Daniel was caught being faithful. The world hates our love and commitment and confidence in God. It is because they know not our Lord Jesus Christ and His love and forgiveness of their sins. Before Daniel was thrown into the lion's den, he heard the king say in Daniel 6:16, "Thy God whom thou servest continually, he will deliver thee." Daniel's faith had given faith to the king. The king did not sleep during the night and went to the mouth of the lion's den and said, "is thy God, whom thou servest continually, able to deliver thee from the lions?" Daniel 6:20. Daniel responded in verse 22, "My God hath sent his angel, and hath shut the lions' mouths."

Should not our faith in God be a tool to strengthen the faith of others? Ephesians 1:12, "That we should be to the praise of his glory, who first trusted in Christ." Ephesians 1:13, "In whom ye also trusted, after that ye heard the word of truth, the gospel of your salvation: in whom also after that ye believed, ye were sealed with that Holy Spirit of promise." Oh, that we would be living our faith in Christ. Ephesians 1:19, "And what is the exceeding greatness of his power to us-ward who believe, according to the working of his mighty power."

As I opened the wood stove door early this morning, the fire had gone out, but I stirred in the ashes and there were some coals. As I added wood and let air come in, the fire took off and there would soon be heat in the house. Proverbs 26:20, "Where no wood is, there the fire goeth out." It is time we stir the coals of faith in our heart, add some wood from the Word of God, and let the fire of faith burn. Psalm 119:89, "Forever, O LORD, thy word is settled in heaven." Let the Word of God burn in your faith for God and watch it warm those around you. We need to live a life of faith that will "dissolve doubts" in the lives of a lost world so that they will trust the living Christ that lives within our heart. Let us throw some wood on the fire this morning.

We need to live a life of faith so a lost world will trust the living Christ.

November 27

Daniel 7-8 Psalm 119:97-112 Proverbs 27 Ephesians 3-4

Reality of Life

Good morning! I walked through several stores yesterday looking for gift ideas and things that are already on a list. I thought to myself as I looked at games and toys. Where are the checker games, the trucks, and tractors? Where are the baby dolls and teddy bears? I felt like I was walking through the aisles lined with demons. Please do not shut me off right now, but what happened to the toys for boys to build things out of wood, and little girls learning to bake things instead of being a beauty queen and turning into some type of monster?

As we read in Daniel how he had several visions, he saw different types of creatures that reveal end prophecies, but we also read in Daniel 7:13, "I saw in the night visions, and, behold, one like the Son of man came with the clouds of heaven." Daniel 7:14, "And there was given him dominion, and glory, and a kingdom, that all people, nations, and languages, should serve him: his dominion is an everlasting dominion, which shall not pass away, and his kingdom that which shall not be destroyed." We live in a world that is whirling out of control. It is high time for God's people to live the truth in Christ, share the truth in Christ and teach the truth in Christ. Ephesians 4:1, "I therefore, the prisoner of the Lord, beseech you that ye walk worthy of the vocation wherewith ye are called." The word "vocation" is our place of service for the Lord. We are challenged as we read on in Ephesians 4:22-24, "That ye put off concerning the former conversation the old man, which is corrupt according to the deceitful lusts; And be renewed in the spirit of your mind; And that ye put on the new man, which after God is created in righteousness and true holiness." Oh, that we would ask for God's wisdom in these days and walk and live in newness of mind. Let us live and teach reality of life for young men to grow up to be men of God and young ladies to grow up and be women of God. Be careful of what your children and grandchildren read, and characters that they try to be in their playing. Proverbs 27:12, "A prudent man forseeth the evil, and hideth himself; but the simple pass on, and are punished."

I remember dreaming and playing as a fireman, policeman, etc. Real people. I remember our daughter and my sister playing house. Real people. The words of Psalm 119:101 need to be heeded, "I have refrained my feet from every evil way, that I might keep thy word." God created us to worship and serve Him, not the things of this world. May God's Word and the Holy Spirit be our guide. Psalm 119:105, "Thy word is a lamp unto my feet, and a light unto my path." Be cautious what you teach and what you live. We do not grow up to be monsters and superheroes. We were created in the very image and likeness of God.

May God's Word and the Holy Spirit be our guide.

November 28

Daniel 9-10 Psalm 119:113-128 Proverbs 28 Ephesians 5

Clean Things Up

Good morning! As I read a phrase this morning, my mind went back to when our children were younger and when our grandchildren were younger. Picture with me going into the bedroom where the children are playing, and as you step into the room you see toys, clothes, covers, etc., all over the place and it looks like a tornado hit the room. There is silence as you stand there and scan the room, and then you speak those often-said words, "What happened in here?." The children look at each other and no one speaks. Then you ask this question, "Who is responsible for all this mess?." The children look again at each other and then at you and say nothing. They were having fun until you entered the room. Truth is and they all know the truth, every one of them is guilty.

Daniel 9:7, "O Lord, righteousness belongeth unto thee, but unto us confusion of faces." Daniel 9:8, "O Lord, to us belongeth confusion of face, to our kings, to our princes, and to our fathers, because we have sinned against thee." Judgment of sin has fallen and the phrases, "confusion of faces," and "confusion of face" are saying all of us are to blame because of the condition of our people that has brought the judgment of God. The children look at you as they sit in the middle of the destroyed room or play area and one will say, it is all of our faults. Daniel 9:19, "O Lord, hear; O Lord, forgive; O Lord, hearken and do." As Daniel prayed, he asked the Lord's forgiveness for all their sins. As a parent or grandparent, we tell the children, now all of you get busy and clean this room up. Not one of those children in that room stood and said, we need to stop and pick up this room. If revival will come to our lives personally, to our churches, our country, and our world, and it can, we need to start proclaiming the truth of God in every way we can by standing, living, teaching, and proclaiming the Gospel of Jesus Christ. Ephesians 5:1-2, "Be ye therefore followers of God, as dear children; and walk in love, as Christ also hath loved us, and hath given himself for us an offering and a sacrifice to God for a sweet smelling Saviour." Ephesians 5:8, "walk as children of light." Ephesians 5:15, "See then that ye walk circumspectly, not as fools, but as wise." We need to quit passing the blame on others, on the times or a world pandemic, and spread the Gospel of salvation to all mankind. We who are saved know what is truth and what is right. Are we living it, proclaiming it, and personally sharing it? Proverbs 28:5, "Evil men understand not judgment: but they that seek the LORD understand all things." Proverbs 28:13, "He that covereth his sins shall not prosper: but whoso confesseth and forsaketh them shall have mercy."

A wise parent will not leave the room until they see all the children helping to clean the mess up. One of the children will leave before everything is all picked up and a wise parent will send them right back in the room until everything is all picked up. The condition of this old world is because of sin and because we have not more strongly, consistently lived and proclaimed the gospel story. The Psalmist wrote in Psalm 119:117, "Hold thou me up, and I shall be safe: and I will have respect unto thy statutes continually." I know I need my heart continually stirred and convicted to keep me going forth with the Gospel story. We taught the children when we made them clean and pick up the room. May we today pick up and clean up our lives, so that we can be more faithful servants of the Lord. As I conclude this morning, I had written on the top of my paper this thought, "Am I living what I teach and am I teaching what I have learned?" All of us need to get in that room and spiritually clean things up. That room is our prayer place. We need to daily pick up our lives and get out the sin.

May we pick up and clean up our lives so that
we can be more faithful servants of the Lord.

November 29

Daniel 11-12 Psalm 119:129-144 Proverbs 29 Eph. 6 & Phil. 1

Faithful, Fervent, and Forward

Good morning! Are you excited about what the Lord is doing in your life? Are you praising Him for the answered prayers? Are you excited what you are asking Him to do in the days ahead? Mrs. Smith and I were driving home from church, and we got to talking about the prayers, blessings, and miracles that we have seen the Lord do in recent days and months. Is your life stirring the hearts of another generation? Daniel 11:10, "But his sons shall be stirred up, and shall assemble a multitude of great forces." Yes, I know that the last two chapters of Daniel close the books on the end times, but my heart was so stirred this morning about this thought. Am I setting the pace for the next generation? Am I as excited about God as I have been?

My faith in God should be stronger than it has ever been. My excitement for camp is as strong as it ever has been. I know I am getting older and maybe not going as fast, and maybe my strength is not quite as strong as it was in my 20s and 30s, but I will tell you, my belief in what God can do is greater than it has ever been. My desire of seeing the hand of God is stronger than it has ever been. I hunger for the power and presence of God more than ever before. We need to be strong in the Lord, strong in our faith, strong in our walk, strong in our convictions, strong in our faithfulness to our God. Daniel 11:32, "the people that do know their God shall be strong." Are we motivating another generation to live for God, or is this generation seeing a discouraged, defeated generation? Ephesians 6:4, "And, ye fathers, provoke not your children to wrath: but bring them up in the nurture and admonition of the Lord." Are you living what you are saying? Ephesians 6:6, "Not with eyeservice, as menpleasers; but as the servants of Christ, doing the will of God from the heart." Ephesians 6:7, "With good will doing service, as to the Lord, and not to men." We, as the older generation, need to live a sincere life in Christ to the generation behind us. Philippians 1:10-11, "That ye may approve things that are excellent; that ye may be sincere and without offense till the day of Christ; being filled with the fruits of righteousness, which are by Jesus Christ, unto the glory and praise of God."

I recently got on one of my grandson's motorcycles and took a ride. I do not have the balance that I used to have, but I rode. I spun the rear tire and played around a little bit, but I knew I had to watch myself. When I got done riding, I stopped and went to lean over to catch myself and I slipped and fell to the ground. I was embarrassed in front of my grandsons, but I had to get past the embarrassment. We need to keep living for the generation that is coming behind us. You know, those grandsons were so understanding and kind; they kept telling me how they had done different things, just to make me feel better. Don't quit, keep living and keep your faith in God strong. Proverbs 29:18, "Where there is no vision, the people perish: but he that keepeth the law, happy is he."

Maybe I can't ride a motorcycle as well as I used to, or throw a football or baseball like I used to, but what example am I setting in my walk with God, my faith in God and my service to God? May our hearts stay tender for lost souls as we see the world getting harder and harder to the things of God. May we stay faithful, fervent, and forward until the end, which is really the beginning. Psalm 119:133, "Order my steps in thy word: and let not any iniquity have dominion over me." I have decided my days are to have four wheels under me and not just two. A four by four and not just a motorcycle. Keep on growing for the Saviour.

Our faith in God should be stronger than it has ever been.

November 30

Hosea 1-2   Psalm 119:145-160   Proverbs 30-31   Philippians 2-3

A Life of Compassion

Good morning! Do you ever ask yourself, why do people change? The change that I am talking about is not the change for the better. Children being obedient in their home and seemingly having principles of life that will lead them down a path with a walk with God, separation from the things of the world, a love for church, and an involvement of serving in their church, and then! What happened? Where are they? What are they doing? Why??? Each time I begin reading the book of Hosea, I take time to understand the picture that God is teaching. A man marries a woman, they have children, she is unfaithful and becomes a harlot, she is forgiven and comes back to her husband. I then dwell on the fact of God's never-ending patience, love and forgiveness of us sinners. Hosea 1:7, "but I will have mercy upon the house of Judah, and will save them by the LORD their God, and will not save them by bow, nor by sword, nor by battle, by horses, nor by horsemen."

We cannot fix anyone else. Have patience with people. Be kind, loving, tenderhearted. The world is searching for what they think will bring peace, happiness, and contentment, but we know that Christ is the only answer. Many a Christian have dropped their standards of separation, quit singing the hymns that they were raised with and have gone to the world. It is not our place to battle this world, but to stand for Christ and truth, which is the Word of God. It is the Holy Spirit that changes lives and not us. Philippians 2:13, "For it is God which worketh in you both to will and to do of his good pleasure." I am the oldest of three children, and I wish I could go back and retrace my tracks and be more patient and kind, especially to my siblings. Quit arguing, quit giving our opinions, especially when it is not asked. Quit burning bridges that do not need to be burned. I am not saying to compromise; I am saying let God and His Holy Word bring the conviction. We have raised too many to follow because we said so, and not because we patiently taught the Word of God.

Think about this, we cannot teach what we do not know and what we do not live. Too many have turned away from the Lord because they were not taught the Word of God, and they look at truth as just opinion. We are living in a starving time of the truths from the Word of God. Philippians 3:7-8, "But what things were gain to me, those I counted loss for Christ. Yea doubtless, and I count all things but loss for the excellency of the knowledge of Christ Jesus my Lord." We must teach a solid foundation from the Word of God and a relationship with Him that will be a growing relationship in a walk with Him. Philippians 3:10, "That I may know him, and power of his resurrection, and the fellowship of his sufferings, being made conformable unto his death." Proverbs 30:5, "Every word of God is pure: he is a shield unto them that put their trust in him." Hosea wrote the words of God by saying a life will not be conquered by the power of an army or weapons, but by God's mercy. May we live a life of compassion for others and stand strong with a loving and compassionate heart.

Psalm 119:147, "I prevented the dawning of the morning, and cried: I hoped in thy word." I do not want my life, my attitude, my spirit, my words, my actions to prevent the Lord's working in someone's heart. I will stand with the old paths, but not with an arrogant spirit. I will stand with the truths of the Word of God, but not with an attacking spirit. Stand with mercy, compassion, patience, a burdened heart, and a love from God, to win, encourage and strengthen a world filled with anger, confusion, hate, and most of all, a world without Christ. Someone needs your help today. Be a messenger for Christ with His love and compassion.

May we live a life of compassion and stand strong
with a loving and compassionate heart.

December 1

Hosea 3-4 Psalm 119:161-176 Proverbs 1 Phil. 4 & Col. 1

God's Signs

Good morning! When I go to the woods to just have a walk, to pray, to just spend some time alone and think about different things, I am looking and watching. No matter the time of the year, I am looking around for signs. When I say signs, I mean animal signs, signs of the seasons changing, signs of an area to develop for a camp activity.

The Scriptures have all kinds of signs for us. Hosea 4:1, "Hear the word of the LORD, ye children of Israel: for the LORD hath a controversy with the inhabitants of the land, because there is no truth, nor mercy, nor knowledge of God in the land." I noticed and thought about the word "hear." It means to listen, to pay attention, to focus upon. Did you ever think of the signs of life that the Lord gives us in our walk with Him, but we are not listening to "hear" Him speak? God was trying to get the attention of His people who had turned away from truth and even turned away from God. Are we ignoring signs from God that He is trying to keep us from being so much like the world? Philippians 4:11-13, "Not that I speak in respect of want: for I have learned, in whatsoever state I am, therewith to be content. I know both how to be abased, and I know how to abound: every where and in all things I am instructed both to be full and to be hungry, both to abound and to suffer need. I can do all things through Christ which strengtheneth me." No matter the trial or the blessing, the testing or the rejoicing, the emptiness or the peace, times when God seems to be there and times when we seem to be alone; are you content knowing He has shown you the signs that He is with you? Do you understand the signs that God is giving you when you drift from walking with Him?

Proverbs 1:23, "Turn you at my reproof: behold, I will pour out my spirit unto you. I will make known my words unto you." Proverbs 1:33, "But whoso hearkeneth unto me shall dwell safely, and shall be quiet from fear of evil." Let God reach out to you today. Listen for His voice, sense His presence. Psalm 119:173, "Let thine hand help me; for I have chosen thy precepts." God is always there. We just need to learn how to see Him, even in trials and testings; not just only when we are rejoicing. "Hear the word of the LORD."

No matter the trial or blessing, are you content knowing He is with you?

December 2

Hosea 5-6 Psalm 120 Proverbs 2 Colossians 2-3

The Comfort of Scripture

Good morning! Is today one of those days that your heart is so heavy? You are doing your best to keep your head up. It seems those you love the most have turned and you do not know how to fix it. Let us allow the Scriptures to bring a comfort this morning.

Hosea 6:1, "Come, and let us return unto the LORD: for he hath torn, and he will heal us; he hath smitten, and he will bind us up." There is nothing like the healing of our Saviour. Let His salve bring comfort to your aching heart. Keep on, my friend, my brother, my sister; keep on. Colossians 2:6-7, "As ye have therefore received Christ Jesus the Lord, so walk ye in him: Rooted and built up in him, and stablished in the faith, as ye have been taught, abounding therein with thanksgiving." Okay, you stumbled, you fell, you feel broken, you feel betrayed. Just know you are complete in Him. Colossians 2:10, "And ye are complete in him, which is the head of all principality and power." Press on. The burden will be lifted, and the brokenness will be healed. Colossians 3:16, "Let the word of Christ dwell in you richly in all wisdom; teaching and admonishing one another in psalms and hymns and spiritual songs, singing with grace in your hearts to the Lord." Get a song and sing it all day long. Sing that song over and over again.

Look around and focus on God's blessing. Cry out to Him and let Him comfort you. You know what to do to get back on top. Just do what you know is the right thing and the spiritual thing to do. Proverbs 2:7, "He layeth up sound wisdom for the righteous: he is a buckler to them that walk uprightly." He sees, He knows, He cares. Psalm 120:1, "In my distress I cried unto the LORD, and he heard me." You know what? The sun is beginning to come up, so let the Son shine in your heart. Have a blessed day.

Press on. The burden will be lifted, and the brokenness will be healed.

December 3

Hosea 7-8 Psalm 121 Proverbs 3 Col. 4 & 1 Thess. 1

Spiritual Mentors

Good morning! Do you like baked potatoes? I have to admit I just like food, but there are some things I like better than others. Think with me for a moment about eating a baked potato. Do you eat the skin or throw it away? How about a sweet potato? Do you eat the skin along with the inside or do you peel it off and throw it away? I understand about calories, but I think eating the whole thing is pretty delicious. How about an apple? Do you peel the apple or eat the apple with the skin on? Why throw away something that has vitamins and nutrients in it?

How about us in our walk with God? Do we cast off some things that are vitally important? Hosea 8:3, "Israel hath cast off the thing that is good: the enemy shall pursue him." Israel had not seen the need to pay attention to some of the most important things God was telling and warning them. Hosea 8:7, "For they have sown the wind, and they shall reap the whirlwind: it hath no stalk: the bud shall yield no meal: if so be it yield, the strangers shall swallow it up." Every step in our walk with God is so very important. Every detail of fighting sin must be watched and guarded. There are those spiritual mentors in our lives that try to help us along the way, and we must heed their guidance, warning, teaching, challenge, etc. They are not perfect, but they carry a burden to help us grow in our walk and relationship with God. Colossians 4:12-13, "Epaphras, who is one of you, a servant of Christ, saluteth you, always laboring fervently for you in prayers, that ye may stand perfect and complete in all the will of God. For I bear him record, that he hath a great zeal for you." Remember we were all told, eat your vegetables because they are good for you. There is always somebody older than us trying to tell us how we should be. Maybe they are trying to help us grow in the Lord and keep us from ruining our lives by allowing sin to destroy us. All of us need those who love us and carry a burden for us to grow in the Lord. Proverbs 3:7, "Be not wise in thine own eyes: fear the LORD, and depart from evil." Proverbs 3:13, "Happy is the man that findeth wisdom, and the man that getteth understanding." Proverbs 3:23, "Then shalt thou walk in thy way safely, and thy foot shall not stumble."

It was very humbling for my brother to ask me a couple of years back to forgive him. I said to him, what for? He said, I used to get so mad at you for bossing me and pushing me about some things. He went on to say that as he has gotten older, he realizes that I loved him and wanted to help him. Let us all look around today for those who love us enough to help us to do right and grow and mature in our walk with God. Most of all, let us look upward toward the Lord. Psalm 121:1-2, "I will lift up mine eyes unto the hills, from whence cometh my help. My help cometh from the LORD, which made heaven and earth." I sure wish my parents were still alive so that I could tell them both that I am eating my vegetables and I love them. Take time and listen to those who are trying to help you in your walk and growth in Christ. Look up and thank the Lord that He is always there for us.

All of us need those who love us and carry a burden for us to grow in the Lord.

December 4

Hosea 9-10 Psalm 122 Proverbs 4 1 Thessalonians 2-3

The Right Path

Good morning! I have walked in the woods many times here at the Ranch, and as I walk, I often follow the trails that were made for years by cattle. Some of the trails have been grown over and some of the trails are still very clear. The thing that I have often noticed is how they picked their trail through and around things. They had no guide, but they had an instinct that was within them. The trails even to this day are so clearly marked because they were walked so often.

The children of Israel continually seemed to go their own way instead of going the way the Lord led. Hosea 10:13, "Ye have plowed wickedness, ye have reaped iniquity; ye have eaten the fruit of lies: because thou didst trust in thy way, in the multitude of thy mighty men." May we not make the same mistake by going our way instead of going the way of the Lord. Those cows followed the path they did because they knew where the good grass was to graze. They also knew where the pond was to water. I Thessalonians 2:13, "For this cause also thank we God without ceasing, because, when ye received the word of God which ye heard of us, ye received it not as the word of men, but as it is in truth, the word of God, which effectually worketh also in you that believe." Paul is praising the people for going in the way of truth and responding to the Word of God. I Thessalonians 3:13, "To the end he may establish your hearts unblameable in holiness before God." As a young calf wants to often get out and away from mom, they will go in a way that is more difficult. I saw a calf caught in a thicket at the neighbor's the other day, and that little calf was having trouble getting back to mom and the rest of the herd. The right path to follow is always a clear path even though there are times it may seem to be a difficult path. Proverbs 4:18, "But the path of the just is as the shining light, that shineth more and more unto the perfect day."

When a herd is moved from one pasture to the other, they seem to follow the same paths as they did before. Why do we not follow the path of those before us who lived a victorious life in Christ? Keep your heart in tune with God. Stay on the right path to blessings from God. Proverbs 4:23, "Keep thy heart with all diligence; for out of it are the issues of life." The path to follow is the path that always leads to God and His blessings. It is the path of faith in Christ. Make sure you stay on the right and proven path.

Stay on the right path to blessings from God.

December 5

Hosea 11-12 Psalm 123 Proverbs 5 1 Thessalonians 4-5

Keep the Fire Stoked

Good morning! I trust your morning is starting off in a wonderful way. We have another day before us to serve the Lord and be used of Him. This morning as I was beginning to read, I came to Hosea 11:7, "And my people are bent to backsliding from me." I stopped right there and read the first part of this verse a dozen times or more. Why?? It is almost like a statement is being made that the purpose was to backslide away from the Lord. Why do we allow this to happen? Why does it happen? Let us go back and begin again and finish the entire verse. Hosea 11:7, "And my people are bent to backsliding from me: though they called them to the most High, none at all would exalt him." "None at all would exalt him."

Have we become so proud and so independent of God that we think we do not need God? Have we learned to go on in life without God? I Thessalonians 4:1, "Furthermore then we beseech you brethren, and exhort you by the Lord Jesus, that as ye have received of us how ye ought to walk and to please God, so ye would abound more and more." It is God's will that we "abound more and more." It is God's will that we grow in Him, be blessed in Him, serve with joy in Him, share with others about Him. The book of First Thessalonians ends with several thoughts for us to keep going in our growth and walk with the

Lord. I Thessalonians 5:19, "Quench not the Spirit." Do not shut off the working of God in your life. I Thessalonians 5:21, "Prove all things, hold fast that which is good." You can watch a child in the early years of their schooling have an excitement about learning how to write and read, then in elementary, learning some science facts and doing some simple experiments and then in the later years of schooling there is the struggle of finishing. It is the same in the Christian life. In the beginning there is a desire to grow, the excitement of first answered prayer, the vision to serve, and then the death of living for God. Why does this happen? Proverbs 5:12-13, "How have I hated instruction, and my heart despised reproof; And have not obeyed the voice of my teachers, nor inclined mine ear to them that instructed me!"

If we do not stay near God in every area of our life, the fire for God will soon go out. It is like putting wood on a fire. If you do not keep stoking the fire and adding more wood, the fire will soon go out. We must keep reading the Word of God, spending time with Him in prayer. Keep your heart tender for hearing preaching and being under conviction of sin. If a child is not bathed, they will get used to being filthy. May I suggest a time of getting alone with God, facing where you are spiritually, and seeking God's face? Psalm 123:3, "Have mercy upon us, O LORD, have mercy upon us: for we are exceedingly filled with contempt." A dog and cat continually cleanse themselves. How about you and me taking a close look at our life to see if the filth of sin has caused us to fall away from being what we need to be for the Lord?

If we do not stay near to God in every area of our life,
the fire for God will soon go out.

December 6

Hosea 13-14 Psalm 124 Proverbs 6 2 Thessalonians 1-2

Expressing Our Affection

Good morning! I heard whimpering this morning, so I went to see my dog, and there she was with her tail wagging so hard that her whole body was like a spring going back and forth. I knelt down and began petting her and the response was her pushing harder up against me. In the dark of the morning and in my reading today, I asked myself, how much do we hunger for the affection of God and how much does God hunger for our affection? Hosea 14:1, "O Israel, return unto the LORD thy God; for thou hast fallen by thine iniquity." Did you see the words, "return unto the LORD thy God?" It is as though there is the hunger for the closeness that was once there. Hosea 14:4, "I will heal their backsliding, I will love them freely." God is saying, I hunger to love you, forgive you and be what I desire to be.

I walked with my wife on a trail the other afternoon and we held hands. It has been fifty-two years since we first held each other's hand, and I still love it very much. Do we only want God for things, or do we hunger to love Him and hunger for His love to us? II Thessalonians 2:2, "That ye be not soon shaken in mind, or be troubled, neither by spirit, nor by word, nor by letter as from us, as that the day of Christ is at hand." The signs of the return of Christ are showing greater each year, month, and day. The signs are all around us. Is our attention more on the signs of the times, than on the love of Christ for winning souls and discipling new converts? II Thessalonians 2:17, "Comfort your hearts, and stablish you in every good word and work." Let us spend more time daily learning to express our love for the Saviour and receiving His love for us. A snuggle of a baby or a young child, a grandchild sitting on a lap and letting their head rest up against you, a wink from a husband or wife, a grasp of a hand as you walk together; are all signs of affection for each other. How about you and I spending more time praising and showing our love to our Lord and Saviour? Proverbs 6:20-21, "My son, keep thy father's commandment, and forsake not the law of thy mother. Bind them continually upon thine heart, and tie them about thy neck."

I thought how proud and honored I was when my wife first wore the engagement ring I gave her. Then through the years she has worn other jewelry that I have purchased. We are jewels in the eyes of our Lord. Should we not express our love by displaying the change Christ has made in our life, because of our love for Him? He is always there to love us and help us. Psalm 124:8, "Our help is in the name of the LORD, who made heaven and earth." I think I will spend more time showing my affection to my Saviour and Lord. You know, I think I will send someone I love a note or call and express the affection I feel for them. True love gives and does not just receive.

Let us spend more time daily learning to express our love for the Saviour.

December 7

Joel 1-3 Psalm 125 Proverbs 7 2 Thess. 3 & 1 Tim. 1

Jesus is Coming

Good morning! I would like you to think about the word "disappointment" this morning. Have you ever been disappointed? You had expectation in someone, you had put time, prayer, and effort in helping someone, and they turned from the Lord and seemed as though they never wanted to be around God's people any longer. The coming of the Lord for His saints seems to be drawing so close. We see the turning away of God's people, the lack of spiritual concern for the lost, families not being faithful to God's house and not realizing they are setting a pattern for destruction spiritually for their children.

What Joel wrote by the Holy Spirit is very convicting, or it should be. Joel 1:14-15, "Sanctify ye a fast, call a solemn assembly, gather the elders and all the inhabitants of the land into the house of the LORD your God, and cry unto the LORD, Alas for the day! For the day of the LORD is at hand, and as a destruction from the Almighty shall it come." Read on down to Joel 2:1, "for the day of the LORD cometh, for it is nigh at hand." We might be disappointed in someone's lack of concern for spiritual things but think what will happen when the Lord returns. It seems like we should be drawing closer to the Lord, and we should be busier about the things of God. God is our only hope! Joel 3:16, "but the LORD will be the hope of his people, and the strength of the children of Israel." May we not focus on the things of this world but focus on being faithful to be watching and working toward the coming of the Lord. In I Timothy 1:19, Paul charged young Timothy and the charge is also for us, "Holding faith, and a good conscience; which some having put away concerning faith have made shipwreck." There are lives that have been ruined by turning back to sin. Proverbs 7:2, "Keep my commandments, and live; and my law as the apple of thine eye."

We might not be able to see it with our eyes, but the Lord is always there to be our strength and guide in the sinful world, our hope for tomorrow, our joy of life, our everything. Psalm 127:2, "As the mountains are round about Jerusalem, so the LORD is round about his people from henceforth even for ever." May we keep in our hearts and minds those words we read in Joel 2:1, "for the day of the LORD cometh, for it is nigh at hand." Be watching. Jesus is coming again.

We must be faithful to be watching and working toward the coming of the Lord.

December 8

Amos 1-2 Psalm 126 Proverbs 8 1 Timothy 2-3

Stay Away From the Cart

Good morning! There are so many pressures in life and sometimes these pressures pile up and seem to be so heavy there is no way that we can get out from underneath them. Money pressures, health pressures, family pressures, job pressures and the list goes on and on. We often say, is this pressure ever going to end? Amos 2:13, "Behold, I am pressed under you, as a cart is pressed that is full of sheaves." As a parent, there are those times that our children, even though we have corrected them, seem to keep doing the same thing over and over. We say, will they ever learn? Think of a large cart full of grain and this cart rolls over your foot and stops. You cannot get your foot out from underneath the wheel. Oh, the pain of your toes and foot being smashed!

Our sin puts us under pressure that is not necessary. That sin will soon hold us so that we cannot pull our foot out from underneath the wheel of the cart. The best thing that could have been done was to stay away from being in the way of the cart. We need to learn to stay away from sin that will press down upon us. I Timothy 3:5, "For if a man know not how to rule his own house, how shall he take care of the church of God?" These are Paul's words to Timothy but as I read them, I thought how we must learn to stay away from sin and if not, we will never be able to find the joy of the Lord and serve in the will of God. Let us go back to the cart where our foot is caught under the wheel. Why did we get so close to the cart? It is like sin. If we get close, it will get a hold of us. Stay out of the way, stay far away from sin. Proverbs 8:32-33, "blessed are they that keep my ways. Hear instruction, and be wise, and refuse it not." The joy of the Christian life is always being far away from the clutches of sin. We must be focused on living and sharing the joy of being born again in Christ. Living and walking with God will keep us far away from the temptations and destruction of sin. Psalm 126:5-6, "They that sow in tears shall reap in joy. He that goeth forth and weepeth, bearing precious seed, shall doubtless come again with rejoicing, bringing his sheaves with him."

Pull your foot back before the cart of sin rolls over it. Stay away from that which will destroy you. Those things that do not cause us to live in the joy of the Lord and help us produce fruit for a joyous life in Christ, must be removed from our life or we will be caught and pressed and destroyed. Live in the joy of serving and living for Jesus. There is a price for sin and God shows us that our sin brings Him to a place of no choice but to bring judgment upon us because of the sin. Think about what has a hold on you and get away from it, confess and forsake it. Thank the Lord that if we come before Him and repent, He will forgive us.

Walking with God will keep us far away
from the temptations and destruction of sin.

December 9

Amos 3-4 Psalm 127 Proverbs 9 1 Timothy 4-5

Are You Ready?

Good morning! The Lord has blessed us with another day to live for Him and to serve Him. As I read Amos 3:6, "Shall a trumpet be blown in the city, and the people not be afraid? Shall there be evil in a city, and the LORD hath not done it?" A trumpet was blown to sound an alarm. The alarm was to alert the people. What if the world woke up this morning and all Christians were gone because the rapture of the church had taken place? Who would be left behind that we know? Are there relatives that we love for whom now it is too late because the delusion promised in the Scriptures has now come, and they will eventually die and go to Hell for eternity?

As we read in Amos chapter four, five different times we see the phrase, "yet have ye not returned unto me, saith the LORD." Yes, as I am writing, I am still on the earth, breathing and serving the Lord, but when will He, our LORD, come? Amos 4:12, "prepare to meet thy God." Should we not be living each day in preparation to meet Him? I Timothy 4:15-16, "Meditate upon these things; give thyself wholly to them; that thy profiting may appear to all. Take heed unto thyself, and unto the doctrine; continue in them: for in doing this thou shalt both save thyself, and them that hear thee." As long as we have life, should we not be living to honor the Lord in every way that we can, being faithful to Him in any way that we can? The way of this world is destroying lives, marriages and families. Jesus is coming soon, and we should be preparing to meet our Lord. Proverbs 9:6, "Forsake the foolish, and live; and go in the way of understanding." Proverbs 9:9, "Give instruction to a wise man, and he will be yet wiser: teach a just man, and he will increase in learning."

Be in the house of God, singing hymns, fellowshipping with the family of God, encouraging one another through testimonies of God's goodness. Grow from lessons taught in Sunday School and respond to the conviction of the Holy Spirit in church services. A generation is before us, and it is our responsibility to carry on with the Gospel story. My heart was pricked as I prayed this morning and every morning for my children and grandchildren and so many more. May we be conscious of the heritage that we must live and pass on. Psalm 127:3, "Lo, children are an heritage of the LORD: and the fruit of the womb is his reward." We must not just live unto ourselves but live for the heritage that God has given us. Live for and serve Him today and every day. HE is coming again. The trumpet will soon sound. Are you ready??

Jesus is coming soon, and we should be preparing to meet our Lord.

December 10

Amos 5-6 Psalm 128 Proverbs 10 1 Tim. 6 & 2 Tim. 1

Beware of Backsliding

Good morning! There are times I wish I could just shut my tastebuds off. Overeating the things you enjoy can be a real problem. Some things that we think are good can be the ruin of us if overdone. As I read in Amos 6:8, "The Lord God hath sworn by himself, saith the LORD the God of hosts, I abhor the excellency of Jacob, and hate his palaces: therefore will I deliver up the city with all that is therein." The people got too much of living in ease and they allowed unrighteousness to come in and turned their backs on God. We must be careful when we live in ease without God. Too often living in ease causes us to give excuse, and the excuse brings us to backsliding from God.

Look at the phrase, "I abhor the excellency of Jacob." Faithfulness compromised brings us to a backslidden state. It seems as though any little excuse will keep us from being faithful, but when it comes to what we want to do, nothing will keep us from the pleasures or recreation that we want. Prosperity has ruined many. Pleasure has destroyed many a servant of the Lord. I Timothy 6:9-10, "But they that will be rich fall into temptation and a snare, and into many foolish and hurtful lusts, which drown men in destruction and perdition. For the love of money is the root of all evil: which while some coveted after, they have erred from the faith, and pierced themselves through with many sorrows." Anything that pulls us away from being faithful to God's house is the very path that will soon destroy us. Proverbs 10:2-3, "Treasures of wickedness profit nothing: but righteousness delivereth from death. The LORD will not suffer the soul of the righteous to famish: but he casteth away the substance of the wicked." What we think we want or must have may not be wicked, but when it controls us, there is the possibility of it destroying us.

May there be a desire and action to please the Lord more than anything we do. Psalm 128:1, "Blessed is everyone that feareth the LORD; that walketh in his ways." Put God first and let Him handle all of your situations. What we love to do cannot be more important than what God would be pleased is us doing. God always blesses faithfulness to Him. I love many things and I am thankful the Lord has provided things for us to enjoy, but we must not let anything ever be more important than putting the Lord first.

Faithfulness compromised brings us to a backslidden state.

December 11

Amos 7-8 Psalm 129 Proverbs 11 2 Timothy 2-3

A Spiritual Famine

Good morning! As I finished our reading this morning, I could not get settled to write, so I went to the back of the camp, deep in the woods, and began to ponder what I had read in our morning reading. My heart is breaking for the world that we live in. This earth is covered with people, some lost and some saved, and yet with the influence of saved people it seems as though we are not seeking the face of our Lord in these trying times. Faithfulness in a church service has gone to viewing live stream services, and yet people can go where they want and do what they want, when they want to.

Read with me again the words we read in Amos 8:11-12, "Behold, the days come, saith the Lord God, that I will send a famine in the land, not a famine of bread, nor a thirst for water, but of hearing the words of the LORD: And they shall wander from sea to sea, and from the north even to the east, they shall run to and fro to seek the word of the LORD, and shall not find it." Even though these words were written about the children of Israel, they can sure be applied to us today. Paul wrote to Timothy in II Timothy 2:3, "Thou therefore endure hardness, as a good soldier of Jesus Christ." Do not let your heart become hard and indifferent to the things of the Lord. Do as Paul wrote in II Timothy 3:14, "But continue thou in the things which thou hast learned and hast been assured of, knowing of whom thou hast learned them." Oh, be thankful for every pastor, missionary, evangelist, or saint that has influenced you for Christ and do not let the famine of spiritual things set in. Proverbs 11:6, "The righteousness of the upright shall deliver them: but transgressors shall be taken in their own naughtiness." Proverbs 11:8, "The righteous is delivered out of trouble, and the wicked cometh in his stead."

May we have a continual thirst for the fresh spiritual water from the well that never runs dry, the Word of God. We need to be on our faces before the Lord, pleading for a lost world and being the righteous remnant that is living and professing the truth of the Bible. The Lord will have His day. Psalm 129:4, "The LORD is righteous: he hath cut asunder the cords of the wicked." Seek Him this very moment, spend time with Him alone, and let His Word be a strength and guide to you today and every day.

Be thankful for every pastor, missionary, evangelist, or saint who has influenced you for Christ.

December 12

Amos 9 & Obadiah 1 Psalm 130 Proverbs 12 2 Tim. 4 & Titus 1-3

A Remodeled Life

Good morning! Building, building, building all around us. Building of homes, businesses, new construction of all kinds. Homes being remodeled and updated. This is a way in all of our lives. As we drive down the road, we see new construction of homes, roads being repaired, and even new roads being built. We see old roads being expanded, widened, or even more lanes being added. What about our lives? Are we growing and building personally? Are we expanding in our study and application personally of God's Word to our lives? A Christian who is not growing is dying. A Christian who is not reading and studying God's Word is going backwards in their walk with God. A Christian who is not faithful to the house of God is backsliding.

Mrs. Smith and I have remodeled several homes. We did most of the work ourselves, but there were certain things that I had to have a professional come in and do the work. Too many Christians think they can do all they need to live the Christian life. That is why they can go from week to week without reading the Bible and being in church. I have been told many times by many people that they can worship the Lord at home, camping, in nature, etc., etc. Amos 9:6, "It is he that buildeth his stories in the heaven, and hath founded his troop in the earth; he that calleth for the waters of the sea, and poureth them out upon the face of the earth: The LORD is his name." Did you ever think about all the times the people of God were called to worship together? They were called to come and bring their offerings and sacrifices, to come together and fast and pray. The temple, the house of God, is plainly seen in the Word of God. It is God that builds all our lives, but it is God's Word that tells us to "forsake not the assembling of yourselves together." II Timothy 4:17, "Notwithstanding the Lord stood with me, and strengthened me." It is God, His Word, the fellowship of His people, the gathering at His house, the singing of hymns together, praying together that we need.

Proverbs 12:15, "The way of a fool is right in his own eyes: but he that hearkeneth unto counsel is wise." Be faithful. Be in your place. Serve together in your church.

Maybe you are going through a difficult time fighting some battles or going through some testings. Stop, listen to God's Word. Psalm 130:2, "Lord, hear my voice: let thine ears be attentive to the voice of my supplications." Psalm 130:7, "for with the LORD there is mercy, and with him is plenteous redemption." Thank the Lord that He is always in His place and ready to hear our pleas. Are we always in our place to worship and serve Him? The happy Christians are the serving Christians. Let God do a remodel on your life or just let Him have everything and let Him build how He wants. "It is he that buildeth."

Thank the Lord that He is always in His place and ready to hear our pleas.

December 13

Jonah 1-2 Psalm 131 Proverbs 13 Philemon 1 & Hebrews 1-2

A Surrendered Spirit

Good morning! I can remember many years ago I was given a young stallion horse, a beautiful palomino horse. He was light brown with a beautiful flowing mane and tail. The only problem was the horse had not been ridden in several years. To walk up to this horse was no problem at all. I could touch him, brush him, and stand there and walk around him, but then it came time to put the bridle in his mouth and the saddle on his back. He did not take to any type of tack being put on him. To look at him, brush him, touch him, even to lead him around with a lead rope was no problem, but to saddle and ride him was a problem.

As I read this morning in our reading, my mind went to those Christians who say they are saved but the fruit of their life, the faithfulness of their life, the service of their life is not there. At one time that horse was broke and ridden, but several years had passed and the horse began to enjoy his freedom and he had come to the point of acting like a horse that was not broken to ride. Jonah was the man of God, the prophet of God, prepared by God to go to Nineveh, but he did not want to, plain and simple. Jonah 1:3, "But Jonah rose up to flee unto Tarshish from the presence of the LORD." The first day I got a saddle, blanket and bridle and went to the corral to ride that horse, he began to run around and act like an unbroken horse. Jonah 1:10, "For the men knew that he fled from the presence of the LORD." I had to start all over and treat that horse just like he was an unbroken horse. Jonah ran from God and found himself at the bottom, just like many a Christian that keeps running away from what they know they should be. Hebrews 2:3, "How shall we escape, if we neglect so great salvation." We cannot escape the reach of God, even though we try everything else there is just to satisfy and justify our flesh. As I began to work that horse in a round pen and my son helped me, in a very short time we began to see that stubborn streak break and we soon began to ride that beautiful horse.

Please don't run from God. The flesh can never be satisfied. There is no place to hide from God. Proverbs 13:6, "Righteousness keepeth him that is upright in the way: but wickedness overthroweth the sinner." Let God be the friend that He desires to be. If you are away, come back. If you have never left that wonderful walk with God, stay strong and in His will. Psalm 131:2, "Surely I have behaved and quieted myself, as a child that is weaned of his mother: my soul is even as a weaned child." You know, when I walked by the corral where that horse was, he used to run over to the fence and act like he wanted us to ride him. All because he surrendered his spirit to the one that would take care of him. Where are you today? Running from God or running to Him? He loves us and hungers for us to fellowship with Him.

Let God be the friend that He desires to be.

December 14

Jonah 3-4 Psalm 132 Proverbs 14 Hebrews 3-5

True Happiness

Good morning! The greatest thing that a born again believer can do is be obedient to Christ who saved our soul. To most all of us this will take a great character change because we are very selfish beings, and we serve self first. I often wonder what we could really do for the Lord if we would move self out of the way.

Jonah 3:3, "So Jonah arose, and went unto Nineveh, according to the word of the LORD." God called, Jonah heard, and Jonah fled. The question through the ages is, why did Jonah flee? The commentaries are full of opinions and yet the fact is, He ran from what God asked him to do. If we would learn to take everything to the Lord in prayer and spend more time on our knees seeking the face of God, we would stay farther away from those things that destroy our spiritual walk with God. Hebrews 4:16, "Let us therefore come boldly unto the throne of grace, that we may obtain mercy, and find grace to help in time of need." Jonah hit bottom and when he did, he paid a price, and that price brought him to seek the face of God. Have the things of this world distracted you from the things of God? Is there a discontentment in your walk with the Saviour? Is there a frustration? Take time and focus on what is the real problem and give it to the Lord. Do not pick it back up. Just leave it with the Lord. So often we try to fix things that are not ours to fix, so we need to learn to leave them with the Lord and let Him show us His mighty hand. Proverbs 14:30, "A sound heart is the life of the flesh: but envy the rottenness of the bones." The word "sound" means content or at peace. We have no peace because we are trying to find happiness where happiness is not. True happiness in serving the Lord is being in the place of His will, doing His will, in the way that His will should be done. Psalm 132:12, "If thy children will keep my covenant and my testimony that I shall teach them, their children shall also sit upon thy throne for evermore."

I love listening to my grandchildren talk about what they are doing, how they enjoy what they are doing, how the Lord is blessing what they are doing. There is no greater joy for a Christian than to see the blessing of God in your life because of being in the perfect will of God. It was a great day when "Jonah arose and went unto Nineveh." May we have a focus on being where God wants us to be at all times. Rise up and be in your place, the will of God for your life.

True happiness is being in His will, doing His will,
in the way that His will should be done.

December 15

Micah 1-2 Psalm 133-134 Proverbs 15 Hebrews 6-8

A Good Listener

Good morning! As I began the reading in the book of Micah this morning, one word caught my eye and I read this verse several times. Micah 1:2, "Hear, all ye people; hearken, O earth, and all that therein is: and let the Lord God be witness against you, the Lord from his holy temple." I kept looking and thinking about the word "hear." Why do we not hear the voice of the Lord? Why do we not work to listen to the voice of the Lord? Then I moved on to the word "hearken." We would discipline a child who did not obey. A parent will say this phrase many times in rearing their children, "Did you hear me?." You know, God loves us and when we face, confess, and forsake our sins, God always forgives. Listen to the words of Hebrews 8:12, "For I will be merciful to their unrighteousness, and their sins and their iniquities will I remember no more."

Why is it that we always want to be heard, but we have trouble keeping our mouth shut and listening to the other side of the story or conversation? We want to ask of God, we plead with God, we beg God, but do we listen to God? We are just as a child who will listen to their parents, but then go and do the same thing that got them in trouble.

I have learned that it is much better to stop what you are doing, listen to what is being said, and do what has been suggested as a help. Our selfish, prideful, sinful heart gets us in trouble so often. Proverbs 15:14, "The heart of him that hath understanding seeketh knowledge: but the mouth of fools feedeth on foolishness." Sin is like a magnet that will not release its power of attraction. We must break this power that controls and listen to God and His Word and hearken to the wisdom that comes from God. If we do not hear and hearken, we will continue to go farther from the relationship with God that will help us. Proverbs 15:32, "He that refuseth instruction despiseth his own soul: but he that heareth reproof getteth understanding." "Reproof" is not for destruction, but for correction. Correction is for our help and strength. Unity of a marriage, a family, a job, a unit, a team, a church, comes when we work together by listening to each other and following the path of unity that is pleasing to God and the teachings of His Word. Psalm 133:1, "Behold, how good and how pleasant it is for brethren to dwell together in unity!" We must quit justifying what we think and listen to what God says and do what God says to do.

Let us work on listening to each other. I have often said, if we will not listen to whom we can see, we will never listen to whom we cannot see. Another way to say what I just said is: if I will not listen to a man whom I can see, I will never listen to God whom I cannot see. Just think about God that lives within your heart and the small voice of the Holy Spirit, as well as the preservation of the Word of God that we hold and the blessing of hearing the Word of God taught and preached to us. May we ask ourselves today where the problem really lies. Am I the listener that I need to be? Could I help my marriage, my family, my children, if I would learn to be a better listener? Could I have a clear path to know the will of God for my life if I was a better listener? Can you hear His voice? Then hearken to Him and obey Him.

If we will not listen to whom we can see,
we will never listen to whom we cannot see.

December 16

Micah 3-4 Psalm 135 Proverbs 16 Hebrews 9-11

Quietness of His Presence

Good morning! Last night when Mrs. Smith and I arrived home from church, the moon was full and bright. I just stood outside for a while and enjoyed the quietness and peacefulness of the night hours. Sin fills the world we live in, and we as God's people must find the time to be alone with our Heavenly Father, to continually renew our strength in Him.

Micah 4:6-7, "In that day, saith the LORD, will I assemble her that halteth, and I will gather her that is driven out, and her that I have afflicted; And I will make her that halted a remnant, and her that was cast far off a strong nation: and the LORD shall reign over them in mount Zion from henceforth, even for ever." Sin will wear us down to the point of destroying our life. Sin will take over in any way that it can. I look forward to the day that the Lord has come and is in control of this world. My prayer and earnest desire is that we, the remnant, would use this time we have left on the earth to stand and grow in God's grace. We must never forget that we are not alone. Christ is interceding for us. Hebrews 9:24, "For Christ is not entered into the holy places made with hands, which are the figures of the true; but into heaven itself, now to appear in the presence of God for us." He is there for us. Glory and praise to His name! May we see the importance of living our life to not only be a testimony for Christ, but to be an encourager to others. Hebrews 10:24, "And let us consider one another to provoke unto love and to good works."

As I stood in the quietness of the night, it seemed as though the Lord had let the lights of Heaven burn just a little brighter so that I could enjoy His power and glory. We have no idea how long our journey will be on this earth, but may it be a journey that pleases the Father. May we live our lives in Godly wisdom and have a heart's desire to please the Lord in all that we do. Proverbs 16:20, "He that handleth a matter wisely shall find good: and whoso trusteth in the LORD, happy is he." Let not your heart fail in faith to God. Live for Him today. Take time in the quietness of His presence. Psalm 135:3, "Praise the LORD; for the LORD is good: sing praises unto his name; for it is pleasant." Let us spend time daily in the quiet presence of our Lord. Listen for His voice and dwell on His promises.

We must find time to be alone with our Heavenly Father,
to continually renew our strength in Him.

December 17

Micah 5-6 Psalm 136 Proverbs 17 Hebrews 12-13

Leftovers

Good morning! Do you like leftovers? I mean do you like it when there is food left from a meal, and it gets put in the refrigerator and another day, maybe even the next day, it comes back out, is warmed and you get to eat it again? There is something very delicious when the meal is first prepared, set on the table, hot and ready to eat and the kitchen is filled with the beautiful aroma. When a person gets saved, there is a Heavenly peace of having our sins forgiven, our name has been written down in the Lamb's Book of Life and we have the peace that only eternal life can give. There is a smile on a face as deep as the heart can make it shine. We sit down and begin to explain the picture of baptism, and we even take them back to the baptistry and let them see all that has been prepared, and they say, sure, I see that I need to do this. Wow, what joy!! When they come out of the baptismal waters, they often will say, I sure am glad I did that. Now we begin a journey. We maybe give them a Bible and write some verses down for them to read and remember, or we even give them a little booklet that will help them to look up Scriptures that will help explain more of what they have just done.

What happens next is what must break the heart of God over and over and over. They come maybe once more, or a couple of weeks, and we pray and we try to work with them. The Christian life can be simple to follow and it sometimes is very hard, but it is the best life on earth. Micah 6:8, "He hath shewed thee, O man, what is good; and what doth the LORD require of thee, but to do justly, and to love mercy, and to walk humbly with thy God?" Please get back in church. Quit making excuses about why you miss. Your head will still hurt on Monday. Please do not miss fellowshipping with God's people and singing the hymns together. Keep the joy of your salvation first in your life. Hebrews 12:28, "Wherefore we receiving a kingdom which cannot be moved, let us have grace, whereby we may serve God acceptably with reverence and godly fear." Quit giving the Lord leftovers. Quit just going when you feel like it. Online services are nothing like really being there and being part of the service. I have eaten many a leftover food from the refrigerator but there is nothing so delicious as when it is first prepared. Let God have first place, the best, the foremost, the main part. Proverbs 17:24, "Wisdom is before him that hath understanding; but the eyes of a fool are in the ends of the earth."

Some reading this devotional this morning always put God first place in everything. My prayer is the words written this morning will cause each of us to think about if we give God first or do we give God the leftovers? Psalm 136:26, "O give thanks unto the God of heaven: for his mercy endureth forever." Mrs. Smith has often said to me, "Supper is hot and ready," even when I say, can I keep working a little longer? I love it when we sit down together and have that delicious meal that has been prepared. Every Sunday morning and Sunday night, midweek and during revivals, missions conferences, there has been a hot meal prepared. Quit giving God leftovers. See you in church.

Let God have first place, the best, the foremost, the main part.

December 18

Micah 7 & Nahum 1 Psalm 137 Proverbs 18 James 1-4

A Constant Companion

Good morning! It was late last night when I finally pulled the tractor into the barn. Earlier, I was out by the cowboy town at the ranch and had to do some work in the office. Laying by the tractor was my dog. As I came out of the office where I had parked the tractor, I needed to go to the Dining Hall and up she got and followed me to the other building. As I came out the door, there she was with tail a wagging. Wherever I was all afternoon and evening, there she was, from one end of the camp to the other. As I drove the tractor back to the barn, that little dog of mine was running right alongside. As I stood in the darkness of the barn and in the light of the moon, there sat that dog that had been with me every place I went.

As I read in Nahum 1:7, "The LORD is good, a strong hold in the day of trouble; and he knoweth them that trust in him." My brother and sister, the Lord is every place that we go and everything that we do or say, He is right there with us. Why do we have trouble submitting to Him? There are times I have to scold my dog and say, get out of that flower bed, quit digging in that place, stay here, etc. Listen to the verses this morning in James 4:7-8, "Submit yourselves therefore to God. Resist the devil, and he will flee from you. Draw nigh to God, and he will draw nigh to you, Cleanse your hands, ye sinners; and purify your hearts, ye double minded." My dog and I have fun together, and when I try to teach her something new or when I have to scold her, there is something that causes her to submit even when she is in trouble. Oh, that you and I would submit to our Lord, even in times when we do wrong and we get scolded by God or, as the Bible teaches, chastened by God. My dog will stick her tail between her legs and most of the time, drop right to the ground and look sheepish. James 4:10, "Humble yourselves in the sight of the Lord, and he shall lift you up." James 4:17, "Therefore to him that knoweth to do good, and doeth it not, to him it is sin."

Mrs. Smith loves flowers and works hard to plant new ones and work with them to help them grow. We made a new place for some flowers and plants and guess where my dog went until she knew she was in trouble? You are right, the flower bed. We need to learn what is right and what is wrong in the eyes of God. Proverbs 18:15, "The heart of the prudent getteth knowledge; and the ear of the wise seeketh knowledge." Yes, my dog is with me until she wanders on a trail that is not always the place she should go. Are you walking with the Master or have you been disobedient and wandered away? Psalm 137:4, "How shall we sing the LORD's song in a strange land?" Come back to God and let Him walk alongside and be with you every place you go.

The Lord is every place that we go and everything that we do or say, He is right there with us.

December 19

Nahum 2-3 Psalm 138 Proverbs 19 James 5 & I Pet. 1-3

Seasons of Life

Good morning! Did you ever say those haunting words, I wished I would have? So many things in life pass us so very fast and there is no turning back, but there is always going forward. The book of Nahum covers the destruction of Nineveh and yet there are words to keep us focused on the importance of going forward. Nahum 2:1, "He that dasheth in pieces is come up before thy face: keep the munition, watch the way; make thy loins strong, fortify thy power mightily."

Do not let yourself be drained by focusing on the failures of the past, or those things that you wished you had not missed in life. There is the future ahead because God has still given us life and that is for a purpose. I Peter 2:9, "But ye are a chosen generation, a royal priesthood, an holy nation, a peculiar people; that ye should shew forth the praises of him who hath called you out of darkness into his marvelous light." Let us clear our minds today and look to God for the future plans He has for us, and not make the same mistakes that we made in the past. Proverbs 19:23, "The fear of the LORD tendeth to life: and he that hath it shall abide satisfied; he shall not be visited with evil." Just think about this verse. You and I still have life. You know, no matter how good or bad the weather is or can get, all the seasons will still come and go. Winter will always come after fall and spring will always come after winter, and we will always complain about the heat of summer and forget about the cold of winter.

So, if God gives us the promise of all seasons, let us press forward with the season of life that we are now in. Psalm 138:6, "Though the LORD be high, yet hath he respect unto the lowly: but the proud he knoweth afar off." You might be in your 20s, 30s, 40s, 50s or 60s; just keep pressing on and living and serving the Lord in your 70s and beyond, until the Lord returns or takes us Home to Heaven. Just praise Him we have today to live and serve Him.

There is the future ahead because God has still given us life and that is for a purpose.

December 20

Habakkuk 1-3 Psalm 139 Proverbs 20 1 Pet. 4-5 & 2 Pet. 1-2

Continue On

Good morning! As Mrs. Smith and I turned in the lane to the Ranch, we were met by about a dozen of the neighbor's mallard ducks that just roam around most of the day. I have watched them on different occasions picking at the grass, just waddling along. These ducks are constantly busy picking away for bugs, worms and whatever they can find to eat. The principle that they taught me is that they continue on even when they do not find something. What if they just picked away at the grass for five minutes and found nothing? They seem to stay after it all day. Those ducks never quit looking for food to keep them alive. Do we as God's people get tired of trying to find our spiritual strength in God's Word? We start off with a desire to see God answer some prayers, and we get discouraged when the answers do not come, so we just quit praying.

Habakkuk had a heart for God and became impatient toward God because He did not bring judgment. Habakkuk 1:2, "O LORD, how long shall I cry, and thou will not hear! Even cry out unto thee of violence, and thou wilt not save!" You know, those ducks will find their needed food. They just keep staying after it. They know it is there and they are going to keep searching and not quit. Keep praying and keep living for the Lord. Keep reading His Word and looking for His promises, knowledge, guidance. and you will receive His strength. Habakkuk 1:5, "I will work a work in your days, which ye will not believe." Habakkuk 2:3, "though it tarry wait for it; because it will surely come." We need to quit putting God on a time schedule and just keep on believing, reading, and praying. What we need is to humble ourselves before God. I Peter 5:6-7, "Humble yourselves therefore under the mighty hand of God, that he may exalt you in due time. Casting all your care upon him; for he careth for you." Those ducks live because they stay after searching for food. Proverbs 20:4, "The sluggard will not plow by reason of the cold; therefore shall he beg in harvest, and have nothing." Keep on for the Lord. The answer to those prayers will come in God's time. Proverbs 20:27, "The spirit of man is the candle of the LORD."

I rolled down the window of the car and, sure enough, those ducks were chattering. I do not know what they were saying but it sounded like they were saying, I know the bugs are here, we just need to keep searching. Or I thought they might be thanking God for His bounty in the earth. How about you and I just keep living for the Lord, praying and spending time with Him, living and serving in His will, and waiting on His timing in taking care of us? Psalm 139:14, "I will praise thee; for I am fearfully and wonderfully made: marvelous are thy works; and that my soul knoweth right well." Continue on, the answers will come.

We need to quit putting God on a time schedule
and keep on believing, reading, and praying.

December 21

Zephaniah 1-3 Psalm 140 Proverbs 21 2 Pet. 3 & I John 1-3

Focused on His Return

Good morning! The focus of the Christian life should be a focus on His return. The distractions of this world and trying to figure things out keeps us from our focus. God is in charge and there is nothing that can change that. We and every generation have difficult times, and those times should be drawing us closer to that relationship in Christ in preparation for His return. Zephaniah 1:14, "The great day of the LORD is near, it is near, and hasteth greatly, even the voice of the day of the LORD." Just this one verse from our reading today should cause us to stop and think about the return of our LORD.

Picture with me some kids playing in the yard after a rain and finding a mud hole. There is something about mud to a little boy and to some little girls. When mom allowed them to go outside to play, she said, now stay away from the mud. At first all the children did. Then there was something that drew them. They walked closer, threw a stone in it, stuck the edge of their boot in it, put one foot in it, then both boots in it, then a little jump to watch the water splash, then a splash on each other and the mud fight has begun. They are forgetting what mom said when they first went out. There will be a punishment because of lack of obedience, and the lack of obedience came because of forgetting what was told by mom. II Peter 3:9, "The Lord is not slack concerning his promise, as some men count slackness; but is longsuffering to us-ward, not willing that any should perish, but that all should come to repentance." You know why mom mentioned the mud hole? It is because she was a little child one time and liked to play in the mud. God knows we are sinners and that is why He shows His mercy, but He also brings His judgment on sin. If the children would have remembered and heeded to the words of mom there would not have been trouble when mom saw them. I John 2:6, "He that saith he abideth in him ought himself also so to walk, even as he walked." Christ set an example for us, as He kept His eyes on His purpose and that was the cross of Calvary. My friend, Jesus is coming again. We must keep our hearts and eyes focused on His return and not on the ways of man. Proverbs 21:8, "The way of man is froward and strange: but as for the pure, his work is right."

As the children forgot what mom had said, have we forgotten what God has said? The ways of man are the ways of destruction. The way of God is for life eternal. Psalm 140:13, "Surely the righteous shall give thanks unto thy name: the upright shall dwell in thy presence." When mom showed up and saw the children in the mud, there was a price to pay. Man's ways are never satisfied, and they lead to destruction. May we be challenged today to keep our focus on the return of our Lord. He is coming again. As mom opened the door and saw the children in the mud, what would Christ do today if He took a long look at you? We need to be living as if Christ is coming today. By the way, He sees everything even better than mom.

May we be challenged today to keep our focus on the return of our Lord.

December 22

Haggai 1-2   Psalm 141   Proverbs 22   1 John 4-5, 2 John, 3 John

Consider Your Ways

Good morning! There have been times in all of our lives that we wish we could have gone back and corrected something or have an opportunity to start all over. We said something we did not mean the way it came out; we did something and it was taken wrong, we acted in a way that was not right and our flesh took over instead of our spirit. Can you relate?

As we read this morning, a thought of rebuilding, repairing, or refurbishing came to my mind. In our walk with God, we must view everything through the truths of the Scriptures. The devil wants us to quit, give up, throw in the towel, admit we can't, just admit the Christian life is not for everyone. Those are lies straight from the devil himself.

Haggai 1:5, "Now therefore thus saith the LORD of hosts; Consider your ways." Haggai 1:7, "Thus saith the LORD of hosts; Consider your ways." It is as if the Lord is plainly saying, just take a good look at yourself. I do not know about you, but I do not like looking at the way I am, but God says, "Consider your ways." I think we need to consider this phrase and take a good look at our life, our marriages, our attitude, our ethics, etc. Now, do not just say, I can't. Take a look and at the same time look at Haggai 1:13, "I am with you, saith the LORD." Haggai was a prophet sent by God to be an encourager to those builders, rebuilding after 70 years of captivity. My friend, we must keep rebuilding our lives for the glory of God. When we fall (sin), we need to seek God's forgiveness, get back up, and go forward. Wounds can heal if we let them. You know a wound will not heal if we keep picking at it. Quite often, if we pick at or mess with a wound it will get infected. Three times in Haggai 2:4, we read the two words, "be strong." This same verse ends by these words, "and work: for I am with you, saith the LORD of hosts." I John 5:4, "For whatsoever is born of God overcometh the world: and this is the victory that overcometh the world, even our faith." It is faith in God, His Word, and the precious Holy Spirit that indwells us from the very moment we asked Christ to come into our heart. II John 11, "Beloved, follow not that which is evil, but that which is good. He that doeth good is of God: but he that doeth evil hath not seen God."

The devil wants us to quit, give up. God challenges us to "Consider your ways," "be strong," and be an overcomer. Proverbs 22:5, "Thorns and snares are in the way of the froward: he that doth keep his soul shall be far from them." Stay away from the snares of the devil. Psalm 141:2, "Let my prayer be set forth before thee as incense; and the lifting up of my hands as the evening sacrifice." The Psalmist was setting the example of "being strong" and pressing on in our walk with the Lord. Quit picking the wound of failure and let it heal. Be strong and get busy in serving the Lord.

We must keep rebuilding our lives for the glory of God.

December 23

Zechariah 1-2 Psalm 142 Proverbs 23 Jude & Rev. 1-3

Wake Up and Smell the Coffee

Good morning! The lines at the stores are long, the parking lots are full, and the patience of people is growing short. Hurry, hurry, hurry and get everything done and ready. It has been often said we miss the true meaning of Christmas. Just two days away, and so much is left to do. I asked myself this morning, is there the same rush by us, as God's people, to be ready for His return? I do not understand why a phrase will come to my mind, but as I was reading this morning, this phrase came to my mind; "Wake up and smell the coffee." That little phrase has been used time and again in my life. I have said it many times. Did you ever wonder where it came from, and why it was ever said? I looked it up and it was first recorded in print in 1927, in a newspaper in Akron, OH.

The reason I thought about this this morning is because of our Scripture reading. Zechariah 1:18, "Then lifted up mine eyes, and saw." Zechariah 2:1, "I lifted up mine eyes again, and looked." Zechariah was writing to bring attention to the mind of God concerning powers that wanted to stop the rebuilding and restoring of God's people after the 70 years of captivity. God wanted the people to "wake up and smell the coffee." Jude 14-15, "Behold, the Lord cometh with ten thousands of his saints, To execute judgment upon all, and to convince all that are ungodly among them of all their ungodly deeds which they have ungodly committed." I am excited to have my wife open a few presents and to eat a special meal, but I cannot lose the real focus on the real purpose of Christmas. I need a new awakening to, "wake up and smell the coffee." Revelation 1:1, "to shew unto his servants things which must shortly come to pass." Revelation 1:3, "Blessed is he that readeth, and they that hear the words of this prophecy, and keep those things which are written therein: for the time is at hand." "The time is at hand," is what needs to be on our mind. I love the singing of the Christmas songs, the getting together with family and friends, the lights, the food, the fellowship, but we as God's people need to "wake up and smell the coffee." Proverbs 23:5, "Wilt thou set thine eyes upon that which is not? For riches certainly make themselves wings; they fly away as an eagle toward heaven." Proverbs 23:12, "Apply thine heart unto instruction, and thine ears to the words of knowledge." These verses also challenge us to "wake up and smell the coffee." God is in full control, and He knows when His Son will return for us who are saved.

Can we, during this wonderful time of the year, use the time with family and friends to talk about why Jesus came and about His soon return? We are all busy and we all want to share our love with those that we love but let us not forget to "wake up and smell the coffee." Psalm 142:3, "When my spirit was overwhelmed within me, then thou knewest my path." The phrase that has been used thousands upon thousands of times is a warning to face up to the realities of an unpleasant situation. What is that situation? Could there be those that we love and spend time with who will be left behind and spend eternity in Hell because they have never trusted Christ as their Saviour? This is a wonderful, tender, open-hearted time of the year to share the love of Christ and the real reason He came to earth to a lost world. Let us decide to "wake up and smell the coffee."

"The time is at hand," is what needs to be on our mind.

December 24

Zechariah 3-4 Psalm 143 Proverbs 24 Revelation 4-7

Day of Rejoicing

Good morning! It is Christmas Eve day and most people are tired from shopping, baking, wrapping, rushing, busy traffic, impatient people, and on and on and on. Stop and listen to the Spirit of God speak through the Scriptures. Zechariah 4:6, "Not by might, nor by power, but by my spirit, saith the LORD of hosts." Stop. We all know Christmas is not about all the business. Tomorrow will be a day of loneliness for some, a day of the first Christmas without the one they love. Tomorrow will be a day where for many years a family was together and now they are separated. Let us begin right now, this morning, to make this day the way the rest of our lives should be; and that is praising the Lord. In Revelation 5:12, let us see the angels exalting Jesus in Heaven, "Worthy is the Lamb that was slain to receive power, and riches, and wisdom, and strength, and honour, and glory, and blessing." Revelation 7:12, "Blessing, and glory, and wisdom, and thanksgiving, and honour, and power, and might, be unto our God for ever and ever. Amen."

May this Christmas Eve be a day of praising the Lord, a day of rejoicing that we are saved, a day of rejoicing that our name is written down in the Lamb's Book of Life, a day to rejoice that our sins are all gone. We have so much to rejoice over. We should be the stable ones in an unstable world. Proverbs 24:5, "A wise man is strong; yea, a man of knowledge increaseth strength." Christmas is a time of strength for us believers. Stop and hear the Heavenly host, see in your heart that day that our Redeemer came to this earth. Rejoice in the star that guided all to the humble place our KING lay. Listen to the Psalmist in Psalm 143:8, "Cause me to hear thy lovingkindness in the morning; for in thee do I trust: cause me to know the way wherein I should walk; for I lift up my soul to thee!" Look at these words in the next verses; verse 9, "Deliver me," verse 10, "Teach me," verse 11, "Quicken me," verse 12, "I am thy servant."

My heart is challenged this morning to stop and spend extra time rejoicing in the Lord. Stop this morning, sit down, sing a Christmas song, rejoice in your salvation. Spend time with the Saviour. Praise Him in song, in your prayer, in your heart, in your speech, in your thoughts. Yes, it is time for the earth to learn to praise Him in all things.

We should be the stable ones in an unstable world.

December 25

Zechariah 5-6   Psalm 144   Proverbs 25   Revelation 8-11

Lift Your Eyes Toward Heaven

Good morning, and a very Merry Christmas to you and yours! I do not know where you are today and what you will be doing, but please make the time to open the Bible to Luke 2 and read about the birth of the Lord Jesus. The house will soon be awakening and the voices of little ones and the excitement of the day and being together and giving presents to each other will soon begin. Maybe you do not have a family with you today and you are all alone, you think. Stop and know that we are never alone. Our Saviour, His name is Jesus, is still present with us and we are never, never alone. He arose from the grave, and what a joy to know that when He went back to Heaven, He still was here in the Holy Spirit, and He lives and dwells with us. Even when we think that we are alone, we are not if we have asked Christ to forgive us of our sins and to come into our heart.

Picture with me this morning the shepherds who were in the field keeping watch over their sheep. What do you think those shepherds did when they heard the voice of the angel? They looked up! In our reading this morning in Zechariah 5:9, "Then lifted I up mine eyes." As I read on, the word "lift" and "lifted" is mentioned six times. That is what we need to do today and every day; lift our eyes and heart up to the Lord. We need to get our eyes off this world and "lift" them up toward Heaven and praise the King of Kings, for He is our Saviour and Redeemer, and He is coming again. In Revelation 11:12, "Come up hither," will soon be said to us. That is why we need to lift our eyes to see and hear the wonderful angelic choir singing today and giving praise to our KING. This world and all its sins will soon pass and the reality of who is in charge will soon come. Revelation 11:15, "The kingdoms of this world are become the kingdoms of our Lord, and of his Christ; and he shall reign for ever and ever." "Lift" up your eyes and heart this morning and sing praises unto HIM. As that angel spoke that day in Luke 1:10, "And the angel said unto them, Fear not for, behold, I bring you good tidings of great joy, which shall be to all people." Luke 2:11, "For unto you is born this day in the city of David a Saviour, which is Christ the Lord." We need to separate the dross of sin in this world. This Christmas we should begin a new promise to ourselves, to every day the rest of our lives, "lift" our eyes, hearts, desires, goals to our Saviour and give Him all the praise. Proverbs 25:4, "Take away the dross from the silver, and there shall come forth a vessel for the finer."

That day the Heavenly host began to sing, and they have been singing since. Luke 2:14, "Glory to God in the highest, and on earth peace, good will toward men." Listen to the words of the Psalmist in Psalm 144:9, "I will sing a new song unto thee, O God: upon a psaltery and an instrument of ten strings will I sing praises unto thee." Psalm 144:15, "happy is that people, whose God is the LORD." Lift your eyes and heart toward Heaven. Tell the story that Jesus has come to save the world from sin. He is our Redeemer, He is our Saviour, He is our Lord. If you have never confessed that you are a sinner and asked forgiveness of your sins, ask Him today, trust Him today. That is why He came. Merry Christmas from our house to yours, and may we praise our KING together.

Lift up your eyes and heart this morning and sing praises unto HIM.

December 26

Zechariah 7-8 Psalm 145 Proverbs 26 Revelation 12-13

Keep Going

Good morning! I read Proverbs 26:7 this morning, "The legs of the lame are not equal: so is a parable in the mouth of fools." I had already read in Zechariah and Revelation and made notes, but when I read Proverbs 26, I kept coming back to verse 7, "The legs of the lame are not equal: so is a parable in the mouth of fools." I sat for quite a long time and thought about my father who is in Heaven. You see, he was born with the disease polio. His legs were different lengths and one of his legs was a little deformed and he had to wear one shoe that was built up so he could walk. My dad was quite a man, never complained about his short leg. Somehow, he took it in stride with life. He did so much for us, worked all his life and provided for our family. I thought about excuses that I hear from people as to why they can't come to church, live for God, read their Bible, live the Christian life. I thought about people I know who have let bitterness destroy them, their families and often even their friends.

Zechariah 7:11-12, "But they refused to hearken, and pulled away the shoulder, and stopped their ears, that they should not hear. Yea, they made their hearts as an adamant stone." Yesterday was a day of joy, cheer, laughter, and thankfulness to many and yet a day of loneliness for others. Don't let situations of life get you down. Don't let hard times, times of confusion distract you from walking with God. Be careful what you put before God. Revelation 13:9, "If any man have an ear, let him hear." Ask God for a tender heart and ear to hear Him speak through His Word, through preaching, and teaching in Sunday School and church. Spend time daily in God's Word, walk with God in prayer. Psalm 145:2-3, "Every day will I bless thee; and I will praise thy name for ever and ever. Great is the LORD, and greatly to be praised, and his greatness is unsearchable."

All of us know or have met people who just kept on going, even when others would have stopped. Our Saviour came, fulfilled the Father's purpose and is in Heaven interceding for us continually. Keep on keeping on and keep your heart tender to the Word of God, the voice of God, and the leadership of God. Keep going!! Jesus is coming soon, and we need to be busy sharing His Word and the wonderful story of salvation to a lost and dying world. Keep going!!

Keep on keeping on and keep your heart tender to the Word of God.

December 27

Zechariah 9-10 Psalm 146 Proverbs 27 Revelation 14-15

We Can

Good morning! As I awoke this morning and went out to the woodstove to stir the coals and add some wood, I just stopped while kneeling in front of the stove and said, "Thank you, Lord, that I can." We teach our children at a young age to not say, I can't. Over and over again we tell the children, you can, you can. Yet when it comes to us adults, it is over and over again, "I can't." We who are saved know the God who can. Zechariah 10:1, "Ask ye of the LORD rain in the time of the latter rain; so the LORD shall make bright clouds, and give them showers of rain, to every one grass in the field." Zechariah 10:12, "And I will strengthen them in the LORD; and they shall walk up and down in his name, saith the LORD."

There are things that I am a little slower at than I used to be, but I thank the Lord that I still can do many things. As we get older, we get a little weary of aches and pains, but I notice that people do what they want to do. Did you ever notice how folks give excuse why they cannot come to church, but they can make it to work? We make excuse as to why we cannot get up and read our Bible and have a time alone in prayer, but we can make it to the dentist, the doctor, the appointment to have our vehicles worked on, at the exact time for the appointment. As I knelt, I thought, I can do many things that I still need to do. I have to wear glasses. There was a time I did not need glasses, but I am so thankful that I have the glasses so that I can see plainly. Think about all that God does for us, and He never says, "I can't." We get discouraged; His Word is preserved to encourage us. We need to know His will, so we go to His Word and to Him in prayer and He guides us. Revelation 15:3, "Great and marvelous are thy works, Lord God Almighty; just and true are thy ways, thou king of saints."

I think we need to quit majoring on what we can't do, or at least what we think we can't do, and do what we can and what we ought to do. Proverbs 27:11, "My son, be wise, and make my heart glad." I want to be around those who will encourage me to do what I can, and those that encourage me to keep on. Proverbs 27:17, "Iron sharpeneth iron; so a man sharpeneth the countenance of his friend." Quit thinking life is over. Quit living like God is not in control. Quit thinking you can't and just keep doing what you can. Your head might be hurting a little, so thank God you have a head to hurt. At the end of this year and pressing on to the next, let us decide we can and God will. Psalm 146:10, "The LORD shall reign for ever, even thy God, O Zion, unto all generations. Praise ye the LORD." I still can, so I will.

Think about all that God does for us, and he never says, "I can't."

December 28

Zechariah 11-12 Psalm 147 Proverbs 28 Revelation 16-17

A Trained Spirit

Good morning! Have you ever had a little puppy? You wanted one so very badly and you told your parents that you would feed it every day and you would make sure to give it fresh water every day, and make sure to clean up any messes. Then the day arrived that that little puppy, so cute, so cuddly, so fun, tore up something of mom's or dad's. You heard your name and the puppy's name, and you knew before you got there something was wrong. That little puppy has a spirit within it and it must be trained. Trained to obey, trained to have boundaries, trained so that you can enjoy it and that little puppy can be loved and not yelled at all the time. I have often said about many an animal, do not destroy the animal's spirit, work with that animal so that its spirit can be controlled.

As I read Zechariah 12:1, "The burden of the word of the LORD for Israel, saith the LORD, which stretcheth forth the heavens, and layeth the foundation of the earth, and formeth the spirit of man within him." Because we are sinners, we naturally enjoy sinning better than not sinning. Little children must have their spirit taught, led, controlled, fed spiritually to be the Godly adults that all of us dream our children to be. Many of us adults have not had our spirit fed of the Word of God to help us in our walk in this world. The puppy can be trained, can be controlled, can be enjoyed; but it takes a heart of love, patience, and consistency. We can learn to love God, His Word, His will. Proverbs 28:5, "Evil men understand not judgment; but they that seek the LORD understand all things." When a puppy does right, we reward it by talking softly and often giving it a reward. That creates a spirit within the puppy to obey because that little puppy is beginning to understand when I obey, I get a reward and I am treated kindly. God can give us strength to overcome our sinful spirit. Revelation 17:14, "the Lamb shall overcome them: for he is Lord of lords, and King of kings: and they that are with him are called, and chosen, and faithful." I know of too many people that want to get rid of a pet because of the mess and destruction it creates, and yet they never took the time to train obedience. Be careful, young parents. If you do not take the time now, you are heading down the road to have a broken heart or a bitter child, or both. Please do not say you do not have the time or the patience because that is selfishness. Proverbs 28:25, "He that is of a proud heart stirreth up strife: but he that putteth his trust in the LORD shall be made fat." When we make time for each other we grow in a relationship with each other, we learn more about each other, and we want to spend more time together. When we spend time with the Lord, we will learn more about the Lord and His love for us, and His desire and plan for us.

I have enjoyed several puppies in my life, but with every one of them I had to give time to train them into a dog that I and others could enjoy. I am not a dog trainer, but I have understood that they have a spirit, and it can be controlled. Why don't we decide that if we are truly going to enjoy the blessings of being saved and a walk with God, we are going to have to allow Him to control and guide our spirit? We need to yield our will to be His will. Psalm 147:9, "He giveth to the beast his food, and to the young ravens which cry." Picture how God provides for all His creation. Did you ever think why? His creation is yielded to who provides. Some things to think about today. Please have a very blessed day. It is time for me to go feed and water some animals. I think I will spend a little time with them.

If we are going to enjoy the blessings of being saved,
we need to yield our will to His will.

December 29

Zechariah 13-14 Psalm 148 Proverbs 29 Revelation 18-19

What a Day

Good morning! Life is full of different events. Personally, we have birthdays, anniversaries, family get togethers, family vacations, graduations, marriages, and the list of possibilities can wear a person out. For little ones, there is the first word, the first step, the first time they rolled over or sat up. We then anticipate the first day of school, junior high or middle school, then high school. Then the major decision of college or heading out to learn a vocational trade and be on their own. Oh, the day a dad gives away a daughter or you see your son waiting for his bride to walk down the aisle. Let us change major directions right now. When that little one was given to you by our Lord, have you been pleading with the Lord for them to be saved? Parents, do not quit praying after they have been saved because there is a world of saved young people that have never given their heart to the will of God or even surrendered their heart to be open to God's leading.

I could keep going but several phrases spoke to me in our reading today. Zechariah 13:2, "And it shall come to pass." This same phrase is found in verses 3, 4, and 8. Zechariah 14:1, "Behold, the day of the LORD cometh." Zechariah 14:9, "And the LORD shall be king over all the earth: in that day shall there be one LORD, and his name one." You might say, Bro. Smith, this is after the rapture of the church and God has come for the final victory. Yes, I know and I understand, but my thought for us to consider is Jesus and His return having as much attention in our life as the next birthday. Does yielding to God daily have as much attention as the next days off or the next vacation? I wish we could sing the chorus together of the song, "What a Day That Will Be." "What a day that will be when my Jesus I shall see, And I look upon His face, the One who saved me by His grace; When He takes me by the hand, and leads me through the Promised Land, What a day, glorious day that will be."

Please do not get me wrong. I am excited about some special days ahead. If the Lord tarries and the Lord wills, Mrs. Smith and I will be married 50 years in 2021. We have a grandson that will graduate and many other special days. Consider the phrase in Zechariah, "Behold, the day of the LORD cometh." May we look forward to His return and us leaving this sinful world. Revelation 19:5, "Praise our God, all ye his servants, and ye that fear him, both small and great." Be looking for that day. Proverbs 29:2, "When the righteous are in authority, the people rejoice: but when the wicked beareth rule, the people mourn." I hear the cry of the broken homes, the aborted children, the emptiness that sin brings. Let us speak of the coming day of our Lord. Psalm 148:13, "Let them praise the name of the LORD: for his name alone is excellent; his glory is above the earth and heaven." Oh, my brother and sister, as this year draws close to the end, may we look even more for the day of His coming.

May we look forward to His return and us leaving this sinful world.

December 30

Malachi 1-2 Psalm 149 Proverbs 30 Revelation 20-21

Proper Priority

Good morning, good morning, good morning! Can you believe another year has almost passed? What is behind us is behind us and only the Lord knows what is ahead, and that is the most important thing that we need to focus on. Our focus must stay on the Lord. He has a plan, He has a purpose, He knows everything that is going on. We need to see the importance of the important. What has our value, what has our focus, what has our time? Malachi 1:2, "I have loved you, saith the LORD. Yet ye say, wherein hast thou loved us? Was not Esau Jacob's brother? Saith the LORD: yet I loved Jacob." After reading the last statement you might think that God loves each of us in a different way. That is definitely not the truth, get it out of your head, do not think that way. As we read on in the next verse, we read the words, "And I hated

Esau, and laid his mountains and his heritage waste for the dragons of the wilderness" (Malachi 1:3). What is being said is Esau valued a bowl of pottage more that his inheritance. Go back and read Genesis 25:34, "thus Esau despised his birthright."

We are at the end of this year and looking forward, setting goals, making new plans. Be very careful where your values are. Be careful what your goals are centered around. Malachi 2:15, "take heed to your spirit." Jesus died for all, and it is not His will that any should perish. The problem we face is we put everything else in life first and God someplace down the line of priorities. We live in a world of lies, sorrow, defeat, confusion, turmoil, etc. God has a better plan, a better ending, and that should consume our goals and our focus of life. Revelation 21:4, "And God shall wipe away all tears from their eyes; and there shall be no more death, neither sorrow, nor crying, neither shall there be any more pain: for the former things are passed away." There is a city being prepared and Revelation 21:23 gives us a glimpse, "And the city had no need of the sun, neither of the moon, to shine in it: for the glory of God did lighten it, and the Lamb is the light thereof."

I am not saying to not set goals. What I am saying is that Christ should be the center of every goal that we set because trying to live without Him is destruction, discouragement, and defeat. As we look forward, make sure a daily walk with God in His Word and time in private prayer is at the top of the list. Proverbs 30:5, "Every word of God is pure: he is a shield unto them that put their trust in him." He is there for us. Psalm 149:5, "Let the saints be joyful in glory." Psalm 149:6, "Let the high praises of God be in their mouth." It is so important to set goals with proper priority. Nothing is more important than putting God first. Ask Him to strengthen your faith in Him this coming year. Let me end this morning with the first words we read this morning in Malachi 1:2, "I have loved you, saith the LORD." Let it be said of us that we love Him so much, we put Him first in everything. Have a blessed day.

Nothing is more important than putting God first.

December 31

Malachi 3-4 Psalm 150 Proverbs 31 Revelation 22

Remembering

Good morning! The last day of another year is before us. Probably in the last month, the last week or the last few days each of us have been looking back and pondering our steps, our accomplishments and possibly our failures or goals that we did not get to accomplish. I heard a statement many years ago that went something like this, "life will go on." That brief little four- word phrase has seemed so cold to me. It is like we are to forget the past and only look to the future. The men that our LORD used to write the New Testament looked back to the law and the prophets. The Old Testament men and women often were reminded of the sin of Adam and Eve. It is not wrong to look back, but I feel it is wrong to live in the past. Let us remember our spiritual and physical heritage. Let us remember to keep a solid foundation of Biblical principles, keep developing Biblical personal character, keep remembering the miracles of the Lord, the answers of prayer.

Remember those things that strengthen your faith in the Lord. The longer man lives, the more rules and regulations are made, and made, and made, and made. Why? Because of sin. It has been said, and I encourage you to write this little phrase someplace that you can often see it and read it, "The Bible will keep you from sin, or sin will keep you from the Bible." I cannot change a lot of things that I would like to change, but what I can do I ought to do, and what I ought to do or be, I should do, and I should be. Malachi 3:3, "that they may offer unto the LORD an offering in righteousness." We all can offer ourselves, our time, and our will to God. Malachi 3:7, "Return unto me, and I will return unto you, saith the LORD of hosts." Okay, we have failed to keep some commitments to the Lord. Return unto Him and make fresh commitments of faith and faithfulness. Another phrase that I have used often is "knocked down, but not knocked out." We have life, so live life for God. Malachi 3:10, "prove me now herewith, saith the LORD of hosts, if I will not open you the windows of heaven, and pour you out a blessing." Prove the Lord or live for Him to receive His blessing in your marriage, in your children, in your grandchildren, in your business, in your service for the Lord, in every area of your life.

Do not ever forget that today and all the days in the future, could be THE DAY that our Redeemer will return. Revelation 22:12, "And, behold, I come quickly; and my reward is with me, to give every man according as his work shall be." Quit looking for the world's approval. Quit looking for others' approval. Quit trying to please the flesh. Proverbs 31:30, "Favour is deceitful." I looked at those three words this morning and thought how many have been destroyed because they looked for the approval of others and not the approval of God. Let us end this year and step into the next year by deciding we are going to give God the praise and glory, in every area of our life. Psalm 150:1, "Praise ye the LORD. Praise God in his sanctuary: praise him in the firmament of his power." Thirteen times the word "praise" is used in the six verses of Psalm 150. My brother and sister in Christ, let us end this year and jump into the next year by a "return," daily decision to "prove" and "praise" our Lord. He has blessed us this year. Look and see and live the blessings of the past year and watch for His return in the year to come. The end is really the beginning of a new beginning.

Do not ever forget that today could be THE DAY that our Redeemer will return.

CPSIA information can be obtained
at www.ICGtesting.com
Printed in the USA
JSHW030720200222
23056JS00002B/2

9 781630 734046